Crowded by Beauty

The publisher gratefully acknowledges the generous support of the Humanities Endowment Fund of the University of California Press Foundation.

The publisher also gratefully acknowledges the support of the Leslie Scalapino Memorial Fund for Poetry, which was established by generous contributions to the University of California Press Foundation by Thomas J. White and the Leslie Scalapino–O Books Fund.

Crowded by Beauty

THE LIFE AND ZEN OF
POET PHILIP WHALEN

David Schneider

UNIVERSITY OF CALIFORNIA PRESS

University of California Press, one of the most distinguished university presses in the United States, enriches lives around the world by advancing scholarship in the humanities, social sciences, and natural sciences. Its activities are supported by the UC Press Foundation and by philanthropic contributions from individuals and institutions. For more information, visit www.ucpress.edu.

University of California Press
Oakland, California

Library of Congress Cataloging-in-Publication Data

Schneider, David, 1951 – author.
    Crowded by beauty: the life and Zen of poet Philip Whalen / David Schneider.
        pages cm
    Life and Zen of poet Philip Whalen
    Includes bibliographical references and index.
    ISBN 978-0-520-24746-8 (cloth : alk. paper)
    ISBN 978-0-520-96099-2 (ebook)
    1. Whalen, Philip.   2. Beat generation.   3. Poets, American—20th century.   4. Zen Buddhists.   I. Title   II. Title: Life and Zen of poet Philip Whalen.
    PS3545.H117Z86 2015
    813'.54—dc23

                                                2015008822

Manufactured in the United States of America

24 23 22 21 20 19 18 17 16 15
10 9 8 7 6 5 4 3 2 1

In keeping with a commitment to support environmentally responsible and sustainable printing practices, UC Press has printed this book on Natures Natural, a fiber that contains 30% post-consumer waste and meets the minimum requirements of ANSI/NISO Z39.48–1992 (R 1997) (Permanence of Paper).

This book is for Kit and Lily.

CONTENTS

ILLUSTRATIONS

PREFACE

This book came about because I'd written another, earlier book about Philip Whalen—a journal of life with him at Zen Center, modeled roughly on Boswell's chronicles of Samuel Johnson. Through recording as accurately as I could Philip's conversations and describing the places these occurred, I hoped to . . . actually I had no real goals beyond the pleasure and practice of writing. I just wanted to be writing *something,* and here was Philip, an accomplished author, an eccentric, whose presence—large body, distinctive voice, and peculiar, learned insights—had provoked many in his company to write about him. At least two other young men, both more-or-less practicing Buddhists, had, at different times, kept exactly the same kind of journal I did. The title of this biography comes from a remark Philip made to one of those writers—Steve Silberman—in a hardware store. Steve wrote it down in his journal. None of us knew about the other's work until years later. We'd all clearly felt, during the time of our writing, that something unusual and valuable was happening in front of our eyes. Philip Whalen was happening.

Shortly before Philip's death in 2002—twenty years after I'd written my journal—I typed it up. Who knows how these things work, but I'd been roused from distraction and laziness to this concentrated labor by a powerful dream visit from Philip. In the dream, he wondered if we might not "lose all those texts we worked on." At the time, he lay in a hospice in San Francisco, nine thousand kilometers from Cologne, where I was working. Typing for those weeks, I may have been unconsciously trying to hold him with old stories.

A respectful time after his death, I sent the journal, titled *Side Effect,* to a few likely publishers. They all kindly assured me that they'd enjoyed reading it very much, but that in today's market, well, Philip wasn't famous enough, and neither was I, and how could they sell it? Even five years earlier they could have, but these days. . . . Shortly after this, though, University of California Press, in the person of my wonderful editor, Reed Malcolm, got in touch about doing the biography.

In the twelve years we practiced Buddhism together in Zen Center's three locations—as well as in the eighteen years after that, when we stayed in touch and continued practicing, sometimes in different traditions, sometimes from different countries—Philip taught constantly. He taught official courses in literature, he taught courses in Buddhist theory and history, he taught a select few what he could about poetry. But this is not what I mean by "he taught." The group of young people, mostly men, who gathered around Philip wherever he was definitely felt they were learning something from him, even if they were not actively studying. It was and remains a puzzle to name that topic: it wasn't literature exactly; it wasn't recent or ancient history; it wasn't how to be a Zen student or a friend, or how to relate to celebrities; it wasn't how to look at paintings, how to listen to music, how to cook and enjoy food; it wasn't how to speak, how to read, or how to open the mind. But it wasn't separate from those things, either. They were all very much included.

The thought of Philip's biography scared me; I'd written one and knew how much work they were. That biography was of a remarkable and kind person— Issan Dorsey—but a person largely unknown to the public, apart from certain local sectors of the gay community. Philip, though not famous, was certainly well known among poets internationally, and among those who cared about the Beat writers. (As one of his circle unkindly put it to him, "You're a name, not a face.") Philip had also left a wide paper trail. Whereas Issan read very little and wrote even less, Philip read and wrote constantly. He kept a journal, and he often wrote several beautiful letters per day. Many of these were squirreled away in the special collections of libraries scattered around North America. They were there because a number of Philip's friends were famous writers. The letters these friends had written back were mostly at the University of California Berkeley's Bancroft Library. I was happily anchored in Germany by a two-year-old daughter and a demanding job. Undecided and uneasy, I consulted a Tibetan lama skilled in divination. Word came back that it would be good to undertake the biography. The prophecy also said it could take a long time, and that that would be fine.

The Philip I knew was of course a poet, but that was not his most important aspect. A number of his publications appeared between 1972 and 2002.

He would sign these if you asked; you could recognize in the poems people and places belonging to Zen Center. But no matter how strange or beautiful the lines were, they made faint impression compared with the living person handing you back a newly decorated book or broadside.

"What relationship does anyone's biography have to do with what they wrote?" Philip abruptly posed this question to a class he was teaching in late July 1980, at Naropa University. He observed, "The person of the poet is often extremely difficult and unpleasant. . . . I can distinctly remember Kenneth Rexroth saying, 'Writers are terrible people. You don't want them in your house!' He says this to a roomful of writers he was accustomed to seeing on Friday evenings."

Because Philip and the class had been studying Hart Crane's work that afternoon, he allowed that Brom Weber's biography of Crane, though "a cranky book," related the facts of the life well enough and might be useful in getting at the poems. The earlier Horton biography had necessarily left out a lot—Crane's mother was still alive—and the John Unterecker biography, at nearly eight hundred pages, could tell you practically what Crane had been doing on any given day, but it "does not help much. You don't read Crane any better, I don't think." Philip was even less encouraging about the two-volume biography of William Faulkner, "by Professor What's-His-Name," as it completely left out an important and obvious love affair—and he savaged one of the Hemingway biographies (discussing two others in the process) for extrapolating and romanticizing what Hemingway thought—even, for example, as he put the barrel of a shotgun in his mouth to kill himself. A contemporary two-volume Emily Dickinson biography received Philip's praise for its appendices and scholarly apparatuses, but he complained about the number of salacious details—"the most incredible tittle-tattle"—of nineteenth-century Amherst. He was relating these with evident pleasure to the class when he suddenly interrupted himself to exclaim: "It does *not* explain how Emily Dickinson was simply a genius who wrote beautiful poetry!"

Prodded then by the class in an all-too-familiar direction, Philip talked about the several Kerouac biographies that had appeared (and the one that had been suppressed) even then, pre–*Memory Babe*. Philip noted when interviewers had been deceptive with him, had gotten facts wrong, or been mean-spirited. He regretted things he'd said, and in one case, even that he'd been involved. "I *never* should have talked to that person!" Philip's digression on the limits and failings of writers' biographies ran an energetic twenty-five minutes and would discourage anyone trying to write *his* life—were it not for the fact that he'd obviously gone hungrily through the books, with close attention. That's all any writer can fairly ask of readers.

Against these sobering reflections, I must confess that I also cannot explain how Philip was simply a genius who wrote beautiful poetry. I pass along at least some of what he said of his methods and writing habits—he was very generous with this information. I must also say that I have not written a literary biography; I do not attempt much literary criticism, apart from brief praise. Philip's poetry appears, but in support of, or in explanation of, his life, not the other way around.

This book does not proceed chronologically—at least not until midway through—so I have included an abbreviated chronology, excerpted from one Philip himself wrote to accompany *Off the Wall*.[1] Its dates have been extended to cover the last twenty-five years of his life.

A note on punctuation and abbreviation: Philip Whalen wrote his journal and most of his correspondence long hand, with pencil, broad-nib fountain pen, or even ball-point pen, on unlined paper. He composed poetry and prose, at least initially, with these same materials. He used many of the abbreviations and other markings typical of calligraphers.

In transcribing his hand-writing, I attempted to preserve these: thus if he wrote an ampersand for "and" I copied the ampersand. The same with "&c" for "etcetera," the same with curly brackets in places one might expect parentheses. His usages were inconsistent, but definite. Trusting the reader would not be confused, I tried to reproduce Whalen's choices. Some of these survived the thoroughly beneficial edits this manuscript received.

BRIEF CHRONOLOGY

1923	Philip Glenn Whalen born in Portland, Oregon, on 20 October, only son of Glenn Henry and Phyllis Aminta (Bush) Whalen.
1929–1938	Attended public grade school and junior high school in The Dalles, Oregon.
1939 ·	Mother died.
1938–1941	Attended The Dalles High School, graduating May 1941. In September 1941, moved with father to live in Portland.
1941–1943	Worked as office boy and laborer in airplane factory and shipyard.
1943–1946	Service with U.S. Army Air Corps as radio operator and mechanics instructor.
1946–1951	Attended Reed College, taking creative writing, graphic arts, language, and literature courses. First poems published in campus literary magazines. Met Lew Welch, Gary Snyder, and many more lifelong friends there; set type, carved linoleum blocks, and printed his first individual publication, *Three Satires. The Calendar,* a book of poems, written in 1950–51 as thesis project required for B.A. Graduated 1951.
	Odd jobs in Portland, San Francisco, Venice (CA).
1952–1953	Residence in San Francisco with Gary Snyder; long visits in Los Angeles with Leslie and Rosemary Thompson, friends from Reed College. Odd jobs.
1953–1955	Residence in San Francisco; summer work as lookout fireman in Mount Baker National Forest.
	Fall and winter 1954, living with Ben Richard Anderson and his wife, Virginia Heath, in Newport, Oregon.
	September 1955, residence in Berkeley. Met Jack Kerouac and Allen Ginsberg. Six Gallery reading on 7 October 1955, with Ginsberg, Lamantia, McClure, and Snyder; Kenneth Rexroth, master of ceremonies; first solo poetry reading later that year at the Poetry

Center, under the direction of Ruth Witt-Diamant, at San Francisco State University.

1956   Reprise reading of the Six Gallery group, plus or minus various participants, at Berkeley Little Theater.

Poems published in "San Francisco Scene" issue of *Evergreen Review.*

Met Gregory Corso and gave him poems for *Cambridge Review.*

Living at Milvia Street, Berkeley; part-time work for University of California at the Poultry Husbandry Laboratory.

1957–1958   First walking trip in Sierra Nevada, with Les Thompson, Robert Walker, and Max Woods.

In September, moved to Newport, Oregon, to work as circuit court bailiff for Judge Ben Richard Anderson of Lincoln County, Oregon.

Leroi Jones solicited book of poems. *Like I Say* completed and accepted for publication.

1959   Returned to San Francisco; participation in a number of public poetry readings (including benefit readings) with Ginsberg, McClure, Wieners, Spicer, Kyger, Duncan, and many other poets.

October reading tour of colleges in New York and New England, with Michael McClure, arranged by Elsa Dorfman and Grove Press. As part of that, visited Charles Olson, Frank O'Hara, Joe LeSueur, and others.

Memoirs of an Interglacial Age completed and accepted for publication by Dave Haselwood's Auerhahn Press.

1960   Part-time work with U.S. Postal Service. *Like I Say* published in New York; *Memoirs of an Interglacial Age* published in San Francisco.

Second New England reading tour, arranged by the Paterson Society.

1961–1962   Wrote *Brain Candy* and *Every Day.*

Moved to Mill Valley to stay with Albert Saijo and family;

January 1962, Poets Foundation Award.

1963   Moved to San Francisco, the Beaver Street period. Wrote a novel, *You Didn't Even Try.*

University of British Columbia Poetry Conference (the "Vancouver Conference"), guest of Warren and Ellen Tallman.

Monday in the Evening published by Fernanda Pivano, Milan.

Recorded *Like I Say* and *Memoirs of an Interglacial Age* for Library of Congress Poetry Collection.

1964–1965   Coyote Books, an offshoot of *Coyote's Journal,* published *Every Day.*

Father died, September 1965.

Completed *The Diamond Noodle,* a prose text.

Filmed walking and reading for the NET series *USA: Poetry.*

Awarded a grant-in-aid by the National Academy of Arts and Letters.

1966–1967	*Highgrade* (graphic works), edited and designed by Zoe Brown, published by Coyote Books.
	Sailed to Japan for part-time teaching job in Kyoto.
	Began a second novel, *Imaginary Speeches for a Brazen Head,* in August 1966, completed May 1967.
	Intransit magazine (Bill Thomas) brought out the Philip Whalen issue.
	You Didn't Even Try published by Coyote Books.
	Returned to United States in November 1967, residence in Bolinas, San Francisco, Stinson Beach, and Bolinas again.
1969–1971	Returned to Kyoto end of March 1969.
	On Bear's Head (a collection of previously published works) published by Harcourt, Brace & World with Coyote Books.
	Grant-in-aid from Committee on Poetry.
	Severance Pay published by Four Seasons Foundation (Donald Allen).
	"Many Happy Returns" commissioned by Tom Clark for his All Stars anthology.
	Second grant-in-aid from Committee on Poetry for *Scenes of Life at the Capital,* published by Grey Fox Press, June 1971.
	Residence at Bolinas.
1972–1973	Moved to San Francisco Zen Center, February 1972.
	Imaginary Speeches for a Brazen Head published by Black Sparrow.
	Ordained *unsui* (Zen Buddhist monk), 3 February 1973.
1975–1976	*Shuso* (head monk) at Zenshinji, Zen Mountain Center, Tassajara, September–December 1975.
	Prolegomena to a Study of the Universe (prose texts from 1959–1960) published by Poltroon Press.
	The Kindness of Strangers: Poems 1969–1974 published by the Four Seasons Foundation, Bolinas.
1972–1984	Lived as Zen monk and teacher in Zen Center locations in San Francisco and Tassajara.
	Moved from San Francisco to Santa Fe, August 1984.
1975–1987	Visiting poet at Naropa University.
1978	*Decompressions: Selected Poems* published by Grey Fox Press, Bolinas.
1980	*The Diamond Noodle* published by Poltroon Press, Berkeley; designed by Alastair Johnston, illustrated by Frances Butler.
	Enough Said: Poems 1974–1979 published by Grey Fox Press, Bolinas.
1981–1982	Resident teacher at South Ridge Zendo, Shogaku-an, San Francisco.
1984–1987	Resided in Santa Fe, New Mexico.

	Two Novels (Whalen's novels reprinted with an introduction by Paul Christensen) published by Zephyr Press, Somerville, Massachusetts, 1985.
	Dharma transmission from Zentatsu Richard Baker, 23–30 July 1987, at Crestone, Colorado.
1988–1990	Resided at Sanchez Street in San Francisco, then Issanji, Hartford Street Zen Center, serving as *Godo* (head of training).
1991	Mountain Seat Ceremony, making him the third abbot of Issanji, 14 September.
1996	Retired as abbot of Issanji on 15 August, remaining as teacher-in-residence.
	Canoeing Up Cabarga Creek: Buddhist Poems, 1955–1986, introduction by Richard Baker, foreword by Allen Ginsberg, published by Parallax Press, Berkeley.
1999	*Some of These Days,* designed and printed by Clifford Burke, Desert Rose Press, San Jose, New Mexico.
	Overtime: Selected Poems, with an introduction by Leslie Scalapino, edited by Michael Rothenberg, published by Penguin Books.
2001	*Goofbook: For Jack Kerouac,* edited by Michael Rothenberg, published by Big Bridge Press, Pacifica, California.
2002	Perished, 26 June, Laguna Honda Hospice.
	Philip Whalen Memorial Reading, 30 August, Presentation Theater, University of San Francisco.
	Passing Over Ceremony, Green Gulch Farm, 1 September.

A number of posthumous publications of Whalen's work have appeared, most notably, *The Collected Poems of Philip Whalen,* edited by Michael Rothenberg (Middletown, CT: Wesleyan University Press, 2007). An invaluable resource, a monumental work, this volume presents the poems in chronological order of composition; it gives as well the original groupings at the time of first publication, in an appendix. The poems are indexed both by title and by first line. Though Philip began one preface, "I don't believe poets ought to write prefaces to their own work," he did. These are also collected and reprinted in an appendix running twenty pages. The book contains a very complete bibliography of Whalen's printed works, including broadsides.

Another posthumous book, a Festschrift, valuable for the photographs laboriously collected as well as the assembled tributes, is *Continuous Flame: A Tribute to Philip Whalen,* edited by Michael Rothenberg and Suzi Winson (New York: Fish Drum, 2005).

ONE

Reflection in Friends

Philip Whalen generally impressed the people who knew him, either through his writing or personally. His literary voice, consonant to a high degree with his person, was large, restless, learned, demanding, fearless, humorous, singular. Not very many people, however, knew him. He preferred a mostly quiet life, with brief eruptions of wild social activity. He appeared to possess little outward ambition. He was extremely sensitive—to weather, art, literature, other people—to influences of all kinds, yet he knew clearly his own way forward, a way that required solitude. On top of a kind, curious nature, his early upbringing left him fundamentally shy—again, with explosions of theatrical complaint, usually accurate and often hilarious, at least in retrospect.

From a humble background in a remote, beautiful corner of the country, he went on to exert a strong influence on American poetry of the second half of the twentieth century. He did this through his own writing, and through the force of his personality and its influence on his students and more famous friends.

In a similar way, his faithful, observant presence, as much as his erudition, helped establish Zen Buddhism in the West. To look at him you might not think it possible: a large man, a fat man, older, scholarly, practicing a style of Buddhism renowned for its strict exertion (bordering on asceticism) and an athletic, quasi-military approach to the spiritual path. Yet there he was every morning—evenings too, in the monastery—day after day, year after year for three decades, until he could not physically drag himself to the zendo any longer.

He stood by his teacher Richard Baker Roshi through the stormy Zen Center scandals of 1983–84, though this was neither popular nor easy. It required him to pull up stakes at the age of sixty-two and move 1,100 miles to the Southwest, to an unformed and unpromising situation, and to live in close quarters with a skeleton crew of similar refugees in a place he found beautiful but trying, not least because of its distance from the charms of the Pacific Ocean.

Four years later, newly minted as a teacher in his own right, he uprooted himself again and headed off to . . . he knew not where. He had the blessings of the lineage but nowhere to live and no source of income, so he wandered in the old-style Zen way: no clear direction forward and no possibility of staying still. He passed the last active period of his life as abbot of the Hartford Street Zen Center, a small, lively temple in San Francisco's Castro district, where, upon ascending the Mountain Seat, he calmed the fears and soothed the ruffled feathers of that sangha, disturbed as they were by worry that the temple would drift away from its initial and primary function as a practice place for local gay and lesbian practitioners. Approaching seventy, beyond or above the issue of gay versus straight and clearly at ease living in the Castro, Philip guided the temple back toward Zen's more central concerns.

Whatever Philip Whalen's accomplishments, when it came out in ordinary conversation that I was writing his biography, the response was very often a blank look and an uncomfortable silence. To furnish identification, I might say, "poet," then "Zen master," and finally "one of the Beat poets." This inevitably led to a list of three of the most famous: Jack Kerouac, Allen Ginsberg, and Gary Snyder. For those who don't know Philip Whalen, it seemed initially necessary to name these names, though they constitute a very incomplete list both of Beat poets and of Whalen's friends. Here follows an apology—in the older sense of that word—for parlaying the fame of those three writers, as well as for not using others. I begin with sketches of Whalen's friendships with Ginsberg, Kerouac, and Snyder. Two more chapters follow—briefer portraits of relations with close friends who, though not perhaps as famous as the initial three, have, through brilliant writing and venerable longevity, come evermore into public view and deserved honor—Joanne Kyger and Michael McClure.

. . .

Teaching a class at Naropa University in June 1982, Allen Ginsberg said that in the mid-1950s he, Jack Kerouac, Gary Snyder, and Philip Whalen all lived together in a cottage in Berkeley. Whether this is strictly true,[1] it impressed itself on Ginsberg's mind: he'd told about it six years earlier, also in a Naropa class, linking it then to a study of R. H. Blythe's four-volume set of haiku translations. Ginsberg stressed to his class how fundamental those texts had been for the young poets—a bible, an encyclopedia, a primer in direct perception and use of concrete details, as well as in the mind that was still enough to catch these and the hand that was confident enough to set them down on paper. Barely more than a few minutes after he finished telling the class all this, a student roused himself to ask for the name of the books again. In a somewhat exasperated response, Ginsberg went through the whole thing a second time. "How many have heard of these books, put your hands up. How many have NOT heard of them? OK B-L-Y-T-H-E . . ." This time he told how the volumes were divided one per season, how the texts were bilingual, how they were arranged on the page, how the covers looked, and he included the publishing information. He extemporized a rather passionate advertisement for Blythe, linking him to the previous eighty years of American poetry, from the Imagists down to the Beats. Ginsberg then recounted how he and his shackmates had treasured the books, shared them, pored over them, incorporated them into a kind of internal mutual vocabulary, eventually writing haikus of their own. "This was when we were all living in this cottage together, Kerouac, Snyder and me, we . . ." This time through, Ginsberg left Whalen off the list.

Perhaps he thought Whalen not famous enough to dent the students' minds; perhaps it was just verbal compaction, spoken in urgency. Whatever the case, Whalen had dropped from sight, mirroring to a certain extent what happened to his public persona in the twenty-seven years since the seminal Six Gallery reading. That event could fairly be seen as a starting point in the poets' careers. It was, for Ginsberg, Whalen, Snyder, and McClure, their first public reading. Kerouac's *On the Road* was still a couple of years from publication.

In the decades that followed, Kerouac, Ginsberg, and Snyder all got internationally famous and enjoyed or suffered fame's effects. Whalen did not; fame never came his way. Despite a number of conflicted efforts to set himself before the public's eye, his relationship to it remained relatively barren. By way of introduction, though, one can place him in the middle of a famous crowd, and this *was* initially group fame. The whole gang got famously entwined, and they brought a sizable entourage to their tangled relations, such that it seemed from outside as though a school was born entire: the

Beats, the West Coast Beats. While Philip was central to the events that pushed the school into the public's attention, he did not catch much of that attention personally.

Part of what made the Beats remarkable was their association with Buddhism. Certainly this was so with Kerouac, Snyder, and Whalen, and soon after also with Ginsberg. Their fame attracted attention, and later also people, to Buddhism. Beyond studying and to varying extents practicing Buddhism, they all told one another about it. And having opened the innermost door of spirituality to one another, they were completely intimate, with little they did not share. These friends passed books and manuscripts back and forth, they typed and retyped one another's work and promoted it tirelessly to publishers and editors. They cared for one another in times of sickness or difficulty, and they lent money back and forth, though this flowed almost exclusively toward Whalen rather than from him—"almost exclusively" because whenever Whalen did have money, he was happy to lend it, and his friends were not shy in applying for it. In crisis, literary or otherwise, they rallied around and gave staunch defense, but they were neither blind to one another's shortcomings nor uncritical: they were real friends.

(It is told that the San Francisco Beats also passed lovers back and forth. It does appear that one or two passed-along girlfriends came Whalen's way, according to poet Joanne Kyger, who explained that "it was under this Beat brotherhood kind of 'My girlfriend is your girlfriend' sort of thing." Kyger began paying attention to that scene in the late 1950s, and she pointed out that "it didn't really work very well, though. It turns out that there *were* all these little territories involved."[2] In the famed orgies at Ginsberg's Berkeley cottage midfifties—the ones promoted by Ginsberg and Snyder, and chronicled by Kerouac—Whalen was, as Kerouac was, a shy participant, if either involved himself at all. Ginsberg let it be known that when such an event was nearly over, Philip would need encouragement to join.)

Whalen was proud of his friendships but lamented being thought of as only "a friend of the great." He was labeled, possibly burdened, with the moniker "poet's poet," and he allowed this role to come to him through half-hearted efforts at promoting his own work, while at the same time exhibiting a manifest energy and devotion for his friends and their works. Whalen started no family of his own, had no long-term lover or companion, and was not deeply involved with blood kin, apart from a solicitous correspondence with his sister, Velna. Whalen's friends, however, meant a great deal to him. Famously cranky, he was a loyal, loving friend who cultivated a range of comrades, of which Kerouac, Snyder, and Ginsberg are only prominent examples. Whalen counted these three among his best friends, and they all in turn loved him and admired him. Philip was someone they wanted to talk to, write to, read, dine with, stay with, hike or hang out with.

These four friends wrote long, detailed, often hilarious letters to one another. The time and energy Whalen gave to writing his friends certainly rivals what he allotted to the composition of poetry and prose, or to keeping a journal. His letters tell of the daily man: the one who suffers or enjoys weather, who has or hasn't money, who must look for a new place to live, who packs to travel or hike, who reports and sometimes gossips about mutual acquaintances, who is reading and thinking about five or six books simultaneously, who is or isn't writing anything interesting, who passes along intelligence of blossoms and landscapes, who has fits of nerves. His letters tell the things he wanted to tell the people he loved.

For these poets, Whalen often played the role of mentor, teacher, elder—and he thought of himself that way. "Not that [Dr.] Johnson was right," Whalen wrote in 1959, "nor that I'm trying to inherit his mantle as a literary dictator, but only the title *Doctor, i.e., teacher*—who is constantly studying."[3]

Looking back from a remove of five decades, Gary Snyder wrote, "He [Whalen] first showed me the difference between talking about literature and doing it, and pointed the way into Asian philosophy and art."[4]

"Phil taught me Stein," Allen Ginsberg told his Naropa class, "and I'm hoping he's going to teach you Stein."[5]

Jack Kerouac may have been too certain of his own literary ideas to take recommendations—maybe too competitive as well—but he did have something to learn from Whalen. As he wrote to him in 1956, "You have always done everything possible to make me feel good; you are a pillar of strength, and why? Because you never get mad, people can shit all over you and you never get mad. If that isn't being a pillar of strength, the Buddha is a load of the same."

McClure also saw that Philip's character was the real lesson, not his erudition, which he found nonetheless admirable. Whalen's extraordinary ability to open himself to people and ideas and sense experience, and to stay open, particularly impressed McClure. "We were all in awe of him."[6]

In a 1958 letter to Ginsberg, Philip wrote, "Everything he [Kerouac] has told me is true, about himself, about myself . . . fantastic. Everything is unbelievable, strange . . . that the 4 of us [Kerouac, Snyder, Ginsberg, Whalen] should have met when we did, that we are inextricably involved together & so completely separated. I can go back to the parinirvana happy, no more question now, I've done what I came here to do, all you other bodhisattvas have helped me . . . you the Bodhisattva Ever-weeping, Jack the Bodhisattva Manjushri (the Writing Bodhisattva), Gary the Lightningbolt Diamondsplitter."[7] Whalen continues the list with increasing fancy and naughty accuracy, including a Nose-Punching Bodhisattva, two Beer-Pouring Bodhisattvas, a Bodhisattva of Gaga, one of Boredom, countless Bodhisattvas of Indifference, Wrath, and Slobism, not forgetting wrathful Protector Bodhisattvas, Musical Bodhisattvas, and thirty-four Bodhisattvas of Sex. Having surveyed his personal pantheon, Whalen goes one Buddhist step farther. "I've loved it; I turn it loose. to enjoy itself. wild horse rolling in the grass, all four feet curled in the air, spine a curling snake against the dirt (curling joy snake) mane & tail spilled over humped over clumps of grass: PHILIP (phil-hippos, 'horse-lover')."

"He's one of the patriarchs, so to speak, of Western Zen," observed Philip's Zen teacher, Richard Baker Roshi. "My own feeling is that there are more lineages in the West that lead us to practice than there are in Asia: lineages in philosophy, psychology, poetry, painting—all these coming right towards Buddhism. But they're broken lineages, because they don't know what the next step is. Then there are also historical moments . . . there are lots of factors. But for me, one of the most important lineages in the West—which Europe doesn't have—is the Beats. Somehow, Allen and Gary and Jack Kerouac and Philip."

Baker then distinguished Philip's role from those of his more famous friends: "These other Beats influenced a lot of people. They had people who wanted to *be* like them, to *imitate* them. Philip didn't have people who wanted to be like him or to imitate him. Rather, Philip gave the people he hung out with the feeling . . . he made them experience themselves. You experienced Philip, but you also experienced yourself, through being with Philip." Baker went on to compare Whalen with priest, philosopher, and social critic Ivan Illich:

> I don't think Philip had the same feeling for mentorship Ivan Illich did, helping people write their PhD theses and so forth, but he did have that same sense of how to just be with people. For Illich, it was "The world is the people I'm in actual contact with. That's the only world I want, and I want to be fully present with them." Philip had that—"Just *be* with people; that's what the world should be"—and it made him, indirectly and directly, a good teacher.

While other people, other Beats, may have been good examples, Philip was a good teacher. To me, Philip was a kind of patriarch of a Western lineage that brought many people closer to Buddhism.[8]

METHODS

Facing the biographer of an articulate, highly trained Buddhist monk are problems beyond those of describing a purely secular life. Behind the dates and doings, relatives and education, institutions, assignations, accomplishments, teachers, friends, lovers, detractors, decline, and death that every biographer must tell lurks the Buddhist conviction—shared in this case by the biographer—that none of this can be pinned down; that it is all, to use the overworked, underexplained technical term, empty.

"This seat is empty. There is no one sitting here," is how Philip Whalen put it from the High Seat, having just assumed the abbacy of the Hartford Street Zen Center. "Please take care of yourself," he continued. And ended.

There is no denial of existence implied by Buddhist emptiness; that would be a logical fault as grievous as flat-out accepting existence, and would also fly in the face of experience. But *how* things exist interests the Buddhist, who must summon a language of impermanence to talk about it. He or she needs a language of transience, of split-second causal conjunction and interconnection, because the Buddhist sees everything pulling on everything else, thereby changing it, ceaselessly and in accord with the laws of karma.

Whalen often saw his life in these terms and described it so. When he said, "There is no one sitting here," it was not an admission of ignorance. He'd looked. The question of identity fairly obsessed him—he wrestled with it in public for decades, long before becoming a Buddhist. He knew there was no one home, but very definite things kept happening to him. Hunger, for one.

One way to handle this paradox inherent to Buddhist biography is to write, as Tibetans have regularly done, more than one history of the same person. In the *namthar* (spiritual biographies) from Tibet, it is not uncommon to read the same story told on three levels: outer, inner, and secret. These levels move from observable facts of daily life to progressively more sublime visions, realizations, and teachings, many invisible to the fleshly eye of readers. These texts can mostly be classified as hagiography, and as such are beyond the goals of this work. While this book does indeed aim to inspire, it will not attempt to do so through idealizing its subject; and although Philip

Whalen did many strange, even inexplicable things in his life, no real suspension of disbelief will be asked of the reader—only a certain looseness or spaciousness, a flexibility of mind: no more than is asked of anyone reading poetry.

Another tool—another three-part division—Buddhists use to get at a person is to section them into body, speech, and mind. These correspond roughly, though inexactly, to outer, inner, and secret. *Body* clearly means the body, but it extends as well to anything connected to form: the literal stuff of a person's life. *Speech* comprises all acts of communication, including how someone talks, which language, how loud, their gestures, manner of dress, attention to grooming, and how they move. *Mind* concerns itself with a person's education, faith, prejudices, perspectives, and conceptual habits, or the absence of these.

This scheme allows a picture to be made at any point in a person's life, without slipping into the fallacy of saying, "This is who they actually *are*." Who they are emerges, almost magically, from the collection of bits. It may shimmer for a quick minute and then devolve back to pieces. Buddhists say this is how we all exist, the assembly and disassembly taking place constantly, many times per second.

Every tool mentioned here will be brought to bear on Philip Whalen, in hopes of resuscitating him. If he does manage to rise from the page, it will be no more true or false than the apparition who walked around for eighty years. That one gave delight, wisdom, beauty, and spiritual guidance to the world. The hope is that this shadow of him might offer a taste of the same.

TWO

Banjo Eyes

WHALEN AND GINSBERG

Allen Ginsberg and Philip Whalen met only days before participating together in what has become one of the most storied poetry readings of all time, the Six Gallery reading in San Francisco, on 7 October 1955. Ginsberg had first seen Whalen's work a month earlier, at Gary Snyder's little shack in Berkeley. Allen had dropped by to introduce himself and to involve Gary in the reading. During the visit, Snyder shared some of Whalen's poetry with Allen, who found it, and thus Whalen, also worthy of inclusion in the reading.

On Friday afternoon, 23 September,[1] Snyder and Whalen rode in from Berkeley on the F train. (In 1955 the lower deck of the San Francisco Bay Bridge was still dedicated to train traffic.) Disembarking at the Key Terminal, they met Allen Ginsberg and Jack Kerouac, who had ridden in from Berkeley shortly before. Whalen and Snyder were old friends from Reed College; Ginsberg and Kerouac were old friends from Columbia University. But Whalen knew neither of the East Coasters, just as Kerouac knew neither of the Northwesterners. Snyder and Ginsberg had only just met. Kerouac had come up from Mexico, while Whalen had descended, both in latitude and altitude, from his summer forest lookout work on Sourdough Mountain in Washington State. Whalen recalled, "We got off, and there standing on the corner of Mission and First streets were Allen and Jack, like Tweedledum and Tweedledee with their arms around each other's shoulders, giggling and bopping, and there we were, and so we all got along very well and ran all round the town."[2] They walked up to North Beach, talking. They had drinks at The Place, then paid a respectful visit to the Friday evening salon held by San Francisco poetry patriarch Kenneth Rexroth, where that evening Kerouac read from his work. (Other, later visits to Rexroth's house would be less respectful.) From a remove of fifty years, the encounter of the four young, unknown poets, as well as their meander through the city, appears almost staged—they even met, poetically, at First and Mission—but at the time it must have seemed just as happenstance as any of the other thousands of connections knitting together the web of the time.

When Philip arrived in the Bay Area late that September, he'd landed on Snyder's tiny floor, in the place he termed "Gary's doghouse," and stayed there about a month. Thus it was that these two were living together at the time of the big event. A large and growing body of writing exists about the Six Gallery reading, to which this book hopes to add only material concerned with Whalen's participation.[3] As soon as Whalen was in the lineup, he shouldered his part of the publicity dog-work. He sat with Ginsberg, addressing what he called "seven million dittoed postcards announcing the reading."[4] Ginsberg's handwriting was an oft-illegible scrawl, but Whalen's hand in 1955 was the elegant italic he'd studied at Reed College. His postcards must have at least caught the eye of those on the Six Gallery and Poetry Center mailing lists. That and word of mouth—everyone associated with the reading had a good big mouth—may have accounted for the surprise overflow crowd of 200–250 people.

Whalen read third, following Philip Lamantia and Michael McClure, and if he appeared shy, as his friend Will Petersen recalled, that would be normal for a man newly down from several months alone on a mountaintop, skittish by nature, giving his first public poetry reading, and that before a large audience. Snyder and McClure recount that Whalen read well, his smart humor engaging the audience. By contrast, Jack Kerouac's *The Dharma Bums* contains a fictionalized account in which his own character—Ray Smith—finds the Whalen character, Warren Coughlin, "too incomprehensible." But Smith has stark criticism for all the readers, even Alvah Goldbook/Allen Ginsberg, who is universally thought to have carried the night with an emotional first reading of *Howl*. Only the hero of Kerouac's book—Japhy Ryder/Gary Snyder—merits praise.

Beyond what anyone else thought of it, Whalen had a great time. He answered Anne Waldman's question on that point in an interview fifteen years later. "It was interesting and exciting," he said,

> because you would read a little bit, and people were actually listening. If they would hear something funny they would laugh. They were a very live audi-

ence and they really seemed interested in what we were saying. This was extremely important to me, extremely exciting that people would respond to what I had written. You know, for many years I had been writing things and showing them to people but the people were all friends of mine. It's one thing to have friends of yours say something is all right, but it's something else to have a stranger, sort of like an audience, pick up on what you're doing. It adds another dimension that wasn't there before. It cheers you up in a certain way.[5]

Kerouac's point stands, though, about the difficulty of Whalen's work. The poem most often cited from his performance at the Six Gallery is "Plus ça change . . ."—an arch, comedic piece about two people turning into birds as they chatter. For all its wit and elegance, that poem remains more or less on its surface, where it can serve as a crowd pleaser. At least two other works Whalen read that night go deeper and function primarily on levels requiring learning and contemplation—though Whalen did take care to make the poems sing.

In thirty-five short lines, "The Martyrdom of Two Pagans" proposes to compare ancient religions, to condemn organized Christianity, and to argue for the sacredness of plant, animal, human, and god realms. Dense with allusion, Whalen's lines confect Greek myth with biblical quotation and Zen legend. Little of this meaning is clear even on first read, much less on first hearing, but energetically the poem possesses what Snyder called "crackle and vigor." Whalen moves the lines along quickly through rhyme and near-rhyme, ending in a catchy ditty:

> Love is better than hate
> Love is better than hate
> Love is better than hate
> & stronger than hell
> for we took our shoes off
> as we fell.

Just as he applied a high or elegant language to great silliness in "Plus ça change . . . ," in this work Whalen reverses the mixture, sketching grand themes with abrupt talk and nursery rhyme.

The next poem he read, "If You're So Smart, Why Ain't You Rich," was also the next one he'd written, earlier in 1955. (All these works stem from a creative burst in the beginning of the year nourished by powerful experiences with peyote.) This poem moves from outside religion to within it, as Whalen closes in on the source of spiritual practice: the observation of mind mixing and colliding with the phenomenal world. As he puts it himself, slowing down the drive of the poem to make sure it isn't missed:

> The effect of this, taken internally
> The effect
> of beauty
> on the mind

If the break of the lines and their placement on the page remind one of William Carlos Williams—and indeed the whole poem is built on the direct address and concrete imagery Williams so prized—it may be because Whalen had seen the great poet frail with age and illness the night before writing it, and had been saddened by Williams's obvious decline.

Titling his poem with a line of slang—something an unhappy housewife might say to her no-good man—and concluding it with another phrase of hard-luck money talk, "I've squandered every crying dime," the body of the poem in between proceeds with relatively formal language, hinging on the act of perception and an urgent attempt to locate mind itself amid the barrage of thought and the appearance of external existence.

The senses and sense objects, the nature of perception, the nature and location of mind—these would remain central to Whalen's work and life. That he cared and studied and wrote about such things made him seem to his companions, possibly unconsciously, like the Buddhist he would formally become only many years later, because these investigations also lie at the heart of Buddhist meditation. It will become clear that Whalen's constant engagement with these classical contemplations also made it possible for him—a large, strange, openly hedonistic man—to undertake one of Buddhism's most rigorous styles of practice, to stay with it through many trials, to rise to the position of abbot and the title of Zen master.

But this moves ahead too quickly: all that happened on 7 October 1955 was that he read his poems to an attentive audience. They surely applauded him politely, then retired to a short break. After that, Ginsberg came on, chanted *Howl* for the first time in public, to listeners who felt, as McClure recalled, they were hearing with gathering excitement a poem that finally spoke to their "actual and real lives" and blew everything preceding him out of the water.

Each one of the poets made his mark that night, including Snyder, who had to follow Ginsberg's *Howl,* but who managed, through physical presence and sonorous voice, to rivet the audience. Each of the poets was invited in the following months to give readings around the Bay Area, including at the Poetry Center, a quasi-official organ of poetry sponsored by San Francisco State University. As a group, they gathered again the following 18 March in Berkeley's Town Hall Theatre, under the auspices of Berkeley professor Thom Parkinson, to reprise the reading. The Six Gallery reading made a dent in the culture, no doubt. Snyder wrote (a couple of decades later), "From that day to this, there has never been a week without a reading in the Bay Area—more like three a night, counting all the coffee shops, schools, the art museum, the aquarium and the zoo."[6] Whalen also reflected, rosily if unrealistically, "Everything went billowing up after that." His own poems that night—with their learned allusions, spiritual contemplations, off-kilter whimsy, and illuminations—could not compare before a tipsy, cheer-led crowd with the rousing momentum of *Howl*'s long lines. It is reported that Ginsberg received a telegram after the reading from Lawrence Ferlinghetti greeting him at the beginning of a great career, but *each* of the poets that night had decisively begun his career. Whalen too had shown his hand—he'd put his cards on the table before the public. It was a hand he would study and play all his life, a hand he would trump.

A coda on the Six Gallery reading: the many accounts, when they offer any physical description of the poets at all, call Whalen something in the direction of fat: burly, portly, big. Kerouac lets Ray Smith come right out and say, "Big fat bespectacled quiet booboo." But photographs of him from the summer before the reading, as well as shots taken the following spring, show Whalen as by any standard trim. Walking and working in the mountains had left him in good shape. He was not rail-thin like Snyder, or muscular like Kerouac—and through the years he did indeed become progressively burlier and portlier, ending up, as predicted, a big fat bespectacled booboo. But in October 1955 he was not fat. Whalen's build gave the impression of fatness, even when there wasn't much extra on him. We would call him an "endomorph" if the term were still in respectable use today. Broader across the beam at the hips than at the shoulder, he had inherited the unfashionable shape of a pear. Sitting on the ground or on a chair accentuated this, and his round face completed the picture. However big Whalen was—Kerouac guessed "180 pounds of poet meat"—it was distributed in an unflattering way. Whether the notion of fatness originated with Whalen and radiated outward from him, or whether it was something he absorbed from his companions, as early as 1956 it enters his poetry, where it would stay. "Small Tantric Sermon" is an overtly sexual poem, requiring physical description:

your foot
Braced against the table-leg beside the bed
Springing your hips to admit
My gross weight, the other foot
Stroking the small of my back:
A salacious picture of a man and a woman
Making out together
Or ingenuous autobiography
"Memoirs of a Fat & Silly Poet"

. . .

In early November, Whalen moved into a room of his own, taking over a little place from lithographer Will Petersen, who was heading to Japan to study traditional printmaking. Thus for the next bubbling months—months described in Kerouac's *The Dharma Bums*—the four poets did not literally live together in that they did not sleep each night under one roof. On the other hand, they spent so much time together—nearly every afternoon and evening—that it felt as if they were housemates, much as Ginsberg constructed it later in his memory.

Along with the room, Whalen inherited Will Petersen's job washing laboratory glass for the Animal Husbandry Department of the University of California, Berkeley. One of the very few jobs in his life that suited him, Whalen profited from it in four distinct ways. First, he was making regular money. Second, the job was a morning commitment, so his afternoons were open. He spent them goofing off with his friends, walking around "screeching and laughing," drinking wine, looking at everything, taking pills, studying Buddhist texts, learning haiku, smoking dope, discussing literature, and writing it all down, as each of the writers seemed to have done sooner or later. A third perquisite of the glass-washing job was that Whalen had a steady supply of eggs within reach. The lab specialized in chickens and eggs, and Philip nicknamed it "the Egg Plant." Given that everyone in the group of friends was living on very little money, a free protein source was more than welcome. Finally, there was the grain alcohol used to sterilize the test tubes. Whalen regularly brought back jugs of the stuff, where it was mixed with other fluids to create an intoxicating if dangerous punch.

Though this period of creative quasi-cohabitation felt important to each of the writers, it didn't last long. Kerouac left Ginsberg's rose-porch cottage on Milvia in a huff in December, heading east for the winter. Snyder decamped from his Hillegasse shack in February to another cabin in the North Bay, in Marin County. Ginsberg moved himself and most of his things west into Peter Orlovsky's place in San Francisco. Whalen kept the steady day job but also bounced around some, moving for a couple of months into Gary's old quarters, then settling in May into Allen's cottage. Because Allen had a lot going on both sides of the bay, he did not completely abandon the Milvia Street digs, and it was there, on 9 June 1956, that he found a telegram from his brother, brought over from San Francisco by Peter. It told of his mother's death. Allen memorialized the moment some years later in his famous poem "Kaddish":

> Orlovsky in my room—Whalen in his peaceful chair—
> a telegram from Gene—Naomi dead—
> Outside I bent my head to the ground under the bushes
> near the garage—knew she was better

Having lost his own beloved mother some years earlier, Whalen would have been a comfort to the bereft Ginsberg.

The physical space that began to grow between Whalen and Ginsberg gave birth to several important patterns in their relationship. First, a written correspondence arose between them, one that would eventually run to hundreds of letters, from 1956 until 1991, after which time Whalen could barely see to write and read. He was at that point serving as abbot at the Hartford Street Zen Center in any case—a stable address with a working telephone.

The easy, open hospitality at the beginning of their friendship characterized its duration. Whenever Philip was in New York, he stayed with Allen; Allen expected and got the same from Philip when his travels took him to the West Coast. Moving into a new flat in 1959, Philip wrote to Allen as enticement to visit that the place had an "enormous bathtub and a huge orgy-bed."[7] Playing host meant of course also cleaning up after one another and sometimes covering tracks. Whalen's "other pair" of pants, for example, went flying across the country several days after he did one time, and he had to forward Allen an alert that "the fuzz cats are stalking you; they want their $10 reward for having caught you *in flagrante delicto* on a certain January evening at the corner of Shattuck."[8]

Beyond opening their homes to each other, they seem to have cared, to a surprising degree, about one another's domestic comfort and daily life. Allen was forever at pains to arrange hospitality during Philip's East Coast reading tours or to set him up well at poetry conferences. He also tried more than once to arrange fellowships and artist-in-residence stays for Philip. In support of an application in 1968, Allen wrote that as Philip was

> of sober scholarly temperament, of middle-age, industrious in letters, experienced in peaceful residence in US West Coast cities and forests and Japan, it occurred to me that the facilities of the American Academy in Rome would be a perfect solution of his immediate perplexity, and a very happy one. It would enable him to enlarge his acquaintance of the world to the European continent which he has never visited, and familiarize himself with traditions and places which he has explored extensively in his learned & varied reading over the decades; at the same time, the American Academy in Rome could be host to a most distinguished poet whose honorable impecuniousness & tranquil penurious devotion to his craft have served as a marvelous standard of patience and dignity by which his many friendly peers in Poesy have measured their own flamboyant aggressiveness with rue.[9]

As much as it appears Allen relished composing this, it did not work out. Nor, alas, did his other attempts. Philip groaned to Allen about his prospects for receiving a fellowship that "some Fellows like me; some do not." Finally in early 1971, when he bought a second parcel of rural land, Allen wrote to Philip in Japan, informing him that

> COP Inc [Committee on Poetry, Ginsberg's nonprofit foundation] has land, 22 acres or so, next to Gary's. . . . I wrote Gary to arrange it for Lew and yourself to take over the land for COP in perpetuity or lifetime, whatever can be legally arranged—that is, you can have half a dozen or dozen acres (depending on how law falls) to come back to, build a house or shack on and call your own. If that's useful, mention that briefly in application, ie apply for land too . . . since Welch asked, and Gary agreed, and since it was bought with you both in mind.[10]

Two weeks later, Allen sent Philip a check together with an agreement from COP that the land would be at Whalen's permanent disposal. This fantasy took more definite shape over the next few years, as Allen engaged an architect and builder, and asked for a set of drawings for the house from Philip himself (which he actually submitted). In a charming letter in late 1973, Allen amends his plans, realizing that he requires more room. "There [must] be an area big enough for Peter to share my space. I hadn't figured this out, because I had the image of you & me retired old poetic characters tending the fire writing haikus. But I'll likely enough for the next decade still be having one kind or another mate around. Also if we do wind up old and senile there we'll need room for a younger attendant to get groceries & chop wood."[11] But as Allen ripened these plans in his mind, Philip was moving ever deeper into formal communal Buddhism, so that by the time this letter arrived, he'd been living on Zen Center property for nearly two years. He'd been ordained, and neither he nor his teacher, Richard Baker Roshi, thought it becoming for a monk to own property.

Advice and practical help also flowed the other way, from Philip to Allen. When Allen first got his farm in upstate New York, he wrote about the faunal joys of country life, and Philip responded with clear advice drawn from his youth in rural Oregon:

> Cows love love & they also dig listening to music while you milk them— radio in the barn delights them. Horses are brilliant but unsound—they are smarter than cows, but giddy and undirected. You must be gentle but exceedingly self-assured & quite firm with them, otherwise they will take advantage of you & try trotting along quite near the fence in order to brush you off, or will go zooming along near trees with low, overhanging branches, with the same object. What they want is exercise & to be told what to do. They respond well to charming speeches & apples & carrots & tobacco {these last three are rare treats, maybe twice a week, if you're messing around riding or working them daily.}
>
> Chickens are congenitally stupid, but respond to pretty words & slow, calm movement. {Don't move fast or talk loud around any farm bird or animal; it scares them & they will bite, kick, stop giving milk &/or eggs if they are nervous.} Egg laying time {hormones or not} won't really get going until the approach of spring. Didn't you ever notice that the price of eggs is lower in spring and autumn, & late autumn and winter the price goes up? There just aren't so many eggs then.
>
> Flowers & vegetables vastly enjoy companionship & chants & prayers. They really do better if you talk to them while you pull out the weeds & cultivate and water them.[12]

. . .

If Whalen and Ginsberg were solicitous of one another's physical comfort, what they really cared about was each other's voice. They met as shy, brave poets, and poetry and bravery bound their friendship together. They offered their apartments to each other, but they also offered their ears. They made room, privately and publicly, for one another's voice. They wrote a steady correspondence, each demanding to hear news, each appreciating and carefully storing the other's letters, each pouring intimate details of his creative and mundane life onto the pages. Allen's letters often convey a feeling of pressure. Sometimes they are virtually telegraphic. He complains of facing stacks of unanswered mail 100, 150, 300 envelopes high. Yet out of the daunting pile, he's writing to Philip. Philip too complains (with the best of them) about unfinished work, but his letters—many written with broad-nibbed pen in a careful hand, move at a stately pace, with time for asides, jokes, gossip, research, music, anachronisms. Ginsberg and Whalen could write to one another about business, they could write about sex, they could write about politics, about protest and practicalities, they could write about infinities. They wrote about money when they needed to, which was often. They wrote about Buddhism, first as appreciative outsiders, then as initiates, finally as adepts.

Early on, in the mid-1950s, Ginsberg especially was active in promoting his circle of writing friends. He recognized that more or less geographical groups had gathered—the Black Mountain school, what he called the "O'Hara group" in New York, the Spicer crowd in San Francisco, and the group around Duncan in Berkeley—but the work Ginsberg took to his old professors, the works he typed up himself or had typed by girlfriends, the poems and prose he read to nearly captive editors in their offices, cut across these groupings. Kerouac, Snyder, Whalen, and Corso: these are the names that appear most frequently, usually together, in Ginsberg's "business" letters to Whalen. These long, margin-to-margin, single-spaced briefs detailed whose manuscripts had gone where. Getting work in front of editors' eyes was remarkably laborious in 1956, but Ginsberg undertook it with vigor, working as a front man in New York, depending on Whalen to serve as the textual repository back on Milvia Street in Berkeley. Whalen also functioned as a link to Snyder, newly in Japan.

Prospective book deals, placement of work in existing magazines, creation of new magazines, recordings—with or without jazz musicians: Ginsberg filled his letters to Whalen with the specifics of these, inevitably apologizing for it as well. He was trying to exploit the crack made by the Six Gallery reading in the front wall of academia and publishing, and to do this, he advanced what he called, startlingly, "a blitzkrieg."[13] Forcing his work and the work of his friends outward with such energy caused even the irrepressible Allen to pause at one point in 1956 and to check with elders. William Carlos Williams thought the campaign a good thing and a timely one. Allen reported this in a letter to Philip, adding that Williams lamented that nothing similar had happened before. Feeling poetry's lineage blessings upon him, Ginsberg forged ahead, stirring up as much interest and action as possible in New York and Chicago, knowing Whalen was solidly back on the West Coast to catch the return papers and anchor the operation.

Mirroring this, but on a deeper, psychological-spiritual level a couple of years later, Ginsberg sailed out on truly brave explorations of mind and consciousness, counting on Whalen and Snyder as the sane Buddhist shore upon which he could drag his psychic dory, there to receive calm but hip instruction—which, it appears, Philip and Gary actually did offer.

As early as 1958, Allen sent his poem "Laughing Gas" to them, writing, "I seem to have become a Bhuddist [*sic*] overnight, much to my embarrassment & chagrin. What the fuck is happening. Have you Bodhisattvas been hexing me? In any case, rush me a reply before my reason gives way in Total Giggle. . . . I can't tell you how grateful I am for your patience with me, tho at the moment I am so confused, write me a letter immediately. It's so funny." Clearly soliciting advice, part of Ginsberg simultaneously and stubbornly resented doing it. In 1960 and the years following, Allen consulted shamans both in South America and in India, sometimes taking psychedelic drugs under their guidance and becoming increasingly distressed by the basic message that his self must die. His correspondence with Philip, recounting horror visions under the influence of *yage* and *ayahuasca* at the hands of a Peruvian *brujo,* are soaked with fear and confusion. In an extraordinary letter from summer 1960, Ginsberg breezily begins by telling Whalen that he'd been thinking of him in a hotel room in Lima two months earlier, and then copying in a sharply insulting excerpt from a long poem in progress, *Aether:*

> Stop Conceiving Worlds!
> Says Philip Whalen
> (My Savior !) (Oh what snobbery)
> (as if he cd save anyone)
> At *least,* he won't understand.
> I lift my finger in the air to create
> a universe he wouldn't understand, full
> of sadness.

A few short paragraphs on in the same letter though, Allen confesses that he's confused, scared, ignorant, and that he needs help. Shrugging off Allen's jabs in the poem (which stand today as written in *Reality Sandwiches*), Philip sent back a funny, caring letter a few days later. It bears quoting at length not only for the insight and range and humor it shows, but because it is typical of the first five years of their friendship. Beginning simply with "YES," Whalen first addressed Ginsberg's fear of death: "Jack told me about the brujo's chant, 'neh, neh, neh' calling (as you heard) on Kali, who IS that reptilian devourer. But think what she will eat: the old, hung-up, bugged, tired-out Self that's merely a collection of sad old regrets, irrelevant passions ('I like rhubarb; I hate spinach').... Buddha did the same thing, he says 'I done tried ever way I could, now I can't go on no way atall, I just going to sit here until I has a breakthrough or perishes.'" Then Philip addressed his friend's pique:

> I know you don't like the terms I use; I want to find new ones, make new stories, poems, metaphors of all this which you & anybody else WILL dig, so's you can get started on the way to figuring out for yourself what you are, what is Heaven (or Enlightenment, or Real, or whatever). You got to do it your own way, by yourself. Find a guru if you can; if you get one you can really know & dig & trust he can help you lots, he will know you & have more skill-ful means than I've been able to scrape together to point out, suggest what you should try. But it will end up with you having to do, to experience, to realize the whole works by yourself. It won't work otherwise; somebody else's poetry is theirs; you make your own; it's like that.[14]

Beyond this accurate advice about locating a teacher, Whalen's desire to find new terms and vocabulary to express ancient, specifically Buddhist truths is something he shared early on with Kerouac, Snyder, and Welch, later with Ginsberg himself, as well as with Kyger, McClure, di Prima, and Waldman. Finding the right language for spiritual experience is, after all, one of the poet's jobs, but the job necessitates *having* spiritual experience.

Many reams have been published on Beat poets and Buddhism. Whatever those pages facilely say, it remains an act of bravery to sit in meditation and engage one's mind, one's raw awareness. But this is the essence of spirituality. The experience, as anyone knows who has tried even a little of it, can be by turns groundless, tedious, frightening, boring, confusing—as well as calm-ing, clarifying, and strengthening. Treading a spiritual path demands a great deal of the pilgrim, and the pilgrim often feels a mess. To then be brave enough to talk about this with another person requires a further act of cour-age. Very few can do it, and very few can hear it. This channel, however, was wide open between Ginsberg and Whalen, and remained so their entire lives, becoming finally the central theme of their intercourse. Both men tried to practice Buddhism very sincerely, and although both men possessed the necessary arrogance of an artist, neither was overly burdened with pride, a leaden obstacle to spiritual communication.

．　　．　　．

Emboldened no doubt by Allen's radical openness to sex with both genders and with varying numbers of simultaneous partners, Philip was able to write to him on this matter. Whalen reports his activity with women neutrally or with a humorous tone. "C.D. and I are chasing one another around the living room. Who will win?" or "She claims it hurt but was great & made everything all right." But he also wrote to Allen, and it seems *only* to Allen from among his closest circle, about action with men, mostly in despair: "Beefcake is bestirring himself among younger, blonder, thinner, richer folks & so I see little of him at present; I do not, however, surrender. . . . Wire immediate advice on my next move."[15]

Allen's letters contain little advice, though they do include regular reports of sex—with women, chiefly as participants in cluster sex, and with men—previous acquaintances, current lovers, and professionals. Sex was such a standard part of his communication that it took on the air of a regular column. When Allen wrote in a quiet period, "Just about no sex at all these days," one has the feeling of turning to the sports page and finding that one's team has been shut out. Horny and outrageous as he showed himself to be in the 1950s, Allen still fell into occasional doubt and guilt about his sexual activity. One letter to Philip about it occasioned a learned lecture by return mail on the history of the mind-body split before and in the Judeo-Christian tradition, the various sources of guilt, what Buddhism might have to say about sexuality, and a funny report on research about masturbation—"No exact description of 'excessive' was given . . . every hour on the hour? . . . twice a day? . . . four times a week? . . . more than once a year?"[16] Attempting to soothe Allen's worries, Philip settles on the biological view: "People are people with sexual drives. They have a physiological need for some sexual outlet. As far as I can see there is no sin about it. Sometimes it is inconvenient, illegal, impossible, & unpleasant for other people to think about or watch. (Let them think of something else or look elsewhere.) But people in their physical makeup will do something or other to get a jolly in spite of the law or Moses or their own notions of what they ought to be doing." The moral? Philip draws out several. He urges Allen to stay busy and take cool baths. He urges him to stop worrying so much. He urges Allen to submerge himself instead in the deepest questions of the human experience—the list that Philip himself was busy with—and above all to keep writing.

The same list shows up again in Philip's response to Allen's politics, though here more cutting practical advice also enters the friendship.

> Politics thing is the objectification of "mental war"—violence & brutality of other tyrants are actually our own carelessness, ignorance, & lack of compassion REALIZED—& we are naturally the victims as well. The real secret is not to hate anyone or anything, not even oneself {it's hardest of all to disconnect from loving or hating self, but must be done}—the final struggle is in myself {yourself, ourselves}: wisdom, compassion & detachment vs. ignorance, desire {all kinds of *wanting*—for peanuts, crystal chandeliers, peace, war—not just sexual desire} & attachment {i.e. the will to *repeat* life (former & future lives ... merely a metaphor) repeat pleasure, keep things, possess people.}[17]

Whalen shared Ginsberg's stance on almost every outward political issue, but he also stood in league with Ginsberg's muse and seemed to feel a chaperone's duty to point Allen back toward her. "STAY THE FUCK OUT OF GAOL," he wrote in 1968, about Allen's participation in the Chicago Republican National Convention protests and riots. "You have too much else to do yet. Don't get sucked into this teensie local idiot game of copsie/hippsie/warsie/dontsies. It will devour you & nothing more will get done; the game will devour anybody."

In the thirty-five years and hundreds of pages of their correspondence, when irritation or needling does arise between them—and their letters are remarkably free of it—it erupts precisely around protecting one another's ability to work, the aesthetic space of composition. Philip required lots of it—undisturbed, elegant space in which to think what he mockingly called his high-class thoughts.

"I have my own cuckoo style of living," he wrote in 1966. "My nerves demand lots of solitude & quiet & occasional short fits of noise & people. But I MUST be able to get away from the people & hide & be quiet whenever I want to." Allen preferred it social, as Philip well knew: "You *like* to live a more complicated & populous existence—don't complain to me about 'you ain't got time.' Take the two girls [Ginsberg has written that he's living in a ménage, with two girls in his bed, and that the tiny flat is crowded, and that he has little room] & a typewriter & a hotel room & go to work, if work is what you *want*. I have exactly the same complaining letter, for the same reasons, from E.v A. & B.B. Why aren't all you married folks HAPPY?"[18] Allen's letters to Philip also contain many instances of flat-out name-dropping. As Philip was unruffled by Allen's jibes, he was equally unimpressed by hyperventilated mentions of the rich and famous. When Allen let it be known, for example, that he was hanging out with, jamming with, even beginning to record with the likes of Bob Dylan and John Lennon, Philip wrote back that it was wonderful that Allen was finally learning music.

. . .

Turning from internal correspondence to more public display, Allen worked hard to get Philip's work and his literal voice before the public. Starting with the Six Gallery reading and the subsequent New York "blitzkrieg," Allen continued for the rest of his life to help arrange readings and invitations for Philip and to shuttle attention, acclaim, award, and emolument his way. Allen arranged Philip's first reading tour—to New York and New England with Michael McClure in 1959—and even had to jump in to read at several venues when McClure took sick with pneumonia. The next year, Allen turned over as much logistical work as he could for an East Coast tour to the young Elsa Dorfman, though he remained staunchly supportive in the background. When Philip's first book appeared in 1960, published by Leroi Jones's Totem Press, Allen stood behind it: he was the one who'd written to Jones from Paris, alerting him to Whalen's work. When, ten years later, Whalen's big book *On Bear's Head* was nominated for the National Book Award in poetry, Allen (together with Kenneth Rexroth) was behind it.[19] When the Vancouver Poetry Conference in 1963 began gathering itself into what looked like an important event, Ginsberg, along with Bob Creeley, sent Philip a telegram to come up and take part, and they sent a plane ticket to make it possible.

The steadiest, most long-standing invitation that Allen issued to Philip began in 1973, as Allen began to study with his new Buddhist guru—the young, brilliant, charismatic, troublesome Tibetan, Chögyam Trungpa Rinpoche. Ginsberg and his guru agreed to a two-way teaching relationship: Ginsberg would humble himself and enter as a disciple the arduous path laid out in the Kagyu tradition; Trungpa Rinpoche on the other side would undertake the study of American and English poetry—and poets—under Allen's guidance. Unbelievably energetic for someone who moved slowly and spoke carefully, Trungpa Rinpoche soon had Allen involved in poetical projects of all sorts: giving benefit readings, teaching seminars, and creating poetic curricula. Allen's attempts to co-enlist Philip in this began just as quickly. "He [Trungpa Rinpoche] asked me if there's anybody I'd like to read with," Allen wrote in 1973, about a benefit planned for October. "You, me and Gary, if there's leisure on your part." Philip accepted the invitation, only to beg off a week later by telegram, claiming it was impossible—there was no time, and besides, he was having a nervous breakdown. (Curiously, Whalen was living at the time in the San Francisco Zen Center, with no duties or responsibilities other than what he assigned himself. Just living there taxed his nerves, though, as he widely reported to his friends.)

At the beginning of 1974, Allen wrote again, informing Philip of Trungpa Rinpoche's plans to found the Naropa Institute that coming summer in Boulder, where Trungpa Rinpoche had established a seat for himself and his organization. Poetics—what Allen termed "spiritual poetics"—were to play a large role. Allen and Anne Waldman were inviting a roster of well-known poets, each of whom was to teach for a weekend or week. When he received Allen's letter, Philip was still mired in culture shock at having joined the San Francisco Zen Center community, which turned out to be chiefly young, middle-class "kids" with strong opinions. Philip also felt that the several exacting periods of formal meditation each day had whacked his head around. He wrote to Allen that he was in no position to teach anything, that he was mostly conscious of his "titanic ignorance," and beyond that, "'spiritual poetics' is not my dish." In response, Allen prodded his old friend good-naturedly, "'Spiritual poetics' was just my romantic title for whatever anyone does. I wrote them you'd not likely come, unless you got an engraved personal invite from Trungpa, transported in the beak of a garuda." Thus Whalen missed the inaugural summer session at Naropa, but by 1975 he'd seen his way clear to visiting, performing, and teaching there, and he continued to do so for the next twelve years.

These one- to two-week Boulder visits opened a new period in Whalen and Ginsberg's friendship. For one thing, it meant that they saw each other every year and had at least a little time to spend together at ease. Whalen much enjoyed being in the mountain air and pretty landscape of Boulder. Some years the visiting faculty housing had a pool, and swimming further lifted his spirits. The differences in the Buddhist communities they'd joined fascinated both Allen and Philip. Ginsberg was helping to create the "scene" around Trungpa Rinpoche, who was a Tantric Buddhist meditation master,

FIGURE 1. Philip, standing and wearing a *rakusu,* at Naropa University, 1975–76. Seated, left to right, are David Rome, Chögyam Trungpa Rinpoche, William Burroughs, Allen Ginsberg, and Anne Waldman. Photograph by Allen DeLoach. Estate of Philip Whalen, Bancroft Library, University of California, Berkeley.

revered scholar, and former governor of a large area in Tibet. Whalen had accepted an invitation to live at Zen Center from its new abbot, Richard Baker Roshi, someone Philip had cheerfully known for years, both in the United States and in Japan. Under Baker's guidance, the Zen Center community was rapidly expanding into the urban life of San Francisco, developing its forest valley monastery at Tassajara, and establishing a farm at Green Gulch in coastal Marin County. Whalen was a reluctant but colorful node in this otherwise quietly streaming network. The comparing and contrasting he and Allen did—of the meditation styles, of the shrines, of the aesthetics, of the approach to classical Buddhist teachings, of the demography of the communities, of the varying engagements with the surrounding world—were part of a larger cross-pollination that enriched both meditation groups, an exchange that had begun several years earlier, when Trungpa Rinpoche came to meet Zen Center's founding abbot, Shunryu Suzuki Roshi.[20]

Philip would come back to Zen Center each year shaking his head and clucking as if scandalized by what he termed the "vajra energy of those kids" in Boulder, but he was clearly impressed. He took a dimmer view of Naropa

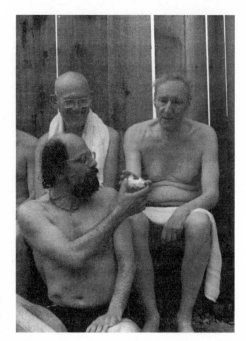

FIGURE 2. "Bathing Beauties,"
Boulder, Colorado, July 1976.
Clockwise from bottom: Allen
Ginsberg, Philip Whalen, and William
Burroughs. Photo © Gordon Ball.

itself, as communication about travel and honoraria did not always run
smoothly, and because he harbored deep reservations about using classrooms
for teaching poetry. In fact, the role of teacher, adjunct to their jobs as poets,
strained both Whalen and Ginsberg, who were both already destabilized by
rather serious shifts in their lives. Both men had recently joined Buddhist
communities—Whalen residentially, Ginsberg administratively. And both
had recently signed on to study Buddhism with serious lineage-holding
teachers. This kind of study is not comparable to a weekend course or even an
extended seminar. The kind of commitments Whalen and Ginsberg made to
their respective teachers can be compared to a marriage—though with a
Buddhist master, it is an explicitly unfair, unequal, unbreakable bond. Both
men were thus struggling with their teachers in the traditional ways, and as
part of that dharma combat, both had been pushed into teaching. They were
differently equipped for the job, but both worked hard at it. Allen had vastly
more experience speaking before a crowd and was something of a natural
showman. Philip by contrast tended to be retiring if he could get away with
it; if he could not, he was theatrical, loosely strung, and Irish. In a recording
of a Naropa class from 1976, one hears Whalen improvising a tribal song
while dancing a literal circle around the class—his voice going away and com-

FIGURE 3. Group at Naropa Institute, 1975–76. Standing, from left: an unidentified woman, Peter Orlovsky, Allen Ginsberg, Allen DeLoach, Whalen (in robes), Jerome Rothenberg and his wife, Diane. Front row: Gordon Ball. Photographer unknown.

ing back to the recorder, the class convulsed in laughter—all this in imagination of a primitive death rite for someone called George. All about how poetry began.

Allen trusted Philip as a teacher. He had Philip take over his classes on occasions when he couldn't make it himself or was feeling worn out. One hears Allen chattering from the front row in recordings of some of Whalen's classes, and several times they taught together. On one occasion, the recording picks up with Allen interrupting friendly gossip to proclaim, "O the glory!" as Philip walks into the room wearing his robes. "This is only part of it," he replies coolly, explaining that he only wears the full Zen costume to scheduled sitting periods. There follows a brief but strange discussion about the times of these sittings, during which Allen, distracted, cannot seem to grasp the schedule, despite Philip's patient but increasingly strained repetition of the information. Finally clear, Allen launches into a praise of meditation generally, of Whalen as a distinguished teacher of it, and of meditation as extremely helpful to understanding the development of twentieth-century poetry. Ginsberg finally assigns the class, as nonnegotiable homework, to learn the meditation technique at one of the free Naropa instruction sessions.

In this and other joint appearances, Whalen and Ginsberg's distinct styles played out. Allen—voluble, dominating, confessional, energetic, demanding—was polite to his guest coteacher, when he remembered Philip was there. Philip, sometimes left with room to do naught but embroider, embroidered beautifully. He supplied Allen with missing names, dates, editions, locations. He chuckled at Allen's intentional provocations, told supportive stories, but had no qualms at all in correcting or flatly contradicting him. If Allen mentioned a particular writer or book, Philip would chime in with facts about the availability of said work or writer in various paperback editions, this one containing the letters, another the journals, a third the variorum. He could as well, and often did, extemporize a further reading list on the theme or writer or period that Allen was teaching.

When Philip or Allen held the floor alone, they would often read aloud or recite longish stretches from works assigned to the class. (Allen could do lots of this from memory, something Philip admired about him.) Partly they both suspected that not many in their classes had completed the assigned reading; partly they just liked to read poetry aloud; and partly they needed to fill out the ninety minutes. With a given work fresh in the air, both teachers might offer a summation of a poem's meaning or general thrust, but then they took different approaches to working with the poem and the class. Allen would frequently isolate a particular device or technique and show how it worked in the poem. He would then engage the class in spontaneous exercises using that very "trick," as he sometimes called such things. An example was putting two very different words next to one another, with the intention of creating a jarring effect or interruption in the mind: "hydrogen jukebox"—an example from his own *Howl,* or Corso's "penguin dust." The aim of these exercises seemed to be to give students a new tool in their poetry toolkit. Whalen preferred to open things out from a poem and then wander a bit, usually asking whether anyone had gotten any good out of the poem at all—if anyone was turned on, made mad, interested in the slightest, and if so why. He mostly despaired of getting intelligent discussion from the class, but this may have been at least partly due to his own cutting erudition and strong opinions; it took a brave student to pipe up in Whalen's seminars. Philip usually tried to put the work under discussion into a larger context by pointing students back to other works from the same author, or to biographies, intelligent criticism, or cultural history. He pointed them back to books and tried to instill in the students a devotion for reading.

Ginsberg seemed to feel that poetry as a skill could be taught. Whalen felt otherwise. He maintained that poetic skill was a magical, inexplicable gift, but that one could draw it out by reading a great deal, listening constantly and noting what one heard, consciously opening one's mind through the time-tested techniques of prayer, invocation, drug use, fasting, physical exertion, sexual ecstasy, time alone in nature, and so forth. Philip shared with Allen the view that one could come to a clarifying knowledge of one's mind and feelings through meditation—though both stressed that Buddhist meditation was not to be simply used in this directed way. In summary, Allen seemed to feel that students could be led. Philip felt students must be pushed to find out things for themselves. Perhaps these positions are not so terribly far apart.

Whatever Allen thought of Philip's teaching—or his poetry (he let it be widely known that he never really understood Philip's work)—he continued to invite Philip into reading or teaching situations. In 1978, Whalen received a letter from John Ashbery asking him to come to New York for a couple of semesters and take over, together with Allen, Ashbery's teaching load at Brooklyn College. Ashbery proposed that Philip and Allen could split the $15,000 pay, and that Philip could stay at the Ginsberg place during the time. Whalen chose instead to spend 1979 at the monastery, but he did end up at Brooklyn College nearly ten years later, during Allen's first year of formal employment there. Philip went east that spring to do the short stint at Brooklyn College as well as to fulfill a number of reading engagements around New York State. He also went to Naropa, at Allen and Anne Waldman's invitation, as he had done for many years. He went for the job and the money it gave him, to escape temple life, to be in the mountains, and to see Allen, Anne, and other friends—but he complained that during this last visit he could "scarcely see enough to cross the street without getting run over." As long as he was at all mobile, though, Philip showed up and was grateful for the gigs Allen and staff put together for him. In later years, Philip began to fill out his itinerary by leading Zen sittings and workshops.

As blindness, infirmity, and religious commitment reined Whalen closer to home, he and Ginsberg continued to want to see one another. The letters they wrote in their own hands, and letters they later dictated or parceled out to assistants—Whalen because of blindness, Ginsberg because of overcommitment—express their straightforward, tender wishes to visit or chat. "I'd love to see you," "Can we get together when you're traveling through?"

"Why don't you come here for a break?" As the letters tail off altogether, little archival notes continue to appear in Allen's files: "Call PW," "Spoke on . . . by phone to Whalen." Until a few months before his death, Ginsberg remained unstoppably on the road and did what he could to keep the friendship alive.

There is no formal record of Allen's calling or coming by during his last San Francisco visit in late 1996, though more than one resident of Hartford Street remembers him being there. Philip had been functionally blind for some years and had long since ceased keeping a journal. Similarly, there is no record of any special memorial service conducted at Hartford Street Zen Center, when Allen passed away a few months later.[21] Most certainly, though, a memorial took place. The usual procedure for these involves the deceased's name and dates being written out in calligraphy on stiff paper and placed upon the altar in the meditation hall for several days. At a time when a fair number of practitioners could gather for meditation and chanting, the service would take place. Integrated into the standard liturgy, specifically into a section of it called the "Dedication of Merit," the name would be read out. The merit of meditation practice and of reciting sacred texts—both thought to generate immeasurable quantities of merit—are then dedicated to the departed's smooth passage from life and good onward journey. At Hartford Street Zen Center, located in the middle of San Francisco's famed gay Castro district, Allen would have been further celebrated in an informal gathering after the chanting, with tea and cookies and stronger beverage as well.

One practitioner at the Hartford Street Zen Center recalled a lunch the week of Allen's death during which Philip expressed his sadness about it, as well as his worry that it had been a loud event, with lamas chanting and many people around.[22] Another spoke to Philip shortly after he'd been told of the death; to him, Philip reported that he felt all the air had been sucked out of the room, as if he were stuck on a musty sofa in the lobby of a transient Tenderloin hotel.[23] Beyond personal recollection, what remains is a record of a talk Whalen gave the following month on the theme of death. Not a lament, Whalen wrestles death in classical Zen style but manages to give it personal feeling:

> To experience death is one of the big teachings in Zen practice. Hakuin Zenji said that you must experience the great death, where you give up, you are gone, you have been carted off somehow by your practice into a new insight or breakthrough.
>
> He said that you must also experience the great doubt. We have this system, the Zen way of doing things, and what is it all about after you've been

doing it for 20 years? We got the robes, chanting, ceremonies and endless sitting, and here we all are no smarter than we ever were. Obviously nothing is happening. Nothing is ever going to get us out of this. So we have this great doubt about Buddhism in general or about the world. We are out on a limb. Years ago I decided that what you do is pick up the nearest saw and start sawing on the limb and see what happens.

We have to doubt. We have to give up our certainty about ourselves, about how Buddha is going to save everybody or the idea that zazen is going to fix anything. Give up everything. Go past life and death, doubt and belief, the idea of salvation or destruction. You have to go clear past all the boundaries into something else and experience some other state rather than trying to figure out pairs of opposites.

How do you do that? Well, you got to make what somebody or another has called the "existential leap." You have to throw yourself over the edge of the cliff. We need to have confidence in our own understanding of what is going on now and what we can do from where we are. And avoid getting all tangled up trying to arrange the world or lapsing into memories of how things were. We have to be careful of what it is we think we are seeing. Are we seeing the present or are we trying to see something else? All we have to be bothered by is how things are now. Starting out from here and doing something new is certainly of more use than trying to reproduce conditions that are gone.[24]

THREE

Buddha Red Ears

WHALEN AND KEROUAC

Jack Kerouac and Philip Whalen stood the same height, and both had piercing blue eyes. Beyond that, the physical resemblance stopped. Square-jawed, dark-haired, handsome, and muscular, Kerouac presented a stark contrast to Whalen, who, in his own words, "always looked and talked like a college professor. And people don't like it." In the three Kerouac novels where a character based on Whalen appears, Kerouac portrays his looks often, giving a fresh description nearly each time he enters the action. It is as though Kerouac can't quite believe that among his circle of fit, young, active, dashing friends, like Neal Cassady, Gary Snyder, and Lew Welch, there would be the stoop-shouldered, round-bottomed Whalen, with looks a bit like a bowling pin.

Despite his softer shape, Whalen was a strong man with remarkable endurance, and the athlete in Kerouac noticed this. He wrote about it in letters when he told people about his new friend Philip, and he showed it in a well-known scene from *Big Sur,* the one Kerouac called the "big axe chopping contest." Here, comrades collect wood for their stay. Real-life models Victor Wong, Lew Welch, Lawrence Ferlinghetti, and Philip Whalen took turns cutting logs. Whalen ("Ben Fagan") was so at ease with the work that he kept his pipe in his mouth while he calmly chopped, very unlike the flashily energetic but inefficient character based on Neal Cassady. Fagan simply labored along using the techniques he'd learned in the Forest Service, "getting the job done, silently, not a word."[1]

When, in that same book, Ben Fagan raises the question of emptiness with the Kerouac/Duluoz character, he reverts to the physical, almost for security. Walking along with arms around one another, Fagan asks Duluoz what makes him think he's not alone at the very moment, "making me realize

FIGURE 4. "Buddha Red Ears," drawing of Philip Whalen by Jack Kerouac, 1955. Bancroft Library, University of California, Berkeley.

the ghostliness of existence tho I feel his big bulging body with my hands and say: 'You sure some pathetic ghost with all that ephemeral heavy crock a flesh.'"[2]

In *Desolation Angels,* Kerouac wove Whalen into a sports fantasy. Posing for pictures with Irwin (Allen Ginsberg) and Raphael (Gregory Corso), Jack began to think of the three as an all-star baseball outfield. He himself would be Ty Cobb, one of the greatest players but an unloved one; Corso's effortless composition would make him Joe DiMaggio; while Ginsberg's earnest nature and success brought Lou Gehrig to mind. Whalen's solid strength and stillness led Jack to write, "Later we posed with the greatest catcher of all time, Ben Fagan, squat-legged Mickey Cochrane is what he is, Hank Gowdy."[3] But Jack also saw the cleric in Philip, drawing him earlier in the book as "a big pink fellow with glasses and great calm blue eyes like the eyes of a Moon Professor or really of a Nun." However he looked—and Kerouac kept trying to get it down—Jack was fascinated. "He sits and meditates in big broken pants—I had a vision of him sitting in empty space like that but leaning forward with a big smile—He writes big poems about how he'll change into a 32-foot Giant made of gold—He is very strange—He is a pillar of strength—The world will be better because of him."[4]

That portrait came after years of knowing Whalen. In *The Dharma Bums*—an earlier book chronicling an earlier time, the period of their first acquaintance—Kerouac called Whalen "a big, fat, bespectacled quiet boo-boo" or, further on, "deceptively scholarly looking or fatty-boomboom looking, but he was a real man." To be fair, Jack noted that Philip was more than met the eye, but he settled on the physical: "One hundred and eighty pounds of poet meat."

Both men often thought and wrote against a background of cosmic proportions—"golden eternity," "the Void," past lives, and so on—but Kerouac and Whalen both rooted around in ethnicity, their own and that of others. The sway it held, the power, interested them. As they strode off to North Beach the first time they met in 1955, Kerouac asked Whalen if he was Irish. Philip responded by blowing up and shouting at Jack. The evening and the friendship continued unharmed, so it appears to have been a typical Whalen thunderstorm, with little consequence. But Jack had touched a tender spot. Philip knew his ancestry well and had decidedly mixed feelings about it. He could identify all the characters in his mother's and father's clans; he saw and admired their many strong points—their industry, their love of music, their toughness, their compassion—but had come to feel about his quarrelsome father's side that "Irishmen can't agree about anything, other than they don't like each other."[5]

Whalen similarly took note of Jack's French-Canadian-Indian heritage. He peppered his letters to Kerouac, and very likely their conversations, with French idioms, and Jack wrote back using them too. Most directly, Whalen respected Jack's ancestry by respecting his mother. The notoriously powerful Gabrielle Kerouac—Memere—with whom Jack lived on and off his whole life, liked Philip Whalen, a rare affection among her son's writer friends.

Whalen liked Memere as well: he liked her stories, her humor, her singing of French and Indian songs, and her cooking. He was not blind to Gabrielle's effect on Jack, but Philip always asked after her politely in letters, and sometimes he and Gabrielle wrote back and forth independent of Jack. This mutual fondness may have derived in part from Whalen's feeling that he had a fraternal connection to Jack. Having only a younger sister himself, Whalen wrote early on in their friendship:

> I know there is a lot more of you than I can see or touch. As far as your writing goes, I think you have done some good stuff and that you can do even better as you go along—and the same goes for your own life, I think you have a great deal more ahead of you than you realise now. If I sound strange or bugged or depressed or what not to you, maybe it is because I feel, in a funny unjustifiable way, older than you, like you are my kid brother to be helped and loved in spite of myself—my own whims or changes of mood. Depend on me. I can't say I will always understand you or agree with you about everything; we are separate individuals, but I will be trying to be the best of brothers.[6]

In reply, Jack discriminated among the various strains in Whalen's complicated tender, first listing out numerous books that he'd already completed, noting that they were good books too, in case Whalen should have doubts. He then accepted and reciprocated without reservation Whalen's vow of brotherhood. Jack also inscribed a book he gave to Philip, "Your Brother."

In a remarkable display of this fraternal care, Philip literally sat as Jack's keeper for the better part of a day. Fragile, on the verge of an alcoholic nervous breakdown (which he did soon have and chronicled to hair-raising effect in *Big Sur*), Kerouac had fallen in love with one of Neal Cassady's girlfriends, Jackie Gibson Mercer. He had taken refuge in her flat, where together they passed the nights in extended bouts of sexual pleasure. She worked days, however, and Kerouac sat through them glumly, waiting for her, rarely moving from a broken-down chair, and drinking himself into a nervous blur with port wine. Alarmed at reports of Jack's deterioration, Whalen turned up one day at Mercer's apartment to haul Jack out into the fresh air. They walked toward Golden Gate Park, both of them being strong walkers, and they paused to buy a bottle of wine. Not far into park, they sat on the grass to imbibe, but Kerouac stretched out first. He instantly fell into a deep slumber, one that lasted six hours, from noon to dusk. Philip simply sat next to him the while, smoking his pipe and enjoying the changing views of the park and its inhabitants. He made no attempt to rouse Jack even when he seemed to stir briefly once or twice. Finally Kerouac awoke fully. The two stood chatting awhile, then headed toward the museum, which they found to be closed. Turning back toward Mercer's apartment, they walked along arm in arm, continuing their conversation.

This afternoon naturally impressed itself on Jack Kerouac's mind. When he fictionalized it a year later, he hewed closely to the physical events of the day but re-created the Zen-flavored postnap dialogue from memory, and from what he imagined Philip would have said. Clearly, on an emotional level, Kerouac was touched. He recorded thinking as he rose to waking consciousness, "I'm in Heaven with Ben Fagan watching over men and me," and as they talked and walked home in embrace, Kerouac felt that Whalen "had blessed me by sitting over my sleep all day and now with these few silly words," acknowledging Whalen as "my real Zen master."[7]

In another instance of brotherly faithfulness, Whalen housed Kerouac's library when Jack and Memere abruptly departed Berkeley in 1957, after a three-week attempt at California life. Whalen hauled these books around with him and in and out of storage for the next twelve years. Finally in 1969 it came to pass simultaneously that Jack had a stable address and Philip had sufficient postage to mail the books. True to his bibliophilic nature, Whalen carefully wrapped them—including an edition of Blake's *Jerusalem,* among other precious volumes—carted them to the post office, and sent them off to Jack, who received them in the house in Florida where ten months later he would die. Jack sent back a letter of thanks and a check. The ten dollars would certainly have surprised and helped Whalen, who was as impoverished as ever, but Kerouac's gentle ribbing about how Philip was a reincarnation of Ben Franklin, "trudging the Bradford road in mud and rain with letters for log cabins," would have pleased Philip even more, with his devotion to the eighteenth century generally, its literature and music specifically.[8]

. . .

In point of fact, Whalen and Kerouac only had two periods during which they spent any appreciable time in one another's physical presence. The first ran episodically from the autumn of 1955 through spring 1957 (with most of 1956 missing). These are the times chronicled in *The Dharma Bums* and the last chapters of *Desolation Angels.* The second period—the *Big Sur* days— occupied another few weeks in 1960. Despite this brevity, Philip and Jack enjoyed a wide range of experience with one another: they traveled and camped together in nature; they drank and got high together; they tripped

FIGURE 5. Philip Whalen and Jack Kerouac, 1956. Photo © Walter Lehrman.

together on peyote. (Though the word *together* may exaggerate the nature of the event as Kerouac recalled it. Whalen wrapped himself in a set of sitting robes, newly received from Gary Snyder in Japan, and conducted his psychedelic adventures inside the Milvia Street house in unmoving meditation posture. Kerouac, meanwhile, worried oil-based paints around paper in the backyard, finally becoming consumed by how to deal with an insect that had literally entered the painting.) They "hot-tubbed" together with a gang of writer friends at Big Sur, and Whalen ribbed Kerouac about wearing a swimsuit. After all, he, Whalen, had gone naked, as had Ferlinghetti, Welch, and McClure. But Kerouac refused; his New England Jansenist Catholic upbringing, his horror at the thought that sperm might be floating in the tub, his worries over a group of gay men using adjacent tubs all conspired against his going naked into the plunge. Neal Cassady, no stranger to getting naked—the famed "cocksman and Adonis of Denver"[9]—also possessed a Catholic upbringing and also refused to get naked, or even to relate to the hot tub scene at all.

Kerouac and Whalen held each other in enormously high regard. One could safely say, as they did themselves, that they loved each other; but there is no evidence, or even any hint, that they slept with one another. There does seem to have been a wrestling match, perhaps of the kind that young, strong, pacifist men might have if they are not having sex and find themselves at the end of the night variously intoxicated and loose. Kerouac mocked Whalen and himself as "two huge thudding rhinos, we'd been wrassling for fun."[10] This bout ended with Whalen's back and leg going out, and Kerouac having to pick splinters from his arm for months. The two men could talk about sex. Whalen told his journal that "Kerouac claims that he must come every day in order to feel well. 'That old stuff in there, it isn't good for you if it stays in.' So if he isn't making out with somebody, he masturbates, or so he claims. He told me that he had discovered a very fast & efficient way of doing it."[11]

A word is in order here on reading Kerouac's books as history. Jack himself vexed the question of their historical accuracy, saying different things at different times about the verity of events in his books, as well as by shifting styles during the course of his career. In *The Dharma Bums,* he explicitly camouflaged characters, also mixing and reworking events considerably. What he says about Whalen/Coughlin there can be confirmed or denied only by looking at other contemporary sources. *Big Sur* and *Desolation Angels* belong to a later period, one Kerouac himself described as picaresque narrative: here he was just telling the story in a series of pictures. In this phase he made little attempt to disguise (his view) of the facts, beyond dubbing friends, lovers, enemies, and others in his circle with whimsical names—and he only did this reluctantly, to mollify publishers worried about libel. Jack wrote to Philip about the composition of these two books, saying things like "I got this and that in there" or "Remember the time we did thus and such ... *that's* in there." Kerouac's astonishing memory does not extend, though, to the dialogue he gave Whalen: that must be viewed as fictional. Most of the physical action checks out.

What is indisputable is that the two men spent lots of their time together as modern-day flâneurs. "He [Kerouac] was pointing out things to me. We'd walk together quite a lot, pointing out things. At the time it was rather buggy, because I could see perfectly well what he was talking about, plus other things. But he thought I wasn't seeing them, so he was trying to tell me about it, which was interesting."[12] Both men habitually carried little notebooks and writing tools with them, and they sketched what they saw—in words and in doodles, and later in more careful transcription. Thus they both spent a good part of each day just sitting still writing. Journals, letters, poems, stories— producing these takes time. Both men had what they recognized as serious writing "habits," exactly in the sense used to describe a relationship to drugs. Complementing this, both Whalen and Kerouac read heavily. One of the prettiest pictures Jack Kerouac gave the world is of Philip reading. Jack and his mother Gabrielle had arrived in Berkeley in the middle of the night. Catching sight of Philip through a window, Jack held back his weary, dispirited mother, so he could watch Whalen enjoying passages from what turned out to be the Lankavatara Sutra: "By God he's just alone in the night smiling over old Bodhisattva truths of India. You can't go wrong with him. He's smiling happily, in fact, it's really a crime to disturb him."[13] That Whalen was not actually reading, or contemplating ancient spiritual truths of India, but rather being amused by a butterfly that had landed on his book, dissuaded Kerouac not in the least. He knew about the butterfly—Philip told him—but he still summarized Philip so: "He's a strange mystic, living alone, smiling over books."

Philip Whalen and Jack Kerouac enjoyed any amount of fun during their brief weeks together in person, but their real connection did not depend on proximity, nor were the hours they passed together uniformly harmonious. The blowup that took place shortly after their first meeting—when Jack asked Philip about being Irish—struck Jack as being more than just show energy. In *Desolation Angels,* he allows that Philip "almost killed me" over the question. No doubt, either, that if Whalen felt bugged by Kerouac's constant tour-guide-to-the-phenomenal-world approach, he would have told him so. Philip loved Jack but felt no intimidation. In the other direction, Whalen related in an interview how Kerouac could descend suddenly into a sour, depressed mood and say very mean things. Philip would be hurt and would get mad at Jack for it, but in the greater pleasures of his company, these incidents would pass. And Jack carefully spared Philip any venom in letters—a form he otherwise used to attack people or to ventilate frustration and pain. Once or twice Philip did catch from Jack a group indictment—mocking, drunken, collective put-downs: "you Buddhists! you West Coast poets! you haiku writers! you readers of Gertrude Stein! you bunch of shits!" Kerouac even once playfully called Philip out to offer a defense: "Bah. Come on Whalen, put up yr dukes and fight. Satori!"[14] In truth, Kerouac himself was no street fighter. To his own physical detriment, he refused to punch back during the well-chronicled brawls in which he actually did find himself; in this letter, even before he mailed it, he regretted his outburst. He suggests in closing that he and Whalen limit themselves from now on to penny postcards. Whalen roundly ignored this, just as he had ignored Kerouac's earlier suggestion of unwinding to one another in long letters. Philip sent Jack whatever size and shape letter he felt like sending, including, some years later, a book-length manuscript entitled *Goofbook: For Jack Kerouac,* about which more later.

For the most part, Jack Kerouac's letters to Philip Whalen are loving, full of praise, at times almost reverential: "You & Gary—The two best men I ever met" and (continuing to link Philip and Gary), "Your poem in *Chicago Review* is best thing in the *Review,* with possible exception (well who compares poetry to prose?) of Gary's marvelous clackety-clack sesshin description."[15] Or, "Dear Holy Old How'll Who'll Ya, You brilliant diamondstar, shining on Oregon beachie.... You old bangle-gaving bo! (that was supposed to be gavel-banging).... Goddamit I already lost your beautiful letter which was the first thing I read for 1958, sitting sad drunk in gloom of room on edge of bed gray New York ... the human voice speaking to me, also the Buddha voice."[16]

Beyond the mutual declarations of brotherly love, Philip's letters to Jack recognize his genius as a writer, and they do their best to encourage, uplift, or simply stand by Jack the author. Whalen knew that as a writer he had benefited enormously from the infusion of creative energy Kerouac brought into his life; he also knew that he could learn from it. He wrote to Jack about this early on in their friendship, in a letter of remarkable self-awareness:

> A couple days ago I got a funny insight. It seems as if I have been carrying on an unconscious dialogue with myself somewhere in a remote passage of my brain—the voices so quiet that I never consciously noticed them before, one saying "I bet you won't see, hear, feel, learn, read, write, do etc" & the second voice agrees, "Guess not. No, I won't."
>
> 1st voice, "Bet *anything* you wont—I bet all the love, illumination, trees, money &c in this world that you won't."
>
> 2nd voice, "Thas right, thas right."
>
> Anyway, I felt I got a clear look at an enemy I'd never seen before—had him for years without knowing his face or nature. Then it seemed I must have scored one point against him, after all these years, just by having seen him, recognized him.
>
> All this goes into this letter because it was partly a response to having met you. I found out that I own a bigger & more complicated system of prejudices & notions than I was aware of. It happens that you have one also. Very few people that I know own them. {Allen is growing one, Gary is possibly trying to avoid doing so—maybe the aging process has something to do with it.} In any case, these few people have been the only ones from whom I have been able to learn anything.... The kind of learning I mean isn't the acceptance of somebody else's ideas, or becoming a disciple, a repeater—it is a measuring &

evaluating process leading to more knowledge of your own interior—& presently, of the world at large, the final product of our minds, &c &c, &c.[17]

The night they met—the night Kerouac, Snyder, Ginsberg, and Whalen all met—ended up with Philip face down on some floor in Berkeley, bawling inconsolably that poetry was shit, that everything was hopeless, and many other such expressions of frustration with his own work. But the lift of the Six Gallery reading a few days later and the steady provocation to literary intelligence through the steady company of Kerouac, Ginsberg, Snyder, and McClure worked as a tonic on Whalen's spirit. In the autumn of 1955 he produced his most oft-quoted poem, the long, profound, funny, beautiful "Sourdough Mountain Lookout,"[18] as well as several other works on love and intoxication. He concluded the season's composition, however, on a very different note: a stern—indeed merciless—meditation on suffering, a poem entitled "Unfinished, 3:XII:55."

The shift in Whalen's theme and tone reflects the dramatic dissolution of that cheerful autumn—a time biographers and critics point to as Kerouac's happiest. First, in late November, Allen and Jack quarreled, the spark being a disagreement over the meaning of emptiness (!) as taught in the Prajñaparamita Sutras. The argument escalated rapidly, the upshot being that Jack threatened to leave Ginsberg's Milvia Street house where he'd been bunking, and Allen called his bluff. Then a few days later—much more consequentially—Neal Cassady's girlfriend Nathalie Jackson committed suicide.

Jack had stayed in Nathalie's flat that evening explicitly to babysit her, while Neal worked a late shift at the railroads. Jack had tried to soothe Nathalie's agitation with clumsy expressions about the Buddhist notion of emptiness of self, but she would have none of it. Finally, sensibly, he rounded up food and brewed tea for the overwrought young woman. Nathalie had been high on speed for several days, and her native intelligence had wound itself into a spiral of paranoid ideas—arising, it must be said, from damaging, criminal actions committed by Neal. With nourishment, however, she seemed to cheer up and calm down enough to rest—enough, at least, that Jack felt he could doze off on her floor. He was the last person to have a real conversation with her. When Cassady came home from work, Jack left. Then sometime near dawn Nathalie awoke, went to the roof of the building, and cut her wrists with glass from a shattered skylight. A short while later, she escaped the well-intentioned grasp of a policeman, leaving him holding only her bathrobe, and fell six stories to her death on the pavement below. Nathalie Jackson's suicide threw an immediate pall over the whole bubbling San Francisco scene. Lapsed Catholics Kerouac and Cassady retreated to Cassady's house in Los Gatos (where Neal's wife and children lived) and fell repeatedly to their knees in mortified prayer.

Thus when Philip Whalen stepped up to the microphone three days later to give his first poetry reading at San Francisco State's Poetry Center, an occasion that should have merited all-out celebration, he cannot have felt much joy.

Unfinished, 3:XII:55

> *We have so much*
> *That contemplating it*
> *We never learn the use—*
>
> *Poisoning ourselves with food, with books*
> *with sleep*
>
> *Ignorance quicker than cyanide*
> *Cuts us down*
>
> *No lack of opportunity to learn;*
> *Flat-footed refusal! Call it*
> *Perversion, abuse, bullheadedness*
> *It is rejection of all we know*
>
> *A single waking moment destroys us*
> *And we cannot live without*
> *Ourselves*
>
> *You come to me for an answer? I*
> *Invented it all, I*
> *Am your tormentor, there is no*
> *Escape, no redress*
>
> *You are powerless against me: You*
> *Must suffer agonies until you know*
> *You are suffering:*
>
> *Work on that.*

The poem slams the door on frivolousness and the crimes of the previous season. It is, as Whalen's most penetrating poems often are, partly a description of mind, in this case mind soured by ignorance, greed, and hatred—the three classical poisons according to Buddhist doctrine. Mention of the particular poison cyanide binds the poem, should it have seemed ambiguous, to the idea of suicide. Mind takes first-person voice in the last, brutal lines, and as the poem thuds to its conclusion, so does the period. So did Whalen's own work. He wrote no further poems for three months.

. . .

What Philip told interviewer after interviewer, biographer after biographer, was that Kerouac *wrote* his books: that Jack wasn't simply a recorder or scribe of the period (nor, as Truman Capote's insult ran, was Jack a mere typist).[19] Whalen insisted that Kerouac chose events with great skill, that he illumined only some aspects of any character, that he deliberately shaped his stories into classical forms, and that above all, he was able to get the sounds and feelings and excitement of the time down on paper. Whalen recounted how the events chronicled in Kerouac's books were actually much wilder and more various and even more confusing than the books make them sound—and the books sound plenty wild. Philip felt that Jack's genius was in roping events and characters to a forward-moving through-line. He could yank up from chaos a coherent and pleasing form. Philip also admired and flat-out envied Kerouac's flow, his speed. He wrote to Jack, "I've still got to figure out some different way that won't get me all hung up in knots of critical paralysis and hesitation. You are lucky & don't know it, having doped all this out for your-self already . . . the way you can write what you're thinking of right now. I get hung up on various memories, different ideas of what the stuff is sounding like (other writers, etc) and there I am, *foutu.*"[20]

Jack often told Philip that he should write novels. Kerouac dispensed this advice freely to members of his circle, but for Whalen it was not a new idea. Philip wanted desperately to write novels. He had tried in fits and starts for more than twenty years and had burned hundreds and hundreds of pages, until he finally got a novel finished on 7 June 1963. When he completed *You Didn't Even Try,* he wrote to Jack, "I wouldn't be able to do anything if you hadn't encouraged me to write whatever it is, bad good & indifferent. . . . You are about 1/4 responsible for this book happening."[21]

But most of what Jack saw and was able to comment on was Philip's poetry—the poems enclosed with letters and those in Whalen's first two books—both published in 1960, oddly enough. About Whalen's first book—*Memoirs of an Interglacial Age*—Kerouac wrote a letter of gushing praise, calling it "really some of the best poetry ever written in the world." Jack waxed on, "There's a style all your own that no one can pin down or define—a style of Seeing and Saying—You're definitely a poet definitely Whalenesque," before concluding, "You don't have to write novels if you don't want to."[22]

A year later, in the spring of 1961, Philip mailed Jack a finished manuscript he called *Goofbook: For Jack Kerouac*. He'd sent excerpts of it earlier, which Jack had praised as "you at yous [sic] best." Kerouac's first biographer, Beat literary historian extraordinaire Ann Charters, regards the manuscript as Whalen's attempt to practice Kerouac's method of spontaneous prose.[23] The book may hearken after Kerouac's method, but on the whole it reads and looks very much like most of Whalen's journals or letters: a mixture of prose paragraphs with verse fragments, all spaced elegantly on the page. There are also drawings throughout, some explicitly erotic. Philip created the book in longhand, but what survives in manuscript is typed. Kerouac and Ginsberg made noises about having it published, which Philip discouraged, saying he hadn't written it to sell it—but that if Jack really wanted to see it as a published book he should send the manuscript back so that he, Philip, could look after that aspect. In the event, the pages lay unpublished until Whalen's final editor, Michael Rothenberg, brought it out as a paperback forty years later. Here again, Whalen engaged Rothenberg in a Zen-style mondo of dissuasion, which Rothenberg bravely used as part of his editor's note:

> Philip: This is a private letter that fell into the wrong hands. It should never be published. but if you have to do it, then that's that.
> Michael: I'd hate to think of myself as the wrong hands.
> Philip: I was speaking metaphysically.[24]

Whalen began writing *Goofbook* after seeing Jack in the depths of his Big Sur alcoholic nervous breakdown. He'd also naturally kept abreast of Kerouac's ongoing troubles with editors, reviewers, money, fans, ex-wives, lovers, health, and the demands of his mother. Thus Philip surely wrote and sent *Goofbook* in large measure simply to cheer Jack up. "Cheering up old so-and-so" was a constant theme for Whalen: he would visit his friends, send gifts, call on the telephone, write letters or postcards or poems—all in an attempt to simply cheer them up. He told about it in conversation and in letters, and he often told his journal, "I went to see old ____ to cheer them up." Certainly *Goofbook* contains a good deal of self-deprecating humor and many wacky drawings such as could not fail to bring a smile. The text also contains many direct expressions of admiration: "Like all the people I love, I think you suffer too much or anyhow more than necessary & in that aspect you're a meathead—while realizing that you're very great" or "I always believe anything you tell me because sooner or later it turns out you were right; however, during the interim, I tend to drag my feet."

Grounding these effusions, giving them perhaps even deeper resonance, Whalen suspects in the manuscript that he and Jack have—as he posits all men have—a secret, possibly unconscious war with another, "even more concisely, 'O MY ENEMY, MY BROTHER!'" The war mentioned here hasn't broken out in pitched battle; it's at the level of myth. Whalen calls in the views of Thomas Wolfe, Robert Graves, and William Carlos Williams to bear on the point, with the sense that this war is not a friendship breaker; it's simply the male condition. Certainly Whalen's close literary friends pressured and jostled each other very hard.[25] Allen and Jack both were pushy and domineering; Philip was opinionated and explosive; Gary could come on as arrogant and didactic. They were each constantly telling the other what he should be doing but respecting and loving one another just enough to hold the circle together. In the letter he sent along with *Goofbook,* Whalen nails Jack as one would hope to be nailed when caught whining about a mean critic: "Besides being a hopeless alcoholic, you are a genius and a bodhisattva, what do you *care* what sad old so and so says."[26]

· · ·

Beyond their literary friendship, though mixed up with it, Kerouac and Whalen recognized spiritual capacity in one other. If Whalen got a lot of good out of Jack the writer, Jack looked more to Philip the spiritual pilgrim. In the novels and in letters to friends, Jack always portrayed Philip, despite quirks, as a person of integrity, faith, and mysticism. He held Whalen to be an approachable spiritual person, a living, struggling Buddhist with whom he could relax and open up. Late in life, in a broken-down state, Kerouac movingly ends a letter by almost literally reaching out to Philip: "Prend ma main, ami" (Take my hand, friend). Remarkably often—eight years of the thirteen they knew each other—Jack began the new year with a letter to Philip, or wrote to him within the first days of January, as if in doing so he could bind himself more tightly to the feeling of resolution that comes with the fresh start of a calendar year. This has nothing to do with Buddhism particularly; it is rather a testimony to the simple human goodness that Jack, despite his own woes, could always see in his friend Philip.

They did write back and forth about Buddhism, but Philip maintained a skeptical view of Jack's involvement with the practice.

> Jack carried a copy of Dwight Goddard's book called *A Buddhist Bible* around with him. As far as I could see, he was interested in the very large, big, wonderful ideas about Buddhism and about the language. He liked the extravagant language that appeared in those translations. They talked in terms of vast distances and vast lengths of time and huge quantities of everything and lots of flowers and doves and one thing and another, so it's quite a fantastical language trip, for one thing. He had had a great many profound religious experiences himself, which he later would tell about, and he picked up on the fact, I think, that the Buddhist scriptures were about experience, that they were based on meditational experience. So this interested him.
>
> He was quite incapable of sitting for more than a few minutes at a time. His knees were ruined by playing football, so he couldn't sit much with his knees up. He never learned how to sit in that sort of proper meditation position. Even had he been able to, his head wouldn't have stopped long enough for him to endure it. He was too nervous, but he thought it was a good idea. . . .
>
> As far as I can see, honestly, his interest in Buddhism was pretty much literary, and the idea that people were actually trying to do it was interesting to him as exhibitions of their character, possibly, as facets of their character. The idea that Gary was this very active man—very learned and very active person who liked to live outdoors and who had a very exciting social life— would be interested in Buddhism and practicing it, or trying to practice it, and presently went off to Japan to start in formal Zen training, this was interesting for Jack as a manifestation of character more than Buddhism as such was interesting to him.
>
> He would go just so far with it, and then he'd say "Ah well, It's wonderful, but I really believe in sweet baby Jesus," or "little lamby Jesus" or "my brother Gerard."[27]

Buddhist or not, just knowing that the other one had a feeling for a cosmic level of experience, and for a world of energies beyond the visible, allowed Whalen and Kerouac to relax with each other and rely on each other in the deepest ways. On 23 July 1957, Whalen awoke from an uneasy, nightmarish sleep. As he came to, he perceived that he was under attack from a being or beings nonhuman. He recognized it as a black magic attack, and the name "Robert Duncan" screamed in his mind. Philip recalled that Allen had suffered a nearly identical experience a year earlier; thus he roused himself, vigorously warded off the attack, and set about writing it up—as a poetic open letter to Mr. Duncan[28]—and also telling Jack all about it in private correspondence. Whalen could have written to any of his friends, but the person he felt would best understand such a thing was Jack.

> I woke up while strange malefic flashes and motions were still appearing & vanishing around the room—I had a head-ache—it was the magical emanation of Robert Duncan, the wicked magic faggot! So I had to exorcise the demon with a thaumaturgic branch, bell music, gun powder, and a short dance. Remember last year when the same thing happened to Ginsberg?—he awoke from sleep with a pain in his eye and the name Duncan shouting in his mind. Like Mila Repa, I am full of remorse for using magic in reply to Robert's enchantments. The notions of power, of victory & defeat are all illusory; born of fear for one's Self. They spawn superstition & the idea of control by magic, control by authority. Law. Tyranny.[29]

Lest the reader think Whalen had fallen into pure paranoia, it should be noted that Robert Duncan, together with Jack Spicer and a number of other San Francisco poets, was at the time actively engaged in a weekly writing group in Berkeley they called the Magic Workshop. The assignments to the group included things like "Write a poem in which the poet becomes a flesh-eating beast," "Write a poem concerning some magic sacrifice," "Evoke magic spirits," "How would you cook a baby?"[30]

Kerouac wrote back quickly, acknowledging Whalen's central point. Jack told Philip he'd immediately used the letter in an article called "About the Beat Generation," in support of his theory that Beat writers were all working with what he termed "religiousness" and that many had profound visions, both positive and negative. Kerouac also alluded to the incident much later in a novel, in which a character based on himself asks a character based on Whalen, "Anybody hex you lately?"[31]

It turns out to be one thing to have "religiousness" and spiritual visions, and another, more difficult thing to *apply* those visions and feelings to actual experience—to integrate the blazing cosmic insights into personal daily life. A traditional Buddhist approach to this problem involves three aspects: hearing, contemplating, and meditating. Kerouac and Whalen both heard: they visited and listened to Buddhist teachers as they could, and they both read a large portion of the Buddhist literature available to an American in the 1950s and '60s. They also contemplated. Through writing and through banter with like-minded friends, they worked with the meanings in the texts they'd come across. Some of what they read was profound indeed: the Lankavatara Sutra, for example, with its exposition of the pervasiveness of consciousness—the so-called mind-only school—or the Diamond Sutra, with its cutting dialectic pointing to "emptiness" and nonabiding. Both these Mahayana texts had been used to seal the Zen lineage transmission from one generation to another. Their "meanings" are well-nigh ungraspable and have given rise to philosophical schools and debate that continues to the present day. Kerouac and Whalen cut their teeth on the contemplations in these sutras, and they let their spiritual exercises color their writings, sometimes quite explicitly, as in the early chapters of Kerouac's *Desolation Angels* or in poems like Whalen's "Mahayana."

But Buddhists say that the third, crucial step to realizing wisdom is the practice of meditation—with one's body. One must devote a certain amount of time to an enactment—to literally embodying the philosophies by sitting still. The tradition warns that insight uncoupled from such steadiness can be dangerous, leading to an excess of concept and mental agitation. Both writers fell prey to this from time to time and told about it in their works, but they had varying ways of dealing with it. One of Whalen's strategies was to actually try to do Buddhist meditation—sporadically at first but with ever-increasing application through the years.

Not so Kerouac. The stability, clarity, and strength that arise from a regular sitting practice help deal with the painful aspects of insight, but Jack rarely had access to these. Seeing one's life, and the world as it appears, very often leads to feeling deluged by suffering. The simple facts of impermanence, separation, decrepitude, insanity, selfishness, cruelty, and death are all around for anyone to witness anytime. All this weighs on a sensitive individual, let alone on those who attract extra helpings of negativity to themselves, as the Beats regularly did, through rebellion literary and physical, and through unsavory, sometimes criminal activity. Philip never involved himself in any of the heavier bad behavior, but he was touched by it through connections with his friends. Jack too tried to act in what he thought of as a good-hearted way, but through drunkenness and miscalculation, he often found himself in bad trouble. The pain of seeing this, and the pain of being on the receiving end of savage attacks—from critics in the literary world, from realtors and ex-wives and lovers in the domestic world, and from outraged patrons in the dim world of bars (these last sometimes in the form of physical beatings) left Jack Kerouac a good deal to balance against the airy notions of emptiness and universal consciousness. From a perspective of fifty years on, it seems reasonable to attribute at least some of Kerouac's deadly embrace of the bottle to his lack of options in handling these huge piles of pain, and the prodigious *amounts* of painkiller he required, to his tremendous sensitivity. When Jack confessed to being a bad Buddhist, Whalen told him that the thing to remember about Buddhism was that it was there, and it worked.[32] But Jack couldn't really work it fully. Soaked in painful clarity about his situation, he lacked some of the best tools for navigating through it. An obvious move, then, was to numb the pain, to intoxicate the clarity.

Kerouac's openness[33]—with its corollary vulnerability—and his refined, ultimately loving view, bound him to Philip, who suffered these same symptoms. Both men began as good boys who loved their mothers. (Whalen's mother died early; otherwise he might well have ended up in a state similar to Jack's excessive, skewed filiality.) Both men longed for peace, for harmony, for gentle, supportive situations—almost as much as they craved release, noisy pleasure, and wild, elevated states of consciousness. Both men loved love itself, and when love of human beings failed them, they fell back to a shared love of words and their mother tongues.

Whalen, by whichever means—meditation, long solitary hikes in the mountains, a decided bachelor's preference for staying put, for reading, for the quiet life—was somehow able to cobble together an acceptance of all he saw and felt. He took it more or less straight. He bitched about it certainly, he filled his poems and letters and journals with the absurdity of it, he scraped bottom a good deal, he swathed himself with thick pads of flesh, swelling at times to a very large shape, but he survived. Kerouac sank finally under the weight of the accumulations, and when he died of a gastrointestinal hemorrhage from alcoholic cirrhosis of the liver at forty-seven years of age, it was not expected, but neither was anyone surprised. Whalen was living in Japan at the time and had trouble getting clear information. He first wrote to Joanne Kyger, "There was some rumor about Kerouac dying—have you heard any such story? It's very embarrassing—how can I cable him in Florida to ask ARE YOU ALL RIGHT? REPLY PREPAID. It would be very hard to adjust to, if true."[34]

Eventually Philip got the story straight, as he told Allen Ginsberg in a letter:

> Roy Kiyooka, the Canadian artist we used to see all the time at the Tallman's house in Vancouver 1963 . . . came over one night to bring me some dope & mentioned something about Kerouac dying—some note in a Japanese paper, very uncertain. Then I found a very short dispatch in the Asahi English edition—later TIME's creepy snide editorial. Anyway, it wasn't too dreadful,

except several days of uncertainty before I could really find out for sure—news here is always bent & cuckoo in transmission translation. Well anyway, I wasn't too surprised—Gabrielle finally succeeded in eating him—& he dug it & kept applying more sauce to make himself nice & tender. I burnt lots of candles & incense at big historic buddha temples in Nara—my sister was dreadfully ill & operated on in Brooklyn hospital at the same time, so I was stirring up the gods & buddhas to help everybody, & Jack would dig candles, since it is part of the Catholic death trip.[35]

Philip then went on to reflect—first to Joanne and then to Allen—on Jack's influence in his own life and in the world: "What he wrote is still funnier & livelier than TIME or anybody else in NYC would like to believe. I don't feel too sad, because he really did a great deal while he was alive—made loopy grand poetic books, & all that is still to the good—no matter how cranky & impossible he could sometimes be 'in person.' And if he & Allen G & Gregory Corso hadn't insisted that Barney Rosset & other publishers should read my poems, & Gary's poems I imagine I'd have remained even more obscure & unknown."[36]

"I feel it was a great release for him; he has seemed so down for the past 5 years. It is impossible to think of him as being dead, though, & all his writing is still radioactively radiating & humming along, & we all remember him when he was beautiful & cuckoo & wild—& that energy or *karma* or whatnot will persist for a long time."[37]

FOUR

Kalyanamitra

WHALEN AND SNYDER

Ranking one's friends in order belongs principally to the realm of grade-school girls, but a quick visit there might be allowed, only to note that Philip Whalen had no better friend than Gary Snyder. Whalen's life would have run a vastly different course had a seventeen-year-old Snyder not first seen him from offstage at Reed College's theater, directing players in a student production, and been impressed with him. Whalen might have taken much longer to run across Zen writings, for example—Snyder brought D. T. Suzuki's books home to their apartment when they were living together in San Francisco. Philip might never have found work in the mountains: sitting in that same Telegraph Hill apartment in the hot summer of 1952, Whalen read one of Gary's regular letters, this one from a Forest Service lookout on Crater Mountain in the North Cascades of Washington State. Provoked by it, and by working—"bad anytime, but especially nasty in summer in the city"—Whalen wrote back to declare, "By God, next summer, I'm going to have a mountain of my own!" This he did, then got another mountain the following year and spent a third summer as a forest lookout the year after that, making this by far his steadiest, most satisfying job until many years later, when he became a "professional" man of the cloth. Whalen would never have read in the Six Gallery reading had not Snyder put Philip's name and poems literally in front of Allen Ginsberg's face. Philip certainly would have floundered longer with unemployment and flirted more dangerously with outright homelessness had Gary not simply taken care of him whenever the two were in the same town at the same time.

They roomed together in San Francisco off and on from 1952 to 1954 in a flat on Montgomery Street, above the city's North Beach district, to which they descended together nearly nightly for beer at Vesuvio and other drinking establishments. Thus Philip and Gary came to know the writers, players, merchants, philosophers, painters, filmmakers, musicians, and scholars circling around the Bay Area in the gestation phase of the San Francisco Renaissance. During this same period, Snyder and Whalen began going together to the American Academy of Asian Studies, where they heard and met Alan Watts, and later also D. T. Suzuki. From among the audiences there, they got to know Claude (Ananda) Dahlenberg, who later cofounded the East-West House[1] and still later became an ordained Zen priest under Shunryu Suzuki Roshi—and they made the acquaintance of an attractive, older, elegant woman called Schändel Parks. Schändel connected them to the roaring lion of the local poetry scene, Kenneth Rexroth, taking Gary to Rexroth's Friday evening literary gatherings. Other Friday evenings found Whalen and Snyder in Berkeley for the study group with Reverend and Jane Imamura at the Buddhist Church of America. Together the Imamuras were descended from the most important old families of Jodo Shinshu Buddhism; they displayed no arrogance and welcomed the young men, going so far in subsequent years as to turn their little church publication—the *Berkeley Bussei*—over to artist Will Petersen for a time. Snyder, Whalen, Ginsberg, and Kerouac all published early poems in its pages. The benevolent Imamura family gave both Snyder and Whalen their first contact with people actually practicing Buddhism instead of purely discussing its philosophies and traditions.

Without Snyder's impetus, Whalen might have made his way out to Pacific Street, to the Asian Academy or over to Berkeley for the study group, but Philip was much given, even then, to the sedentary life. As long as he could, he spent hours each day reading, writing, drawing, playing music, doodling, staring into space—and wondering from time to time where and how he could find a job that wouldn't drive him crazy. He ventured out when he needed to—for cigarettes or food or for fresh air, but he had nothing like Gary's get-up-and-go. It is in fact difficult to think of anyone with the drive and sense of adventure the young Snyder had. These propelled him up mountains, up trees, down the holes of tankers, out into deserts, back into libraries, into universities, into monasteries, across the country, out of the country, across oceans; they armored him against the many outer and inner obstacles an unmoneyed young man might encounter in such travels; they sustained him as he went where he needed to go, saw what he wanted to see, studied what and with whom he needed to study, worked as he had to, and cut loose when he could. If this sounds relentlessly energetic, it is partly the fault of compression generated by looking back at the time through sixty years. The fifties were a slower time, and Snyder was of it: he studied and lived in serious, methodical rhythms.

Whalen certainly profited from Snyder's solid discipline and steady energy. Gary's confident style also worked as a magnet: Kerouac was magnetized, for example, as were a number of young women. Shy, socially awkward Whalen profited from this as well, in the sense that it afforded him much more contact with females and feminine energy than he otherwise would have been able to arrange for himself. Falling in love, wearing out love, having imaginary affairs and occasionally consummating them—these essential emotional territories for a young poet were much more accessible to Philip because of women who were initially attracted to Gary. Signal among such introductions, enduring and completely transcending any other was the introduction Gary made between Joanne Kyger—his future wife—and Philip in 1958. Not the first night but soon after, Philip fell helplessly in love with Joanne, and stayed that way for his remaining his forty-two years. Gary observed Philip's crush on Joanne, possibly underestimated its profundity, but correctly gauged that it presented no threat to his own relationship with her. Philip, though, writhed with guilt, telling Ginsberg, "Joanne and I are still having some sort of felicity, you name it. I didn't see her most of the day today & missed her, wondered how I'll feel when she goes away [to Japan, to be with Gary] & all that jazz, my god. What a mess. Am completely unable to write to Snyder."[2] Gary saw that Philip was attracted by Joanne's wit, her creativity, and a matching style of "bitchiness."[3] True as all this was, Whalen's sexual energies were also understandably engaged by the beautiful Miss Kyger, evidenced by his going on to tell Ginsberg, "Maybe Chicago & New York balling will fix all this. Good grief." Whether or not there was any balling in New York, nothing much seems to have helped. Philip remained impractically in love with Joanne; she went off to Japan and eventual marriage with Gary. Philip stayed home, haunted.

Philip's own two sojourns in Japan—so crucial to his writing and his Buddhism—came about through Gary's agency. Knowing Philip to be impoverished in 1965, functionally homeless, unhealthy, and depressed, Gary arranged a teaching job for him in Kyoto, instructed him in all he would need to know to negotiate visas and transportation, and gave him a place to live for several months.

By 1971, both men back in California, the obvious outer good turns Gary had given Philip's life ceased to be so necessary, to occur so frequently, or to be so easy to trace. With Philip soon settled in Zen Center housing and Gary getting phone service in his Sierra Nevada home, their letters to one another tapered off. Such hard evidence as does remain shows no lessening of affection, though, no diminishment of respect between them. They were simply absorbed in the demands of their parallel lives: Gary with raising a family, working with a zendo, publishing continuously, and teaching at the University of California, Davis; Philip, roughly 150 miles to the west, with learning the routines and population of the San Francisco Zen Center. He spent the days educating himself and students about Zen history and working with and for his teacher, Richard Baker Roshi. The poets managed to visit each other during these years. They exchanged seasonal letters and holiday wishes. Gary arranged teaching gigs or readings for Philip—both at UC Davis and up at Ring of Bone Zendo, the meditation hall near Gary's family homestead. The last big service Gary offered was to help officiate, together with Zen teachers Baker Roshi and Norman Fischer, as well as poet Michael McClure, Philip's funeral service at Green Gulch Farm in September 2002.

Relaxing by a hair the strict Japanese ceremonial rigor, these four conducted a memorial both traditional and warm. Flashes of humor took place; tears flowed. Gary dressed for the role, looking exactly who he was: an outdoors man wearing with craggy elegance a dark suit, white shirt, and tie, his dignity and city clothes conveying deep respect.[4] After Baker Roshi's opening rituals and remarks, Gary spoke. He bowed crisply to the shrine with Philip's ashes upon it and, still facing it, told him, "Hey buddy, I'm going to say some words about you." Snyder then turned to the audience and read slowly from prepared remarks—an essay he'd titled "Highest and Driest: For Philip Zenshin's Poetic Drama/Dharma." In this trenchant eulogy, it is possible to see some of the other side of the friendship.[5] This chapter so far has focused on what Whalen got from Snyder, but for a creative friendship to last more than a half century, surviving contraction and expansion, proximity and distance, for it to remain loving and humorous and bright at whatever remove, both parties have to be getting something. For the friendship to allow a living man to address, with utter naturalness, a box of his dead friend's ashes, saying, "Hey, buddy," the path between their hearts has to be a well-traveled, two-way route.

"Being part of Phil's circle [at Reed College] was like being in an additional class—having an extra (intimately friendly) instructor, one with nutty humor and more frankly expressed opinions. He extended us into areas not much handled by the college classes of those days, such as Indian and Chinese philosophy. . . . Philip led the way in making conversation possible, and then making poetry out of the territory of those readings."[6]

Seven years his senior, Whalen was more accomplished than Snyder in almost every academic field when they met. Through industry and native intelligence, Gary made huge strides in learning, catching, and—in Oriental studies and languages certainly—surpassing his older friend. Still he maintained a deferential tone: "Cher Maître" was not an uncommon opening for a letter from Gary to Phil, even if the respect in it is coated with a dollop of fun. What Snyder acknowledges in the passage above is how Whalen both broadened his mind and pointed it, or confirmed it, in the direction of poetry. That Snyder continued with astonishing energy to broaden and deepen his own mind and that he developed into a Pulitzer Prize–winning poet can largely be attributed to his own powers. But Snyder thinks historically and systemically (among other ways), and he knows that a slight bump here, a little pivot there, a turn of a couple of degrees early in life affects the whole course of that life. Gary had begun to read from Oriental classics but was a raw beginner in poetry. In Philip he found someone older, familiar, strange, and friendly who'd been studying classics of all kinds for much longer than he had, and who was undeniably already a poet. In another short essay, Snyder states this more explicitly: "He first showed me the difference between talking about literature and doing it, and he pointed the way in Asian philosophy and art."[7] Since Gary Snyder spent most of the rest of his life "doing" literature, most of it profoundly affected by Asian philosophy and art, this is no small responsibility to lay at Whalen's feet. If it seems an exaggeration of Whalen's importance, and it does feel bold even to suggest it, then consider that this excerpt comes from the author's introduction to *The Gary Snyder Reader,* a six-hundred-dred-page summary volume assembled after more than forty-five years of publishing poetry, prose, and translations. The whole big, fat, rich book—the essential texts from a life's writing—is also dedicated to Whalen. "For Philip Zenshin Whalen," it begins, right after the copyright information. Then Snyder adds as an epigraph the opening lines from Confucius's Lun Yü:

> K'ung said:
> To learn and then put it in practice—isn't that a delight?
> To have friends come from afar—isn't that a joy?[8]

(A good deal of meaning is being teased out of few words. This can be justified with poets. Snyder and Whalen both absorbed many of Ezra Pound's dicta early in their lives, including this one: "Great literature is simply language charged with meaning to the utmost possible degree."[9] Beyond this, note Snyder's lifelong practice of reading, studying, and writing Chinese and Japanese characters—these "ideograms" are each a marvel in condensation of meaning. Reading Snyder's deceptively simple poetry or prose *without* allowing for the surface meanings to expand or deepen would amount to disrespect.)

Both in his eulogy for Philip and his author's note dedicating *The Gary Snyder Reader* to him, Snyder uses Whalen's Buddhist name, calling him Philip Zenshin Whalen. For Gary, as for Philip, names and naming held real significance (a theme that will reappear more fully later). By including Whalen's Zen name, Gary was pointing to more than Philip's literary endeavor. A different man answered to "Zenshin Ryufu" than to "Phil," "Philip," "Philip Glenn Whalen," or "old buddy." Philip felt, as the ceremony insists a postulant should feel, that his priest's ordination cut him off from previous history and gave him a new start in a life. Together with the new name, ordainees received new robes, new eating bowls, new or renewed vows, and new family ancestors, a lineage. Buddhism is casually associated with rebirth, but the ceremony that made Whalen a priest is called *tokudo,* which translates as "home departure"—emphasizing its disentangling effects. A person emerging from *tokudo* is known as an *unsui:* not monk, not priest, but "cloud-water person," one who should henceforth float, constantly changing like a cloud, and reflect, like clear water. In actual practice, one still drags around a good deal of baggage, and the *unsui*'s new role as "a child of the Buddhas" brings with it binding specificity about deportment. It may be an enlightened family he or she has just joined, but an *unsui* is still subject to family dynamics. The path forward consists in balancing the liberating and binding aspects of the new role, and in unpacking, sorting, and using or discarding the contents of the luggage. Snyder knew this well, having gone through *tokudo* himself in 1956 in Japan. When he dedicated his big collection of writing to Philip, it was to the man doing just this work. When he eulogized his old college pal, it was a eulogy for an *unsui.*

Discriminating Snyder's words this way would be unfaithful to their sense if they were not reintegrated in summary meaning. For Gary did not see Philip's Buddhism as separate from his work or his life generally. These were not conflicting parts of Philip; they had been braided together.

Once a priest, it was clear that this was Philip's true vocation. He had the dignity, the learning, the spiritual penetration, and the playfulness of an archetypal Man of the Cloth, of any tradition, and yet was not in the least tempted by hierarchy or power. Philip never left his poetry, his wit, or his critical intelligence behind; his way of poetry is a main part of his teaching. His quirks became his pointers, and his frailties his teaching method. Philip was always the purest, the highest, the most dry, and oddly cosmic, of the Dharma poets we've known—we are all greatly karmically lucky to have known him.[10]

Gary went to a Japanese monastery years before the idea even occurred to Whalen. He learned the people and places of Zen years before Whalen set forth to the old country; Gary developed a meditation habit before Philip did, and he led Philip into Zen's literature. Nevertheless, Gary appeared to harbor a feeling about him, as all Whalen's close friends did, that whether or not he had gone through the ceremonies, whether or not he wore the robes, there stood in Philip Whalen a spiritual man. Gary confirmed this one evening at a dinner with some poets and other friends. Overhearing a remark addressed to the Chinese poet Bei Dao about how Whalen was a sort of brother figure, Snyder's literary sibling, Gary nodded: "Older brother. And also *kalyanamitra*. Philip was my good spiritual friend, my *kalyanamitra*."[11]

.   .   .

The first time Gary and Philip lived together was in their college days, from 1949 to 1951. Housemates but not roommates, they shared a residence at 1414 Lambert Street—about a mile from the Reed College campus—with as many as sixteen other students. Gary as house manager lived in a basement room he'd renovated; Philip was up a couple of floors. Economically sensible (and necessary); socially avant; possibly a model and certainly a forerunner for the many urban communes of a decade later; politically left-wing to the point of FBI investigators dropping by and very likely running a tap on the phone; intellectually serious and stimulating, and religiously open, the house and its residents have been written about to surfeit.[12] But when people congregate in particular places, they may, if the constellation is right, attract certain inexplicable, temporary "blessings," so that the group and its members stand out as memorable, influential. Certain string quartets rise this way from the ranks of string quartets, certain dance troupes, sports teams, cultural salons, military units. Certain places appear to carry this energy for a time as well, places as generalized as San Francisco's Haight-Ashbury or as specific as New York City's Cedar Tavern. For no apparent reason—almost as if an angel had come along—people and places click together in a way that lifts all involved for a time. History remarks such pattern highlights, and the Lambert Street house seems to have been such a place. Whalen's closest lifelong poet-pals, Gary Snyder and Lew Welch, lived there with him. Poet William Dicky lived there; novelist and Zen student Don Berry lived there. The circle of many other talented friends—professors, musicians, humanists, and scientists—that radiated from the house have remained in affectionate contact for more than half a century.

At Lambert Street, Philip and Gary's friendship took root. The teenage Snyder climbed up to the room Whalen shared with his army friend Roy Stilwell for improving conversation and companionship. Attending Reed on the GI bill, these men were considerably older than Gary, and though they got the respect accorded all returning GIs, they also suffered the disorientation (or worse) resulting from wartime service. Both knew a lot: Stilwell was an accomplished musician, playing violin with the Portland Symphony, and Whalen was already deeply learned, having spent any free time in the army—and he had a lot of it—feeding his intense reading habit. Gary endured good-natured scholarly correction from these and the other ex-GIs in the house, but the intellectual stimulation and the magnetic life experience these contacts provided were worth it. Besides, Snyder was tough and resilient, and had also been around quite a bit himself. It must have been here that Gary and Philip began to discover some of what they shared: an upbringing in the low-rent Pacific Northwest, rural and urban, as well as a specific affection for the heritage, characters, and vocabulary of those places. This included the strong influence of Native American, Chinese, and Japanese populations.

For anyone who can see it, the country around Portland—the sheer scale of those landscapes—impresses and broadens the mind. As a child, Philip disliked being forced by relatives to look at this or that view, but he developed nevertheless an allegiance to the huge sloping hills, wide plains, big rivers, dark forests, and snow-covered mountains that a child being driven through western Oregon would have seen. Whalen felt it to be "his country." Snyder was practically born an outdoorsman, an enthusiast of hiking and mountain climbing from early minority on. Whalen and Snyder both understood that to imbibe the philosophic and literary wisdom they wanted meant they would have to leave that country and go not only to the "virtuous town" but also to the "wicked city."[13] They went willingly and thirstily. But the wild, the trail, the mountains, and the big country were in their bones. Both required regular draughts of mountain air and long views of stone and forest for emotional health, as well as for their work as writers. A week or two-week backpacking trip, sometimes together, became a seasonal entry on their calendars. Gary ended up living in the foothills of California's Sierra Nevada mountains, and Whalen spent years at Tassajara Zen Mountain Center. Both men would grumble, though, if forced to compare either the Sierra Nevada or Los Padres National Forest to the massive country of their youth.

An example trip together would be one they took in July 1965, with Gary back from Japan for an extended visit. He and Philip embarked on a trek of about a week, together with writer Drummond Hadley, heading into California's mountains above Kings Canyon. Whalen's journal pokes occasional loving fun at Gary: "The Granite pass appears (of course) to be quite near. I suppose it's a trip of several hours hard climbing. There's lots of snow up there. The Dr. Leitswics school of snow traveling and Neo-Nomadism . . . "[14]

Whalen also pokes fun at his own bent of mind and shows how he and Gary pick up conversations and activities from fifteen years ago:

> This morning we argue metaphysics & do our laundry. The mosquitoes are many & fierce. The Horse Shoe lakes & basin aren't quite as beautiful or various as the State Lakes {Why not?}
> . . . Ice formed on Wolf Tit's sleeping bag after he came out of it. Although there were clouds & thunder yesterday, there was no more rain. We slept in the open, after consuming 1/2 pint of cognac. Gary & I spent much of yesterday sitting in the high meadow above the lakes. I've re-read *Timon, Troilus,* & *Pericles.* The print is defective in the first two of these. . . . A few yards from this camp the ground is littered with flakes of obsidian. Sometime or other people sat here trying to make arrowheads. I found an imperfect one.[15]

After graduating together from Reed in the summer of 1951, Gary and Philip went separate ways: Whalen to San Francisco to try his fortune (where it was found wanting) and Snyder to work at a lumber company on the Warm Springs Indian Reservation in Oregon. At summer's end, they met for dinner in San Francisco before going even farther afield. Philip was heading to Los Angeles, where he could enjoy a sunny climate and stay for free with friends, reading, writing, and pretending to search for employment. Gary planned with mounting reluctance to hitch off east to a scholarship at Indiana

University—reluctant because he'd already been bitten by the Zen bug and had resolved that his life's direction should be west—to Japan, to the monastery—not east to academia.

Spring of 1952 found them living together again, back in San Francisco in the Telegraph Hill apartment Gary had rented. Gary, provident, held a day job; Philip held a number of them—night watchman, stockroom worker, printer's assistant—none significant, none memorable, none for very long. "He had such a hard time with employment," Snyder recalled. "He had a number of different pick-up jobs at different times, and he hated them all. He would do what they told him to do, but it made him upset. He somehow had a lot of stress and anxiety when he worked." Pressed as to why this might be, Snyder added with a tender chuckle, "Because Philip was kind of nuts. He never adapted to reality, quite. He never took the idea of making a living by publishing or teaching seriously. Philip did not have patience for things that did not interest him. He couldn't have gotten a law degree, because to do that, you have to read things that aren't interesting. . . . He'd always say 'A real writer or thinker shouldn't have to work anyway!' The zen approach—that naturally you should do whatever work comes to you, and that will become part of your practice—hadn't entered his consciousness."[16] Whalen suffered badly from unemployment and the resultant poverty all his life, and he offered many bitter criticisms of the systems—political, economic, academic, and military—that he felt forced him into such straits. The only psychological analysis he made of his own side was the no doubt accurate "I suffer a poetical indisposition."[17]

They entertained little in their North Beach flat, though Claude Dahlenberg came by for chess games, and eventually for go matches. During the year's cohabitation, Snyder recalls Whalen taking considerable trouble to wrestle a small pump organ up to their flat, the better to continue his hands-on study of Bach, which he also pursued on the recorder. Though Gary thought Philip played pretty well, Whalen's own view—which did not vary through the decades—was that he played badly. Profiting from the many bookstores in San Francisco and Berkeley, the two young men built up their libraries, including their Asian and Buddhist collections. Gary already owned D. T. Suzuki's *Essays in Zen Buddhism* (volumes 1 and 2) as well as R. H. Blythe's *Zen in English Literature* before he left for Indiana, and had packed these with him for the trip out and, a semester later, the trip back. The Metaphysical Bookshop, where Snyder had found the texts, yielded further D. T. Suzuki writings, as well as the Blythe four-volume *Haiku* series. These early classics, together with translations of the Diamond Sutra and renderings of Chinese poetry by Arthur Whaley, Ezra Pound, Witter Byner, and Lionel Giles, provided the raw material for many a pointed talk between Snyder and Whalen. Gary reported that he and Philip discussed these texts "elliptically. Poetically. Unpredictably. We didn't hold seminars," adding, though, that the ideas put forth in the books found their way into Philip's poetry. They can be seen, for example, in his approach to the teaching of emptiness. From a remove of fifty years, Snyder observed what he could not have known at the time: "There are some very key ideas in Buddhist philosophy, that you almost *have* to work with poetically. Either that, or you just repeat, like, 'Because a sweater is not a sweater, therefore we call it a sweater,' the basic logic of the Diamond Sutra. You can have a lot of fun with that." It is precisely at this point that logic—at least the Greek version of that science—runs out. This apparent dead end leaves an interested person who wants to go further one option: trying out Mahayana Buddhist philosophy personally, trying it on oneself by doing it. Thus it was at their Montgomery Street flat that Snyder and Whalen first practiced zazen—sitting meditation—together.[18]

By autumn 1953, Gary had moved to Berkeley to study Oriental languages at the university. Philip kept the San Francisco apartment for a couple of months before leaving suddenly, with no notice to his still key-holding friend. Gary registered a mild complaint in early November, writing that he'd "let myself in to your place on Telegraph Hill and walked in on two fairies in bed. They very kindly told me you were in Los Angeles."[19] Philip indeed had gone to L.A., the charms of which he'd explained in a letter to Gary: "Ah Horace! Quelle Faiblesse! The spell of the South is upon me. It is a languorous warm day & the breeze in the palms whispers softly of dolcefarniente."[20] Gary remained at Berkeley for the next several years, studying seriously during the semesters and using summers to get into the country for lookout work, trail work, or logging. Whalen also spent the three summers from 1953 to 1955 in the mountains, in his case the North Cascades of Washington, working as a lookout for the Forest Service. The rest of the time, Philip migrated among the homes of friends in Los Angeles; Newport, Oregon; and Seattle. He continued to subsist, as he later put it with Tennessee Williams's words, "by the kindness of strangers." He contributed little or nothing to the economy of whichever household held him, beyond help in the kitchen and the charms of his conversation and company. When these were no longer sufficient, when the indulgences wore thin, Philip would feel obliged, or indeed be obliged, to pack up and move on, sometimes abruptly.

His route generally took him through San Francisco, which meant a visit with Gary. They had some time but not much near one another at the Marblemount Fire School in 1953, before their summer lookout stints on different mountains of the Skagit. Their workdays were long and strenuous, and left little energy for philosophy or socializing—enough, though, that their friendship was remarked on. According to John Suiter, they were seen of an evening sitting together in a truck, earnestly parsing and debating an Asian text. Word went around that "them guys're Buddhists." The rumor must have originated with Snyder and Whalen themselves, as it is an unlikely deduction for young men of the Washington State countryside to have made, with no external evidence, in 1953. Private religious beliefs did not seem to count for much in the Forest Service camps. Political beliefs came to play an increasingly heavy role, but what really counted in camp was a man's attitude toward work and his ability to do it. Snyder recounts that everyone there could see that Philip was a little different—always with a book nearby and writing materials to hand—but that he worked well and without complaint during the weeks of trail clearing and construction the lookouts did before being packed up to their posts. Whalen's corporal strength may have been wrapped in a scholar's flesh, but strength sufficient it was. That, his appreciation for rural eccentricity and for Northwest vocabulary, as well as a hidden talent for telling jokes, made Whalen well liked in camp. Conversely, the physical exertion in mountain air, the eccentric crew working around him, the immediate prospect of time alone with long views and long books, and the camp cooking in quantity cheered Whalen. Lots of these impressions appeared in his writing, especially in his first breakthrough "big" poem— "Sourdough Mountain Lookout," where in arch complaint he notes:

> I always say I won't go back to the mountains
> I am too old and fat there are bugs mean mules
> And pancakes every morning of the world
>
> Mr Edward Wyman (63)
> Steams along the trail ahead of us all
> Moaning, "My poor old feet ache, my back
> Is tired and I've got a stiff prick"
> Uprooting alder shoots in the rain.[21]

After Whalen's third summer in the mountains, he came down to Berkeley—with speed, at Gary's urging—to participate in the Six Gallery reading, landing in Gary's very small "hojo" and bunking there for several weeks. Originally a gardener's shed, Kerouac described the place as being about twelve feet square, furnished with orange crates for shelves and a low table, and with straw mats as floor cover.[22] Snyder's pack in the corner, with camp-cooking utensils tied up on the outside, completed the decor—and the kitchen amenities. Whalen would have had his own pack, as well as a raft of new books recently purchased in Seattle with his lookout pay. It must have been snug. But when Snyder tells of the places he and Whalen shared, he reserves the description "tight quarters" not for the Hillegasse doghouse but for the time a decade later when Whalen landed on his doorstep in Kyoto.

Gary had invited him. It was planned: Philip would live there until he found his own place. The two went around town. Philip enjoyed being shown the old capital—being taken on hikes in the hills and shown the old temples and shrines, as well as spots made famous by events in Japanese cultural history (a surprising number of these known to him from reading). He also enjoyed Gary's introduction to the eating and drinking establishments in town, as well as the public baths, where they would sweat out the inevitable hangovers. Pleasurable as this all was, Philip was aware that something was off. He reported to Allen Ginsberg that he liked it at Gary's, but he'd be much happier in his own quarters. He felt he "made Gary nervous, living at his place."[23] Several years later, Whalen came back to these awkward feelings, sparked into memory of them by waiting in that same house for its new tenants—Richard and Virginia Baker—to be ready to go with him on an expedition. He told his notebook,

> I find myself looking at the SW corner of the big room—that spot which Gary had fitted up with a work table & foot warmer for me. This is what I was looking at—that *fusuma* & corner of shoji—the first few weeks I was in Kyoto, in 1966. There was some sort of failure. And there was the earlier "failure" of Joanne & Gary's marriage & divorce. All that was clearly {from the outside, looking in} a very minor kind of failure, an extremely common sort among Americans of every class. Yet, on the same level, it was important or significant or harmful to all of us.[24]

Kyoto apartment hunting was not easy, but within a couple of months Whalen found rooms of his own—rooms he kept for the rest of his first (twenty-month-long) Japanese residence—across town from Snyder's place. This restored their harmony: "Now we are all happy," he told Ginsberg in a letter. Whalen's departure from Japan in mid-November 1967 marked the last time he and Gary lived with or near one another. By the time Philip

FIGURE 6. Gary Snyder and Philip Whalen in Japan, 1966. Photo by Ken Walden.

returned to Kyoto in 1969 for a second stay, Gary had left; when Philip got back to San Francisco in 1971, Gary had been living in the Sierra Nevada for some time.

When not living together, Philip and Gary still tried to do things together, pretty much whenever possible. Their most famous hike together took place in 1965—Friday, October 22, to be precise—and included Allen Ginsberg. The three poets spent a day circumambulating Mount Tamalpais, a very pretty mountain ridge rising from the Pacific to a peak dominating Marin County. They walked with ceremonial intention, following a tradition of pilgrimage and circumambulation as old as recorded human history. Because Mount Tamalpais was already a magical mountain for the local Native Americans; because Gary and Allen and Philip all continued ritual walks around the mountain in subsequent years as their fame grew; because they had connected their initial circumambulation to Buddhism and because Buddhism in the Bay Area continued to grow; because it is a gorgeous way to exert oneself among the varied California ecologies hosted by the mountain—for these and other reasons, the circumambulation has continued to the present day and has given rise to many poems, articles, essays, and at least two full-length books, complete with photographs, drawings, woodcuts, trail maps, elevations, aerial views, journal entries, and poems.[25] "It's been of interest to us to construct it very slowly into a magic mountain," Whalen told a class at Naropa in 1980,

> or to restore its magic by very traditional means—not black magic, but magic magic. We started this process around 1959 by performing circumambulation of it and reciting sutras at various points around it. Actually Locke McCorkle started and then the rest of us continued from time to time.
>
> There was one time when Ginsberg and Snyder and I actually set up specific altar spots around the mountain. It's funny, that sort of formal trip was done first in maybe 1964 and we all wrote poems on that occasion, at each of those places. It wasn't until much later that the Zen Center was given, at a greatly reduced price, the Green Gulch Farm, which is right at the bottom of Mt. Tamalpais and more or less includes Muir Beach where the wobbly rock is that Lew writes a long poem about. It was a place where we had gone in the early '50s to collect mussels and roast them on the seashore, drink wine, and laugh a lot, before Gary went to Japan the first time in 1956....
>
> If you live outdoors enough, and stay alone enough, and walk around enough, you tune in on landscape and it becomes important to you; and you like places, you like the way things go together.[26]

Gary and Philip had been walking on, camping on, and sometimes living on Mount Tam for as long as they'd been in the Bay Area, but the first mention of a walk all the way around appears in a 1959 letter from Philip to Gary in Japan: "On Friday and Saturday [April 17–18] Locke and I performed a proper circumambulation of Mt. Tamalpais—overnight camp at Laurel Dell. The whole trip a delightful flowery excursion."[27] Whalen's calling it "proper" refers to the fact that he and Gary both had been sketching out and hiking sections of a circumambulatory route since much earlier in the decade. They insisted that these early outings were not specifically ceremonial,[28] meaning that they were not yet copying any formally established ritual. But whoever chooses to spend time on a mountain, particularly a fabled magical mountain, finds that the boundaries between spiritual and mundane, between a pleasant hike and an extended walking meditation, are porous boundaries indeed. Which is sort of the point.

Whalen knew the tradition of *parikrama* (circumambulation) and *pradakshina* (circumambulation to the right) from his extensive readings in Indian religious literature. Snyder encountered the contemporary version upon his arrival in Japan, when he began hiking on Mount Hiei. Gary learned from his Zen friend Walter Nowick of a walking meditation (*gyodo*, or *kaiho gyo*) carried out by Japanese mountain monks of the Tendai school. These walks included stops at certain shrines for prostration and recitation. Soon after that, Snyder connected with what he called "a very old Shinto-Buddhist mountain-walking brotherhood"—the *yamabushi*—and was initiated through a rigorous set of ceremonies into their membership.

Whereas Philip could only read about it, Gary and Allen (with respective partners Joanne Kyger and Peter Orlovsky) witnessed circumambulation of stupas and other holy sites in India and Nepal in 1962. They also learned about more ambitious routes around entire mountains or rivers. Some suggest that these trips went clockwise, or "to the right," because this is (somehow) the sun's path. But to speak mundanely, in India the tradition certainly also had to do with manners: one ate with one's right hand and used the left hand to clean oneself at the other end. To show respect, one would thus present one's right side to the object or person of veneration, keeping the left side away. Together with prostration, this bodily veneration is mentioned in a number of early Buddhist texts; Whalen and Snyder may have known it from the Diamond Sutra: "Then many monks approached to where the Lord was, saluted his feet with their heads, thrice walked round him to the right, and sat down on one side."[29]

Snyder's and Whalen's poems from that day tell what they chanted and where. In their brevity, concrete imagery, humor, and present tense, the poems exhibit the effects of long rhythmic walking and mantra recitation. Ginsberg's poem seems never to have surfaced. The three poets had no prior plan about where their shrines would be; these they divined on the spot, through sensitivity to elemental powers—the "magical vibrations," they called them. To the recitations, however, they gave thought. David Robertson, an English professor colleague of Snyder's from UC Davis and a Tam hiker himself, recalls that in a lecture about the hike, Snyder listed four basic types of chants, from Hindu as well as Buddhist liturgy: "First of all was a statement of the 'total truth of the universe' as the three of them understood it. They chose the Heart of Perfection of the Great Wisdom Sutra. Second was a magic spell *(dharani)* that would push disasters away and at the same time 'spread protection and well-being throughout the universe.' They also selected short verses that addressed specific powers: 'rocks, animals, plants, human beings, watersheds, upthrusts, all spiritual beings.' Finally, they recited the 'Four Vows' of Buddhism, in order to 'dedicate their lives to work for the benefit of every other being on earth.'"[30]

They hiked as an act of translation, in the old sense of the word, carrying something religious from one place to another; in this case they carried a walking meditation practice. By 1965, Whalen and Snyder had both engaged with Buddhism—Snyder classically by entering a temple and studying with a teacher, Whalen through private, extensive reading and semiregular meditation practice. Both had also worked with the language of Buddhism—Snyder, again formally, translating liturgies, as well as, like Whalen, weaving language and meaning from Buddhist literature into his own compositions. Both understood that certain things would require the lineage stamp of approval before being imported to America, whereas other aspects of the Buddhist culture could be adapted more freely. In 1953, Whalen issued a lusty mock challenge to Snyder about his interest in Zen: "Why don't you follow an antient example, viz. that of the Puritans, & simply announce the establishment of the Neo-Orthodox Purified Anabaptist Nonepiscopal Zenshu of Inward Grace (as derived directly from scriptural authority) & I will damn well weed the tomato patch once a day, out back of the zendo."[31] But Gary knew that to actually do that—to establish a teaching line, a temple, and temple forms—would require a great deal more than "scriptural authority." It would require personal, close practice and study with a teacher in situ, until the teacher said it was okay. Whether or not he had importation in mind, by 1965 Snyder had accomplished the steps of heading to the old country and working with a Zen master.

In opening the mountain, as they called their hike, the poets had found something more flexible—a practice that yoked ancient Asian traditions to local Californian deities and power, a serious practice roomy enough to accommodate a lot of play, a lot of experimentation, and a certain amount of nonsense. It was Buddhist, but bigger than Buddhism, in the way that tantric Buddhism is thought by some to be "beyond Buddhism" because of its inclusion of shamanic elements. The trio of poets certainly carried magical shamanic implements that day: conch-shell trumpets, long- and short-handled *shakujos* (a staff adorned with three metal rings), claws, beads, bangles. They also later sturdily resisted the notion, proposed by Robertson, that hikes should be carried out in a formal Buddhist or Hindu manner. "How do you feel when you are there?" Whalen asked his interviewer. When hearing that Robertson felt wonderful on Mount Tam, Whalen advised, "'Well then, you say, 'Here I am at Rock Springs and I feel wonderful. Let's hop up and down and sing 'Happy Days Are Here Again.' You don't have to recite some dharani." Contrariwise, this sort of happy behavior might actually have fitted Whalen's definition of Buddhism. "Actually Buddhism is very physical," he went on to tell Robertson. "Not only is Zen physical, Chinese Buddhism in general is something people *do*. It's a way of living, it's a way of looking at the world, it's a way of being. To me, anyway, there is a great deal to it of feeling. About how you feel about things, how you feel about people, and how you feel toward yourself."[32]

How did Whalen feel about the hike? It cheered him up—at least it stopped him, temporarily, from worrying. Whalen was "worrying about a whole lot of things right then."[33] He was, as usual, poor, sometimes literally penniless. For complicated reasons of loyalty to friends, he had been "hiding under the bed to avoid the Berkeley Poetry Conference." He was in the throes of pulling up stakes in San Francisco to seek employment and improvement in Japan (which was unknown to him). He had several manuscripts out to publishers—one of these titled "Different Ways of Being Nervous"—and he felt nervous about their treatment. His father had died a month before the walk, and Philip had had to remain in Portland, among relatives, for several weeks. So without parents, without funds, without prospects, leaving one of his most stable residences, ensnared in the complex bureaucracy of travel to a new residence, Whalen went walking. "I didn't have to worry as long as I was busy walking around the mountain. I could feel relatively at ease with myself. I was able to just open up to things and see them and feel comfortable, instead of feeling that I'm no good, or that I'm great. You're just there, a part of the scene." For Snyder, the hike must have functioned as a farewell of sorts—to Allen Ginsberg, with whom he'd been hiking earlier that year; to Whalen, with whom he'd been hiking in the Sierra, and to Mount Tamalpais, the power spot of the San Francisco Bay Area. Two days later, Gary flew back to Japan.

It bears noting that although a great deal of poet hiking took place during Gary's year and a half in the States, other things happened as well; specifically, Vietnam War protests were in full swing. All three Tam circumambulators had variously taken part in protests. One of the most unusual forms of this was the all-day zazen session Gary organized at the Oakland Army base. Philip told his journal, "On Tuesday 22 June I went with Gary to the Oakland Army Terminal. We sat outside the fence beside the highway, doing zazen, from 7:20 in the morning until 4 in the evening. There were 25-minute periods & ten minute breaks & an hour for lunch. No formal kinhin."

Snyder noted later that although there was no walking meditation, they did have work meditation—*samu*—both morning and afternoon, during which time they patrolled the area for garbage and collected it in plastic bags. Whalen continues:

> Richard Baker, Jim Thurber, Robert Gove, Silas Hoadley, a man called Chuck (Reader? Rieder?) sat with us, & in the afternoon a man called Max joined us. Although many people photographed us & a few news-men came around, none of us gave our names. Snyder had thought it best for all of us to remain anonymous Buddhists. While we sat, some of the people who drove past (on the street behind us, or on the street in front of us inside the Terminal) laughed or yelled insults or jokes. No one seemed to know what it was we were doing, except for the Police & Military Authorities who had been informed in advance.

Three months earlier Whalen, in the same spirit of promoting peace by being peaceful rather than by shouting about it in masses, had composed a couple of broadside manifestos and enlisted Gary's help for the distribution. The first piece seems not to have been collected in anthologies of Whalen's work, but he was proud of the idea, if not of the actual composition. In elegant calligraphy, it reads,

> Nobody listening to YOU?
> Stop yakking.
> If we STOP Everyone will know:
> We want peace & quiet & liberty for all.
> Celebrate GENTLE THURSDAY, March 25 1965
>
> *Don't leave home except to attend church.
> *Don't go to work—don't open your store, your office
> *Stay home from school
> *Don't buy or sell anything
> *Phone only in case of emergency
> *Don't do ANYTHING until Friday March 26
> SPEND THE DAY CALMLY. BE GENTLE. BE KIND.
> Send this message to your friends. Mail it to President Johnson, to congressmen and senators.

The other piece, also a broadside printed from Whalen's calligraphy, reads in all-capital letters:

> DEAR MR PRESIDENT,
> LOVE & POETRY
> WIN—FOREVER:
> WAR IS ALWAYS

A GREAT BIG LOSE.
I AM A POET AND
A LOVER AND A WINNER—
HOW ABOUT YOU?

> Respectfully Yours,
> Philip Whalen 10 : III : 65

With its saucy flair, this piece *has* made it into Whalen's collected works and is to be found posted on walls and refrigerators to this day in the San Francisco Bay Area, where, with Snyder's help, it achieved its widest distribution. President Johnson's response has not been recorded.

. . .

Dear John . . . Dear Long Pan . . . Dear Uncle Bud . . . Nanki Poo
The letters between Philip and Gary in the early to mid-1950s are frequent; a couple of letters a week each way is not unusual.
Dear Siva . . . Dear Mogambo . . . Ossian . . . My Dear Governor Wei . . . Dear Nuthatch
They often wrote by hand, especially Philip, and have as one of their themes handwriting, both Occidental and Oriental. Whalen studied calligraphy under Lloyd Reynolds at Reed, but his italic handwriting soon departed from the model. It achieved perhaps the more important calligraphic aims of being clear, legible, beautiful, distinctive, and remarkably expressive. Snyder, who never took Lloyd's course but taught himself, wrote classic, fluid Italic—an elegant hand by any measure. Their letters sometimes contain Chinese and Japanese characters, as well as drawings. Gary and Philip come close to having a quarrel in letters over sumi painting and aesthetics generally.
Dear Lentil-Head . . . Dear Popjoy . . . Dear Sze . . . Dear Bimbashi Sahib . . . Dear Nightingale of the Far West
They try to keep track of their Reed friends, including professors. They try to keep up with old lovers—mostly this is Gary, but Philip joins in. They gossip naughtily. They talk about how and when to visit one another and said friends.
They describe what they're reading and how they feel about it. Very often they're reading Pound or Rexroth and, not coincidentally, their translations, since both Gary (formally, in school) and Philip (generally not in school) are reading in and about Oriental classics. They're both reading many kinds of classics, as many as they can.

Dear Dismukes . . . Dear Chutney . . . Dear Dirty-Boy . . . Dear Peach-Stone-Boy . . . Dear Claude

They talk about jobs, whether or not they have one and how that feels. One reason, certainly, that Philip writes to Gary so often about his employment status is that he owes Gary money, either money borrowed outright or shared rent money, unpaid. When Whalen borrows money from Snyder, he does it charmingly and writes of paying it back, and does sometimes manage to pay back some of it. Once Gary borrows money from Philip.

Dear Crazy Horse . . . Dear Kabir . . . Dear Gilgamesh . . . Dear Zoraster . . . Dear Waxwing . . . Mon cher maître Balthasar . . . To one in the Southern Province . . . Dear Vishnu . . . Blue-necked One

Partly it seems they're trying to come to grips with their education. Both had been recently extruded from the college system into a postwar America the politics of which neither liked. It was mutual. Snyder's problems with the House Un-American Activities Committee began during his years at Reed and dogged him, wasting his time right up through getting a passport for travel to Japan in the mid-1950s. Philip's own brush with the political Right came a decade later, in 1964, when his poems caused an outrage in Oregon.[34] They write to one another of the trials of just getting along, and they wonder what, if anything, their education has prepared them for. As early as 1953, Whalen pens a line to Gary he will later use as a title for a poem, "If you're so smart, why ain't you rich?"

Dear Gaygo . . . My Good Kamo Chômei . . . Dear Whipsuade . . . Dear Sebastian Melmoth . . . Dear Hemingway . . . Dear Tiger . . . Dear Apollonius . . . Dear Penrhyn . . . Dear Waterchestnut . . . Dear Julius . . . Dear Felix . . . Dear James . . . Dear Terrence . . . Dear Timber-Beast . . . Dear Lemon Head . . . Dear Egmont . . . Dear Sage . . . Dear Pilchard

Dear Gary

Dear Philip

They continue their education. It seems clear to both that they need to, though Philip wonders in his letters if vast knowledge improves moral character or not. From this, one can see that he not only wanted vast knowledge but was concerned with being a good person. Such a dichotomy did not apply to the Confucian and other classic Chinese texts Gary was studying at Berkeley and seems not to have exercised him. Whalen toys with idea of going back to school. He announces plans to do so but never does. He does continue to read and study all the time.

As their circle grew to include other friends and writers, Philip and Gary reported about these as well: Alan Watts and Kenneth Rexroth and the fire lookout guys from Marblemount early in the 1950s; Ginsberg, Kerouac, McClure, Creeley, Ferlinghetti around the mid-decade Six Gallery reading; Cid Corman, Albert Saijo, Leroi Jones, Gregory Corso in the later 1950s. Sometimes their letters sound like simple dispatches from the social scene, telling who is doing what to/for/with/against whom and the various opinions arising from that.

The salutations and signature lines cited here—a random sampling, drawn from both sides—show that play and gentle mockery figure centrally in their letters. These two were dedicated to having at least literary fun with one another and to provoking, through pun and allusion, an elevated atmosphere of intelligence. Their very bright minds seemed to shine most intensely when they relaxed into humor. The wit does not stop after the greeting or pick up again only at closing; their letters are shot through with it—almost as a philosophical stance, almost as if to say that despite poverty, despite hard employment or unemployment, despite loneliness or lovesickness or the stresses of school or homelessness, despite nationally held political, economic, and religious attitudes that largely disapproved of them, they were going to enjoy themselves anyway. They did not ignore their difficulties, or any of the darkness they felt in the national climate, but through humor and intelligence and pleasure in writing, they thwarted them.

Faithfully yours, Sohi . . . Malignantly . . . Indigently . . . Pendulously . . . Faintingly . . . Snobbishly . . . Tiddley-poo

The running gag with naming was not something they ever discussed. They simply did it. They did it with enormous energy throughout the 1950s, letting it fade away only in the later years of that decade. Whalen had used some pet names with earlier correspondents, but the consistency and variety he and Snyder showed with one another was wholly unmatched. Gary thought perhaps their readings in Mahayana Buddhism inspired them to it. In some of those texts, one does find extravagant lists of names for just about everyone—including, as Snyder noted, names for each wind spirit and each spirit abiding at the tip of each blade of grass. For his part, Philip often cited Gertrude Stein's blunt dictum: "Names are always interesting." Names fairly obsessed him. He knew the roots and meanings of his given names and had researched many names in his family tree. He pored over multilingual dictionaries to puzzle out the messages coded into names he received in the course of his Buddhist ordinations. Later he was confronted with the challenge of giving out such names himself.

In a 1976 class he taught at Naropa, Philip broke into a fifty-minute riff on naming, using another Gertrude Stein pronouncement as point of entry: "A poem calls on the name of something." From here, Whalen went on to consider the vision quests that some American Indians and other tribal peoples undertook. He explained that in the best cases, a sacred helper would arrive, and bestowing protection and power on the supplicant through ritual song and dance, the helper would grant a name, or possibly two names: a secret name, as well as a name that could be openly used. He then sketched out the series of names a young Chinese gentleman of classical times might have had—from being called at the beginning something like "son number 4" up through a chosen name, a school name, a civil service name, artistic names for whichever disciplines the gentleman practiced, honorific names, and possibly a posthumous name. He dwelled at some length on the tradition of names being secret sources of power, much as one finds in the Rumpelstiltskin tale (though Whalen doesn't specifically mention that one). "With lots of people, if you can find out what their name is, and call them by it, they have to give up. At that point, they either have to submit to having you kill them, or do whatever it is you say you want them to do. Because names are secret— a person's name is a sacred possession, a secret he doesn't tell everybody." Having thus expatiated on the tradition of secret names and a corollary of this, false names, Whalen proceeded contrariwise to tell the class all about his own names, including how he received a secret totemic name from an encounter with an animal in the middle of a full-moon night, in the middle of a lake, in the middle of the mountains.[35] He didn't tell them the name but explained that it was secret insofar as it was only written out in Chinese. He'd had a seal made from it, which he used to identify his books and prints.

Remember me to the animals & trees. Phrenetically . . . Feverishly . . . Tropically . . . Illiterately . . . Si monumnetum requeris [If you seek his monument], Snowball . . . Desperate measures are called for . . . Hoping our product pleases you . . . With many happy singing uguisu-birds, cher Bête, La votre . . . In short, I am sliding across the edge of a larger Blank than usual, with little hope of emerging ever again. Forgive me, Sylvestre Bonnard

Write me, S. T. Coleridge . . . I retire now, with germ. Septically, sick sick sick . . . Selah! . . . Amor omnia vincit [Love conquers all] . . . Prophetically

What to make of this years-long name game they played? The act of using so many false and funny names seems at minimum to be a rousing of intelligence, but following Miss Stein's near identification of poetry and naming—going the other way with it—it is possible to see the game as a veiled calling on poetry herself. Mixed in among the nicknames and nonsense names are many literary allusions, some obvious, some hidden. Even discounting literary reference, the delight and seduction of the game are clear attempts to channel the stream of language their way, toward them. That Snyder and Whalen did this intensely together, and pretty much only with one another, points to a perceptual agreement or an aesthetic fraternity—something Snyder groped to explain in a 1955 letter to Philip: "I feel the sensibilities you and I have—in somewhat different ways—been employing in our poems, there is something really very new historically, and [they] mark a new beginning."[36] Pop-quizzed about this letter some fifty years later, Snyder was understandably cautious. Using the half-century's perspective and thinking also of other poets,[37] he finally said, "Apart from the characteristics of the content, in Philip's and my work there's an attempt to use elegant, spoken language—without being excessively colloquial, but still very down to earth—reflecting usages here in the western United States. And trying, thereby, to find ways to say complex things with the most straightforward and physical vocabulary." He reflected awhile, then added, "There's probably a lot more to it, when you start thinking about it."[38]

One other way to think about it here harks back to the old Buddhist bugaboo: emptiness. The shocking notion Buddha put forth early in his career, that the self is empty—that no singular, enduring, unchanging "self" can be found, but rather only a shifting collection of feelings, concepts, and impressions all housed in impermanent flesh—has sometimes been taken in a nihilistic sense, leading to a depressing view of Buddhism. Closer to the original intention of the emptiness teaching is a view that does not deny an *experience* of self but does not limit it to a static thing. Seen positively, emptiness can mean that human life is more multiple and varied than the usual notion of a "self" would allow.[39] With this more relaxed, spacious view, a person could try on—like costumes—the attributes and attitudes of people throughout history since, as Walt Whitman also said, one contained multitudes. If one young poet addresses a letter to To-no-Chujo, for example, he might indeed be so completely involved in the world of Lady Murasaki's *Tale of Genji* as to want to write from that place, especially to another young poet who knew that place and could go there. If Philip signed a letter "Sebastian Melmoth"—code for a feeling of humiliation and rootlessness—who could argue that the author was separate from the state Oscar Wilde found himself in when he took that name upon his release from prison? If one wrote in formal, calligraphic book-hand at the bottom of a letter, "Exit, pursued by a bear," is the comedic impulse of that moment so different from Shakespeare's, when he penned the same? Presuming that a feeling for emptiness did underpin Snyder and Whalen's use of so many names and personalities, it was never intended to be solemn or monumental. Confrontation with emptiness does not lead only to dreary negation. An equally classic response, reported in the lives of Buddhist worthies throughout the centuries, is a feeling of liberation, spontaneity, and humor.

In the strange, beautiful essay he contributed to a 1991 Festschrift for Gary, Philip tells of their language games. The piece in fact seems to be wholly about language, about getting a word or phrase stuck in your head, following it into English until you get satisfaction, or not, and all that happens along the way. Whalen shows the reader a playful obsession with language, as well as obsessive play. He mentions Snyder's name just once, as member of the Adelaide Crapsey–Oswald Spengler Memorial Society at Reed, an ad hoc group who jousted at writing five-line poems using five strange or difficult or unknown words freshly drawn from the dictionary or another book. After conducting a tour of reference works, Whalen tacks on a sobering coda about Buddhism's paradoxical view of language: "The study and practice of Buddhism tends to clarify the boundaries of speech, what can and cannot be said. But even Buddhism sets up a paradox: Silence is best; contrariwise we must use words to teach Buddhism and to communicate with people in the 'real world.' Zen people, who are very polite and very refined—at least as much so as the *OED* and *The Riverside Shakespeare*—simply say, 'Sit down and shut up!' and so I do."[40]

The piece doesn't seem to be about Gary at all.[41] He's hardly there, though Whalen composed it specifically for a book called *Gary Snyder: Dimensions of a Life*. But here, instead of telling about Gary, Philip demonstrates. He takes the reader's hand and in effect says, "Come along. Here's how Gary and I have worked at being writers: we've read, we've made notes, we've memorized, we've found the books and cracked them open and looked things up; we've gone down the trails the words pointed out; we've loved (and used) the bawdy jokes, the slang, the songs, and anything else we've needed from Anglo-American. Now, after more than forty years of exerting ourselves in this joy, we've joined the ranks of the caretakers of this language." One of the phrases Whalen has stuck in his head is from Shakespeare. He uses it to title the piece "Liberal Shepherds."

When Snyder went to Japan in 1956, a shift took place in their letters. For one thing, the materials changed: they began to write on ten-cent aerograms, and, to fit as many words as possible onto the blue sheet and the two side flaps, they typed. Philip moaned about this. He cited his lack of skill as a typist, the cost of the air letter, and the distinct likelihood that what he wrote would be so worthless as to end up costing him a dime when he tore up the paper. Still, except during periods when he really didn't have the dime, Philip kept up his end of the correspondence. (He did, however, interrupt an otherwise pleasantly discursive letter to Gary with the blast "FUCK ALL TYPEWRITERS!")

Snyder had much exotica to report: about Japan, about the particulars of temple life, about his teacher, and about his patron, the notoriously challenging Ruth Fuller Sasaki. They played the name game for a while, but this gradually gave way to a more serious tone and more factual accounts. The letters continue to be absorbing and beautifully written but become more earnest, in respect perhaps of the several thousand miles of cold water that now separated them, and the stark cultural differences.

For some unknown reason, Whalen answered Snyder's first round of letters from Japan—letters to himself, to Kerouac, and to Locke McCorkle—with a scolding corrective, telling Gary, "You sound dangerously near to indulging in a great maudlin fit of sentimentality and nostalgia, coupled with even unhealthier broodings of a masochistic nature.... Have your mental faculties decayed in that incense-laden air?"[42] The rest of the letter continues with a typical Whalen mixture of bright, grumpy observation, strong literary opinion, and social reportage. Announcing that he must go "think about committing some new literary extravagance," Whalen abruptly ends, "Try to be a better bonze. Quit trying to stop. Mordantly, Philip." It is difficult to understand how Philip, sitting on his broad rear end in the comfort of his Berkeley home, working an easy part-time job, with time to write and food to eat and even, unusually, getting laid regularly (thanks to an introduction from Gary), could write such things to Snyder, who was certainly undergoing some sort of culture shock and enduring the always challenging, often brutal life of a junior student at a Japanese training temple.

To his credit, Snyder sorted the matter quickly, admitting he may have "shot the wrong language at you by mistake," and thanking Philip for having "the presence of mind & integrity enough to protest," adding that this was "not by way of compliment, but simply recognition of the indispensable astringency you have always been kind enough to show me." Whalen's imperious tone he gently dismissed as "Johnsonian."[43] Gary learned early on in their friendship to ignore Philip's tantrums—the red-faced, foot-stomping kind, as well as their written equivalents, seeing them simply as heightened emotions without much substance. "They didn't even mean we were having a real argument. We *might* have been having a debate, and sometimes he'd build a little soap opera around it."[44]

Just as he did for Ginsberg in the eastern direction, Philip kept track of manuscripts and forwarded mail westward to Gary. They also sent fresh work to one another, Snyder particularly seeming to need it: "Man, send me your poems—please—they may help keep me sane in this crazy scene."[45] After waiting to be asked one more time, Philip sent rather a lot of material, and Gary's praise by return mail "quite overwhelmed" him. Gary's remarks back then have stood up through the decades. Snyder saw the essential virtues of Philip's poetry as clearly as anyone ever has. "Well man, I read THE SLOP BARREL last night having just received it & was simply stoned. I mean I can't say too much—that little bundle of poems is elegant, spontaneous, balanced, everything they mean by classical & without no stink of the lamp. You're miles ahead of me or Ginsberg, simply because of that balance and style. . . . Pivotal poetry brings a fresh mind to the reader & he is neither partisanly delighted, nor offended and annoyed, but minorly awakened. This is what this complex of your stuff seems to work like for me. The balance between discipline & spontaneity is almost perfect, & the exciting inner tension of the intellect which the academics wheeze about is solidly, but discreetly there."[46]

This sort of praise ran both ways. Consoling Gary about Barney Rossett's rejection of *Myths & Texts,* Philip wrote, "It is my opinion that Mssrs. Grove Press have fucked themselves by not accepting it for book publication. Nobody else's first book of poems is such a complete & unified composition, presents such a total effect, has so much finish, so much definite point."[47]

They could also be critical, Whalen especially. "I must now commence beating you about the head and ears," he wrote, after reading a ninety-two-page letter from Gary to his sister telling of Snyder and company's adventures in India and the Himalayan foothills. "I never suspected that you was an undercover agent of HOLIDAY magazine. I never seen such longeurs in prose anywheres else. Good Grief . . . but I am enormously disappointed. . . . I really am unfair. . . . I apologise, but drat it, I hope that after while you will have time to write more sharply & exactly about whatever. . . . That letter is just exactly 45 pages too long. TOO MANY WORDS. AAAAAAAAAGH!"[48]

With Snyder, of course, Philip only meant to encourage; he understood his friend's tremendous talent and potential. "From you or any other writer I want to hear what he is, what his world is, clearly or complicatedly, however he can do it, preferably, (in the case of contemporaries) simply. I want you to sound like Gary; sometimes in this piece you sound like yourself singing through your nose, not your usual bel canto."[49]

Following hard on such criticism—either the exaggerated kind or the more considered take—Whalen would spend a paragraph apologizing and confessing his own literary shortcomings. Philip's critiques were never personal arrogance; they were literary strictness, and he held himself to at least the same high standards. "For my part, I like to imagine that I'm not so much interested in my opinions, stands, stances, any more, but the questions: 'What do I really know? What do I really feel? Who's knowing &/or feeling?' etc. ending up with Rabbit horns. Oh well. In other words I get sillier every minute I'm alive." Gary's criticisms of Philip's work took a gentle form, very possibly in consideration of Whalen's self-critical nature and his emotional lability. The most he would say was that this or that piece didn't seem to him to work as well as the others or that he couldn't quite get (or dig) what Philip was driving at.

They wrote about weather. Both were influenced by it: Snyder because of Japanese temple architecture and building materials, and his habit of hiking; Whalen too because of hiking and because his pronounced mood swings were tied to whether the day was bright or dark, hot or cold, dry or damp.

They sent things back and forth: vital papers stashed at old apartments, books—lots of books. Gary sent robes and bells and ritual implements, including eating bowls, from Japan. Philip sent magazines and records and bicycle clips (presumably for keeping wide pants fast around the ankle) from the United States to Japan.

They reported about sex, and beyond this, Gary theorized about its place, or lack of place, in the Zen Buddhist path. In one letter he observed with approval the Japanese way: his Zen master was married, and he was not alone in this. Philip seized the occasion to deliver a lecture, similar though shorter than the one he'd sent to Ginsberg: "[Ginsberg] has, like you, been worried in mind about religion vs sexual continence &c. Now goddamit, two of you on my hands with this damned Manichee twaddle is too much." With the goal of making clear that they all carried around unconscious acculturation, Philip laid out three possible worldviews and urged Gary to choose. The choices were (1) a Judeo-Christian-Platonist view "of the split man: the bright spirit in dull gross filthy clay routine"; (2) a Buddhist view of a person's nature as "the product of his own karma and of his own mind, with the possibility of busting into something else (namely zen, in your case,)"; or (3) "man [as] the semi-automaton of the biological scene." Philip opined in pretty bawdy talk that "old golden face"—Lord Buddha—probably wouldn't mind if Gary had sex. Unable to resist clucking at his younger though vastly more experienced friend, Philip went on: "You gave me the impression that if you are going to really work at zen, you do not expect to be practicing the finer points of bull fighting at the same time, not because bull fighting is a sin or is forbidden, but because you are simply occupied otherwise."[50]

If he came off sounding boorish, Whalen knew it, later telling Gary, "I wish you were nearby so I'd have somebody to pick on: I guess I shall have to find some way of becoming enormously rich so I can fly to Nippon & pester you there some weekend."[51]

They wrote about meditation. Gary had undertaken in Japan the practice and lifestyle of meditation about as seriously as it is possible to do and remain within a social context. Philip also kept a little meditation habit going, but with nothing like the depth, in nothing like the environment, and without the constant instruction that Gary had. So Philip used his friend as a source. "As I understand it, there is a secret method for doing zazen. I don't know, from reading [D. T.] Suzuki exactly what zazen is, in the first place & now Watts says, in his book, there is a patented surefire secret of success which is to be learned only from a Mahster. I am not asking you to divulge the secrets of the Lodge."[52]

Gary's reply—oblique, tactful, clothed in anthropological terms, left enough threads trailing for Whalen to grasp. After making the useful distinction between meditation traditions with form and those without form, Gary wrote on the side flaps of an aerogram,

Zen meditation is "formless," i.e. it has no definable subject, & the mind is not actually "concentrated" on anything, but rather gently removed from hanging up on logic-chopping & reasoning; useless imagining (which includes unconscious thought associating, memory associating, etc. surrealist & Jungian shots); & all forms of discriminating, not a process of squelching the surface play of associating & conceptualizing, because it can't be actually stopped, but ceasing to hang up on it & follow it. The koan, as a subject of concentration, is just a device to keep you from taking thoughts as they turn up as though they mattered. Advanced koans handle aspects of dealing with things after you once break into the cool; but first koan is just "a brick to knock on the door with."

Formless or form, with or without koan, just sitting still & watching the mind is a real illuminating process. Very obvious & simple, & also for Occidentals I guess fantastically hard. I have all kinds of blocks against zazen, even though I know it's a Good Thing. If one sits properly & manages to breathe fairly evenly, at least for the first year or so it doesn't matter what he tries to do or think about. Just watching & realizing the general inconsequentiality of what he sees (the precious "personality," ho ho) & getting the physical intuitive sense of his own body & the breakdown of the sense of difference between mind & body—is enough.[53]

Whalen thanked Snyder for his "account of non-objective contemplation, zazen etc" and added a few distracted, scholarly remarks, such that Gary saw fit to write back, "The point is, in a sort of self-sanzen process, to be hardpan sincere with yourself & tolerate no cleverness or verbal trickery, like every moment was the last. & at the same time not getting hung on that process always—a very common state among Zen monks who have progressed a bit—a state of constant inner discipline & tension that gives the sense of POWER but is basically nowhere because it can't include undiscipline, messiness, late-sleeping & spilled beer, etc in its insight."

Snyder's intimate, clear writing about meditation in jargonless English—a very difficult thing to do, and probably no one has done it better than Snyder—seems to have encouraged Whalen. In any event, he kept on with meditation and a few years later confessed to Gary, "I try to do right, knowing my idea of 'I' and 'right' are IDEAS but continue to try doing the right thing & am ashamed when I goof. . . . I can see no earthly use in my sitting, I have no guru, no initiation, don't know nothing about meditation or koans but I feel like it has to be done, so I sit anyway. Probably wrong, probably perversely, probably swindling myself & the world, but do sit. There."[54]

These remarks to Gary bespeak a refined spiritual friendship—the *kalyanamitra* that Snyder mentioned. Beginning adepts are generally taught to regard their teacher as an elder—someone wiser for being farther along the path—a spiritual aunt or uncle. As the relationship develops, the teacher figure shifts from elder to friend, the signal difference being that with an aunt or uncle, one might be tempted to inflate one's report of progress on the path. This can't even be tried with a real friend. The way it is sometimes (crudely) put, you might be able to fool an elder, but you can't bullshit a friend. Because Whalen and Snyder spent their lives in Buddhist-dosed literature, philosophy, anthropology, and art, because these fields were thoroughly swirled together, and because they each had at times more wisdom than the other in various of them, they took turns in the teacher role. While both could show stubborn, even territorial sides, they did little of this with one another. Throughout the years of their friendship, they seemed willing to cede a position or a point, though not sometimes without pointed defense.

They lamented how Beat seekers overran North Beach in the late 1950s. Both thought that the loving, poetic, breakthrough good times they'd shared with friends for a while in 1955 and '56 had been blown out of proportion by media attention and that whatever scene might have been there had departed. They also recognized that with the 1958 publication of Kerouac's *The Dharma Bums,* things would get stranger. "KATY BAR THE DOOR!" Philip wrote to Gary about it, adding, "Book is beautiful, but god only knows how the young of the Bay Area (or elsewhere) will understand it & how they'll react (not to mention the Luce organization.) Be brave."[55] Snyder wrote back a few days later, less impressed than Philip with the literary merits of Jack's book but equally aware that their scene had been exposed: "I hope we won't all be arrested."[56]

In the years following publication of *The Dharma Bums,* Snyder appeared to distance himself somewhat from Kerouac and declined to attend Jack's funeral in 1969. One can imagine reasons: shyness at having been portrayed in a novel, sadness at Jack's physical and emotional decline, distaste for political views attributed to Kerouac. But Gary maintained respect for the work Jack had accomplished and was deeply saddened by his death. None of this was lost on Philip. About halfway between the appearance of *The Dharma Bums* and Kerouac's death a decade later, Philip passed along intelligence of Jack to Gary and proposed, only half-humorously, a way forward:

He's begun to write a new book & is feeling much better but still wonders WHAT MUST GARY THINK OF ME? Apparently you don't write to him

very often. For some reason or other he wants your *approval,* sympathy, etc....
I don't mean that your approval & sympathy are not delightful to hear & to
receive. I mean it is hard for me to see why J-LK DEPENDS so upon it some
moments. Why not, on the other hand. I hope (quite confidentially) that when
you get your INKA as a roshi, you will immediately finally & totally save, illu-
minate, transform & horrify Mr. K the moment you see him in person (although
I wish it could be done by mail or telegram,) because he is really terribly unhappy
& bugged by himself so much of time, and he will, (I fear) demand nothing less
from you on that day. There's a koan for you, with my apologies & love.[57]

Gary replied that he'd written to Jack "and told him I thought highly of him,
but no response yet."[58]

The other "JK" they kept in view was Joanne Elizabeth Kyger; they distin-
guished her as "JEK," while Kerouac remained "JLK."[59] Of Joanne Kyger
they wrote carefully, owing on Whalen's side to his intense, enduring, but
ungrounded love for her, and on Snyder's to several years of somewhat
strained marriage with her. Both men esteemed her native intelligence, her
sense of daring, and her skill as a poet; neither was insensible to her consider-
able beauty. Philip knew, in keeping a separate, parallel correspondence going
with Joanne, that Gary would likely read the letters. Similarly, he used letters
to Gary to send messages to Joanne. They all played with this. Responding to
Joanne's having written "lies lies lies" at the end of one of Gary's letters,
Philip instructed, "Say to her that I expect a full accounting from her person-
ally of the true state of her health & language studies instantly; otherwise I
must accept your version as it stands." In Joanne Kyger's own writing—
Strange Big Moon: The Japan and India Journals, 1960–1964—her first entry
mentions Philip being at a party a month before she departed for Japan and
Gary. The last entry, four years after the first, finds her arriving by boat back
at San Francisco, the marriage with Gary effectively over. The book con-
cludes, "Only Philip Whalen was waiting when I disembarked."

So they went on through the years, writing to one another—less frequently as
they aged and had steady access to telephones, but sending regular (oft) hand-
written letters anyway. All the big moves Philip made occasioned reports to
Gary: Whalen's landing in America after leaving Japan in November 1967, his
various, unsatisfying California residences, his return to Kyoto in early 1969

(Gary had left town by then, and soon thereafter the country), with faithful accounts of the festivals, theater, landscapes, weather, temples, and company they'd enjoyed together. Philip sent congratulations on the births of Gary's children, as well as birthday greetings to Gary himself every year, though Philip remained uncertain of the date. Whalen reported to Gary his whereabouts when he came back from Japan a second time and when, in early 1972, he took up tentative residence at the San Francisco Zen Center, and again a few months after that, when he decamped to the monastery at Tassajara. Snyder naturally received an invitation—several, as the date kept sliding—for Philip's ordination, which in the end Gary could not attend. Poetry continued to go back and forth as it always had, as well as invitations to readings and performances, but now instead of manuscripts, they sent finished books and fine prints. They praised one another's work as they always had, but now included kudos for the awards and honors their writing attracted: Whalen's nomination for the National Book Award, Snyder's receiving the Pulitzer Prize.

From the mountain valley monastery at Tassajara, where telephone connection was sketchy at best and discouraged in any case, Whalen wrote of plotting visits to Snyder's Sierra homestead; and he called on Gary's multilingual command of Zen literature when his own memory of a story failed or when research materials were lacking.

Philip's adventures in 1981–82 running his own zendo in the Noe Valley of San Francisco, the closing of that zendo, his abrupt relocations following those of his teacher Richard Baker in the wake of Zen Center's 1983 schism[60]—all these he related to Snyder in a language calmer and more objective than he could usually muster in everyday speech. This is possibly because after thirty years of a rich, varied life, the correspondence had a power of its own. It absorbed the outer shifts and inner turmoil of the Zen Center scandal rather than dissolving into them. It was swollen, to be sure, like some reptile gorged on another creature entire—but there remained room for plans, gossip, appreciation of landscape and flora, book reports, and dispatches from the inner spiritual journey. Whalen moved with Richard Baker first to a Potrero Hill zendo, and then, in a much more significant displacement, to Santa Fe: far from the ocean and (painfully for Philip) far from fresh seafood and Chinese cuisine.

Although the New Mexico winters tried both his patience and his health, life in Santa Fe gave Whalen a great deal more study time with his teacher than he'd had since the formation of that relationship. The crew who'd moved to New Mexico along with Richard Baker lived more or less on one property and convened for regular classes in Zen's specific literature, the koan collections. They did not study koans in the classic one-to-one-dharma-combat-with-the-master style, but given the material, struggle was inevitable; it was inherent. Because he knew both the koans and Richard Baker, Snyder made the perfect listener for Philip. They'd been writing to one another about koan study for three decades and understood that there is very little one person can do for another engaged with a koan. Still, writing about the process seemed to support Philip. He praised Baker's handling of koans as "really remarkable, considering he makes no claim for having studied them in the systematic way,"[61] but describes his own work as "fretting & fiddling. . . . I go at it like a monkey playing with a looking glass. Turn it over to see where did he go, can't reach him, etc."[62]

Baker Roshi's removal from the Zen Center left him and his loyal students thoroughly unmoored. As Baker considered what kind of group or institution to put together—or *if* to put one together at all—every aspect of the training and much of Zen's received wisdom was put under examination. In open discussion, they all considered what sort of role an ordained person could really play, especially in the United States. What did the term *unsui* mean for modern practitioners? Musings about this to Gary prompted an unequivocal series of responses: he declared himself against "priestly and monastic Japanese-type orders in the U.S."[63] Gary pointed to the difficulties such a system would make for women and children, among other things. Snyder had naturally been thinking about this cluster of issues for a long time, as it affected both his personal path with a larger, structural perspective. He and Philip had knocked it around in letters as early as 1953, with the you-run-the-zendo-I'll-weed-the-tomatoes drawing from Whalen. The short citation above comes as part of Gary's criticism—mixed in with congratulations—for Philip's completion of the transmission process, which empowered him to be a lineage holder and a teacher in his own right. Gary continued to make his views known, even as Philip took up residence at Issanji, a Zen temple in San Francisco's Castro district, and later assumed the position of abbot. On the surface, it seemed a role reversal: Philip was running the zendo; Gary, 150 miles out back, was weeding tomatoes.

At some respectful time in the future, the letters between Philip Whalen and Gary Snyder should be published. That thick book will serve as a memorial to a time when writers wrote letters. It will instruct in the art of opening oneself in writing to another person and in demanding and getting openness in return. It will provide clear pictures of the nourishment an infant Western Buddhism got from English and American literature; it will of course also show how American literature was enriched by access to the spiritual poetry and other writings of Asian Buddhism. It could be a somewhat scandalous book, if it gets past lawyers. It will be frequently hilarious. It will almost never bore.

If it is produced properly, this book will look beautiful, since it will reproduce pages and pages of original handwriting by two of America's earliest and most ardent calligraphic revivalists. Looking at the writing—just looking at it—will give the sensitive reader direct emotional information about the correspondents, before the agency of words and concepts. Thus the reader may be moved, as this one was, to watch Whalen's hand descend into unsteadiness and finally, abruptly, to stop. Coming to the end of this long future book, the reader may be moved to see how Whalen, blind and sick, was forced after nearly fifty years of handwritten pages, to dictate to an amanuensis his last letter to Gary—and how, at the end of a full page of close type, he insisted on signing but was only able to scratch out, with a ballpoint pen, a very shaky blue "P." The reader may be moved to tears.

· · ·

The author's introduction to *The Gary Snyder Reader,* cited briefly earlier, concludes: "And finally nine bows to Philip Zenshin Whalen, retired Abbott of the Hartford Street Zen Center in San Francisco. Phil has been a friend and mentor since undergraduate days. He first showed me the difference between talking about literature and doing it, and pointed the way into Asian philosophy and art. Later we both came to zen meditation. Over the years we've shared bare-floor flats in Portland, Berkeley and San Francisco, tight quarters in Kyoto, plus some huge and funny spaces of the mind."[64]

Proceeding as Snyder does from physical spaces shared to mental ones, this section considers those "huge and funny spaces of the mind." Conjecture necessarily plays a role, since mind is famously ungraspable. Not being solid, it still leaves traces, some subtle, some obvious, the way a moraine makes obvious the departed glacier.

Philip and Gary shared Zen mind, meditation mind. This is not a personal possession, and such a space of mind belongs to everyone, consciously or unconsciously. But Whalen and Snyder meditated together, sitting next to one another; they shared the basic method of accessing Zen mind. They shared as well an influential respect for the lineage that had delivered to the present day this method and others, the lineage that pointed out Zen mind and trained it. This is to say that they shared a practice of Zen that to most all of its disciples does not feel like the complete realization of Buddha mind, but which—according to not a few enlightened teachers—is exactly identical with it. Thus they shared Buddha mind. They knew this.

Oddly, given their very different styles—Snyder energetic, peripatetic, strict; Whalen still, slow, indulgent—they shared a taste for discipline and repetition. For many decades, both men simply rolled over the resistance to getting out of bed in the early dark for meditation. They trampled as well on the pesky resistance to going back into the meditation hall on, for example, a sultry afternoon, during extended practice sessions. Quite apart from the semimagical (but true) explanation that one's ego is threatened by meditation and therefore puts up resistance to doing it, there is the feeling, known to all who try it, that one does not meditate well. The actual experience does not compare well to one's imagination of what meditation is supposed to be or to descriptions—meant to be supportive—that one might read in a book. One feels a failure at it, and who needs more failure? But to continue for years to practice, and to glean the undeniable benefits of meditation—among them mindfulness, empathy, self-knowledge, insight, flexibility, and humility, as well as the occasional entrance into refined, illuminating absorptions—one needs to come to terms with the feeling of failing. In Japan on New Year's Day of 1967, Philip got most of a poem out of the insight that the feeling of failing simply belongs to the life of a practitioner (of any serious discipline) and that whatever one does to avoid it is simply delay or detour. He develops the insight in typically cuckoo fashion:

FAILING

The practice of piety. The practice of music. The practice of calligraphy. These are exemplary pastimes. The practice of rereading the novels of Jane Austen. The practice of cookery. The practice of drinking coffee. The habit of worrying and of having other strong feelings about money. All these are vices. We must try not to write nonsense, our eyes will fall out.

In answer to all this my head falls off and rolls all messy and smeary across the floor KEEP TALKING squelch slop ooze.[65]

Philip and Gary shared, obviously, "poetry mind": they shared a mind that clearly records and artfully arranges sense perception mixed with insight. In service of poetry, they also shared something it might be better to call "musical" or "rapturous" or "ecstatic" mind—a possession, a positive madness, a creative craziness—part of what worried Plato about the art of poetry in the first place. Snyder often described entrance to and departure from these states with a language of shamanism. Some consistent portion of his works have from the beginning portrayed shamanic ritual and trans-species journey. They have done this from the outside—how it looked—as well as from the first person: how it felt. A number of his poems are explicitly shamanic in affect: they use repetition, chanting rhythms, and generous helpings of Sanskrit, Tibetan, and other mantric speech to literally entrance the reader. Snyder wears all this lightly. It's the sky to his poetry's earthiness. But any even casual reader discovers in his poems that the author is a traveler at home in many realms, including invisible ones.

Whalen tended toward more mundane, identifiably Western vocabulary in describing his heightened spaces of composition. A "take," he would say, "a great taking." He might even say "tripped out." In teaching, he usually cited Gertrude Stein's "I am not I, when I write." His poems record numerous appeals to gods and goddesses for their presence, and especially the Muse, for him so undeniably a living force that he sometimes used a domestic tone with her: "You're late today."[66] Abrupt shifts in perspective, discontinuities in meaning and perception, disembodiments, invasions, flights, possessions— these occur so often in Whalen's oeuvre as to be the fact of it rather than the exception. Far from being shy about this side of their work, both poets fronted it. At their first performance—the Six Gallery in 1955—they tipped their hands, Whalen reading "Plus ça change . . . ," in which humans morph into speaking birds, and Snyder reading "The Berry Feast," telling of Bear and Coyote and Magpie and bipeds and their various intermatings, productive of wisdom.

One classical entrance to exalted states of mind is ritual use of hallucinogenic drugs. Inexpensive, not illegal, available, and traditional with American Indians, peyote presented itself in the mid-1950s as an ideal psychoactive. In a series of remarkable letters from the first half of 1955, Gary and Philip shared with one another their experiences with the drug—their visions as well as their hesitations. Gary went first, tripping on New Year's Day, to "an entire world, which is left-handed, baroque, dripping with jewels, & where I for one met Baudelaire, Rimbaud, William Beckford, Morris Graves, Edith

Sitwell, Aleister Crowley, Frederick Prokosh & hosts of others, to whom Peyote (almost a distinct personality) introduced me, as a sort of initiation. . . . I'll send you some, if you'd like to try it."[67]

Citing instability, Philip declined: "Don't need no more hallucinations than I got already. All you addicts can go right on debauching yourselves."[68] Besides the jewels and the introductions, Gary mentioned that his first trip was "almost terrifying," and this cannot have bolstered Philip's desire for peyote. His living situation was unstable—he would be ejected from it without warning about eight weeks later—and his psychological health posed a bigger problem. Months later, having finally ingested peyote, Whalen wrote, "I had been apprehensive about taking the stuff: as I've told you before on various occasions, I consider myself dotty enough without doping myself—I was afraid of seeing only horrors."[69] Describing physical aspects of his trips, Whalen compared them to what he'd read about insulin shock therapy (also known as insulin coma therapy). He matched up the physical responses in two separate letters, written months apart, indicating that he had been at least researching treatment options for schizophrenia and depression. And horrors he did see—at least conventional horrors—when, having eaten three fresh peyote buds in the company of friends, having waited, having given up and gone out for pepperoni and beer, having tired of the conversation and gone home alone to his basement rooms, he began to come on. As he wrote, he was

rapt away. In the early stages, I was in the midst of various ceremonial rites— there were drums & chanting & processions. Sometimes I was a pillar of the temple, sometimes one of the priests, sometimes the idol of the god before whom the ceremony took place.

A couple times I was the bound & mutilated fertility god high on the oak while the priest circled round, wailing and doing the limping dance—the measure /- //-//-//- etc. Then I was born several times.[70]

Here Whalen's journey entered even more mythical and religious realms rather than literary ones.

I was the giant Vishnu on the waters, while in my belly there was a cold, brilliant sun.

I was a giant tortoise, then I was Ganesha.

The prevailing, or recurrent image was that of identification with the giant Vishnu, enormously powerful but divinely, consciously resting.

Sometimes I was Shakyamuni under the Bo tree being tempted by Maya [sic] but resisting effortlessly—impossibly easy because, like Shakyamuni, I knew Maya had mistaken me for someone else, while knowing at the same time we were both relatively unreal. . . .

sometimes the vision was simply confused light & color & music—{not really "vision"—again, identification}—all very fast & bright, with sudden jolting stops—brilliant silence—& start again. Sometimes, being music & motion, I was the dancing Siva—and correctly dancing asleep but aware.

Alternations of life & death of the rival brother gods, rivals for the Goddess. [She was the only thing I never identified with completely]

Visions of people as mechanical creatures, pointless, deceived, supposing they had free will, &c—but who were actually automatons. It was this *saha* world, the only ugly vision. I hated that one, but accepted it.

About 4 AM, Abe kitty woke me. I got up & fed him & watched him and kitty Ogelthorpe smile & scintillate &c., saw the walls with holes opening & things crawling in & out, but not particularly bad or good, just there.

To the astonishment of his friends from the party the night before, Philip had accomplished this staring down of horrors, and indeed the whole trip, completely alone. Gary told him, "Peyote is pure magic. But what it does for you, I'm convinced, depends, just like the Indians say, on how pure your heart is. [You must have a very pure heart. I never doubted it.]"[71] But Philip's heart was not just pure: it also was oriented to cosmic scale and spiritual creation. In a follow-up letter to Gary, Phil framed peyote in a spiritual context but argued against making too much of it. He acknowledged feeling "a lot better having tried it; discrimination sharpened, a few more insights," but went on to point out, "As the old original rice bag said, 'Meditate. Smarten up.' and so we must. Peyotl is another finger pointing someplace."[72] A scant two months later, though, Philip was ready to be pointed again. This time, in addition to the shock-therapy-like symptoms, he admitted he'd been "fearfully sick and barfed most grievously, consequently spoiling, I believe, the intensity & duration of the effects." Even so, the cosmic aspect remained: "Lots of jewels, & a mandala or so. Great fun reaching (from a position in deep space) to touch various suns & receive great charges." But Whalen placed this trip squarely in the context of his work as a writer, both negative—"I am busy trying to write my story, & having this whee has put me off my schedule"—and positive: "When I am sober now I feel that I can sort out the realities and unrealities of this particular world more distinctly than I ever have before. I am more conscious of being conscious—that sounds literary, but take it literally—more aware that here I am with a lot to do. Best of all I find that I can work on things now & that I am working." He also felt sick enough from the cacti— "loathing at the thought"—to not want more of it anytime soon.

In Japan twelve years later, Philip had the chance to sample psychotropic drugs again—LSD, psilocybin, mescaline—and kept a notebook devoted to recording what he could of his trips. Being unable to write during the central ecstatic section, Philip's entries describe any ceremonial preparations he'd made beforehand. The writing then fades out and picks back up only as he comes down enough to write again. It appears that he had some trouble judging when to attempt human contact or adventure into the outside world after a trip. The notebook tells in amusing detail of missteps, chagrins, and swift retreats. One of these involved Gary, if only in absentia. "Took a trolley & bus safely to GSS his house, but he wasn't in—also wondered if I had the right number of heads, arms & legs showing."[73]

Philip and Gary knew early on that being poets meant an active engagement with poetical elders. They understood the power and function of lineage from the Zen context, and even if one wrote one's poems alone, they saw with increasing clarity that poetry too had lineages. In the spring of 1955, as they corresponded about peyote, Philip and Gary were absorbing what they could from these poetical lineages but at the same time trying to find ways to distinguish themselves from them. They particularly wanted a way out from under the heavy influences of their immediate forbears, including Pound, H.D., Eliot, Stein, Joyce, Williams, Jeffers, and Stevens. "You felt everything had already been said. It had all been done," Whalen told a Naropa class about the poetry scene of the time, adding that this scene had also come under the fairly tight control of university academics.

In D. T. Suzuki's martial language describing Zen training, they'd read of "dharma combat"—spiritual life-and-death-style encounters with the master—and they understood that this kind of differentiation from the previous generation can only take place in a atmosphere of mutual respect. Forms to ensure this respect are built into Zen ritual. Not so in the poetry world. The tricky balance of gratitude and arrogance and irritation and pride one felt toward one's lineage needed to be worked out for oneself. With one of the giants, however, this was straightforward. William Carlos Williams had shown Snyder and Whalen only kindness during his 1950 visit to Reed College. He'd spent social time with them, read and critiqued their work, and pushed them onward as poets. Thus when Dr. Williams—weakened by two serious strokes and a hospital stay for depression—came west in 1955 for a reading tour, they made sure to see him. Philip approached the great poet after his reading at the University of Seattle on 16 May, and reported to Gary that Williams had been "most friendly and gracious."[74] That Philip regarded Williams as a father and that he'd been secretly thrilled when the old man had remembered him, Philip only admitted in a poem eight years later, upon the occasion of Williams's death.[75] In the letter to Snyder, Philip merely said that while Williams seemed "much enfeebled," Philip still found him mentally and poetically sound.

Gary too thought Williams "did well" when he read some weeks later, despite technical ineptitude on the part of the University of California Berkeley's sound department, which Gary described as "the fucking school tried to ruin his talk."[76] The clownish behavior of the aides so irked Snyder that he devoted a long paragraph to it in a letter to Philip, concluding, "Jesus I was mad, I practically got up and beat the shit out of those English department snots that did it to him." Philip sent wishes by return mail that Gary might see Dr. Williams under "some less irritating conditions."[77] He added that Williams had also received strange treatment in Seattle. "He was introduced here by Roethke with a rather florid gesture—'one who teaches us that a poet must be a man'—and here was a MAN—not a long speech but rather fancy—yet delivered with great passion &c. Rather embarrassing. One expected W in a cod-piece."

.   .   .

Although the labels comprise dauntingly wide spectrums of meaning, it must be possible to say something like "Buddha mind" and "poetry mind." It *is* possible to say these things to people who try to practice either one. Meditators and poets talk like this all the time and only rarely force precision on one another, probably because the open meanings make conversation possible and fruitful and amusing, and because once definition starts, it takes over. People who try to practice Buddha mind and also write poetry talk like this because there is a rub between these two minds.

Ridiculing Literature

Humans are endowed with the stupidity of horses and cattle.
Poetry was originally a work out of hell.
Self-pride, false pride, suffering from the passions—
We must sigh for those taking this path
to intimacy with demons.

That's Zen master Ikkyu, himself a fine and famous poet, writing in fifteenth-century Japan. That's also Gary Snyder, using Ikkyu's poem (and later giving a commentary on it) at a conference he organized with Zen abbot and poet Norman Fischer in 1987, under the title "The Poetics of Emptiness."[78] Whalen allowed himself to be corralled into attending, though he told the audience on the opening night, "I'm here under false pretenses on about four levels. You're going to have to deal with that however you can. I'm quite willing to talk to people and explain things if they have a question or a problem. Or sit doltishly looking out the window. So if you want something from me, you're going to have to try to get it. Because I'm not going to offer anything. I don't *have* anything to offer. I'm sorry. That's the emptiness part."

The record includes preliminary written statements, circulated before the conference, followed by transcripts of at least three panel sessions, during which the main poets presented further material.[79] The conference meditated together; it ate together and heard Zen talks together. Discussion groups formal and informal took place. Philip wrote in his statement that he had developed both a writing habit—explicitly comparing it to a drug habit—and a meditation habit. "In my experience, these two habits are at once mutually destructive and yet very similar in kind. I write for the excitement of doing it. I don't think of an audience; I think of the words that I'm using, trying to select the right ones. In zazen I sit to satisfy my meditation habit. It does no more than that. But while sitting I don't grab onto ideas or memories or verbal phrases. I simply 'watch' them all go by. They don't get written."

Snyder wrote, "When I practice zazen, poetry never occurs to me, I just do zazen. Yet one cannot deny the connection."

Whalen said, "I became a poet by accident. I never intended to be a poet. I still don't know what it's all about.... As far as meditation's concerned, I'm a professional. I have to sell you on this idea that it's a good idea to sit. That's where poetry maybe comes into all this, that it has to be an articulation of my practice, and an encouragement to you to enter into Buddhist practice."

Snyder said, "I have to confess that like Phil, I don't have the faintest idea what my purpose is or what's going on, and I never have. I became comfortable with that mystery a long time ago—that I would never know how any of these things fit together in any explicit way." In subsequent panels, however, Snyder offered several brilliant if somewhat contradictory theories of "how these things fit together." Whalen kept to his word and didn't say much more on the topic. He declined to even attend the final panel.

In the undefined, sometimes uncomfortable edges between the meditator's mind and the poet's mind, both Snyder and Whalen availed themselves of classical solutions. One of these, brought forward at the conference by both Anne Waldman and Andrew Schelling, is devotional verse: praise and offering to higher powers—to wisdom itself, to ethereal as well as earthly embodiments of wisdom, to the lineage of wisdom, and to protectors of that lineage. Whalen and Snyder both wrote oblatory poems to the goddess Tara, national protector of Tibet and one of the rare female figures seen as holding the rank of a Buddha. Snyder went so far as to call his monumental poem *Mountains and Rivers without End* an offering to Tara. Both wrote poems in praise of Zen teachers: Snyder's breakthrough translations of Han Shan and Whalen's famous "Hymnus ad Patrem Sinensus" are ready examples; there are more. In these works, they imported as well the playful, teasing, or even mocking style of Zen. Whalen portrayed his heroes—"ancient Chinamen"—as "conked out among the busted spring rain cherryblossom winejars, happy to have saved us all."

Beyond this, both hewed (Snyder explicitly, Whalen intuitively, especially as time went on) to a Chinese preference for expressing sublime truth through mundane subject matter and plain vocabulary. It was lost on neither Snyder nor Whalen that China's greatest poets had been either Zen monks themselves or friends with Zen monks, belonging to an elegant circle of spiritual, literary, and calligraphic geniuses. Indeed the existence of T'ang dynasty poets like Wang Wei, Du Fu, Li Po, or (from the Song dynasty) Su Shih—as well as subsequent Japanese writer-practitioners like Sesshu and Basho—had at the outset made Zen immediately attractive to Whalen and Snyder as a spiritual path. When they began, both had been looking for ways to talk about insights, emotional disturbances, concept-melting encounters with landscape, love, literature, and art; and both had been looking for spirituality, Whalen very forthrightly so, to fill the gap left in him by abandoning his mother's Christian Science. In the Chinese and Japanese Zen-style poets they found perfect models. By the time of the 1987 conference, they'd achieved, in different ways, a level of mastery as poet-meditators, and they recognized this in one another. Snyder told the participants how moved he was to hear Philip—his original model for how to be a poet—talk about teaching meditation. A few years earlier at Naropa University, Whalen and Ginsberg had fielded a question from a class in which they were lecturing: did they have favorite Asian poets? Ginsberg recited from memory some Indian and Arabic verse and names were batted about, but in the end both admitted that one of their favorite Asian poets was the Zen man Gary Snyder.

Whalen and Snyder shared calligraphy mind; it's not possible to say only "brush mind," because Philip favored the chisel-edged tool, and Snyder used it extensively too. Being calligraphers, they shared the mind that exists in the hand. Calligraphic mind leads and follows black ink around on white paper; it understands how black marks, even simple ones, as well as the white spaces described by them, convey meaning in a way that precedes and interrupts discursive mind. This is true for the writer as well as the viewer. Calligraphy has long been another of the mediators between the spacious, formless, pregnant Zen Buddha mind and the manifest, explicit, communicative poetry mind. The Chinese and Japanese masters cited above produced works admired as much for the way they were handwritten as for their meaning. Strictly speaking, it's impossible to separate these. Whalen complained bitterly about how "dead" he felt his poems looked set in type and crowded on book pages. Many of his books do reproduce at least one or two handwritten poems, and *Highgrade* collects a great many of his doodles: playful handwritten and drawn works that exist on the edge of meaning. Two short books published by Irving Rosenthal in the late 1960s—one a children's story, one a pornography, both rowdy and funny, both containing only pages of handwriting or drawings or both—would today very likely qualify as short "graphic novels."

Even though handmade letters seem to work differently on the mind of both writer and reader than do their typed counterparts, they remain in their place as letters, for the most part incomplete in themselves and needing company to make a word, a lot of company to complete a line of poetry. More effective than Roman letters in creating a complex visual field on the page and a series of haunting, nonlinear meanings in the mind were Chinese and Japanese characters. Whalen and Snyder both knew the Ezra Pound edition of E. Fenollosa's essay, "The Chinese Written Character as a Medium for Poetry." Beyond that, they worked personally at learning characters. Snyder, typically, went at it early, organized and disciplined. Whalen, typically, engaged the characters much later in life and haphazardly, really only knuckling down to serious study when forced to it by living in Japan, and then later by needing to understand Zen texts in the original. Asked once by eager students what they would need to learn Tibetan, the great meditation teacher and scholar Chögyam Trungpa Rinpoche replied, "A new mind." Not unconnected to calligraphy, Snyder and Whalen applied themselves to obtaining and sharing the "new mind" that could function in Japanese. About the study of Japanese, Whalen remarked to Allen Ginsberg that he found it "entertaining to try, & [it] keeps my head from gluing itself totally shut and senile."[80]

FIVE

Your Heart Is Fine

WHALEN AND KYGER

Late 1958 saw Joanne Kyger—twenty-four, beautiful, stylish, and smart—living alone above La Rocca's, a bar in San Francisco's North Beach. She rented the top-floor apartment and worked at Brentano's bookstore downtown to pay for it. Through the bookstore during the day and in North Beach bars and clubs in the evening, Joanne came to know the poets of that turf, a well-established group orbiting around Jack Spicer and Robert Duncan. Predominantly but not exclusively a collection of gay men, they accepted Kyger—"Miss Kids," as they called her, after her habit of entering a room with a general greeting of "Hi kids"—into their workshops, classes, and social life. Spicer particularly seemed fond of her and recognized her native talent and learning. From Kyger's side, these developments were not purely accidental. She'd been involved with the first literary publication on the University of California, Santa Barbara campus, a direction that appealed to her although "I hadn't really written anything that could be published at that time." Her undergraduate education there included study of W. C. Williams and Ezra Pound under critic Hugh Kenner; another of her professors, philosopher Paul Weinpahl, taught Wittgenstein and Heidegger.[1]

This rich fare propelled her to San Francisco, which she understood to have a more cosmopolitan intellectual and artistic atmosphere than Santa Barbara. She soon found the Spicer-Duncan group, a lively poetry scene in which passionate criticism—constructive and destructive—focused each week on fresh work.[2] In a more loosely organized San Francisco poetry scene, this one around poets of the Six Gallery reading and their friends, she found Eastern ideas, especially Zen, very much in the air. At a Poetry Center function, Joanne Kyger met Gary Snyder—the Dharma Bum himself—and though Snyder moved around the West Coast a good deal that year, they started a love affair. Soon Gary began praising his "great friend Philip Whalen" to Joanne. In the other direction, Gary wrote to Philip that his holiday visit to San Francisco was awaited with "great excitement" by John Wieners (whom Philip actually knew) and Joanne Kyger, whom he did not.

Related to this, Jack Kerouac's novel *The Dharma Bums* also appeared in 1958, shuttling unwelcome tourism and unwanted attention to the (relatively small) North Beach literary scenes. Like Philip up in Newport, Oregon, and like many readers since 1958, Joanne Kyger devoured the novel in a single sitting. From it she constructed a mental picture of the writers in its pages— poets and novelists who had since felt swinged in public by angry literary criticism. These writers, including Kerouac himself, wished to duck back to a smaller, more collegial, more productive, more anonymous time. Thus when a Reed College friend of Gary's appeared in The Place one evening, Joanne assumed his denials of being Philip Whalen were camouflage, part of a quest for privacy. She chatted him up warmly, bringing him and other friends to her flat for further conversation. Only reluctantly, in the face of vigorous and repeated denials during the course of the evening, did Joanne accept this person's identity as Clarence Les Thompson. Even so, she insisted on calling him thereafter "the false Philip Whalen."

Very soon she met the true Philip Whalen. That evening began politely but did not go well. "Gary brought Philip up to the apartment, brought him to the door, I was very nervous. We went to a Chinese restaurant and just everything went wrong. I couldn't use my chopsticks. I was trying to be arch and witty, but whatever I said crashed. Finally Philip said, 'I can't stand these . . . sorority . . . type . . . *girls!*' got up and stalked out."[3] Philip's explosion may have been rooted as much in discomfort at what Gary was *not* saying as it was in what Joanne was trying to say. Snyder wrote later to Philip about the time, saying, "You don't know how bad I felt about no chance to talk to you during Xmas: also when I was in Newport I wasn't very communicative either, the fact is all the time I was in America with the exception of the last few weeks (being w/ Joanne was very sane) I wasn't in my right head, i.e. a real verbal block which was made worse by people who wanted me to say something: & the root of it is that I *can't* say anything where my work on koan is right now & it hangs me up."[4] Whether from frustration at feeling distanced from Gary or from being overwhelmed at the sudden proximity of a stunning, verbal woman, one can only imagine Whalen's chagrin out on the street.[5] But Joanne recalled that "a little later, either that night or the next, we all met up— abjectly apologetic—and agreed to be friends."

The finally amicable constellation lasted only briefly. At the end of his Christmas holidays, Philip returned to Newport, where he worked as a court bailiff, assisting an old army friend—novelist and now circuit court judge Ben Richard Anderson. The work gave him a steady paycheck and left him adequate free time in scenic coastal surroundings, but Philip was unhappy. "I'm still here but wish myself away," he wrote to Allen Ginsberg. "I am going buggy. I want to live in my own dream world & all I get is somebody else's dream world which I don't appreciate. . . . I must AWAY {flap, flap, flap} O where o where o where?" At various times Philip had complained to Allen and to other friends how difficult it was to write in Newport, yet he produced a steady stream of works, including some of his best known. Perhaps riding in on the mists, old trees, rocks, and water, Chinese Zen masters enter his poems more frequently here, exemplified by the brilliant, funny, but serious "Hymnus Ad Patrem Sinensis." In any case, Philip now had Joanne Kyger to think about in San Francisco, as well as the other people and things he pined for. Kyger did not make it easy on him, writing long, deceptively evenhanded accounts of her girlfriend dramas with Gary—that relationship had a rough-and-tumble aspect—then throwing in lines like, "Come back. Come back. . . . Come back and spawn."[6]

Gary also left California only weeks into 1959, heading back to work, study, and Zen training in Japan. From there, he sent Joanne a formal pro-posal of marriage. By April, Joanne herself had moved out of North Beach and into the East-West House, near a part of San Francisco that would later be called Japantown. The East-West House, she explained, "hoped to be a continuation of the American Academy of Asian Studies (which opened in 1951 and closed in 1956). It was started by a group of students who hoped Alan Watts could continue giving lectures there, and that it could be a place to study and prepare oneself for travel to Japan to study Buddhism. The culture of the late 1950s was very much reveling—at least on this coast—in what Japan had to offer in the way of cultural history: gardening, tea ceremonies, beautiful folk crafts, music, a sense of nature."[7] Mixed with these lofty aims and at times overpowering them was a vigorous social life in the East-West House—one that thrived on the study and discussion of philosophy, litera-ture, language, and religion, held in every room but primarily in the com-munal kitchen, where a steady supply of alcohol was near to hand. In *Big Sur,* Kerouac describes the East-West House, or its overflow annex, the Hyphen House,[8] as a place where residents "all live in different rooms, with their clutter of rucksacks & floor mattresses & books & gear, each one taking turns one day a week to go out & do all the shopping and come back & cook up a big communal dinner . . . they end up living comfortable lives w/wild parties & girls rushing in, people bringing bottles. It's a wonderful place but at the same time a little maddening. . . a regular nuthouse actually."[9] Kerouac continues praising the place, telling of an encounter with Whalen, who lived there in 1959: "You can rush into any room and find the expert, like say Ben's room and ask, 'Hey what did Bodhidharma say to the Second Patriarch?'— 'He said go fuck yourself, make your mind like a wall, dont pant after outside activities and dont bug me with your outside plans.'"

Before he became the Zen-wisdom habitué of Hyphen House, however, Philip made stops after leaving Newport, all of them connected to Joanne. Even knowing he had to move, Philip dithered for several months about where to go. A postcard to Gary reveals his thought process, if that term applies: "AG wants me to come to NY. You all invite me to Frisco—today I have money enough to come to Frisco & the sun is shining."[10] In the event, Philip did move to San Francisco, arriving breathlessly in time for Joanne's first poetry reading—7 March 1959—at the Bread & Wine Poetry Mission and bearing as a congratulatory gift a ripe pineapple. Perhaps it was simply the most extravagant-looking thing he had time to buy in the rush of packing, traveling, and installing himself in poet Kirby Doyle's recently vacated flat. Perhaps he simply hadn't wanted to arrive empty-handed. Two years before, Philip had written a touching poem—"For C."—from the similar circumstance of a last-minute gift standing in for emotion:

> lacking the courage to tell you, "I'm here
> such as I am; I need you and you need me"
> Planning to give you this flower instead—
> Intending it to mean "This is really I, tall, slender
> Perfectly formed" . . .
> I had to see you
> If you were out, I'd leave these flowers
> Even if I couldn't write or speak
> At least I broke and stole that branch with love.[11]

It is not immediately obvious which aspect of himself he wished the pineapple to convey. After the reading and the no doubt long and spirited postreading celebrations, Joanne accompanied Philip to his new flat. She arrived fully clothed, she left next morning fully clothed, and from Philip's account, she remained fully clothed the whole night. The evening's accommodation fell

FIGURE 7. Joanne Kyger at Stinson Beach, 1959. Photo by Tom Field.

rapidly and completely from Joanne's memory—it was not at all an unusual arrangement of overnighting among friends in her crowd—but it had an impact on Philip. In surprisingly guileless prose—perhaps another instance of what she would later call the "Beat brotherhood 'My girlfriend is your girlfriend' kind of thing,"—Philip reported to Gary, "Miss Kyds gave a lovely reading & then crawled into my bed where I was panting w/desire & she wdn't take off her clothes & it was sad but I forgive her & maybe she will tame down after a little more cultivation."[12] To which Gary replied with advice—seriously outdated by today's standards—as to how a man in Philip's role should relate to her, including, "Be very firm w/Joanne & don't do anything she tells you," ending, though, by noting, "She's a magnificent woman."[13]

No one among Philip's oldest friends—not Gary Snyder, or Michael McClure, or Joanna McClure, or Dave Haselwood, or Joanne Kyger herself—can ever remember Philip's having a girlfriend or a boyfriend. No one ever saw him appear in public anywhere as part of a couple. No one doubted that he had sexual feelings, even sexual relationships, but when it comes to partners' names, everything goes vague. If there *is* any name that people suggest, even skeptically or half-disbelievingly, about Philip's love life, it is Joanne's name, and that because of the connections Philip made and deepened with her in 1959. A little more than a month after her reading, Philip wrote to Gary, "I spent all of last week-end & Monday as well with Mlle K., who is improving nicely in deportment, attitude towards the outside world, appreciation of Nature {all last Sunday in GGPark} & fancy fun & games. She made a rank scene Tuesday night {drunk & screaming on the phone} because I had to busy myself with getting Ms. into the mail on time, but wrote me a long apology the next day. We continue on a mutually pleasant footing. I shall devote big chunk of tomorrow to her—Monday being the goddesses day anyway."[14]

Through weeks and months, Philip continued to devote his time to her and soon moved the two blocks from Kirby Doyle's flat into the East-West House, taking his own room there. Still, the picture he first sent to Gary—of being physically very close to her, even during the nights, but (at her instance) sexually apart—seems to have held. Describing it years later, Joanne's voice starts and halts, and starts again toward facts until arriving at a portrait:

> I was never "with" Philip. I think that we really liked each other, you know. We were living in this communal household, and Philip never had any money. I was trying to live, and not have . . . a rough edge. I was taking

dexedrine and going to work and trying to figure out how to learn Japanese and study Zen, and staying up late carousing and drinking wine with friends . . . and getting over. . . . I had had this really *bad* peyote trip before Gary left, over La Rocca's bar, in which I was just not in the right place to be taking peyote. I fell *into* the void and came back *out* again, and I didn't know what the void was, everybody had animal faces . . . it was just *really very* schitzy. I had flashbacks from that during this year, in which everything was tilting, and it was very weird. . . . At one point it felt like my brain was cracked in half for about a week. All perceptions were just all changed . . . and I went over to try to tell Philip, "You, know, I'm having this really hard time." His prompt reaction was to have a *harder* time, so he went and had a *bigger* nervous breakdown. He was going, "Oooooh, aaaaah"—there's that poem where we're walking across town and his arm stretches really long—because all this perception altering was going on. So I thought, "Oh, you're not going to be any help at all! You're just going to try to outdo me!"

But he was warmly generous, in that that was not the end of our relationship. We continued to have this very specific relationship. We had a specific relationship, you know, that had to do with reading and writing and having nervous breakdowns, together.[15]

A Distraction Fit

I walk around town with my baby
While I'm sound asleep in the middle of a nervous breakdown

Big pieces of the world break off
Slowly
Sleeping
she didn't know the right way home, I lead the way
with my eyes closed.

Pieces of myself plaster & stucco walls
Potemkin facades
drifting away

Lungs breathe me out
Heart circulates me through pipes & tubing
Brains imagine something walking
asleep
She holds this man by the arm it stretches
across the world
Hand in his pocket
Dream of love in 2 houses
asleep
She breathes me in

4:V:59[16]

Breakages in their connection did not sit well with either of them. Joanne demonstrated this with pique. Beyond the "rank scene" mentioned above, Philip's withdrawal from the East-West House for a stay in Marin and a long hike in the Sierras provoked another example: "Miss Kids isn't too pleased with my departure; I guess she'll get used to the idea in a day or so," he wrote to Gary. But Philip told his journal it had been a "wretched parting quarrel."[17]

Philip's own reactions to time apart from Joanne trended in another direction. As soon as he got into the mountains, he writes in a notebook,

> I was thinking of the different kinds and qualities of sexual sensation & response felt by a person at different times of his life—in childhood, adolescence, early maturity & middle age ... and how many I could remember vividly & could I remember every instance of sexual contact with another person.... I nearly can.... I suspect I know (& sincerely care about) little more than pleasure. However, I did remember ... a number of unpleasant past events, for a change—getting slapped in the face on various occasions as a grade school student—getting punished on various occasions for sexual activities ... various wretchedness in the army & at Reed & later—& I've kept worrying for months now over the question "What have I learned from all this?"—taking for granted the notion that "experience teaches" and the idea that I have some capacity for learning ... what?[18]

Later in the year, when a poetry tour took him to New York, he wrote a series of letters to Joanne. Interrupting the first—a cheerful flow of impressions of the city and new acquaintances—Philip shifts to capital letters to abruptly complain,

> I MISS YOU. NOBODY HERE IS AS PRETTY AS YOU. I AM
> SEXUALLY FRUXSTRATED (your word)
>   & SOON WILL
>   PERISH
> FOR WANT OF LOVE. (*YOUR* LOVE)

The letter just as suddenly returns to normal typescript and stories of friends, plans, and logistics. His next letter, written the next evening, lists out a daunting itinerary and concludes,

> then the AIRPLANE to your door, beside which I trust you will be awaiting
> the return of your faithful but feeble servant, Philip
>   with grand devotion, love & kisses, a pleasant goodnight. X X X X X X X

A final New York dispatch tells of seeing a painting in the Museum of Modern Art: "One HUGE & very beautiful Bonnard that I like. I'll bring it home for your room. How is the rubber plant? How is everybody? How do I live without seeing you? I'm tired & want to come home, i.e. among your ferns and ivy." If Philip here seems to imply, even in jest, that Joanne's room is his home, he went beyond that back in San Francisco. Aware that she was steadily preparing to go to Japan and Gary—possibly not aware that this would mean Joanne and Gary would have to marry[19]—Philip proposed another plan: Joanne should stay in San Francisco with him. The two of them would get an apartment. "I was *leaving* you know, and he didn't want me to leave. He suggested we get an apartment together, but his asking me was just kind of like 'Please don't leave.' I could not see how Philip was going to be able to be a domestic partner, in the way that somehow, at the age of 24 or 25 . . . I was still thinking that marriage and baby carriage was some sort of formality that was going to happen."[20] Joanne clearly understood that Philip had no appetite for a job and no practical sense of money. Part of the reason he left the East-West House, aside from the social hubbub, was that he couldn't pay his share of the rent. He hiked for about a week with Les Thompson (the "false Philip Whalen"), then lived at Gary's old zendo—Marin-an—until the county health inspector ordered the place closed for lack of standard sanitation. After that, he boarded with the McClure family in San Francisco for several weeks, then took his sleeping bag out to Mount Tam again and slept in various camps, going down to Homestead Valley and his friend Albert Saijo to "beg for food." Finally Joanne found him a job in the City of Paris department store, where she worked. He lasted a week in the Brentano's bookstore shipping department, but meanwhile he'd roused himself to pass a civil service exam and had lined up part-time work at the post office. This trickle of income sufficed to get him back, by autumn, into the East-West House and then Hyphen House. A rootless, impoverished lifestyle may fit the life of a poet—many have lived this way in the service of literature—but it did not impress Joanne Kyger.

Though Gary also wandered as a poet, scholar, and half-monk in Japan, he at least had steady work and a place to live. Beyond that, he was adventurous, energetic, and charming. Joanne was taken with Gary in a way that, however much affection and admiration she might feel, she was not taken with Philip.

A chapter about Joanne Kyger might have seemed a good place—since it involves love—to discuss Philip's sexuality. It turns out to be no better than anywhere else. Joanne claims not to have even secondhand knowledge of the topic. "What did Philip do about sexuality? Well, I have no idea; he was a very discreet person. He was not an aggressively sexual person. That's not to say that his emotions weren't tied up in it. I was wondering once if he and Tom Field weren't . . . if they had anything. Everybody was so sexually discreet during the fifties anyway. Philip certainly wasn't someone like Ginsberg, who was completely and totally out front, or someone like Neal Cassady. Most people were discreet—even the Beats, especially the gay Beats."[21] Then, for clarity, she added, "I never heard of *anybody* who *ever* said they had a physical relationship with him."

Joanne's view, and that of other female writers, is that whatever Philip did about sex, it was not an issue of overriding importance for him. She and poet Alice Notley point to Whalen's novels as a place to learn how he would have *liked* to be. The couplings there—marital, extramarital, pretty much all heterosexual—are managed with little physical complication and a certain worldly diffidence. They are respectably numerous. Notley in particular dismisses even the palpable jolt of randy energy in Whalen's early poems as being there for his male writer friends, put in because he thought he should.

Years later, Philip lived at the San Francisco Zen Center during a time of at least local relaxation of the prejudice against homosexuality: the celebratory (gay) nature of the Castro district waxed. Harvey Milk rose to political prominence. The influential columnist Herb Caen often wrote about gayness without shock or quibble in the *San Francisco Chronicle*. A splinter group of gay Zen Center students—jocularly known as the Posture Queens—regularly practiced meditation and held discussions in the Castro district. The topic was in the air. Thus it happened one morning that someone baldly interrupted Philip's newspaper time in the Zen Center's annex kitchen to ask where he saw himself along this spectrum: straight, gay, what? After a painfully long pause, Philip said, "I think I'm what you would call polymorphous perverse." This brought relieved laughter from around the coffee table since it seemed no more than a typically witty, self-deprecating remark. No one in the room besides Philip understood that he was quite serious and that he was citing Sigmund Freud.

Broadly, Freud theorized that human sexual response and libido are not at birth localized anywhere in the body and that infants move through phases of oral, anal, and genital orientation during their first five years of life. With time and social training, people come to situate sexuality in these areas. But not everyone does; this is the meaning of "perverse" in Freud's definition—the word implies only that the condition is unusual. Philip seemed to be saying that he, like very young infants, received sexual pleasure from a range of receptors throughout his body and senses. Friends point, for example, to his near-erotic relationship to food, and his own work evidences at least a conflation.

Litany of the Candy Infant of Geneva

Sweet jewel baby
Darling candy crown
Sticky luscious orb
Sparkly scepter
Golden bib of holiness pray for us
Chocolate baby pray for us
Tears of KARO pray for us
Creme Yvette wee-wee pray for us
Fondant fundament pray for us
Rum slobber pray for us
Snot of slivovitz pray for us
White creme de menthe sweat pray for us
Yummy baby pray for us
Gown of marzipan shelter us
While we suck you forever!

On the brink of departure for Japan, Joanne sent Philip a letter—an eight-page handwritten document set down in the evening before her ship's midnight departure. Full of abrupt mood swings and funny family portraits, the text reflects on an apparently painful telephone call:

> But what a shit-fuck-screw conversation on the telephone. I still have a lump in my chest, and can't take a hot bath because it relaxes me too much and I feel sick and want to cry.
> However you have Sue Rosen and Annie to comfort you and I have no one except a smelly looking Japanese purser. Can you please write to me right away so I will have a letter waiting. However perhaps you won't want to. But I will feel fretful until I hear from you. I feel dreadful and will have an ulcer by the time I cross the Pacific.[22]

The penetrating and wacky humor in the rest of the pages seems an attempt to cheer up both Philip and herself.

If she did have a letter from Philip waiting when she made land some weeks later, it has not found its way into the collection. Philip next wrote to her provoked by the San Francisco newspaper: "Dear Bertha-Marie," he began, conjuring not the slender ingenue he knew Joanne to be but a stout

Midwestern farm wife, possibly of Nordic descent. "Let me wish you and Dominic all joy and gladness." Beyond the distance Philip managed with these names, he addressed the aerogram to Joanne *Snyder*. Indeed, it was having to sign her name this way on a form that alerted a disoriented Joanne to the fact that the civil procedure she'd just sat through three days after her arrival had been an official wedding. Philip continued by teasing her with the paper's news: "The accounts published here lead one to believe however that it was your husband who got married. . . . The Chronicle described him as 'San Francisco's Gary Snyder.'"[23] Philip's taunt was not far off the mark, as Joanne told him: "He said we have to go to the Consulate in Kobe and so help me this is the truth, got TRICKED into getting married by the Vice-Consulate there. Gary Snyder knew but he said this doesn't really count this is registering but it Does count because that made it legal and you have a certificate and I was reading Life magazines from last fall the whole time and just got up to sign my name only G said put down Snyder instead of Kyger so that's when I KNEW."[24] But if Joanne continued with enraged criticism of Gary—she did—she also, fairly, told of her own shortcomings in the relationship: "I am very foul-mouthed, and my EGO is suffering an intense amount and I must admit I become insanely jealous at all the attention he gets being used myself to it & I feel nowhere or part of Gary Snyder's Plan to prove that a family & Zen can work together & I fell on my face & gagged this morning when Harold Snyder sent a clipping from the Examiner which said Beat Poet wed to Vallejo girl with a picture of him looking like Pancho Villa. How does one ever become humble. I want to be gently-rotundly humble like you, at least to outward appearances."[25]

Most of the correspondence between Philip and Joanne took place during the following four years—her stay in Japan and India. Before looking at that and how they supported one another's voices generally, it bears noting that Philip was never again as physically close to Joanne as he was during 1959–60. That marked the longest continuous time they lived near each other. Through it, Joanne was vaguely long-distance-betrothed, though she lived alone. When she returned from Japan four years later, after marriage, she was again alone. Only Philip met her at the dock, and whatever he did or didn't know about the disintegrated state of their union, he knew that Gary would arrive a month or so later.

Back in a city where she could easily speak the language and navigate the streets, where she was no longer living in close quarters with an intense poet-husband, no longer taller than everyone, Joanne began to blossom. "I just took off on this big energy cruise. I had lots to say to everybody, and it wasn't like playing second fiddle anymore."[26] Editor Donald Allen solicited a book of her poems for publication, and though he'd excluded her from the first edition of *New American Poetry,* he included her in the next ones and in the British edition. She took up with old friends from the East-West House and borrowed an apartment. Still calling her Joanne Snyder, even in his private journal, Philip noted, "I am to lunch with Joanne tomorrow. She looks very well, seems much more composed, less giddy and demanding than 4 years ago. I still love her in some way or another." A few weeks later, he reports, "Joanne . . . wants me to telephone her daily. I am of course hugely flattered." Telephoning may have to do with location—Joanne no longer lived in easy walking distance—or it may very possibly reflect Joanne's having a new love affair. The understanding that Gary's life and interests lay in Japan for the foreseeable future whereas hers did not led Joanne and Gary to a definitive split. But a twenty-nine-year-old woman of Joanne's beauty, intelligence, and magnetic energy will soon attract suitors. In this case, Jack Boyce arrived—handsome, blond, physical, a painter—with Lew Welch providing the advance praises and necessary introductions.

Philip's journal always records strong admonitions to himself—not to worry about money, for example, not to get into debt with friends, or to bore people with repetitious talk, or to impose upon them, or to transgress any number of social boundaries—as well as frequent exhortations to rouse himself from moodiness, laziness, and self-indulgence so he could do the thing he knew he should do: work on his writing. Across town from Joanne's burgeoning relationship with Jack Boyce, Philip warned himself against jealousy: "I MUST try to govern my tongue and my temper. Why should I come on so jealous, embittered, calumniating everybody, gossiping &c? What's it to me if each person I think of as silly, worthless and wicked should get money, gifts, love, trips, dope &c &c &c. The money and goodies haven't been taken out of my pocket—there's quite enough left for me—what IS this envy & bitterness routine?"[27] A month later, he records pointedly that his options are closing down, especially with regard to domesticity: "I keep behaving as if I were 17 years old, just out of high school, with every opportunity open to me. I forget that I am well into middle age, that there's no longer time in which to make a fortune, climb the Himalayas, learn several classical languages, learn to play musical instruments, paint pictures, write books, travel, marry, beget a number of children."[28] Through the next two months, he developed this sense of constriction, making a series of twelve poems called

"Dying Again: Destruction, Death, Depression, Dismal & Up Again with Any Luck at All: Funerals, a Set of 12." The fifth of these reads:

> During the day I'm all right. I understand
> We no longer see each other.
> In dreams I go to pieces—
> Four times I see you in tears, running away from me
> I can't stand it, your hating me—
>
> I wake up, eat breakfast, the day's filthy, we're apart
>
> If we meet, later, you'll be gentle.
>
> This is all wrong, the dreams are true, our kindness when we meet
> A waking dream, the consolation, the booby prize.
>
> 15:VIII:64[29]

Jack and Joanne married in 1966. They departed San Francisco for an extended tour of Europe, following which they lived in New York for part of the next year. Back in San Francisco in late 1967 after so much time in big cities, they longed for country life. A tent on Mount Tam, a cabin in Lagunitas, a brief move up the coast to Bodega Bay in 1969—they tried all these before finally homesteading in a yurt in Bolinas while Jack built their house.[30] Although Philip too bounced between San Francisco, Stinson Beach, and Bolinas during the sixteen months between his two Japanese sojourns (February 1966 to November 1967 and March 1969 to June 1971), the next time he had anything like settled time near Joanne came in 1971, when he returned from Japan for good. Starting in June 1971, Philip lived with a series of friends in Bolinas as he wrote, pondered plans, and sorted through his Japanese plunder. He wrote some poems simply listing the stuff he brought back but included in this one a poignant human element:

> *Home Again, Home Again . . .*
>
> She says, "Where are all your gods and goddesses?"
> I said, "I've got them in the closet on a shelf."
> "Are you going to take the closet door off its hinges?"
>
> THAT is what I traveled 6000 miles to hear
> Her voice and beauty and total batty logical inexorability
> I'm suddenly dunked in jealousy although Peter is a splendid fellow
>
> 20:VI:71[31]

What jumps off the pages of letters between Philip and Joanne is velocity: not frequency—there were often gaps of weeks or months in their correspondence—but the speed of the diction. In retrospect, Joanne thought she might have been under the influence of Kerouac's novels. Certainly she was reading them in the first half of the 1960s, and their surface of run-on, urgent talk penetrated many a writer's style. Joanne concludes a 1961 letter to Philip by explaining how, having read the New York section of Kerouac's *Lonesome Traveler*, "I wish I was there Now & am trying to practice now being a mad beatnik sophisticate, wise-cracking prancing around in red highheels brass-tipped & in a magnificent conversation with G. Corso, in which I am overly brilliant. Actually now I read Adele Davis & cook high-protein breakfasts."[32]

Kerouac's influence may have heightened this tendency in Joanne's writing, but the verve, humor, abrupt shifts, mind-stopping juxtapositions, and flat-out speed seem to be inherent characteristics of her work, also witnessed by writer Alicia Ostriker. Reviewing Kyger's second book in the *Partisan Review*, Ostriker proposed "that Joanne Kyger is a genius, though a weird one. Handling her work is like handling a porcupine traveling at the speed of light. She is not 'disciplined' but a radically original combination of symbolist and comedienne."[33]

Philip also had access to numerous channels running parallel in his mind and could switch nimbly among them if it interested him or moved his writing forward. Especially in longer poems, he displayed this mobility but often decorated or restrained it with antiquated language. In letters to Joanne, thinking of her, under her influence, he just let it rip:

> All the world is delighted with your poems & Robert Duncan says he really ought to write to you & how to begin? The editors & I ate together on Thanksgiving at Bill Brown's house, turkey & champagne &c. Donald Crow is getting married today at the Soto Zen Temple in Bush Street, and I guess Mr. Suzuki will perform the gong-ring & blue-smoke solos. Albert has begun to put the flue on his hand-made fireplace this morning, very complicated and beautiful. Brian is out of the Army at last, officially, but now in a state of nervly tremorousness about the Problems of the Outside World. . . . Horrible idiot squeals & grimaces continue about Spicer's book. Everybody mad at everybody else and enjoying every minute & squeak of it.

Whalen continues this exact if disorganized reportage for more than another full single-spaced page before concluding with no warning, "What are you thinking about. How are you. I give up, I am too distracted to write letters today. Maybe later I'll write to you again. Or move to another town & change my name. I don't know. Everything is actually very nice indeed. I'm just nervous today. (Even Jay has been reading books, imagine! What's the world coming to?) Love, . . ."[34]

Aside from the style, this rattling excerpt exposes a number of their usual topics—writing work, friends, enemies, details of their personal lives. Whalen passes along praise of Joanne's newly published poems—part of a larger, very constant purpose in writing to her: to encourage her work, and especially to shore up her oft-wobbly sense of artistic self-worth. Philip seldom sent her any letter that did not directly or indirectly aim to staunch her doubts and cultivate her courage as a poet: "Seriously, the poems are something. I never saw such ones . . . yours are superb, & I want you to let me give copies of them to R.D. for his new mimeo-magazine."[35]

In writing about Duncan and Spicer, Philip acknowledged Joanne's role in bridging the separate, jostling schools of Bay Area poetry. Duncan and Whalen maintained a distant, moderate mutual admiration, punctuated from time to time with barbs, as well as with flashes of connection and warmth. Between Spicer and Whalen there was outright hostility, obvious from Spicer's side. In 1962, Jack issued a cruel public put-down of Philip, offering to pay eleven dollars if Philip would *not* read at a poetry festival, in lieu of the ten dollars he would be paid *to* read. Yet Philip dutifully reported whatever news there was of these old friends of Joanne's. He did not bother to keep his reports free of opinion, however, and he responded equally frankly about advice they sent to Joanne. "I still don't think that Stanley Persky or Jack Spicer are in total control of poetry. Their ideas about it have all been expressed long ago by Paul Valery, & Jean Cocteau . . . sad, bankrupt European poo-poo. Don't you believe it."[36]

In their letters, Philip and Joanne discussed books—usually whatever she was reading: Dostoyevsky, other Russians, Henry James—generally prose, not poetry, though Philip expostulated frequently upon poetry, usually, again, in response to Joanne's questions. (The theories Philip put forth were often forcefully stated but lightly held; later he thought something else.) They did send actual poetry back and forth, lots of it: Joanne as to a mentor, also with the knowledge that Philip was actively connected to small-press and magazine publishing. Philip sent poetry for possibly more complex reasons, one of which was that despite her relative youth, her relative inexperience, and her self-professed literary insecurities, he valued Joanne's thoughts. He wrapped what he sent in self-deprecation and related the many travails he'd had in producing it. Though he took this tone with other friends about work he sent them, he heightened it with Joanne, likely to assure her that her own writing difficulties were neither unique nor unusual. Philip also harbored a theory, voiced from time to time, that women were inherently more talented at writing than men. He states this succinctly in his graphic short story "The Invention of the Letter," when, after recounting Adam's many difficulties in learning to communicate with words or in writing, Whalen describes how the newly extracted Eve, "being a lady, knew perfectly well how to write." Murasaki Shikibu, Sei Shonagon, Sappho, Jane Austen, Emily Dickinson, Gertrude Stein, Virginia Woolf—these women reigned as queens in his literary pantheon, as did, later, a number of contemporary writers: Alice Notley, Anne Waldman, Leslie Scalapino, Diane di Prima. Wherever Joanne was in her development as a writer, Philip held her here; he placed her in his lineage of writer-goddesses.

He sent flowers. On his hiking excursions in the Sierra Nevada, Philip collected wildflowers—often delicate, fugitive species—pressed them carefully, attached them to thick paper, bound the pages into covers, decorated those with collages, and sent them to Joanne. Works of many hours, these books served for Gary as a botanizing record of Philip's mountain treks. What they meant to Joanne is less clear. A laborious object of floral beauty arrives from across the sea; neither Joanne nor Gary felt them to be love letters exactly, though later viewers could not help but see them in that light. "Would you be threatened if Philip sent *your* wife flowers?" wondered Gary aloud many years later. Clearly he was not.

Philip sent recipes and practical advice about cooking. He possessed a great store of kitchen wisdom, whereas Joanne, in the course of her upbringing and bachelorette literary life, had not yet needed to master such skills. *Chinese bean paste is not miso. X vegetable, lightly stir-fried with Y and Z, is delicious and easy.* With Gary in the Zen training hall or at the translation office so often, a large part of the domestic work fell to Joanne. It's hard to keep house for any young Zen monk or to feed one satisfactorily. These difficulties are magnified when one has an uncertain grip on the local language and currency, when one is overwhelmed by the complexities of the nearby public transportation, and especially when one is—as Joanne was— considerably taller than most Japanese and definitely different looking, thus making her the constant object of amazed, even mocking, scrutiny. The recipes Philip sent were part of an attempt to provide practical support to the couple. Beyond the literary lifeline his letters extended, parts of them read like strange tips for young homemakers. Some recipes must have been composition exercises.

Coddled Eggs (for one person)

2 fresh eggs

Tiny sliver of fresh garlic

1 pint of fresh rich milk

1/8 pound of butter

Salt

Pepper

Paprika for decoration; As many shakes of cayenne pepper as you can stand
(or as many squirts of Tabasco as you like.)

Melt the butter & tiny cut-up bit of garlic in the bottom of a pan that will
hold one quart of fluid. When the butter is melted, (gently . . . not violently
frying), add the milk and heat it to nearly a boil, but not quite. Break the eggs
into the milk, keep the milk from boiling, agitate the mess so that the eggs
don't stick to the bottom of the pan, add salt, pepper & cayenne or Tabasco,
and when the eggs are set but not tough, pour the whole works into a warm
earthenware bowl & slowly eat with a big spoon & pieces of buttered toast. If
you are a milk-toast freak, break up the toast into the bowl. I prefer straight
paprika as a decoration for this dish. It is hard to keep from boiling the milk,
it is hard to have patience to not stir the mess so hard that the yolks either
break or become absolutely dissociated from the whites, & become vagrant
eyeballs among the soup. I do this for breakfast especially on rainy sad morn-
ings when nobody loves me. & of course it is unbelievably fattening. But one
can read as one eats. that's one thing that governs what I cook . . . if I'm eating
by myself, I always cook something I can eat while reading or writing.[37]

Because the great bulk of their letters were sent while one or the other was in
Japan, Philip and Joanne reported about life there. Philip spent the last thirty
years of his life as a Zen monk, but it was Joanne who first saw and practiced
in a proper Japanese zendo. She recorded her difficulties with zazen (sitting
meditation) as well as with the hazing-like discipline in the hall. Recounting
how monitors would whack sleepy or fidgety sitters four blows on each shoul-
der with a long, flattened stick, she paused to note to Philip how the many
layers she wore to protect herself from these rigors, as well as the cold, made
her look "dreadfully unstylish—unglamorous."[38] Still, during certain sea-
sons, Joanne went on with it two or three hours each night, and certainly not
only because Gary was there.

She tended to write about domestic life and social connections (or their
lack) in Japan. She continued this art of observation as she and Gary traveled
to India, making no secret at all, for example, of her low opinion of Mssrs.

Ginsberg and Orlovsky as travel companions or—and here her remarks are particularly devastating—as table companions.

Philip, writing from Japan at the end of that decade, noted as well the strangeness of his personal relations there and the resultant misunderstandings and spells of alienation. But his letters also contained more standard epistolary accounts of the landscape, festivals, architecture, temples, and monuments. He had not gone to Japan as part of a couple; he was not constrained there in ways Joanne was. In his spare time he could simply wander as a tourist. On the other hand, Philip came to Japan and found work by Gary's good graces, and if his letters to Joanne sometimes sketch rather than portray more fully, it is because he could count on her foreknowledge of the places and things he was seeing. Philip also began his stays in Japan living exactly where and with whom she had lived—in one house with Gary Snyder.

Philip and Joanne wrote to one another about Kyoto weather, especially in deep winter or high summer, and they reported it as a force. It affected them, sometimes flattening them. One of the many reasons Philip admired the world's first novelist—Murasaki Shikibu—was because even though she wrote about a Kyoto ten centuries before he visited, she "got the weather right. That weather is always THERE."[39]

One of Philip's letters from Japan offers Joanne a different kind of travel writing: the report of a tourist to other realms. Joanne had had an out-of-body experience during a psychedelic journey and made part of it into a poem called "Last Night." She had also queried Philip about the experience by mail—was it sane? crazy? what did it mean? and so on. Philip wrote back in a vein reminiscent of his descriptions to Gary Sndyer from fourteen years earlier, but mixed in a good deal of literary and anthropological reference (which has, for the sake of conciseness, been pruned from the citation below).

> First of all, you might simply sit down quietly & decide, from your own intuition, whether this experience "means" anything at all—"who experienced it"—what after all is meant by "experience"—and "is experience ultimately real?" And next, at your very earliest opportunity, pack up & INTENTIONALLY go there . . . the experience (if you don't worry about the NAMES applied (God, San Juan de la Cruz, the yoga system of Patanjali, the Bhagavad Gita, Dai Nichi Nyorai, Zen-ola kidsville USA) has happened to lots of folks. They made shamanism & poetry out of it—see translations by David Hawks, (What do you think those people were ON) & now a days the psychoanalysts call it "schizophrenia." . . . but if you read lots of Shaman poems, even the Revelations of St. John the Divine at the end of the New Testament, you find out that quite

specific realities are involved, realities and teachings far removed from "psychopathology." All I know is that I have been there myself a number of times, & it is very upsetting, sometimes, but a necessary & instructive trip. I always go there intentionally, whenever I get high, one of the things I customarily do, & recite the Mahaprajnaparamita Sutra for the benefit of all the inhabitants of that world. . . . I don't stay there, but I go & say my piece & then go someplace else— other brighter worlds. So it is "all about" wisdom & compassion & detachment, as usual—unless you decide it is about ignorance, attachment & desire, as usual.[40]

At least once in the forty-four years of their friendship, they read their poetry together, just the two of them, in front of an audience. And once they did not: that time they were scheduled to read together at the 1965 Berkeley Poetry Conference, but Philip backed out. A team of professor Thom Parkinson, editor Donald Allen, and poet Robert Duncan had organized the conference, together with its manager Richard Baker (in a pre-Zen manifestation). The gathering echoed themes from Don Allen's watershed anthology *New American Poetry,* which had appeared five years earlier; the conferees reflected the schools of poetry from which Allen had made his selection. Whether the poets were from the Black Mountain school, the New York schools (first or second generation), the San Francisco Renaissance, the Beats, or the Tulsa group, they were united in not being academics. Many of the best-known names of counterculture poetry appeared among the participants in the twelve-day gathering. Many but not all. Because feelings ran high between different poles of the San Francisco groups, invitations carried a political charge. According to Joanne's memory of it, Michael McClure took offense that he and Philip had only been invited to give readings; they had not been asked—as others had—to lead seminars, give lectures, or participate in panel discussions. Thus disrespected, Michael urged Philip to join him in boycotting the whole conference. Philip owed the family McClure in many ways—beyond the outright, unpaid loans, he dined with them gratis when he had nothing to eat, and he stayed with them when he had no other place to sleep. There was no real way to refuse. Philip and Michael had also developed a strong friendship and a mutual admiration that extended to Michael's wife, Joanna, and, upon her arrival, their baby Jane. Loyalty exerted its pull.

When Richard Baker learned of McClure and Whalen's planned absences, he called Joanne to see if there was anything she could do. There was not. She tried, also for her own reasons: Philip's cancellation meant she would be paired as a reader with Lew Welch, and Lew, by every account a marvelous performer, "always CRIED at his readings," as Joanne lamented. Disliking the idea of being upstaged, she implored Philip to relent. He told her he would just love to help, but he'd promised Michael.[41] In a letter to Diane di Prima, Philip wrote that he'd been "hiding under his bed" to avoid the conference and all associated with it.

Joanne and Philip did participate in a number of group readings through the years, but little record remains of these. A contemporary account exists, though, for an evening featuring just the two of them—in early May 1981, at San Francisco New College, part of a reading series organized by poet Leslie Scalapino. The highly personal account does not list the works they read; it describes Joanne's contribution unhelpfully as "zippy Bolinas-life stuff," but it does record the shape of the room, the size and composition and general level of intoxication of the crowd, as well as what the readers wore. Most of it focuses on the dynamic between them: Joanne in no hurry, having come the long way down from Bolinas, with a large contingent of admirers in tow; Philip, also with a group of admirers, but at the end of a day that had begun for him at four in the morning, and looking at just such a schedule for the next morning as well.

They came in together about 8:15, Philip holding a bowl full of nasturtiums, and they began to complain immediately. Philip started up about the lack of air in the room, and Joanne too about that, and the light. Couldn't they rearrange the room she wanted to know. . . .

The fact that he wanted to go home early and get to bed was a point of contention in his repartee with Joanne. She announced that she would read first, though only for a short while; then before the break Philip would read, "so he can go home and go to bed." After the break she would read again. "Did that take long?" she asked Philip in front of everyone.

He slowly and elegantly raised his arm, turned his wrist, inspected his watch. Joanne asked several times, after finally beginning to read, how long she'd been going. Sometimes Philip just laughed at her and waved her on; sometimes he told her. Once he gave minutes and seconds. Joanne began to warm up to her work and forgot to ask about time. She read very well and, once going, seemed reluctant to stop. "Do I have time for one more?"

Philip frowned a giant theatrical frown, raised his watch to eye level, squinted at it, her, it, the audience, and finally smiled. Joanne, of course, had already begun the poem. . . .

Early in his reading, which ran forty solid minutes, Joanne interrupted him and said, "Do you realize, Philip, that you haven't *once* looked at your audience? Not once. You just keep looking down that book. You've *got* to look up at people ... " She trailed off, laughing hard. As soon as she started this little speech, Philip had taken a bookmark from *On Bear's Head* and walked toward her, holding it with his arm extended in front of him, as if he were approaching Dracula with a silver cross. ...

At the conclusion of his reading, Philip received a fine ovation and made ready to leave. Joanne rushed to the front to clutch him. "You're not leaving now, are you? Please, please stay. You remember, we made a deal. You can't leave now; just stay for a while. It won't be long."

Everyone hushed to see what he'd do. He turned slowly from packing his books and said loudly and distinctly, in the voice of an ancient prophet, "The tongue of a strange woman is sweet as honey, but her latter end is bitter ... as ... *gall!*"

The last words were an emotional growl. The room sort of exploded. Philip calmly packed his books and sat back down. Joanne called for a *short* break.[42]

They also wrote and published poems for one another. Beyond the several quoted already, Philip wrote "Poem for a Blonde Lady" in May 1959, when he was in the throes of love for Joanne. Given that and its early date in their acquaintance, it reads as oddly summarial, portraying the frustrating, mixed nature of their connection.

> Clearly I must not (on any account) stir one muscle
> Until it moves
> a real necessity
> interior
> to it,
> towards or away from
> You
>
> I don't mean "love" or "sanity," I want to answer
> all your crooked questions
> absolutely straight
>
> & if away
> Only a pausing a thoughtless rearrangement
> to include you
> As we really are.[43]

If Philip's poem moves and halts with broken phrases and non sequiturs toward a precise inconclusion, Joanne's best-known poem to Philip buzzes along on the surface in straight talk. It is not, however, a simple poem.

Philip Whalen's Hat

I woke up at 2:30 this morning and thought about Philip's
hat
It is bright lemon yellow, with a little brim
all the way around, and a lime green hat band, printed
with tropical plants.
It sits on top
of his shaved head. It upstages every thing & every body.
He bought it at Walgreen's himself.
I mean it fortunately wasn't a gift from an admirer.
Otherwise he is dressed in soft blues. And in his hands
a long wooden string of Buddhist Rosary beads, which he keeps
moving. I ask him which mantra he is doing—but he tells me
in Zen, you don't have to bother with any of that.
You can just play with the beads.[44]

Joanne pretends to be describing, with some irritation, Philip's clothes, his hat, how it is too loud. She's observed it exactly and is nearly obsessing, awake in the night thinking about it. She complains that it has minimized her— and everyone's and every*thing's*—presence, and now it's stealing her sleep too. The critique crescendos with the line "He bought it at Walgreen's himself." Mock amazement that Philip could actually walk into a low-priced pharmacy and effect a purchase *all by himself.* She corrects the implied insult in the next line but leaves the insult in. Her poem softens on the word *soft.* Joanne continues a close observation of Philip, who now seems to have fully appeared in her middle-of-the-night vision, able to converse. She remarks his mala, his beads. Knowledgeable but junior in the world of formal Buddhism, she shifts to being questioner, and then curator, giving her readers a taste of the bright, playful Philip. From interest to insult to exhibition, Joanne's poem talks its illogical way to a mixed message not unlike Philip's.

One last point about Philip and Joanne's connection through speech— which is that there does have to be a last point. If someone has read all his life, then dies, some book is his last book. An account from one of Philip's caregivers at Laguna Honda Hospice, on his last night: "Philip had been moved to the dying room. Many of Philip's close friends came and went during the day. At some point I retrieved the Kyger book *Again,* which Philip and I had been reading and rereading together for the past few months, and read some poems to him. (It was on the nightstand beside his bed in the ward where he'd been living for the past year, not far from the dying room.) He was, as I said, out of it, but a couple of times during the day I read him poems from the book he particularly liked."[45] So after more than seventy years immersed in English and American literature, the last poems Philip heard on this earth were Joanne's.

· · ·

The description of the New College reading begins with a vigorous complaint. Many of Joanne's and Philip's published works also complain, formalized into poetry or journal entry. Their letters to one another were shot through with complaints, and surely their conversations. Gary Snyder called this their "way of being bitchy together." They complained to each other of life aboard ship to Japan in differing yet similar ways.

Joanne went first:

> I put an old Japanese '78 record on a nasty-looking little plastic player the size of a portable radio but so light each rock of the boat makes it slide on the couch beside me....
>
> There are two potted palms at the end of the couch and everything in here and in the dining room is covered with these white linen-covers w/pleats around the bottom. I peeked underneath and the upholstery is of very nice velvet which they are saving for the day when the emperor and his wife fornicate in the middle of the dining area. The other side of the record is Stars and Stripes forever and it rocks and the record player rocks, it is so GREY outside and the ship rolls and the typewriter slides across the table & back & the tea slops, the ship rocks in time w/the music, the only march-stepping ship in the entire asshole universe world.
>
> Now it is raining and we are entering the heart of the Hurricane, I had thought to read Mickey Spillane this afternoon which I found in the ship's well stocked library of 1957–58 Reader's Digests....
>
> The bath is the greatest thing in the world. The object is to get as much water on the floor as possible, and Out of All the Containers. The floor is tile with drains all around. I washed my hands in the bathroom sink the first day and couldn't understand why my feet were wet until I noticed the pipe from its drain ends about a foot above the floor.[46]

Philip went six years later:

> You might have TOLD me this boat was an Iron Maiden—& food the like of which I haven't seen since the Army! And the seasick pills don't work. And there's no place to put anything. And I am persecuted by insane Philippinos & hectored by the table steward & I feel awful & the sea & sky are incredibly gorgeous & Commodore Ehman is receiving this afternoon. I can't imagine

why GOD invented Philippinos. And seasick. And I eat CONTINUOUSLY. We didn't go to L.A. like the book said we would—instead we are driving through a hurricane which will undoubtedly drive us all to a watery grave long before dinner time. And I have a sore throat, and the other patients are hustling me for more seasick pills because they forgot theirs. I shall weigh 500 pounds by the time we arrive in Yokohama—which of course we won't. You ought to have warned me.

As well as insults to creature comfort, the sea-bound complaining points up their helplessness and disorientation. In the middle of the ocean, you are exactly nowhere (though presumably the captain knows degrees latitude and longitude). The focus goes to local, specific details, part of an attempt to gain a sense of place. If these specifics feel unpleasant and unchangeable, then at least a person can exert intelligence against them by complaining, in writing. Both Philip and Joanne knew that to express these things was possibly childish, possibly un-Buddhist, certainly alien to the tough spirit of Gary Snyder,[47] at whose instance they were each traveling to Japan. But exactly because complaint arises from a self-centered, somewhat threatened mind, it is needle-sharp and alert. The wit they practiced with each other in complaint also served to brighten dullness. Like the name game Philip played with Gary, the complain game with Joanne smartened both of them. With each other, they rubbed against their worlds like knives on whetstones.

But Philip and Joanne are both known, accurately, as Buddhists. Buddhism being a wisdom tradition, it would diminish them to point out that they shared a tendency to complain and leave it at that. It appears that the very states of mind that gave rise to complaint and speed were the states of mind they developed into wisdom, or at least into generous, insightful accommodation. As Snyder said (of Philip), "His quirks became his pointers, and his frailties, his teaching method."[48] Behind such an assertion sits a great deal of Buddhist philosophy. Also debate, composition, and meditation—many centuries' worth. The short form follows.

If Philip and Joanne physically floated on boats in the middle of the ocean with only rudimentary bearings, Buddhism says that in truth we are mentally, emotionally, and psychologically always afloat in the middle of an unpredictable ocean. Lord Buddha pointed out impermanence as a core truth at the beginning of his teaching career, and with this he laid the foundation for a series of spiritual and philosophical developments, culminating in a teaching called "emptiness." Part of what is meant by emptiness is that nothing *really* exists—certainly not in the gross way we usually perceive. Close examination is meant to reveal how everything in the world, including bodies and minds, falls apart and rearises constantly, in nanosecond-long patterns of energetic exchange. Joanne and Philip often wrote from this perspective.

> *Haiku, for Gary Snyder*
> IS
> Here's a dragonfly
> [TOTALLY]
> Where it was,
> that place no longer exists.[49]

Both writers knew the haiku tradition—Joanne's journals overflow with them—as well as the more complex styles of earlier Japanese court poetry. Both had their perceptions influenced, if not altered, by living in Japan. This in no way implies that their work was reductive. On the contrary: the attention required to *have* a clear perception, and the skill required to get it down on paper, afforded both poets a lot of room. It opened things out. It presented them with a lot to notice.

> Sun on the hand so deeply spotted
> Yours for the duration, though[50]

Critics refer to this quality in Joanne's work as "nowness." Indeed, her 2007 volume of collected poems is titled *About Now*. The word Philip used for this in his own work was *takes*—the kind a camera makes. There is no one kind of Philip Whalen poem, of course, but many of his shorter works are "takes," and some of the longer ones—most obviously *Scenes of Life at the Capital,* written in Japan—are series of takes, arranged and overlapped, and decorated with running jokes. You could say "snapshots," but they aren't only visual.

When the lens of emptiness rotates from the "outer" world back on the perceiver of that world, the meditation becomes extremely personal. Thoughts and even emotions—so blindingly overpowering—are regarded as temporary constructs:

> A zillion little butterfly thoughts
> simultaneously flap
> . . .
> Feel the myriad little bits
> of sensation
> that make up emotion[51]

Through reading, through meditation, even through misjudgments with psychedelic drugs, Philip and Joanne had both been introduced to the empty nature of mind by the time they met. The explicit knowledge of nonexistence makes a strange bond, but it's one they had. The empty nature of mind does not mean no mental activity. Words famously fail here, but the words point to a nonsingular, nonpersonal, nonlocalized intelligence; the alert have access to it. Exalted as this may sound, from the beginning it has proved uncomfortable. Legend says that when the Buddha first introduced emptiness—an event so momentous it was called the "Second Turning"[52]—a number of his senior disciples perished on the spot from heart attacks. Others rose and left the hall. For highly educated Western adults, such sudden dispossession might easily lead to insecurity or panic—maybe not so different from feeling your ship is about to go down. This would naturally be worse for those who had already cut themselves away, as Philip and Joanne both had, from much of society's security and were trying to follow the nerve-wracking path of a young artist. An experience of emptiness—however much the sutras may praise it—can be profoundly disorienting.

Joanne records a portion of her struggle thus:

> Giving in:
> to *whom* does one give into
> what does one give up
>
> acceptance is a *loss*
> of a superficial hold on the world
> however, is acceptance giving in
> How can I be something. specific
> yet undefined
> fall back into the world
> What is that nothing. It is something very close. Why do we
> use the expression, "I am *afraid* to let go."
> Self aware:
> *What* is aware of *what*
> I am aware of myself: *who* of *who*[53]

Among the classic responses to emptiness is an attempt to notice and comment on everything, water-bugging between perceptions at great speed. The hope seems to be of establishing control or, minimally, a sense of location. It's possible to attribute some of the quick-cut shiftiness and acceleration in Philip's and Joanne's correspondence and in (especially) their early work to this kind of mental pattern.

What I hear is not only water but stones
No, no, it is only compressed air flapping my eardrums
My brains gushing brown between green rocks all
That I hear is me and silence
The air transparent golden light (by Vermeer of Delft)
Sun shines on the mountain peak which pokes
The sun also ablaze &c.[54]

From one point of view, such a response to basic panic might seem neurotic, but Mahayana Buddhism does not condemn or reject it. In almost unbelievable allegiance to human goodness, the teachings say rather that wisdom is in that style (and in all the other classic styles), especially when uncoupled from the tiresome job of maintaining a small "ego." Joanne began to meditate in her twenties; she continued that and active readings in Zen and Buddhist philosophy all her life. Her works show that she spent a long time looking at mind and integrating insights into her life. Through getting used to it in meditation, through conceptual support delivered by study, through the simple passage of time, and—for writers—through writing, it is possible that the jerky speed of piecing everything together can slow, that the mind can relax open into a kind of spacious, still awareness.

what I wanted to say
was in the broad
sweeping
form of being there

I am walking up the path
I come home and wash my hair
I am bereft
I dissolve quickly
I am everybody[55]

The experience of emptiness, the panic, the coping and relaxing do not occur just once. They happen over and over. Technically speaking, it's happening constantly, right now, for example. Joanne came to share with Philip an experience of mind comparable to a broad field, more loosely organized (and more highly populated) than suits a standard "ego." Yet she also realized—more clearly than Philip—that a person had to function practically to live in the world. This simultaneous large-and-small experience of mind, sometimes called "absolute and relative," is known to give way to a sense of humor about life's ironies. Or complaint. As with Philip's work, Joanne's playfulness and her hard-won light touch may disguise from some readers her profundity. She did not spend thirty years as a Zen monk, but like Philip, she pursued truth—dharma—with remarkable persistence.

Writers record what they notice—in their minds or in the outside world. If, through Zen practice, altered perception, or accidental breakthrough, the distinction between "inner" and "outer" is no longer so sharp or so valid, this changes the writing. It means one thing to describe a beach, moon, or tree as an external object. It goes in another direction to understand these as mind and to use them in writing as part of the communication of mind—like, or equal to, a thought. If mind is not purely contained in the physical bounds of a person—if it extends at least to the environment surrounding them, then describing that environment does not differ from pointing out mind. This is part of how haikus work: the rock, bird, blossom, branch, or mountain inseparable for an instant from the mind of the writer. Recognition of that produces a poetic smack. It must be written down in fitting form, but it is a complete statement, in the same way that, more slowly, a painting—of a room or landscape—reveals the painter as much as the room or landscape. This presumes the artist's depth of understanding and their personal style; it reflects training and skill in portraiture. Joanne Kyger spent a life developing these, as Philip did. They shared this.

Late Afternoon

I'm coming down from a walk to the top of Twin Peaks
A sparrowhawk balanced in a headwind suddenly dives off it:
An answer to my question of this morning[56]

A further consequence of the emptiness of the individual is the emptiness of individual enlightenment. If a person can't really be said to exist independent of the bigger karmic pattern, then their individual enlightenment also cannot exist independently. Without denying anyone's experience, complete perfect enlightenment must be a broad, interlocking affair, something in common with others. Overmuch emphasis on one's own enlightenment is seen as an hindrance; it belabors a misapprehension. The hero of Buddhism's Second Turning is nominated a bodhisattva (literally, an "enlightenment being") because they raise their sights and aim for the enlightenment of all beings. Philip and Joanne did this, Philip ceremonially. Earlier, though—in 1960—realizing the enormity of it, he balked. His poem "A Vision of the Bodhisattvas" portrays his dawdling:

They pass before me one by one riding on animals
"What are you waiting for," they want to know . . .

What am I waiting for?
A change in customs that will take 1000 years to come about?
Who's to make the change but me? . . .

What business have I to do that?
I know the world and I love it too much and it
Is not the one I'd find outside this door[57]

Five years later, he wrote about it another way, emphasizing the view of impermanence and interpenetration:

Mahayana

Soap cleans itself the way ice does,
Both disappear in the process
The questions of "Whence" & "Whither" have no validity here.

Mud is a mixture of earth and water
Imagine WATER as an "Heavenly" element
Samsara and nirvana are one:

Flies in amber, sand in the soap
Dirt and red algae in the ice
Fare thee well, how very delightful to see you here again!

5: IV: 65[58]

Ever since the eighth-century scholar Shantideva uttered his passionate poem on the conduct of a bodhisattva[59] (parts of it spoken from the middle of the air, if the legend is to be believed), Mahayana[60] view and poetry have had a fecund relationship. As Whalen took up the formal practice of Zen, his poetry became increasingly suffused with this view. Less famous perhaps for her own formal bodhisattva path, Joanne's surpassingly beautiful poem below shows profound understanding and stands at ease with the best of Mahayana literature.

Your heart is fine feeling the widest
possible empathy for the day and its inhabitants

Thanks for looking at the wind
in the top of the eucalyptus
dancing like someone you know
well 'I'm here I'm here I'm here!'

The wind picks up
a rush of leaves waving
wildly for your understanding
—apple, plum, bamboo
rooted and flourishing
next to your home

in the air awake

without defect

June 17, 2000[61]

SIX

Hail Thee Who Play

WHALEN AND McCLURE

They made one another's acquaintance in October 1955 as two of five readers at the Six Gallery event, but Philip's real friendship with Michael McClure began a few weeks later, when Philip came to tea. Michael and then-wife Joanna lived in a large, rambling apartment in San Francisco's Polk Gulch neighborhood. A number of painters lived and worked in the same building—2324 Fillmore Street[1]—and many others lived close by. Philip had come to town from across the bay to visit one of these, Robert LaVigne. The simplest route for the twenty-minute walk from LaVigne's to the McClures' would have taken Philip through Japantown. Whichever route he took, Philip arrived bearing powdered green tea and a tea whisk. Following protocol lifted from the Zen books then newly around, the two were soon "high as kites"[2] from slurping cups of the strong, hot drink. According to McClure, they entered on a discussion of Tibetan air demons, because they were actually seeing them swooping around the ceiling. This visit would be the first of a great many Philip made to the McClure household, in a friendship that ran forty-seven years. It's not clear at which point Philip and Michael realized they shared a birthday (with Arthur Rimbaud)—20 October, Philip arriving in the world nine years before Michael.

Their visits took place in almost tidal alternation. For the first fifteen years, Philip was the guest, dropping by the McClure household for social or existential reasons. Without money for food, sometimes without a roof over him or a bed to sleep in, Philip would show up at mealtimes. He was welcome to do so, and to stay the night if he needed to. Michael, Joanna, and their young daughter, Jane, looked upon him as part of the family: eccentric Uncle Philip. Friendly all round as it was, the arrangement gnawed at Philip. He recorded this in May 1959:

Haiku for Mike

Bouquet of HUGE
nasturtium leaves
"How can I support myself?"[3]

Michael recalled another poignant example of Philip's unease, even shame, in the midst of happy family relations: "It's Christmas and the food's cooking, and dinner's getting ready, and it's like, 'Where's Phil?' 'Did we invite him?' 'Does he NEED an invitation?'" At this point—the mid-1960s—the McClure family lived on one side of Corona Heights above Haight-Ashbury, and Philip lived down the other side of that same red rock outcrop, on Beaver Street in the Castro. As preparations continued, Michael grew more uneasy. "He was always welcome, particularly on holidays. He was like our priest, our uncle, our Santa Claus or Easter Bunny. I mean that in the best sense . . . so this was just not right."

Michael finally jumped in his car and cruised down to Philip's place.

> I knocked on the door, then I pounded on the door. Something told me he was in there. I got the door open and I walked into the back, where his room was. I walked through the kitchen and opened the door to his room, and saw this big pile of covers over this large mound on his bed. I say, "Phil?"
> "Yeah?"
> "Time for Christmas dinner . . ."
> "No, I have no money, and I'm going to stay here and starve."
> Finally I got him to come.[4]

Beginning in the early 1970s, as Philip took up residence in the Zen temples where he would pass the next thirty years, he appeared less often chez McClure; for a holiday meal or celebration, yes, but the visits began to pattern themselves so that Michael or Joanna would come to where Philip was living. They'd collect him with an automobile and take him to whichever restaurant he'd been thinking of, there to "scarf" whichever dish he'd been fantasizing about. These were mostly Chinese, sometimes Japanese or Mexican. "If I want honky-food," he remarked, "I'll cook it myself."

Through the years, Philip grew progressively more blind and, as a result of illnesses and infections, progressively more bedridden, but Joanna and Michael kept up the tradition of mealtime visits, now going by restaurants for take-out, dishes not infrequently specified by Philip himself. In

Continuous Flame, a posthumous Festschrift for Philip, Joanna's contribution tells of such a visit.

A Phil Whalen Specially Requested Evening Meal

7:30 pm—coffee with cream and sugar—medium strong, please.
apple pie—with ice cream if there is some.
9:00 pm—roqueford cheese and crackers from the cupboard.
french olives—both kinds, please.
glass of Merlot, 1999.
9:30 pm—hash browns with sausage and catsup.
. . . .
Critiques: pie has too much cinnamon.
not too much cheese on each cracker, please.
Merlot a bit sour, but okay.
olives quite fine.
hash browns and sausage—better than those burnt meatballs.

Menu recorded at Zen Hospice by J. McClure, sometime in 2001.[5]

Gathering for meals with friends and family is among the oldest human rituals, but Philip and Michael took their pleasure in eating and drinking, especially with one another, beyond that. They celebrated hunger and its satisfaction with animal intensity, sometimes using a vocabulary of intoxication to describe it: they went to "score" the superburrito at El Faro; they went on a kimchi "run" to the outer Sunset. (This latter practice was finally banned by Joanna—not the runs for kimchi, which they called "the Korean death-radish," nor for the fermented tofu, but opening either of these in her house, so penetrating and durable were their odors.)

When in 1959 Michael and Philip set off on a reading tour of New York and the East Coast, it must have been with tremendous excitement. They envisioned making money as poets, being feted and admired, meeting old friends, making new ones, and building connections to publishers, all of which happened. But looking back forty-five years later, what arose first in Michael's mind was the food they packed for the flight. "Phil brought several large salamis, lokum (Turkish Delight), things in cans, several cans, Gouda cheese, some sliced ham, rolls, crackers—for the flight! In those days flights were not so crowded, so we took our seats in the back; there was a seat all the way across the back, and we just sat there and ate the entire way to New York. I think Philip may have been doing this to calm himself down. I don't know that he'd ever flown before. For him, this was poets' soul food." Philip's travel journal of the flight, as far as it goes (Chicago) also keeps a close record of comestibles, particularly the string of coffees, soda pops, and waters brought by stewardesses. His journal notes as well that the plane smelled like "a funeral parlor or hospital."[6]

On the surface, one might not imagine McClure and Whalen as feast buddies. Bodily, burly Whalen trudged along, where slender, graceful McClure seemed to swirl, a beautiful man with long hair, flowing clothes, and even from time to time a cape. But both men were fascinated by animals—their power, actual and totemic—and they were interested in the fact that they too were animals. Animal shapes, colors, habits, and sounds figure in McClure's work as one of the principal themes, and the first poem he ever heard Philip read was about animals, one in which two people discuss their helpless, unstoppable metamorphosis into birds. At that same event, Michael read "Animism" and "For the Death of 100 Whales."[7]

Poet/novelist Keith Abbott also picked up on this primitive aspect of their connection: "I did not see PW & Michael together very much, but I noticed that they shared an animal presence when they were together. Their Turkish pastry fest was like watching a bear and a wolf share a rich mound of food." The fest to which Abbott refers took place in the Zen Center hospice, with Philip lying in bed, blind. Even though Philip and Michael were animals, they were highly educated, irreverent ones. "Michael came in and started feeding Philip Turkish pastry sent from Joanna, kneading each square into lumps and claiming that each shiny sugary lump was a Catholic Martyred Saint relic, while the blind PW exclaimed, and raved loudly how delicious & yummy each dead Catholic was."[8]

Deplaning from their transcontinental feast/flight in the early cold hours of 6 November 1959, the red-eyed poets went first to Allen Ginsberg's apartment to drop off their bags, then on to Grove Press, where Philip made two signal acquaintances (not counting Grove's owner, Barney Rosset, for whom Philip only had less-than-flattering words, both before and after meeting him). The two introductions that did count that day were to Don Allen, an editor at Grove, and Richard Baker, a young employee. At the time, Don Allen served as editor of Rosset's *Evergreen Review,* and that scandalous magazine's second issue—*The San Francisco Scene*—had in 1957 put both Whalen's and McClure's poetry before the reading public.[9] Later widening the circle of writers he'd put in that issue, Don Allen published the ground-breaking classic *New American Poetry, 1945–60.* The magazine and the anthology in their own ways shivered the literary world, especially driving a wedge between poets working inside academia and those outside it. When

Don Allen resigned the editorship of *Evergreen* to move to San Francisco as Grove's West Coast editor, he continued his contact with Philip, as a friend, literary adviser, and publisher.

Richard Baker would also move to San Francisco within a few years of meeting Philip, and take up the practice of Zen. Following advice from his teacher Suzuki Roshi, Baker would then also in the late 1960s move to Japan for an extended stay. In Kyoto, his acquaintance with Philip—also living there—blossomed into a real friendship. But it was when Baker returned to San Francisco to inherit the leadership of the Zen Center that he commenced a job in which he would play not just a friendly but a defining part in Philip's life. Richard Baker became Philip's teacher, his Zen master. Of this, more later.

Back in New York that November day in 1959, McClure and Whalen's poetry tour began with a reading at City College of New York, followed by one the next night at Muhlenberg College. At Muhlenberg, regrettably, the professor who'd invited them lost his job, mostly over Michael's spirited reading of "Fuck Ode." Philip described the Princeton stop as "an ugly reading scene" and the crowd at Wesleyan as "unreceptive genteel." From there, an all-night drive landed them in Gloucester, where they'd gone to pay respects to the outsize Charles Olson. By this point in their journey, both poets sagged with exhaustion and poor health. Nevertheless, Michael went in the morning with Charles on a day's trip to Dogtown, imbibing the great man's outpourings: "This is how Charles was working with people at the time," Michael recalled. Philip stayed back and rested, passing the day on Olson's couch.

Philip had read Charles Olson as early as 1956, corresponded with him, and finally met him in 1957. It had been prickly. He'd shown the respect due Olson's learning and accomplishments but refused to accept things as gospel simply because Charles said them. Philip offered informed resistance, sometimes publicly, as in a 1957 series of readings in San Francisco. So they wrangled some.[10] Several places in his own work, Philip cited Olson's jibes at him, including them in his poems and riffing on them but not seeming to take the shots terribly personally, for Charles quarreled in print or in conversation with any number of well-regarded poets. If there was perhaps a bit of extra jostling between Whalen and Olson, it may have been rooted in this visit and a story of Charles's jealousy: how he'd somehow come under the (extremely unlikely) notion that while he was out walking and talking with Michael, Philip was back at the house getting together with his wife. In truth, Philip was only lazing about, recovering and hoping to ward off sickness. If Olson had really understood Philip's tastes, he would have worried more about the contents of his library or his refrigerator than violation of his wife. The depleted McClure did come down with pneumonia the next day, which, complicated by an allergic reaction to penicillin, forced him to fly home early.

Training on to Boston, Philip read at Tufts and spent the rest of his time there enjoying the museums and libraries at Harvard. For the Boston reading and the subsequent five—Brooklyn College, Queens, Fordham, Connecticut College, and the Living Theatre—as well as a big-weekend-drink-and-sleep-over party hosted by John Clellon Holmes, Philip was joined by the tour's main promoter, Allen Ginsberg.

Two more connections Philip and the McClures shared on the physical level bear mention: a wedding and a funeral. When she came of age and found the right suitor, Jane McClure asked Philip to perform her wedding ceremony, and he agreed. Thus on a warm, sunny third of July in 1982, Philip followed Jane and William Eggiman into a Zen Center Buddha Hall crowded with about one hundred guests, including many celebrated literati. The ceremony—adapted from the most basic Buddhist vows of taking refuge and agreeing to live by precepts—runs a scant twenty minutes, but it's somewhat complex and requires rehearsal. Choreography must be managed, timing must be worked out. The couple follows a fairly straightforward set of responses, mostly prompted by the priest, and the ceremony contains both scripted and spontaneous speeches for the officiant. The audience can extemporize. Red-faced at the end of it from heat and from dealing with details, slightly flustered, Philip nonetheless executed his role with aplomb and—given the years of their acquaintance and the nearness of it—with genuine warmth. Only at the wedding reception did he tell Joanna McClure it had been the first ceremony he'd ever performed.

It was surely the first Buddhist funeral that Michael McClure ever conducted when he entered the zendo at Green Gulch Farm on 1 September 2002, as one of a quartet of officiants for Philip's funeral. As Philip's dharma teacher, Richard Baker Roshi led the ceremony. Backing him and speaking very nearly as much during the rites were Norman Fischer, Gary Snyder, and Michael. Gary and Norman had long been fully ordained Zen priests, whereas Michael had come—officially at least—much more recently to the path. He'd been as close to the sources of Buddhist enthusiasm as any of the midcentury poets. He'd read and absorbed such dharma texts as were available, and he'd integrated their messages and put them back out before the public transformed into theatrical works. His own religious bent seemed to

FIGURE 8. Whalen and Michael McClure, May 1980. Photo by Peter Holland.

be—for lack of a better label—a kind of Blakean mysticism. Thus when he did formally go Buddhist, he worked on the enormous Flower Ornament Sutra, with its all-encompassing view and extravagant descriptive language, as his main study.

Throughout the years of their friendship, Michael had taken a jocular approach to Philip's Buddhism—fundamentally respectful but with a roasting edge. As he did in many other works, Michael juxtaposed images and language from wildly differing social structures to achieve humorous effect—and in this case, possibly, to keep Philip from becoming overly serious. For example, McClure titled one of his plays *Minnie Mouse and the Tap-Dancing Buddha,* in the same way he mock-advised Philip, newly established in his own temple, how they could, with this fresh place, at last "set up operations and run all the drugs and girls out of there." When again, after decades of study and service, Philip finally received the complete dharma transmission from Baker Roshi, enabling him, nay obliging him, to teach, Michael accosted him with offers to purchase it. "Hey Phil, sell me the transmission. Come on, man, sell it to me. I'll give you $500 for it. Come on, sell me the transmish . . . at least cut me in on a share." Philip would redden to the top of his shaved head and dissolve in tears of laughter.

At the funeral, though, Michael comported himself in a manner neither lighthearted nor overly somber. Obviously moved, he spoke calmly and concluded his address to Philip by hearkening back to times they'd spent together: "You're leaving me with a lot of pleasure of your company. As for poetry, there are clearly quite a few here who've been taught by you—whether you wanted them to be or not. So the poetry world is okay. Don't worry. I'm going to go on eating Korean red pickled radish, just like we used to do at dragon lunches at Hartford Street. Toodles."

. . .

Michael may have ended by recalling their physical connection, but the main thrust of his remarks at the funeral was about Philip's speech, his poetry. Going back to the first time he heard him read, Michael told the assembly,

> Though Phil's poems were built on classical and modernist foundations, I was quite astonished and delighted by their resemblance to the cartoons—the newspaper cartoons—that I'd grown up loving: Toonerville Trolley, Smokey Stover, the Nutt Brothers, Ches and Wal.
>
> These poems were defiantly outspoken in their love of the mixture of the ordinary and the erudite. We were all laughing with these serious poems; and we were listening hard, not to miss a word. Phil was reciting the most new poetry I'd heard from a fellow poet. Here was this chubby, husky fellow, standing with me, doing it.

When the funeral procession entered the Green Gulch zendo, each of the leaders carried, as is traditional, something to call the departed one present: a photographic portrait, flowers, a beloved cloth, the actual remains of Philip himself in an elegantly wrapped box. McClure carried manuscript pages. "Philip's early books, with his notes on them," Baker Roshi announced to the audience, as he placed them on the shrine.

The admiration for one another's poetry that began at first hearing remained throughout their friendship. Some writer friends will talk about anything *but* writing when they're together. Possibly because of Michael's blunt, unembarrassed way of posing questions—just coming right out with things—they were able to have frank discussions about literary technique, the how-are-you-doing-that? level of exchange. Philip explained what he knew of haiku form and aesthetic; Michael rapidly mastered it. Michael picked up on Philip's notion of "takes," renamed them "slices," and proposed the humorous subtitle for Philip's first long poem, "Slices of the Paideuma." They talked about their use of lines of capital letters, distinguished the reasons for and ways in which they both frequently used them. In correspondence, Philip praised Michael to friends who didn't yet know his work, and reported on his progress, sometimes jealously, to friends who did know the work. The passing remark to Allen Ginsberg in early 1957, "Michael is writing beautifully & in quantity,"[11] is typical. Philip lamented the obstacles—psychic, financial, logistical, legal, or otherwise—to Michael's writing. Legion though these sometimes were, family life did not rank among them. Joanna McClure harbored a deeply poetic sensibility herself, as her books later showed; she took an active part in the Beat literary scene, and later in the hippie movement, as they developed. Their daughter, the sunny Jane, proved to be a source of poetry (and prophecy) rather than a distraction from these. Early in her life, Michael had a habit of showing his daughter, nicknamed Boobus, cards from the Tarot deck and eliciting her responses. Watching this, Philip flashed on mythic echoes and recorded these in two poems, both of which set Jane's utterances in sacerdotal context:[12]

> Oh hidden!
> (Vestal maenad bacchante)
> among the leaves bright & dark
> " . . . a rubber baby . . .
> " . . . a plastic baby . . .
> " . . . cloth baby whose eyes
> close . . ."
> . . .
> & the Sybil also, her eyes closed under the cloth
> & the covered baskets containing that which none but the initiated
> may look upon
>
> " . . . I have one
> I have two
> I have a pencil
> I'm going to get another chair
> & stand up
> I need
> I need to push it
> THERE!"

Dave Haselwood, a boyhood friend of Michael's from Kansas, gave a great lift to both Michael's and Philip's careers, and he helped promote other poets and artists of the time as well. Haselwood had worked his way west to San Francisco (via a stint in Germany after the war), where he, like Michael, enjoyed the artistic brew of the late 1950s and '60s and helped cook it. Poet himself, connoisseur of painters and gallerists, Haselwood manifested in those days primarily as an elegant printer of the new poetry. He produced small editions of creatively designed books, and he used works by artists like Robert LaVigne, Bruce Connor, Byron Gysin, and Wallace Berman for the covers. He wanted to do fine printing, and he wanted to see his writer friends in print: McClure, Whalen, Welch, Spicer, Olson, Burroughs, Creeley, Meltzer, di Prima, and John Wieners—these are just some of the poets on Haselwood's list. His aspirations necessitated that he found the Auerhahn Press. For Philip, as for others, Dave Haselwood printed his first book. Long gone into the hands of collectors, Auerhahn Press editions were from the beginning understood as collaborations of the highest order among poet, painter, and printer. McClure treasured his copies, including his copy of Philip's *Memoirs of an Interglacial Age*. This volume unfortunately attracted the attention of the McClures' large borzoi (named Brautigan), who gnawed on it.

That copy sat on our shelves for years, kind of chewed up. And then one day I decided I just had to have a new one, and it had to be signed. I kind of demanded it. Phil had one and he gave me this one: "For Michael McClure, corrected by the author, 11.11.78. Philip Whalen"—there are three chops here, and one in the back too—"Not much of an improvement over the one your wolfhound ate." He'd gone through, and put in all of his additions, corrections, changes and so forth. He changed the dates of some poems; made some very interesting changes, apart from spelling.

Before the dog ate the book, before *Memoirs* was even printed, Philip and Michael collaborated on it.

Haselwood said, "We have to have a press release. Can you get Philip to do one?"

We had this big flat, with the typewriter sitting there. I told Philip we needed a press release. Haselwood—who by this time was printing these books himself—needed to get these distributed. I told Philip, "I'll type it."

So he sat there, in this big dark Biedermeier rocking chair we had at Fillmore Street, and I sat at the typewriter, poised. He sat there a long, long time. Then he said, "*This poetry is a picture or a graph of a mind moving,*" and I typed it and waited for a long time, and looked at him, and waited . . . "*which is a world body being here and now which is history . . . and you.*" The *longest* pause. I said, "You want me to read it back to you?"

"No."

"*Or think about the Wilson Cloud-chamber, not ideogram, not poetic beauty:*"

Long pause . . .

"*bald-faced didacticism moving as Dr. Johnson commands all poetry should, from the particular to the general.*"

Pause . . .

"(*Not that Johnson was right—nor that I'm trying to inherit his mantle as literary dictator . . .*)"

. . . right through to the end. I never read back to him. He was carrying this thing in his mind, which is as complex as any ideogram it's possible to imagine. And when I got it done, I said, "You want to make any changes?"

"No."

It was a wonderful experience.

It's worth noting that while Michael admired—was at times even awed—by Philip's poetry, he did not feel the same way about his prose. In the nervous weeks following completion of his first novel, Philip showed it to friends and sent it out to a few publishers. He recorded the results in a letter to Gary Snyder: "My novel is unloved; so far nobody wants to print it. L is very hard to please, but he thinks it's rather good, give or take a few faults; the entire Duerden family likes it; the entire McClure family hates it; Don Allen only says he likes the first part better than the last part, & that he won't send it to Barney."[13]

Nor did Michael always like Philip's performance style. Philip often just rattled out his poems, reading with a velocity, volume, and flatness that ill matched the words. Later in his life, it appeared as though Philip may have been simply bored by the act of reading aloud—put upon—and was willfully acting this out by throwing the reading away. But Michael recounted that Philip read in this mechanical fashion before audiences as early as their 1959 East Coast tour. It has been suggested that this was a coping mechanism for shyness. Philip made clear that he wrote for the pleasure of the act; he wrote because he liked doing it, and the reactions of an audience were low among his considerations. This is distinct from the reactions of his *readership*. It is also in sharp contrast to Michael's reading style, which was famously beautiful. McClure would sometimes recite verses from Chaucer in Middle English, before crowds waiting to be blasted by psychedelic rock bands. As a playwright, Michael strove to compose in a way that reached his audience. As he (more beautifully) put it,

Actors grow bright
golden scales
and coil
their stingered tails
as they fire
their souls
through the space
from stage
to
mind.[14]

. . .

From his school days, Philip adored theater. He studied and absorbed Shakespeare and the other Elizabethans, he performed in high-school productions, and by the time he was at Reed College, he directed plays as well. Decades later in Japan, Noh—its staging, costumes, and music—knocked him out. He devoted no small portion of his journal there to recording and analyzing the impact Noh theater had on him.

Michael wrote plays. From early one-acts staged in clubs and galleries, Michael developed his art so that by the mid-1970s, productions like *Gorf,* *The Pink Helmet, The Grabbing of the Fairy,* and *Minnie Mouse & the Tap-Dancing Buddha* were drawing large audiences and serious critical attention. Working with director John Lion, Michael enjoyed an eleven-year tenure as playwright-in-residence at the Magic Theater. The notoriety of his earlier work, *The Beard,* with its rumored pornography, its long string of arrests and police closings, its status as a battle worth fighting in the running censorship wars of the day, and its eventual triumph, no doubt helped propel Michael to celebrity. Beyond this wearisome path to fame stood the fact that Michael was simply a marvelous playwright. His visions ran to cosmic time and place, his language mixed the sublime with the gutter-blood, and his language often went beyond, or before, human speech by including roars, growls, and other nonstandard vocalizations. Sets and costume included whimsy, wild fantasy, and generous amounts of nudity. Yet for all this, the plays were about what men and women did: cyclical gender wars, politics, spiritual quests. The satire in the plays bit sharply, even as the shows dazzled. Michael's plays offered fun; they were lively in every way, but they were also very serious.

Philip loved them. He attended them whenever he could, and could be a loud audience member. He praised Michael's dramatic work to his circles of friends, and in at least one case, Philip performed in one of Michael's plays. In the days before Christmas 1960, Philip joined twelve other actors—poets, painters, and musicians—in reading the first two performances of *The Feast*. Pictures from this event at the Batman Gallery show the actors exactly as described in the text: "Seated at a long table. The actor in the center is the tallest. His hands are beneath the table on his lap. Each of the actors is bearded and with long hair. The actors at each end of the table are women with beards. The actors second from the end, at each end, are Negroes. All are dressed in robes of shining cloth—cerulean blue, gold-orange, etc."[15]

Each actor was responsible for making his or her own beard. Philip's was long, reaching down to midtorso, elaborate and neatly groomed. Seated next to Joanna McClure, he'd applied a very dark blackface and sported a robe of sparkly, patterned gold. He spoke many lines in the symmetrical play, though none in English or even in human language. Like all the characters, he gave from time to time a spirited recitation of his name; in Philip's case, "OHTAKE." Beyond that, his most frequent line was "NGROOR," though this was said with varying degrees of emphasis and musicality. The bestial speech—probably 80 percent of the text—sets off beautiful verses of lyric poetry. Somehow plot develops: crisis, resolution, denouement, conclusion.

Philip's own poetry also contains theatrical or dramatic elements: his characters give speeches, make and fend off ripostes, have conversations, sing songs, and break into sudden exclamation, these latter, like McClure's, sometimes in recognizable words and sometimes in pure sound. Philip wrote little beast-talk, though, preferring machine sounds and comic-book-bubble sound effects: "CHONK," "BOOM," "KRUNK," "tinkle," "squelch, slop, ooze." Given that both poets were, and felt themselves to be, struggling against many strictures at the time—including the grip of academia and formalism on poetry, censorship, conservative American politics, personal financial poverty, and occasional critical rejection—it must have felt extremely good, liberating, to rise and intone lines like the ones Michael gave Philip: "BEARTHIM SUNDANN TIKO soweet VYLE GRAATARB!"

. . .

Before the 1983 scandal that tore the Zen Center apart, evening events were scheduled there with some frequency. Beyond the Zen talks given by the abbot or senior teachers—more or less required—students might be treated to lectures by visiting scholars, luminaries from other Buddhist traditions, writers, especially poets, and the occasional theater performance. Thus it came to pass in the early 1980s that Michael McClure came to read and to offer the Zen student community a bit of cultural uplift. Very likely Michael and Philip and Baker Roshi had dined together before the reading, and they entered a crowded Zen Center dining room as a group at eight o'clock. Baker Roshi took a front row seat off to the side, and Philip stood awkwardly by, robe sleeves dangling, as Michael settled himself and arranged his books and papers for the reading. Once calm reigned, Philip, clearly acting under orders, began an introduction of his friend. "Michael McClure is a great poet. He's someone who's created an absolutely new sound and . . . "

"He's a great playwright too," whispered Baker Roshi, rather loudly.

Philip stopped with shocking abruptness and turned toward Baker, reddening. In a rare, possibly singular, public display of displeasure with his teacher, Philip then turned back to the audience. He paused a long time, then said slowly—phrases hitting like knives thrown into a board at a circus, barely missing the assistant, "There are *many kinds* of poetry. Dramatic poetry is *one* of the kinds of poetry. Michael McClure is a master of *all* of the kinds of poetry. I hope you will join me in welcoming him here this evening."

. . .

What principally united their minds was a quest for openness and a sensitivity to beauty (thus also to pain). This meant keen appreciation for cutting-edge work: in painting, for example, people like Clyfford Still and the abstract expressionists; in music, jazz—Miles, Monk, Coleman, et al.; in literature, of course, their Beat friends and companions, among others. Their love for whatever was breaking loose—a classic reaction to the conformity of the 1950s—was not limited to contemporaries. Painters, musicians, poets, dancers, and actors have been breaking loose for a long time. Blake was a natural hero for Philip and Michael. The Elizabethans. The impressionists. Schubert. Mozart. Both men had high standards and knew from direct experience that breaking loose required grounding in the tradition. Thus both had imbibed large stretches of the canon of English literature.

Michael and Philip also shared a love of physical science. From one perspective, they saw science as a continuous breaking loose from inadequate explanations of the phenomenal world into fresher, more fitting ones. Both read widely and deeply in earth sciences, and Michael counted scientists Sterling Bunnell and Francis Crick among his personal friends. Beyond the

thrill of discovery or the overthrow of established opinion, Michael and Philip's fascination with science reflected an inner question—one that gripped them—about how the mystic or spiritual state could take manifestation in . . . meat, to use one of Michael's favorite words. Having early on rejected a simplistic mind-body split, they saw instead a continuum, and cycles of manifestation, reaching from sublime thought to meat; literally from primordial wisdom to incarnation.

This flows as a major theme through McClure's work, as in this excerpt from "The Bow":

> that is only
> a soft, flesh facet
> of whirling, cytoplasmic meat clouds
> and spirit fires that jet
> and flow from the mosaic
> sub-beings in
> some flash of the perfection
> that we are.

Or more trenchantly:

> THE DIVINE IS PRACTICAL
> The gods are dripping
> with our blood.
> The flood
> of what we do is run
> through grooves
> of beauty.[16]

Or most reduced: "ALL SPACE WILL TWIST ITSELF TO SHAPES OF MEAT." Whalen tropes this notion, going in a different direction:

> *Grace before Meat*
>
> You food, you animal plants
> I take you, now, I make you wise
> Beautiful and great with joy
> Enlightenment for all sentient beings
> All the hungry spirits, gods and buddhas who are sad.[17]

Both men took pleasure all along this continuum, from earthy sensuality (as in eating) to rarest thought and most refined perception. Additional to their writing, this latter is evidenced in a shared fondness for the purifying and broadening effects of getting high. However cosmic their view, though, both men understood their place as artists and the duties attendant. Philip put it in his journal this way: "I know that the greatest pleasures are acts of creation: sexual intercourse, writing, drawing, painting, making music, dancing, reciting poetry, acting on the stage."[18]

It is one thing to admire newness in art or science; it is another thing to produce it. Beyond the anxieties of putting out anything at all are the terrors of stepping away, beyond the sanctioned. Hunters, warriors, explorers, shamans—all garner justifiable praise for stepping outside borders. An artist making a parallel step more often attracts—at least initially—criticism or outright attack. A hunter's, warrior's, or explorer's journey appears to conserve and strengthen the culture. Artists making new images—new ikons—seem to destabilize the culture. To make such work then demands a redoubled bravery and an explicit recognition that these creations are, on some level, political, if not revolutionary. Philip and Michael understood these consequences, and neither backed down from the fights—with critics, with other artists, or with censors—that creating really new work provoked. Both men fiercely and repeatedly demonstrated artistic bravery. Michael endured the nightly police sieges against his play *The Beard,* and he triumphed. Philip toughed out a censorship fracas some years later in Oregon and emerged in a much stronger position for it.[19] Despite harboring something of a "bring-it-on" attitude with regard to these battles, Michael and Philip's was a quest not for a fight but for openness. A creative state without fetters. Philip set the matter at a transcendent level:

> What do I know or care about life and death
> My concern is to arrange immediate BREAKTHROUGH
> Into this heaven where we live
> as music.[20]

If putting out new work requires bravery, then living with the mind that produces that work demands courage as well. An open mind is not an easy thing to acquire or maintain. Poets on the level of Whalen and McClure are generally conscious of the sources of their vocabulary and craft, and they can speak about these. The sources of their talent—their genius—are much more difficult to identify. It is not, however, hard to see or feel attacks against it. Conventional thought, mental provincialism, a subconscious narrowing of scope—these attach themselves to an artist's capacity like barnacles to a ship. Staying open or spacious requires real work and guarantees little. Viewed from outside, a person attempting this might be called, politely, "loosely strung." Less politely but more literally, a person trying to crack out of closing intellectual shells could be described as "crazed." Philip put this succinctly in a poem from 1960:

> To J. about art &c, that you must break yourself
> to create anything, this I, this self, holes have to be
> punched, cracks made in it to release the
> power, beauty, whatever; the act
> breaks us, a radical force like sex not lightly
> to be used[21]

Michael and Philip knew this requirement of themselves, and if it is too much to say they were comfortable, they at least had made peace with it, and art out of it.

> my thoughts that are feelings
> move out like a purring truck
> AND THEY PLUCK
> UP
> THE SOFT RUG
> OF
> WHAT
> I
> AM
> by the edges
> and shake together
> the elf, the mammal, and the man.
>
> I sit so calmly you'd never dream it!
> How crazy I am![22]

. . .

The openness under discussion—the taste for it and the embodiment of it—was what distinguished Philip from his other remarkable friends, in Michael's view:

> I always thought he was the most sensitive of all of us—he was as sensitive as a schoolgirl, but I mean this in a beautiful way. We'd go to the movies, and he'd sit there and cry, he'd be so deeply touched. These would be sophisticated films. . . . He'd try to hide it, but he was just so open—to the highest levels of sentiment.

He was sensitive, but at the same time . . . just his presence could domineer you. It wasn't that he was *being* domineering, it was that you just had such tremendous AWE of him.

And I don't know why.

Because he was also just a big booby, just a big silly booby a lot of the time. But we'd get—everybody I know—was in awe. We all just had great respect for him. People like to say it was his learning or his erudition, but that's only part of it, some kind of shortcut for what the real issue was. The real issue was that he was *so* open—instead of it minimizing him, or making him smaller, it gave him some kind of stature.[23]

. . .

A creative state beyond fetters—the chance to experience this, to express it, to promote it, is perhaps something of what Michael meant with the title of his epic poem (for Jim Morrison) "Hail Thee Who Play." Said experience can arrive in the act of composition or in performance. It can arrive sometimes in sexuality and release, and in other physical exertion. The experience arrives fairly reliably, though in dependence, with use of psychedelic drugs. The path of Buddhist meditation is designed to induct people at a reasonable pace into a state of freedom and openness. It is designed to give them strength and health to relax with it, and it imparts practical advice and training about how to integrate it into a daily life.

Michael, who'd created more consciously than most the persona of a mystic artist, was not likely to simply buy the entire tradition, or even a particular cultural version of it. As mentioned, the outsize language and all-encompassing philosophy (if that is the word) of the Gandavyuha Sutra and the Hua Yen school attracted him similarly to the way the language and thought of the Diamond Sutra attracted Jack Kerouac. But Michael was able to go the crucial steps beyond Jack and establish a regular meditation practice. Influenced no doubt by Philip and Gary's examples, encouraged by Richard Baker Roshi's gestures of acceptance, joined and supported by his second wife, Amy, Michael undertook the practice of daily sitting. In 1999 he published a book of what he called "Dharma Devotions,"[24] and while the publisher claimed these were different from anything he'd published before, they appear to be natural extensions of his work, with poems swarming this time around meditation. They concern themselves, in Michael's unique way, with insights and perceptions arising from zazen practice. In the tradition of Zen poets like Su Tung Po or Hakuin (to which he now legitimately

belonged), Michael dedicated various poems to his friends and teachers.
The book itself is dedicated to Philip. The poem specifically for him begins
this way:

THE POSTURE ITSELF IS THE SUBSTANCE

of

the search.

Compassion like crossed

legs may flow from the

MUDRA

Thumb touches thumb,

back is straight,

and there's a dim screen

for the movies

that flock

to

the theatre.

I

KNOW

ALL

EACH

TIME

SEVEN

Early

1923–1943

This book so far has attempted to place Philip Whalen, among his friends, in American letters of the second half of the twentieth century. It has also pointed to his role in helping to establish Zen Buddhism in the West. In so doing, the text has several times covered Whalen's life from 1952 until his death. More standard biographical chapters—childhood, army service, college education, sojourns in Japan, ordination as a Buddhist priest, work with his spiritual teacher, his own teaching, and his death—now appear in order, with a caution: Philip Whalen was, and knew he was, an anachronism. He felt he existed as easily out of time as in. He mentally traveled to and felt invaded by other times, particularly the fifth and fourth centuries B.C. in Greece and the eighteenth century in and around London. The following typifies a kind of experience Whalen records more than once in his writing:

> As I was sitting in Allen's kitchen, listening to him explain something to Alan Russo, I talked a little with Charley Plymell and someone else. I was doodling on the margins of a newspaper. I made a number of curly marks and found that I was actually seeing the countryside around Lee Vining, someplace east of the Sierras, the northern end of Owens Valley and the mountain meadows above them. The sun was shining. This happened to me at night, the lights were on in the kitchen, several people were there, I was able to move and to speak with them, yet I was, simultaneously, seeing another place, looking out over another landscape in a different time.[1]

Remembering his boyhood, his sister said, "He was always a MAN."[2] In middle age, he chose to be ancient—to look and act old, with old-fashioned manners. Actually old, he often manifested as a stubborn, goofy kid. He suspected time but acknowledged its importance. A long list of "worlds" he knew—this list abruptly wedged between other autobiographical passages in a book—gives primacy to time this way: "a) The world of the common experience wherein reigns the clock, the schedules based on the existence of an ideal clock, which lends money its value, pays the police, the world of 'strangers' 'the public': that world in which I am an object."[3] The list of worlds then runs for pages, with many sidetracks and subcategories, most of them referring back to "a)," where time reigns. When he lived in Japan and needed to work with Japanese descriptions of time, Whalen experienced them as very different. Actually, his comment was that their sense of time was "all cockeyed."[4]

Philip's anachronic bent is not frivolous. Time was for him a serious question, a religious or metaphysical one. He employed in speech and in writing some of Buddhism's most difficult philosophical notions on the topic: that time can run in both directions; that, strictly speaking, everything is happening at once; that time is an unprovable illusion.[5]

Philip tacked dates on his poems and their revisions; he dated his prose, frequently with both a starting and completion date. A number of his journals bear summary chronologies on the last page. When asked directly about it, he said: "I'm just staking out territory in time, so that if I happen to be writing about something on a certain day, even though somebody else [also] has a poem about daffodils or paratroopers, I can be either later or earlier. I want to know what I was doing then."[6]

Dating compositions follows the convention of earlier periods in literature—for instance, the eighteenth century—but the citation above shows that it also provides, at least to himself, points of reference. It must be said that Philip Whalen often felt himself as lacking them. "Sprung loose from all moorings," is one of the most graphic ways he describes the state. Practitioners in the contemplative tradition frequently experience this, but it is not simply a case of being spaced out. It is rather an instance of subtly, accurately noticing a state—a space beyond or before conceptual mind, and thus of great spiritual import—a state much of the world speeds by with all haste. The Zen practice of returning one's attention to the present moment conduces to this, as does regulated temple life, as does, even more so, monastic life:

> Here our days are nameless time all misnumbered
> Right where Mr. Yeats wanted so much to be
> Moving to the call of bell and semantron
> Rites and ceremonies[7]

FIGURE 9. *Left:* Philip's mother, Phyllis Arminta Bush Whalen, her arm around Philip, her baby daughter Velna in her other arm, 1928–29. Estate of Philip Whalen, Bancroft Library, University of California, Berkeley.

FIGURE 10. *Right:* Philip with his father, Glenn Henry Whalen, 1928–29. Estate of Philip Whalen, Bancroft Library, University of California, Berkeley.

Philip Whalen was born 20 October 1923, in Portland, Oregon, about eighty miles down the Columbia River from where he grew up in The Dalles. He appeared as the first child and only son of Glenn Henry Whalen and Phyllis Arminta Bush Whalen; five years later they produced a daughter, Velna Blanche. Philip arrived in the world on his mother's twenty-sixth birthday.

He loved his mother; she was kind, loving, a committed Christian Scientist. "Mama used to say: 'Goodness Godness Agnes!'; she had an Irish temper and she worked hard to control it. She really felt the necessity to love everybody—enough so that she might live happily with all the world. Her hair was black and very fine; it lay in deep natural waves above her broad forehead. He skin was white and pink, very delicate, easily sunburned. Her eyes were grey or blue or green, depending on her health, her costume and her mood."[8] She was also sick a great deal and died from acute peritonitis at forty-two. Philip was in his midteens. She may have struggled with an Irish temper, but Phyllis Bush descended from English, possibly Welsh ancestors, a band of seven Bush brothers arriving in Kentucky before the Civil War. Various branches of this family migrated westward, coming through Missouri and homesteading by the end of the nineteenth century in Oregon's Willamette Valley, where Phyllis was born.

Philip's father's side, the Whalens, not only possessed quarrelsome Irish tempers, they *were* Irish, and note of them appears in a family Bible as early as 1800, in Vermont. They too came in bounds across the country, so that Philip's father, Glenn Henry, was born in Dubuque, Iowa, but had arrived in western Oregon by the time he was marriageable. Philip wrote of him that "his own face was craggy, like an Indian's, but he had wavy black hair and eyes the color of Michaelmas daisies." In pictures, Glenn Henry looks striking and wolfish, a sharp dresser with suit and tie, hat, polished shoes, a watch chain across his vest. He worked as a salesman in a store, and then traveling, for Honeyman Hardware. Phyllis worked as a telegraph operator. Though Phyllis and Glenn Henry calculated later they'd probably gone to grade school together in Rickreall, Oregon, they met as young adults in Portland. Philip speculated about his mother that, having seen her older sister marry an Englishman of lesser nobility—an unhappy union, ending in swift divorce—Phyllis chose instead to marry "my father, a man from her own neighborhood, & {perhaps she thought} her own class & was prepared to accept a lower station in life?"[9] Philip then criticizes his own thinking as "oddly Victorian & Christian & creepy."

In any case, marry they did, and while still living in Portland, they produced Philip. The new family moved to Centralia, Washington, and then set up house in The Dalles, Oregon, in a style that rose above poverty—they lived in a real house, the children had their own rooms—though not above worry about poverty. In *The Diamond Noodle,* Philip pictures his father on a ferry, "sitting in his car, on his way to Goldendale, blue eyes watching the line of hills ahead, the mountains downriver, no doubt worrying about my mother, my sister & me, remembering his own childhood poverty and loss of mother, brother, childhood horror ... now stuck with the job of hustling devalued money (what is the Roosevelt fellow going to do?) to pay the rent, buy gas, feed everybody, Depression."

The strains Whalen elaborates here manifest in predictable ways. Glenn Henry was very often on the road—a week at a time was not unknown, three days was normal—and when he was home, he passed the days in an office in town. During his absences, he left Phyllis almost no money—a couple of dollars at most—to run the household. When he got back, he would go shopping with her, controlling what she spent. Like his father before him, Glenn Henry drank hard, often getting obstreperous. He got rough with Phyllis at home, and this scared the children, who hid in their rooms. Sometimes he'd take them to the bar, where they could play punchboard while he drank.

On the other hand, family life included visits with relatives, weekend outings, and vacations by the sea. Pleasanter, these excursions still held trials for Philip. "We would always go for Sunday drives, which was something people liked to do then. Just to drive through the countryside. I was always bored by the whole business. I wanted to be at home reading books, listening to people talk, rather than being hauled around in an automobile while the scenery went by very fast. Someone would say, 'Look at that!' and I'd turn and look, but they'd shout, 'It's back there you dummy!' I'd feel infinite regret at such a moment. I can't imagine where my attention was when the waterfall went by. My distraction was probably the result of great boredom."[10] Telling a Naropa class about similar outings, he offered constant car sickness as another source of distraction, adding that being told to look at views was often connected to threats, and that failing to really see them and being accused of ingratitude was "very hard to live down."[11] He could see the parts well enough, he said, but could not yet compose them into a view. Musing further about these early failures in perception and appreciation, he lamented that (possibly therefore) he had also been unable to develop proper group feelings, like "going to pieces at Christmas." In general, he resisted being told what to like and what not. Though he loved to sing, for example, he hated to be told to sing along in a group. Such independent-mindedness, laudable in a young person trying to develop his own values, was and would remain a source of vexation in community life—with his large extended family, in the army, at college, and at the Zen Center.

Yet another reason for country drives was one of his aunt's favorite occupations, one on which she evidently dragged young Philip along: visiting relatives' graves. Said aunt would clamber around cemeteries to find the graves, clean them, and deposit fresh flowers. Philip compared this unfavorably with similar customs of Chinese ancestor worship, ruing that his Oregonian relatives omitted offerings of smoked meats and dumplings for the departed.

If the young Philip could not properly compose what he was seeing into a "view," he did mentally record the images and later, in journals and books, wrote pages of beautiful landscape description. Being a kind of prose he admired, Philip also understood that the landscape was built into him: "That River which is too wide, too heavy to flow . . . all of a piece it turns with the world towards the day; along with a great deal more material of the same kind: rock, outcrops of square fractured basalt dull yellow, blue, grey-green lichens, thick mosses, and at the top a flat field of weedy grasses. Rock stairways and thrones looking down mountain on my street and over the tree tops to the River, up to the mountains to the peak of Mt Adams; these cold basalt thrones of dream, rock-child pose, looking out."[12]

Pictures of Philip from childhood show him wearing glasses from a very early age, early enough to still be buttoned into a one-piece, lace-edged garment over stockings. Summer photos—especially in swimsuits—reveal the broad-hipped, narrow-shouldered frame he would carry throughout his life. His eyes would have appeared bright blue and his hair red, had the pictures been in color. Together the photographs present a genuinely happy-looking child: curious, amused, affectionate—often with an arm around his sister or mother—and able to hold a frank gaze toward the camera.

His early and voracious taste for reading led him to sedentary days, and as he grew, he felt clumsy. "When I was a child they laid it on me that I had to remember and to act out, this thing about, 'Up up in the sky, the little birds fly/down down in the nest, the little birds rest/with a wing on his left and a wing on his right/the wee little birdy will sleep all the night.' I did the left and the right wrong, every time. It took me the first 10 years of my life to learn which was my right and left. And also how to tie my own shoes; I was very slow with that operation."[13] None of this seems to have fazed him much. He was socially at ease, spending time with friends both at his house and at theirs, and enjoying the feeling of being one of the guys. He objected (without effect) to wardrobe decisions that set him apart: rubber galoshes, for example, instead of logger boots for winter wear. He put himself forward to perform when required and appeared to relish it, mounting papier-mâché theater pieces at home and for the benefit of the local public and church.[14]

At The Dalles High School, Philip encountered a teacher named Albert Hingston, who encouraged the creative energies of his students. "He organized a lot of interesting plays for the drama club, he had a choral speaking group, he got a magazine going to teach creative writing—and he was, you know, jumping all over the place. So I took him on for my first teacher having anything to do with writing as something you could do or learn. . . . He taught us the usual forms—sonnets, and ballads, and various French forms like triolets and so on. It was a lot of fun to try to make stuff in these shapes."[15] In these years, Philip wrote his first poem, "a high-school-kid poem—something about birds, the stars and tra-la-la," handing it to the girl sitting in front of him. The young lady apparently liked the free verse and wrote him back a nice note.[16]

Philip's mother died on 27 May 1939 and was buried in a graveyard in Salem, south of Portland, in an area where her relatives still lived. Philip, fifteen, was near completing the tenth grade. Given his sister's age—Velna was ten at the time—Philip's own minority, and the fact that their father was away so much, Velna went to live with her mother's sister (she of the rapid divorce from English nobility). This sister, also called Velna, had now married a man named Nicolas Versteeg and lived with him on a farm in Independence, Oregon, near the rest of the (maternal) family. Philip, abruptly deprived of both mother and sister, thus lived alone with his often absent, often temperamental father. The situation would have at least given him free time for his studies and his well-developed reading habit; it would also have enforced on him the necessity of handling solitude. Possibly because he loved his mother so much and saw her so sick so often, Philip thought of learning medicine and becoming a doctor. His father encouraged this plan and said he would do what he could to make it happen. Philip modeled his fantasy on another doctor with literary ambitions: "When I got out of high school, I thought I would do like Dr. [William Carlos] Williams. I would become a doctor and write poems—because I thought at that time that I really wanted to be a doctor more than anything."[17]

He graduated from high school in May 1941, but events conspired against Philip's hopes. Honeyman Hardware went bankrupt, leaving his father jobless. Not only was there no money to "manufacture me into a doctor," as he put it, but there were no funds for college of any kind. Glenn Henry moved downriver to Portland for work in the new Kaiser shipyards, and Philip necessarily went with him. Despite his strong preference for sitting home reading, he too was forced into the job market, and he held three successive office jobs, doing a stint in an airplane factory, and ending up like his father in the shipyards. Aspects of these jobs interested him—learning to repair office equipment, run a telephone switchboard, or research property title claims at the courthouse. He continued to write poems during this time, and his reading veered toward the Far East.

Whatever grounds he may have had, Philip didn't complain about his father in print—nothing stronger than telling an army friend in a letter that he'd "been feuding again with the old man."[18] The few times his father appears in his work (beyond the sympathetic snapshot of a man worrying about money), it is as a foil or straight man. Glenn Henry comments during a museum visit on the small genitalia of Greek sculpture. He also remarks, "Them pots are older than Jesus Christ. What do you think about that?" To which the poet answers, "I could remember buying that pot in the sunshine of the Corinthian agora, something to hold olive oil, my father had forgotten painting the legend of Heracles and the Nemean lion. I remembered all the rest of my lives that day."[19]

His father remarried. Philip tracked his relatives closely in his private writing, but he recorded almost nothing about this woman. He mentions her only as "my step-mother," until in an unpublished journal from 1965, he enters her name. "Ruby writes, 'He has something in the upper part of his chest that makes it hard for him to swallow.'" Philip borrowed funds for a bus trip and was there when Glenn Henry died ten days later of lung cancer.

Music sounded in the homes of Philip's childhood, song particularly. "People liked to sing when I was growing up, and they sang to me as I was going to sleep. My father belonged to a barbershop quartet, my mother liked to sing, my grandmother also. She used to sing with them."[20] As soon as he was able, Philip accompanied the adults on piano. Relatives on both sides were musical. His grandfather Bush played old-time fiddle—dance tunes and reels—and Philip's great-uncle Happy "was a musical prodigy. He could just pick up any instrument and play it."[21] But it wasn't only the melodies and rhythms that attracted Philip: "The words people used in songs puzzled me . . . the task was to find a connection between these words for objects, and sentiment."[22]

"What does it mean—'If a body meet a body, coming through the rye'? I'd thought a body was right about here. My mother used the word as a euphemism for 'penis.' . . . 'Don't play with your body!' Then they told me [about the song], 'Well, it's all in Scotland, it's dialect.'"[23]

His relatives sharpened their intelligence with verbal play and a heavy emphasis on language generally: "Everyone in my family was always making jokes about words, so I was very conscious of speech. People would sit and work crossword puzzles. . . . When I got into high school I started doing them myself."[24]

"I was crazy about words and sounds. . . . My grandmother used to be a freak about correcting my grammar all the time. She'd tell us not to say 'ain't,' for example, which was very funny because her own speech was quite vivid. Being a peasant lady she used speech of the people, though she did have very definite ideas about the way proper people should talk."[25]

> Words had this effect—if I said, "God damn it," my mother would come at me with the Ivory soap and shove it in my mouth. If I said, "Up up in the sky, little birds fly," everybody would be pleased. If I said, "I want a T-bone steak" in a restaurant, everybody would laugh, because how could a little guy like me eat a T-bone steak? So these words all did different things.
>
> Then there was the thing about lying, about how you didn't tell lies. "Stories," my mother used to call them. "Don't tell stories." "Don't tell fibs." "Little white lies." Yet of course that's the whole thing that lends charm to our existence—the stories we tell, real or imagined, to ourselves or other people. And the ones that come back to us, that other people tell about us. They have a strange effect on our psyche. Actually "story" is a very important part of our lives. But for a long time that word was contaminated with me: the absolute connection of "story" with untruth was very heavy.[26]

Part of his family's lively engagement with speech naturally focused on names. The games Philip later played with naming—most remarkably with Gary Snyder—started early. People on both sides of his family possessed interesting names but often were not called by these names. Philip's father would sometimes "call my mother Phyllis Ben Bolt or Bridget O'Flynn or Mrs McTavish, or Mrs (or Mr) MacGillicuddy & I would be Oppodildock or Fred, and my sister Old Roosabill."[27]

Philip's great-grandmother was named Thirza; an aunt was named Way; an uncle named Clarence was called "Happy"; there lived a Pleasant who had a child called Lud who had a sister named Ida whom everyone called Pink. Simpson, Dovey, Provine, Pernell, Adna, and Diment—these were given names. Cecil Alfred was called Bill, Rose was called Mears, Alvah was Dusty, Kenneth was Dick, another Phyllis was Pinky, Philip called his sister Velna "Rosie" and it stuck. His aunt Velna was Nana. Everyone called Philip himself "Pat."

These names and the relations among the people bearing them come from a genealogy Philip handwrote across a couple of large sheets of paper, together with much marginalia, for his sister sometime after 1965. About their family name, it states:

> In Irish, the name was something like "O'Faoláin." It is written in English as O'Phelan, O'Whelan, & without the "O". {"O'" is for the Irish word "Og"

which means "descendant of" or "son of"} In modern Ireland & USA & Canada &c "Whalen" is another variant spelling. . . .

In Irish, "Faolláin" means "seagull." It was the totem, & common name for a tribe of people, not all of them relatives by blood. Technically it is a "sept" {as distinguished from a Scottish "clan."} They seem to have come from the north of Ireland—our branch of Whalens—for they were Protestants.[28]

Philip understood from an early age that his education had several prongs: on one, he recognized forms of cultural indoctrination coming his way— American, Irish, Protestant, rural Northwestern. On another prong, he worked to clear himself of these or at the very least to make them conscious. He did this partly by trusting his own perceptions above what he was told. On a third prong, he consumed whatever literature, history, science, and philosophy he could find in books as a corrective and as supplemental material. He got "nourishment" from this reading, he said, sometimes referring to it as "vitamins." Philip's boyhood relations with American Indians in The Dalles provides a good example of how these different prongs worked, or didn't, in his education.

> They were mysterious beings, mainly because they were quiet, and you couldn't understand them. And also because my parents told me they were dirty, and bad, and they stole dogs and did all sorts of dreadful things. I was not to talk to them, or associate with them, just to stay away. But they were just there, buying things at the dry-goods store, or standing in front of the bank—large, monumental people; very quiet.
>
> Then in the books, of course, they were somebody else. . . . The schoolbooks in Oregon were all printed in New England, and there they were noble red men—creatures of the Hiawatha type—and later, in high school, *The Last of the Mohicans.*
>
> It was a very strange feeling to be in these different worlds—the world of Indians in the schoolbooks, and the real Indians who stood around. They spoke as if they had a mouth full of mashed potatoes. They spoke some brand of Chinook—very interesting sounds. Very quiet people. They just stood there. The gentlemen had braids on each sides of their face and a Stetson hat with a flat brim.[29]

Whalen also understood the inherent dissonance between his own perceptions and the rules governing them. As this mounted, he cast an example of it as "drama," with an unusual (if not unique) literary list:

Cast of Characters in a Drama of my Childhood...

The Sewing Cabinet. (Borrowed from our Aunt. It looks like a table but it contains many moving lids and drawers. Don't touch.)

The Tool Chest. (Galvanized sheet-iron. It contains Daddy's tools. Never open it. Never borrow the hammer, &c. Never touch.)

Daddy's Chair. (The Big Chair, leather bound, with wings, a rocker. Don't put your feet on it.)

Mother's Chair. (A 'Windsor' rocker. Don't put your feet on it.)

The Smoking Stand. (Has a door that opens; you can see light through the green ashtray when the door opens. Daddy's pipes and tobacco pouch are inside. Don't open that door. Don't touch Daddy's things.)[30]

Of the twenty-eight objects in the full litany, most of them conclude with a proscription from touching or exploring. With the final one, the terms are very certain: "The center of this drama was between my legs. It is the temple of the Holy Ghost. All those little things are to be left strictly alone. They must not be touched. They are not to be played with. They must be covered up. They must not be mentioned. Allow no one to touch them. Don't look at those which belong to another. You must learn to control yourself."

Philip learned to read early, and went to his room with what his sister called "pounds of books" he'd brought back from the library. These pounds comprised much more than children's stories or even young adult literature. Philip told a Naropa class how he'd read through Shakespeare the first time at the age of eight.[31] According to Velna, he spent most of his time in his room reading, to the consternation of their father.

> ("Hello there, Loose & Unnecessary," coming up
> the walk from the car
> me slung in a lawn chair reading)[32]

Philip read his way through much of the Wasco County library in The Dalles. Because of his penchant for the Greeks, he happened soon enough onto books from the Near East, and from there the Far East: Asian history, philosophy, and religion.

"I first got interested in Buddhism and Hinduism just after I got out of high school. . . . I stumbled across Madame Blavatsky's work in the library. It didn't take me long to figure out where she was getting her material—out of the classical Indian philosophies."[33] Philip then devoured the Vedas, the Upanishads, the Bhagavad Gita, as well as early Buddhist texts. He continued on into the Chinese poets. Of his informal education during this period, he remarked, "That changed my life about as much as anything ever did."[34]

"Who are we? Where are we going? How'd we get here?" Paraphrasing the title of Paul Gauguin's masterwork, Philip thus began a lecture at Naropa on 1 August 1977. Initially focusing on eighteenth-century philosophers Locke, Berkeley, and Hume, and the novelist Laurence Sterne, Philip tried to interest the class in the questions of how perception works and where ideas come from. He felt that for aspiring poets—as for philosophers, painters, and other artists—Gauguin's questions should be of essential interest, going as they do to the root of the human condition and creativity.

Philip also knew that two and a half thousand years earlier in India, the Buddha, concerned with the problem of suffering, had engaged these questions in meditation. From what he found, the Buddha developed a system of oral instruction and practice. Much of Philip's own oeuvre naturally attempted to work with these same profundities. Certainly *The Diamond Noodle,* a text much cited in this chapter, attempts to sort out, among other things, the question "How'd we get here?"

Three years later at Naropa, Whalen took a different tack: after studying with his class Wallace Stevens's poem "The Bed of Old John Zoeller," he assigned them the task of writing poems about their own grandfathers. The point, he later confessed, was to get them thinking about the people from whom they'd descended. "One of the hidden themes of this class is 'lineage.'" he said. He intended his students to look into their biological lineages but also into their verbal, intellectual, and religious lineages. He cited his own, with regard to Shakespeare: "I have been trained to read Shakespeare by a competent teacher. The competent teacher's name was William Alderson. He was a disciple of Bertrand H. Bronson, Bertrand Bronson was a disciple of Lyman Kittredge, Lyman Kittredge was a disciple of Frances Child. So it's a very respectable lineage of scholarship. So I know what to do about Shakespeare. I know how to look at it, I know how to look things up about it."[35] Philip understood that everyone in the room expressed their individual genetics, but also that they expressed—largely unconsciously—collective philosophical and theological heritages. He called it "the history that's still there," and noted that it was "still working." He strongly felt that unless his students tried to free themselves from the inherited streams of thought that ran through them like blood—unless they at least became conscious of them, as he had done—they would be unwittingly controlled by them. Beginning in defense of Wallace Stevens, Philip unspooled to the class:

> He's interested in what is he seeing. He's always testing, "Am I really seeing this glass of water, am I really seeing these flowers in bowl or what? And if I am, what's really happening, what's it about?"
>
> It's very entertaining, about what is perception, what is reality, what is the nature of reality? Any person with any imagination is going to wonder, "What's happening?" "Where am I at? How am I dealing with it?" Anybody who's thinking about it, anyway.
>
> Because all of us have been TAUGHT a whole bunch of things when we were young. And if you have any brains at all, and look around a little bit, and read a little bit, you slowly discover that you've been hoodwinked, purpose-fully, ever since you were knee-high to a duck—by everybody else's ideas, and religion and prejudices of all kinds. We are dipped in our culture.[36]

Once Philip got away from Portland, which he did after college, at about twenty-eight years of age, he took a dim view of the area and its inhabitants. He ranted against his broader family's "dumb Republican politics," their conservatism, and their poverty, but he nonetheless mined his childhood for insights into his situation, for subject matter, and explicitly for help in unraveling the inherited ties that still bound him. In the midst of just such a talk about his history, he abruptly interrupts himself to point out that by being ordained as a Buddhist monk, he had been "cut away from all that." He meant that as an *unsui*—a cloud-water person—he had ceremonially floated free of biological and cultural ties, joining instead the family of the Buddha.

"But you don't feel still . . . ?" Anne Waldman asked him from the audience, incredulous.

"Of course! I'm still human," he replied, launching into another ten minutes of reminiscences.[37]

It would be improper to conclude without asking what kind of book *The Diamond Noodle* is, since a significant amount of material in this chapter comes from it—and asking if it is useful as a biographical source. Much in the text can be connected to fact. Beginning to write it in 1956 and working on it for the next nine years, Philip collected childhood memories. Descriptions—including portraits of geography, flora, fauna, human beings, and inanimate objects—come forth in a clear, adult prose and line up with other accounts, Whalen's own and those of friends. Beyond these "true" things, some of the text records dream sequences; some of it arises from excursions and is drawn from hiking journals; and some of the book defies category. Philip once said of a musician who was soloing extravagantly that he was "out there, walking around."[38] This praise could be applied to some of the metalogical passages in his book. Altogether it is a difficult semiautobiographical work. The epigraph from Chinese poet Su T'ung Po implies the book is doomed to failure—not because it lacks fact, memory, reflection, or commentary, but because it attempts the impossible:

> *Where are the pleasurable and unpleasurable moments after they are past? They seem to be like a sound, a shadow, a breeze, or a dream. Even these four things are somehow more tangible. Besides, how is one ever going to find happiness by countering one illusion with another illusion? I wish I could express this deep truth to you, but I cannot. (5 August 1088)*[39]

The title—*Diamond Noodle*—juxtaposing two incompatible words, points as well to problems the book engages. Diamonds refract light, are beautiful and valuable; they are indestructible, hard: the hard facts. For Philip, *diamond* alludes as well to the Diamond Sutra, a famous, trenchant exposition of Buddhist emptiness—simultaneous appearance and nonexistence of phenomena. *Noodle* of course means nourishment, but to Philip it also implied play or frivolity, resonating with *doodle* or with a favorite slang word, *canoodle*. He once shouted at the radio and turned it off, complaining that the musician on air was "just *noodling!*"

EIGHT

Forced Association

ARMY LIFE, 1943–1946

Philip didn't record what he felt before going into the army in January 1943, though the circumstances were clear enough: the country was in a bloody war on several fronts, young men his age were being killed, he was to report for duty. On the other hand, he'd never traveled beyond his corner of Oregon or out from under his extended family; now he would. From the window of a train from Chicago to Mobile—on his way to basic training in Biloxi, Mississippi—Philip had his first look at the American South. The poverty he saw—run-down buildings and beautiful landscapes ruined by the relentless harvest of cotton and tobacco—was utterly alien to him. He understood these conditions as the ongoing wreck of the Civil War. One of the principal causes in that war, the emancipation of slaves, also looked to him only very partially accomplished. The racial discrimination he'd known in Oregon had been between white people and Native Americans. Now he saw—"with my own eyes!" as he would later say—the pernicious and stubborn remains of Jim Crow, starting with segregated train cars and stations. "I had been brought up to believe that America was a very enlightened country and that there was great progress being made on every front. Franklin Roosevelt had solved all our problems. Then here you look out the window at these terrible shacks people were living in, and these weird segregated railway stations—it was like a foreign country."[1]

Bookish, peaceable, playful by nature, Philip very much disliked the rough jostling and berating of boot camp; he disliked life in general on an army base, comparing it later to being in prison. He confessed to one of his army friends that for years he suffered nightmares, not of battle or personal destruction—he was mercifully distant from these—but of simply not being released from the army. He admitted though that it was broadening: he got to know young men from all over the country, boys who'd been brought up in circumstances quite different from his own, sometimes more privileged, often with better educations. He also had his eyes and ears open for the amusements of military life. Years later at the Zen Center, if it came time for a new pot of coffee, he might boom in imitation of his drill sergeant, "Yous guys clean out them coffee urn'ls!"

After basic training, he was stationed in Yuma, Arizona, and later in Spokane, Washington, not understanding any more than any other low-rank solider the reasons for his numerous displacements. His assignments also included time in Alamogordo, New Mexico, and Colorado Springs, Colorado. Early on he cottoned to the fact that he had a talent for work with electronics and that this would be to his advantage. Further training in the field authorized him as a teacher of radio equipment and communication for the Army Air Force and got him promoted him to the rank of private first class, as far as he ever got on that ladder. For about six months in 1945, his job required him to teach in situ—that is, in flight. His students were being trained for a dual role as radio operators and waist gunners, meaning that they were also to shoot a fifty-caliber machine gun from the middle of the plane. Philip worked as one of four trainers aloft: he taught them about the radio; the gunnery instructor taught them the weaponry; and in front two more teachers worked, one with the pilot, one with the copilot. Though Philip lived in some fear of being shipped off to actual combat in Europe, he rather enjoyed the risky work of airborne instruction.

In fact, physically, army life was good to Philip. He never left the United States, never saw battle; he never had to worry about a place to live, clothes to wear, or food to eat. He worked a relatively simple job that afforded him time for reading and writing, and in some of his assignments he had extraordinary amounts of time off. Writing to a friend near the end of the war, he described his schedule: "This outfit is on the verge of breaking up. I have still done no work for them. Today for instance, I got up at 8:30, spent the morning at the library writing some stuff for the biography, then had lunch & went to the service club to play the Ravel Concerto (left hand)."[2]

En route to a new assignment in Spokane in mid-1945, Philip made his first visit to San Francisco. As any tourist might, he wrote about the day and noted for the first time several pleasures and activities there that would occupy him for fifty years: "SF was cloudy and cool. I walked up Telegraph Hill and then up into Coit Tower for a look see. From there all San Francisco, both bridges, Oakland and San Rafael can be seen. You feel as if you were in

FIGURE 11. Philip in army uniform with his sister, Velna, 1944–45. Estate of Philip Whalen, Bancroft Library, University of California, Berkeley.

the midst of one of those comic animated maps. Afterwards, down Telegraph Hill to Fisherman's Wharf for lunch at the Fisherman's Grotto, . . . there a great sea-odorous bowl of bouillabaisse with Italian bread and beer. Truly A Great Thing."[3]

After a last scare about European deployment in November 1945, he finally felt in January 1946 that discharge was in sight. "They'll cut the orders & I'll be on my way . . . possibly in a week . . . ten days at the most. Just think! A civilian! No more merd de poulet . . . no more saluting . . . no more details, chow lines, forced association with idiots, morons & sex fiends. Hot dawg."[4] It took longer than hoped, but Philip was discharged in February, having served three years, a month, a week, and a bit.

His technical teaching brought him into association with educated students—soldiers who could by dire necessity express themselves clearly and well, even under pressure. Additionally, several were active readers, and from them, Philip learned of books and authors he'd previously not known, the most important of which was Thomas Wolfe. "I felt great affinity for Wolfe, because I too came from poor people in an obscure part of the country, and yet was aware of the great natural beauty of that section and of the peculiar lives and speech of the people in that region, and so I began to try to write novels in the manner of Thomas Wolfe. I never got too much beyond 40 or 50 pages of it, and it was always pretty much the same. But I thought that was really what writing was about, was to write novels."[5]

From among his new acquaintances, several had literary or musical ambitions of their own, and over time these connections grew into real friendships. The longest-lived of these, a young composer named Stanworth Beckler, one day went to find out who was "painfully outlining" chords on the chapel's grand piano. There sat Philip, "bent nearsightedly into a volume of Debussy's preludes . . . a plump young man in khakis which fitted him like lampshades. A crimson-patched broad face, terribly Irish features, with owlish spectacles, & a modest precise part in his rug of hair . . . head tilted almost imperiously. I instinctively associated him with a stern scholar. When he spoke, he seemed stilted, reserved—speaking through a protective wall of poise & indifference, not speaking down, but speaking around, vastly serious. . . . He had a salty, self-sufficient air."[6]

As Beckler worked on his music, also around his army day job, he involved Philip in it. He told how "together we finished the second movement of the sonata. His moral & intellectual sustenance is immeasurable. He is so well-read & retentive, a stickler for accuracy and sincerity—and a demon attacker of preciousness, pseudo-intellectualism & other forms of musical & literary drivel."[7]

Philip too held Stanworth (whom he called Dan) in high regard. He admired his music; more important, he learned music from him. Beckler introduced him to branches of composition he hadn't known and showed him how to read scores, including the orchestral scores he himself was studying. He taught Philip the rudiments of counterpoint and harmony, and showed him a great deal about playing the piano. These lessons affected Philip's writing profoundly. "Reading scores gave me some notion about form in a subliminal way. I don't really understand theories of harmony and counterpoint, they're very abstruse, but I do have some inkling of what form in time is, which is what music actually does—a form that happens in time. This is something that happens in poetry, at a faster or slower speed."[8]

Teaching with Ginsberg years later, Philip told the students, "My sense of the shape of words, and how they go together, and how blocks of words will go together to make a stanza or make a chunk of poetry, is drawn almost entirely from music, from my experience of music—playing music, and listening to a great deal of music. The idea of what a composition is is all drawn from music."[9] He added painting, sculpture, and architecture as disciplines from which he'd learned about assembling elements of different sizes and weights and times, but said he "depended upon music." The book generally regarded as Philip's first, *Like I Say,* was dedicated to Stanworth Russell Beckler.

Another army friend whose life continued to involve Philip beyond their service days was Ben Richard Anderson, a young Oregonian with a taste for flying. Ben had washed out of the training to be a pilot and landed instead in the radio instruction class, where he met Philip. It soon came out that Anderson was also trying to write during his evenings and weekends, though, unlike Philip, he had an eye toward commercial success and was working on detective fiction. Recognizing Anderson's talent, Philip gave him a hard time "about how writing's difficult enough, and why not write something real, since that's what you ought to be doing, as long as you were going to write at all. Try to do something goofy and marvelous of your own, and worry about the money later."[10]

After the war, after law school and marriage and a trip around the country hauling a trailer, Anderson actually had a novel published by one of the big New York houses—a book Philip much admired, called *Down River,* about an Oregon salmon fisherman. The New York publishers declined, however, to bring out Anderson's second novel, and somewhere through his third he gave up on the writer's life and went with his wife back to Newport. There he took up lawyering, first in his father's office, then on his own, and finally as circuit court judge for the area. During this time, he gave Philip a job as his bailiff. More explicitly, Dick Anderson and Virginia Heath drove down from Newport to Berkeley in August 1957, helped Philip close up the fabled Milvia Street house—Philip had taken to calling it Casita Encantada by then— loaded him and his belongings into their vehicle, and drove back up the many miles on small highways, which at that time were lined with rural redneck bars and restaurants.

This was the third time Philip had stayed with or near the Andersons for an extended period, an arrangement Virginia tolerated, though uneasily. At the very beginning of the 1950s, Philip lived with them in Venice, California. He riveted bolts in an airplane factory for money, reporting that "chimpanzees could do the job without any trouble at all,"[11] and suffering mightily from the constant noise. Again, between his summer lookout work on Sourdough Mountain in 1954 and 1955, he stayed with the Andersons in Newport. During this visit, he makes no mention of employment. In the 1957–59 Newport period, Philip did not actually live with Dick and Virginia, other than when he was between lodgings, which happened at least twice. During the days, he worked closely with Dick: Philip was, for example, the one who called, "All rise," when Judge Anderson entered the court; together, Philip and Dick went through a victorious "mud-slinging" campaign for Anderson's reelection in 1958, with Philip as campaign manager. In return for these services, Philip had a place to live, food to eat, a pretty coastal town to look at, and thirty dollars in 1950s money to burn each week.

Although they spent time together easily and pleasurably—including outings in small airplanes on the weekends—Philip worried endlessly in his journal about the psychological balances of the relationship, as the following (highly condensed) excerpt shows:

> Coming here I simply became further indebted to him; I can't begin to repay even the least of his beneficences. . . . I've spent a great deal of time having to listen to B [Ben] and V recount endless instances of B's having squandered his generosity on unworthy objects. I feel obliged to classify myself with these, mistakenly or not. Contrariwise, I refuse to believe that I am capable of deceiving him—he is much more intelligent than I. He's known me for many years, seen me & my actions & reactions in great number & variety of situations. . . . And I amuse him—does he suppose "Well, all amusements are expensive. P is expensive but I can afford the amusement?"
>
> I waste quantities of valuable time & freedom doing nothing at all. . . . I can't stay interested in my own projects, much less in politics, even though I suppose I should, out of gratitude, be working myself to the bone on the political scene. I can't. Time away from the bailiff job is short enough—there is scarcely time to waste comfortably, much less in which to write anything but the few scattered poems & sheets of babble I've done since my arrival.
>
> I am overwhelmed or something, with feelings of remorse &c. . . . I am Ungrateful Wretch etc. Traitor to my friend & to my own Genius &c. . . . The way I'm seeing & interpreting the present scene is absurd. . . . I spend so much time being occupied with these feelings, these false analyses, that I scarcely am aware of the present moment, my present identity, powers, consciousness.[12]

In early March 1959 these and other strains mounted to the point where Philip abruptly exited Newport—his job, his friend, and the scenery—for

San Francisco with its different scenery, different friends, and no job. It is unlikely he ever saw Ben Richard Anderson or Virginia again. She died a year later in 1960, at the age of forty-nine, a fact that Philip, perhaps not knowing of it before, only entered in his journal four months after it happened. Then in early May 1961, Dick Anderson and a new plane he'd bought went missing; Philip worried about this to Gary Snyder in a letter, passing along the little information he had. The wreckage was found two weeks later.

The third name Philip mentioned when asked about his army days was Paul Fetzer. Paul had been a friend from The Dalles; Philip had known him in high school as his only contemporary with an interest in writing. Paul moved away to Portland with his family, and when Philip landed there a couple of years later, they rekindled their friendship, as well as their encouragement of one another's writing. During the war, Paul served in the European theater, and he and Philip stayed in touch through letters. But in 1944, Paul Fetzer did something significant: he arranged for his mother to send Philip a copy of Gertrude Stein's *Narrations,* which, Philip said, "really wigged me out."[13] In an essay about his education, he continued this thought: "Reading the book gave me great encouragement and pleasure. I read as many of her books as I could find. I wanted style, I wanted a theory of writing, I wanted to be able to explain, to whoever asked me, how come I should be a writer and why writing was important to me."[14] Philip eventually wore out his need for—even his respect for—theory, but not for Gertrude Stein or for Paul Fetzer. The teenage discussions with Paul, capped by Miss Stein's provocations, led Philip to understand eventually that writing occupied a cross-wired but undeniably powerful place in his psyche. "I was having trouble interpreting my religious feelings—if that's what they were; perhaps they were only some kind of Druid backlash from all my antique Irish genes, I don't know. I thought of myself as 'modern' agnostic rationalist. . . . On the other hand, music and poetry and pictures and novels could move me profoundly. I would experience exaltations, 'highs,' and strange knowledges which seemed to correspond with what I had read about in the *Upanishads,* and the *Bhagavad Gita.*"[15]

Philip received his honorable discharge on 23 February 1946 and opted not to live with his father in Portland's wet, gloomy weather. He traveled instead to Escondido, where he stayed with Stanworth Beckler, basking in music and the warmth and sun of suburban San Diego for the month of March. May found him back in Portland, living apart from his father and running out of money. At the end of his service days, he'd written to friends about hopes of attending one or another of the East Coast schools, but by this point he'd narrowed his scope to the West Coast—"Berkeley or U Washington." Finally, in mid-June, he resigned himself to attending Reed College in Portland; he was able to pay for it because of the foresightful GI Bill. At nearly twenty-three, he was five to six years older than the normal freshman. Consoling himself that at least Paul Fetzer and Ben Anderson would be going to Reed too, he entered school in the autumn.

NINE

Reed's Fine College

1946–1951

The Willamette River runs pretty much south to north through Portland and divides the city in half; city planners and cartographers divided it further, into quarters. The summer of 1946 saw Philip living alone in an inexpensive garret in northwest Portland, about fifteen minutes walk from his father's place but quite far—two hours on foot—from Reed in the southeast. The distance didn't matter much until school started, and then it became a problem or a factor in the problem. Location didn't matter because Philip was trying, in an unbalanced way, to write a novel—the "GAN" (for Great American Novel), as he called it in correspondence with Beckler. He was quickly running out of any money he had left from army pay, and he was getting strange. "I would sit home and write and I really found that it was true what Thomas Wolfe said, that if you get going, if you write all day, like nine hours a day, when you stop it still goes on in your head, you hear all these voices and you hear your own voice describing scenes and it becomes horrendously obsessive, you really do go dotty at times. It was very interesting to do it, and I ended up with 150 pages of something that looked more promising than anything I had done in the prose line before."[1]

When school started up, Philip found that excepting a sculpture workshop and a theater class, he neither liked nor respected most of his academic assignments. The distance from his room to campus contributed to his resistance, as did his poverty. "I would get the GI check [$65 at first, then $75] and I would spend the money on books and then I would have nothing to live on. So a lot of the time I was staying at home, because I didn't have carfare."[2] As a plan for getting through college, Philip's was ill conceived and unhelpful in the extreme. When he did make it to Reed, he would most often be found in the coffee shop, talking. He did poorly in his classes, and if he hadn't depended on the GI Bill money, it's unlikely he'd have had the perseverance to graduate. Against this, Philip had his few army friends, and he also appears to have been simply pulled forward by several salubrious encounters. In order, these were with the Vedanta Society, which led him to meditation; with his faculty advisor at Reed, Professor Lloyd Reynolds; and with new friends, most especially Gary Snyder and Lew Welch.

Though he claimed to have come across the Vedanta Society entirely by accident, Philip had been worrying "what to do about religion" since his mother died. He first tried her Christian Science, but found the sect's mixture of scripture and faith healing theologically vague. Worse, Mary Baker Eddy's prose struck him as "mewly."[3] In a poem to his mother, Philip compared the structure of Christian Science beliefs to Yeats's "bent gyres and cones and pulleys and belts and geary numbers," saying that both were "unnecessarily complicated." He saw (movingly) how her faith had sustained *her*, and how she'd been able "to make it iron all our clothing, cook our meals, provide us with total security and love," but—and he apologizes for it in the poem—he rejected her form of worship. He did not reject her example, though, or the heart of Christian Science, which he understood to be "God is love." Contemplating "love" would move him later by degrees toward the classical Buddhist virtue of compassion, as he suspects in the poem. "I guess it doesn't matter so much what it all means, the thing is more like how do I treat other people, how do I use myself?"[4]

To make his religious investigations practical, Philip had begun—first in The Dalles and then in Portland—"visiting various churches of friends of mine. I thought it very interesting, but when I found out about Oriental religions, they seemed to make much more sense than the Christian stuff. But I kept wavering for several years." Finally Philip saw that he was "temperamentally incapable of believing in many of the things you're supposed to believe to be a Christian,"[5] and later he came to attack organized Christianity's methods of subjugating its followers.

The Vedanta Society in Portland had "their own captive Swami who had been ordered from India,"[6] as Philip put it, and he wrote that he'd "returned to the fold, namely sitting at the feet of the Swami Devatmananda at the temple here. . . . Swami Devatmananda represents the Ramakrishna Mission here, just like Prabhavananda did in Hollywood. . . . The swami is a wise, cultivated gentleman with a sense of humor and considerable understanding. We get on excellently."[7]

Philip was well aware of the literary crowd associated with the Vedanta Society in Los Angeles, which included Christopher Isherwood, Aldous Huxley, Gerald Heard, and Krishnamurti, among others. If Philip hoped for a similar society in Portland, he must have been disappointed. Instead of young, smart Englishmen, he found a group of old American ladies who were "into the mysteries of the antique Orient." He complained how "they would play the piano and sing 'In a Monastery Garden,' which is a terrible old song." Despite this, Philip ventured far enough in to visit the society's rural retreat, but when he realized that regular participation and membership would require dues, he dropped away. He had, however, begun to meditate in the way of the yoga system. "There were times when I discovered that something really does happen to your head when you try to do it. You change, somehow. Your attitudes change."[8] The similarity between this description of the effects of meditation and his report about the effects of excessive novel writing bears noting. The 150 pages of novel he later burned; his attention to the potent and malleable nature of his own mind stayed with him.

LLOYD

Whenever Philip spoke about his time at Reed, he gave a variant of the same praise:

> My adviser is a professor of literature, etc, name of Lloyd Reynolds—a political liberal, a printer, woodcut-maker, book illustrator, and a good Joe. We soak up coffee and Gertrude Stein by the gallon, and talk over everything and everybody.

> The really great thing that happened to me at Reed was meeting Lloyd Reynolds.

> The greatest teacher I ever had died a couple years ago. He was called Lloyd Reynolds, and he taught at Reed College.[9]

Philip went on to give the Naropa class a succinct account of Lloyd's work: "Mainly he was a calligrapher; he taught different kinds of pen calligraphy, manuscript writing. He also was good at teaching graphic arts in general, but then earlier, before he got the graphics arts going, he taught regular courses in the humanities. I worked with him doing 18th century writers and doing a creative writing class." Philip then told them what anyone who studied with Reynolds for any stretch would say: "Although he had these subjects and could teach them, and could organize the material and put it across very well, what he was really good at was teaching enthusiasm. He taught people to be interested and excited about the subject he was trying to lay on them."

Another student echoed this, pointing to a more primary effect: "Whatever he was teaching, he was giving you the feeling that it was important, and wonderful that it existed; and that the world existed. And that *you* existed and were wonderful."[10] When he described enthusiasm, Reynolds harked back to the original root—*en* + *theos*—to be inspired by or possessed by a god. An infusion of enthusiasm would have been very welcome to young men and women stunned by the century's second world war and looking to make sense of their future.

Born in Minnesota, Lloyd Reynolds came with his family to eastern Washington State as an infant and, when he was twelve, moved with them to Portland. He thus grew up affected by the natural environment of the Pacific Northwest; his first university degree was in botany and forestry. After college, he worked not in the woods but in a studio, doing commercial lettering. Intellectually restless, possessed of a nearly insatiable thirst for engaging ideas with others, Reynolds then changed course, going back to school for graduate work in literature and beginning to teach high-school English to support it. With his master's degree, he came on the Reed faculty in 1929.

Lloyd was not a large man, and he was often still, engaged in fine movement, but his body bristled with energy. As if he were himself one of the black letters he inked onto white paper, he looked edged: bold, black glasses; hair groomed carefully back; beard trimmed into angles. He understood space and counterspace, and he stood out. Favoring aphorisms in conversation or lecture, he spoke excitedly, volubly, generously. He wrote visually beautiful letters, lines, paragraphs, and pages, a result of constant observation and daily, critical practice. He read deeply and widely, and he covered his books in marginalia. These discussions with the authors must have helped keep their notions available to him. "He had all this information right HERE,"[11] one of his students recalled, moving her hands and fingers around her hair to show circulation. He made the ideas, regardless of their century, sound fresh and applicable.

Reynolds's most direct impact came from his indefatigable promotion of italic handwriting and calligraphy. Even in the present digital period, when the very act of handwriting is in steep decline, his influence survives: giving a commencement address at Stanford, a person no less consequential than

FIGURE 12. Lloyd Reynolds
outside the Reed College
calligraphy studio, 1969,
photograph by Jim Stewart.
Courtesy of Rick Levine.

Steve Jobs pointed to the presence and power of calligraphy at Reed during his own time there, recounting how he included it in his vision for Macintosh computers.[12]

Important as it was, calligraphy was only part of what Lloyd Reynolds presented. To borrow an analogy from his forestry days, calligraphy could be compared to an eye-catching mushroom, the aboveground signal of a huge, underground, mycorrhizal network, invisible to the eye but a streaming connector of forest life. The network from which Reynolds's calligraphy arose included the poetry, paintings, and prints of William Blake; the clear-eyed essays, anti-industrialist stance, and refined aesthetics of John Ruskin; the invention and sheer cultural force of William Morris. The Arts and Crafts movement spawned by Morris comprised book-arts specialist Edward

Johnston and the Asian art interpreter Ananda Coomaraswamy. Particularly Johnston's classic *Writing, Illuminating, and Lettering* sent Reynolds on a lifelong study of the Roman alphabet, "pen in hand." But all the above were acknowledged lineal ancestors for him. To study calligraphy with Reynolds was to be steeped in their vision—and their practicality, for they were nearly all "makers," as well as thinkers. To map, however briefly, these central influences on Lloyd Reynolds is necessary because he not only absorbed them, he impressed them with great energy on his students. Love of nature, sharp critique of industrial materialism, admiration for eighteenth-century literature, an exhortation to make and do—such lines of thought from Lloyd appear in Philip's work with near-genetic clarity.

Philip's degree thesis, for example, completed for Lloyd, was called *Calendar*. The complex series of poems shows great learning and mental suppleness, as a Reed senior thesis must. It is dense with an impressive range of allusion and—typical of Philip—leavened with bawdy old songs and slang. The Arts and Crafts heritage shows itself in that Philip printed three of the poems himself as broadsides, using an old letterpress Reynolds had salvaged and installed in his top-floor workshop. Philip struck the type and pulled the sheets, then carved and printed linoleum block decorations as well, for an edition of thirteen.

To imply cultural patrilineage to Lloyd Reynolds would be to place Philip in a considerable group who held Lloyd as surrogate or second father. Reynolds didn't discourage this; he took parental interest and pride in his students' lives, both at college and beyond it. In a real sense, at Reed Philip replaced his family. Certainly by the time he was living in the Lambert Street house, he'd created brothers of Gary Snyder and Lew Welch; he made aunts and uncles of other housemates, upon whose hospitality he continued to depend for the next twenty years. He also found a literate, political, artistic, "enthusiastic" father in Lloyd Reynolds.

Even a student as undisciplined as Philip, whose distraction and poor attendance required him to stay at Reed an extra year, did not discourage Lloyd. There is no record of a break, or even of harsh criticism from Lloyd— Philip aimed that at himself. When Philip passed the necessary exams to be admitted to his senior year but was denied registration because of his poor record, he tried many things. "I pulled wires and I chanted spells, and did dances where you appease the gods," but he remained out for the academic year 1949–50. His reinstatement "depended almost entirely upon Lloyd Reynolds and Marianne Gold [his sculpture teacher], who believed in me."[13]

Being out of school meant no GI Bill money for Philip, which meant no money at all. Thus broke, flunked out, and stalled in the novel he kept trying to write, Philip needed help. It came in the person of Roy Stilwell, an army friend—as well as a violinist in the Portland Symphony—who simply moved Philip into the 1414 Lambert Street house. Descriptions of that place usually say Philip and Roy were roommates. The nearer truth Philip tells is that "Roy let me live in part of his room."[14]

In the summer of 1954, at the height of the McCarthy era, the House Un-American Activities Committee sent a committee to Portland. Some allege the Velde Committee came specifically to target Reed; in any case, they called before them Reed professors and college administrators in their search for Communists. Like many in these years, Lloyd refused to give the committee what they wanted: he invoked his constitutional rights and remained silent. For simply not answering, he was suspended from all teaching by Reed's president, Duncan Ballantine, and the college trustees. He was not fired, as was Professor Stanley Moore (also an important teacher for Philip), but Lloyd was cut off from his students, his workshop, and his livelihood.

At the time of the hearings, Philip was migrating from Los Angeles, where he'd been staying with the Thompsons, to Seattle, where he would be staying with the Matsons, before heading to fire lookout work in the Skagit. He kept abreast of the humiliations the Velde Committee inflicted on Reedites (as they were then called) mostly through correspondence with Gary Snyder, who had been tarred by other bristles on that wide brush. (Unable to get Forest Service work because of being blacklisted, Gary watched the televised hearings with pointed interest.)[15] Lew Welch was also accused of being a Communist, though he was at that point living in Chicago, married, with a house, a mortgage, and a car, commuting daily through traffic to his nine-to-five job at an advertising agency. Philip's preference for laying low, often physically, kept him from notice, but he wrote to Gary how he and the Matsons "are worrying about you, and Lloyd, figuring you have some chance, but that everybody should get on their horses and do something about Lloyd. Fortunately everyone is properly exercised about that."[16] Lloyd's suspension caused internal politics at Reed to boil up: the conservative trustees on one front, who didn't want the college harboring Communists; an assertive, eloquent faculty on another front; and an agitated student council on yet a third front collided to force President Ballantine's resignation. By the autumn, Lloyd was back teaching.

In the correspondence that grew up between them after Philip graduated are many letters from Lloyd asking after Philip's work. These range from simple inquiry—"You [two][17] written any good books lately?"—to gratitude: "What a wealth of writing, you are most generous," to praise, "You have the ability to hit the mark! . . . this is one of your best poems," to perspicacity, "Your beautiful books arrived today. I read right through both of them w/great delight and have started rereading. . . . I like the way you *seem* to go maundering along, disorganized & discontinuous as ordinary haphazard experience & then WHAMMO—you clobber the reader with an insight that makes a poem out of it. Yes!"[18] Whatever mixed feelings Philip had about his work— and he expressed these openly to Lloyd—he sent every book, broadside, announcement, and pamphlet to his teacher, as well as pointers to poems published in journals.

Post from Lloyd Reynolds could intimidate; the letters and even the postcards are surpassingly beautiful, written in his italic hand, sometimes decorated with a monogram or calligraphic border, small design exercises. Nor did Lloyd's formal elegance impede personal expression: his pages contain crossings out, underlining, and exuberant punctuation, all signs of a mind at work in the hand, at speed. Philip's script, on the other hand, and his calligraphic doodling bear strong traces of study with Lloyd, yet they meander from any norm. Philip's writing was gracefully personal, quirky, sometimes spiky, communicative; it unmistakably revealed its author and his moods. McClure especially urged Philip to publish his poems in original handwriting, and this came to pass a number of times. It is one thing to have friends admire your handwriting; it is quite another to send it off—perhaps written in exhaustion or hurry—to the master who taught you writing. Proud of being a calligrapher but ashamed of his calligraphy, Philip apologized to Lloyd for his own "crumby" writing about once a decade. In a 1963 New Year's letter, Philip wrestled the issue to the mat, taking both sides of the match. "O Lloyd. Why don't I write slowly?" he fairly wails, at the bottom of a chaotic first page. He then answers himself: "Because I am silly & nervous & have a great deal to tell." Soon he's replying to a query from Lloyd—if "pushing letters around" helped him loosen up for poetry—"Yes, I sometimes doodle before I begin to write, & sometimes it develops into a poem or not ... or into stray lines which I save & put into a poem later ... poem which arrives & has blank spaces in it where this matter fits."[19] Lloyd's question and Philip's answer both point to the old conflation of the two arts. Philip then worries the issue of the source of his poetry before abruptly breaking off, "I'm sorry I write so poorly. I may grow better writing by growing more patience, by spending more time at it." Against this humility he immediately objects, "NOT NECESSARILY, however." If it has been vague whether Philip meant by "writing" handwriting or poetic composition—he'd studied both with Lloyd—he then limits the topic to calligraphy. "I really am sorry, having had your best instruction, that I don't write Cancellaria better." That is, even if he can't imitate it very well, Philip shows his old teacher that he at least remembers the name of one of the Renaissance palaces where the script developed. Then, as if standing up and dusting himself off after knocking himself down, Philip concludes the discussion and the letter, "Screw it. I guess it can be read ... When I write a letter it's because I want to TALK to the addressee ... Love to you."

As Lloyd approached retirement after forty years of teaching, the question of a Festschrift for him arose. That the thought of it occurred to Philip—"It had to be done"—is not surprising; that he took it upon himself to organize and do it, is. "I began," he wrote in the preface, "characteristically by worrying about the project for several years." He uncharacteristically enlisted practical assistance, involved the college, and struck a large committee to solicit funds and oversee production. He also got Lloyd's approval during a short visit to Reed for a reading in 1965 (at which Lloyd introduced him to the large audience). Philip composed a fundraising announcement of the project and sent it to the alumni administrator, saying, "I'm sorry to have taken so much time in composing these letters, but I am very giddy & naturally lazy & monumentally slow. But I did enjoy our talk and really believe that I can do this job without going to pieces."[20] The resultant book, twelve inches square and one hundred pages long, contains many beautiful calligraphs—all the great scribes of the day sent something—musical scores, poems, photographs, and essays. Philip was doing "a hundred other things" in late 1965: preparing to go to Japan for the first time; typing and revising *The Diamond Noodle;* readying his first novel, *You Didn't Even Try,* for publication; being filmed for National Educational Television's series on poetry; corresponding patiently but painfully about a manuscript a publisher (and friend) intended to bring out; writing a good deal of new poetry; and grieving, on some level, the recent death of his biological father. That he found the

FIGURE 13. Philip with Lloyd Reynolds at his home, 1963. Photo © Allen Ginsberg.

time and energy and attention to spearhead the Festschrift for Lloyd shows the depth of his gratitude.

On a road trip through Portland,[21] Allen Ginsberg once snapped several pictures of Philip and Lloyd together: both look extremely pleased. In the shots, Philip is turned to Lloyd, attentive to whatever Lloyd is expressing; Lloyd is expressing at least part of it by simply beaming. The years, the miles, and declining health moved their communication steadily in this direction. Tobacco figured heavily into the Reynolds mix, cigarettes and a continuously present pipe. His breathing was often audible; he sometimes panted. Remarkably, many of Philip's letters to Lloyd begin or end with wishes for a speedy recovery. Between the ambitious workload Lloyd always took on—he said once he had so much on his shoulders it bowed his legs—and his smoking, Lloyd was down a lot. Philip's last letter to him, in May 1977, congratulates him on release from the hospital, "the harpies & vampires w/their well-intentioned knives & needles." When Lloyd died the following year of respiratory failure, Philip traveled up from Zen Center and is listed among the speakers, together with Lloyd's widow, Judith, the poet Mary Barnard, and Reed's president, Paul Bragdon, at a memorial.[22]

But Philip's connection to Lloyd no more depended on his physical body than Lloyd's own philosophy had depended upon shaking inky hands with Edward Johnston or walking with John Ruskin. Lloyd had recognized the *theos,* the god, in Philip (as in so many others). He'd cleared around it, protected it in storms, and taught Philip how to develop it. Philip understood what he'd gotten and tried his best to pass it on.

> When he taught the poems of Blake, he made you feel that Blake was very important and exciting and you should drop everything and go read every word that Blake ever wrote, and think about it, and look at all the pictures he drew and all the paintings he made, all the letters he wrote and whatever else you could find out about him. And read all the several biographies and other paraphernalia. And you'd really feel good about all that, and you'd go read.
>
> Well, I think that's what teaching is about, is to *move* students; to move them into educating themselves. Because I can't educate you. I can't teach poetry to you, or anything else. But I'd hope to god to prod you into looking at stuff and working on your own material, and to build up your confidence to work, to learn, and to keep working.[23]

LEW

Philip met Lew Welch in late 1948 by getting up on the seat of a booth in the Reed College coffee shop and looking over into the next booth to see who was talking so loudly, who it was saying things like "red glass birds" and "thin brass dome." Lew Welch sat there. He'd been singing a country tune to friends about a murderer attacking his victim's "thin breast bone." Philip, liking what he'd heard better, told Lew he ought to get that good line into a poem. It fits that Lew—for whom language spoken and sung was the explicit basis of his poetry—and Philip, whose poetry often built in "found" language fragments, especially misheard ones, should commence their friendship this way. It evolved into a fraternity dear to them both, and it stayed grounded in mutual encouragement to poetry.

Both men were redheads, but Lew was wiry, with a runner's build. For a list of reasons he elaborated in essays, lectures, and interviews, Lew felt himself domestically damaged early on and responded by turning to alcoholic drink and away from food. He'd ruined his liver this way by his mid-thirties, and though he managed periods of abstinence, he continued to fall into drinking binges until his disappearance at the age of forty-four. "All I know is I am wiped out every six months or so. I die. I have died hundreds and hundreds of times. It is always the same death. I do not know what dies. Why must I always begin again and again—always with the same high hopes, the identical death?"[24]

Philip and Lew lived together several times: for Philip's last two years at Reed, in the Lambert Street house; at the East-West House in San Francisco in the late 1950s;[25] and again briefly in what Philip termed his "Beaver Street period," in the early 1960s. In Welch's unfinished novel, *I Leo*—a barely disguised account of his college years[26]—he portrays Philip in his early college days. Welch called him

> Roger MacLeod, portly poet laureate of the school. There was nothing official about the title, it was simply obvious that he was by far the best writer. Roger lived in an ugly little room 'way down town. There was a hot plate to cook on & many, many books.
>
> Once Leo went to see him and found him lying in darkness in the middle of beautiful Portland summer on a bed covered only with damp, nearly brown, bachelor sheets. Naked, Roger rose. He explained with great forbearance and all his innate elegance: he didn't feel well, had no money, hadn't eaten in perhaps three days, was writing a novel "but it's all talking about money, so I've stopped."
>
> Roger was frequently peevish, but Leo only visited him when his own torments were so great there could be no question of welcome. Then Roger listened sagely, making a pot of tea, while Leo roared away. Sometimes Ben Edwards came by with a can of beans or chili.... When he showed up with these simple cans of food, Leo ... would realize how desperately poor Roger really was.[27]

Lew was vain, in a light, self-effacing way. In letters and published works, he reported on his beauty—its effects (or lack of them) on women and especially his hair and haircuts. He touched these topics with Kerouac, Snyder, and Ginsberg, but he mostly spared Philip such observations, perhaps sensing they would be uninteresting, even painful. He did report to Philip his regular symptoms of sickness from drink and his manifestations of health during dry periods. A near-fatal accidental poisoning also gets a long account.

As poets, Philip and Lew developed their work separately and in different directions, though keeping in close touch about it. Philip hoped that Lew's dissertation at Reed, a work on Gertrude Stein, would eventually be edited and published, noting that it was a clear, original consideration of her work and pointing out that Dr. W. C. Williams had said the same thing to Lew.[28]

Philip and Lew invented a literary game one college afternoon, trying to make a point about poetry to a young woman Lew had brought to Philip's garret room, one Kate Ware. The discussion hinged on vocabulary. They were not yet worried about forbidden words—the fight with censors would come later—but rather about the range and scope of vocabulary available to poets:

> Kate had the idea that there are certain words that were absolutely intractable—you just can't use them in any way, especially not in poetry. . . . Lewie and I started screaming and saying no, no, you use the entire resources of the English language and several other ones and if that won't do you invent some. And Kate said no you can't do that. . . . I said, well we have to show you that we can. So we picked five words out of the dictionary and we said OK, we're going to be poets and let's use all these words in a poem. We'll sit down right now and make poems of the them. . . . Gradually we decided we should have a club and it would be the Adelaide Crapsey–Oswald Spengler Mutual Admiration Society.[29]

Welch's recollection, when he gave it in a talk at Reed twenty-two years after the event, was more specific. He chalked the words they'd used that first time on a blackboard: *flamen, liripipionated, bema, geode,* and *propolis.* Lew admitted that because all three were so widely read, they had trouble finding words none of them knew, and so relaxed the rules to allow *geode* and *propolis.*

> We had 15 minutes to make up a poem using all those words, and Whalen comes up with:

> > Sated flamen
> > Liripipionated
> > Paces, chanting in the bema
> > While demented hillside bees
> > Pack geodes w/propolis and honey
> > Sweet rock eggs
> > Tribute to no walking god.

> Isn't that incredible? Wow. Boy that guy really has it. That Whalen is so good you just can't believe it.[30]

The society continued to meet for a while (under a variety of names) in groups ranging from two or three people to as many as ten, sometimes taking words from literature, sometimes from the dictionary. Philip collected the poems each time and later gave the folder to Reed's library; it contains a poem by W. C. Williams, who, during his 1950 visit to campus, accepted the challenge, joined the society, and composed it.

Beyond conviviality and wit sharpening, the society led to Lew and Philip's first public poetry reading. Feeling himself "absolutely cuckoo"—a not-uncommon state for Philip, or for college students generally—Philip decided to flee Reed. For that, he needed funds. Lew, Philip, and the violinist Roy Stilwell secured permission to use one of the social rooms—one with a piano—and mounted a fundraising afternoon of music and poetry featuring the poems of the society. "I thought I was going to pay my back rent and go to San Francisco and never come back," Philip recounted. "Of course the money all got spent on food and books, and so everybody said, 'Are you still here?' which was a little bit embarrassing for a few weeks."[31]

Dr. Williams had come to Reed at the invitation of Professor Reynolds; this short residence took place long before the era of regular college reading tours for poets, and Philip speculated Lloyd must have "wrangled" money from the college. They hosted Williams and his wife, Flossie, in the relatively grand Portland Hotel, which Williams commented on in a remark that struck Philip as only half-joking: "After all, that's what we live for—splendor! Extravagance!"[32] Another Williams pearl that impressed Philip was the advice to "never throw anything away. Put it in a shoebox for later." That he was able to hear any of Williams's ideas at all came from Philip's having been invited, together with Lew and others, to a reception at Professor Reynolds's house. The young men were still near the beginning of their literary education, but they certainly knew enough to appreciate Williams as a distinct, fierce voice in American poetics, and they'd read him sufficiently (also in a course from Lloyd) to admire the work. When Williams reciprocated— when he spoke to them seriously as poets and listened to them; when he took, read, marked up, and returned their writing, it gave them an enormous lift. More important by far than the few suggestions Williams scrawled on Philip's poems was simply the fact of Williams having taken the time. Whenever he spoke of it—Philip recounted the story in at least two classes at Naropa, as well as in the Zen Center Buddha Hall—he emphasized the sense of confirmation he'd gotten, as if one of the gods had embraced him and pulled him bodily into the rank of poets. For his part, Williams wrote of the Reed visit that he'd met and taught "good kids, all of them, doing solid work,"[33] singling out Welch's thesis on Stein for individual mention.

In 1971, Lew disappeared into the woods near Gary Snyder's house in the Sierra Nevada, taking a pistol and leaving at least two suicide notes—one, handwritten in the pages of his journal, left behind in his van; the second, a beautiful poem called "Song of the Turkey Buzzard," published earlier. Like Philip and Gary, Lew was a good hiker, at ease spending days or weeks alone in wilderness. Many neighbors and friends—some of them highly skilled woodsmen, including Gary himself—immediately mounted search parties, but nothing of Lew was ever found.

Philip heard the story of Lew's disappearance, the note, and the search parties more than a week after it happened, first in a letter from Allen Ginsberg and then in a sad note from Gary saying it appeared "our Lewy has killed himself."[34] Living alone in Japan and nearing the end of his time there, Philip took the news hard. He devoted a long passage in his journal to feelings about it, and these eleven numbered entries are decidedly mixed; they run from anger at Lew, to worries about his motivation, to understanding and acceptance, to questions about the technical aspects of using a pistol, to wondering if he, Philip—also depressed and cynical, also feeling himself a prospectless failure—could commit suicide, and deciding that he could not. Confusingly, Philip then received newspaper clippings from a friend that reported how Lew had been seen in a bank in Nevada City not far from Gary's place. Gary himself wrote to speculate that Lew was only off drinking somewhere. Philip was not much assuaged, writing to Allen, "If he wants to kill himself by drinking instead of by shooting, I can't blame him. I certainly couldn't do it. But I wish we could help him to live & not want to sap himself headlong into boring grave & tedious tomb &c. I don't mind being dead but I can't stand the taste of embalming fluid."[35]

Many more letters survive from Lew to Philip than in the other direction. They begin shortly after Reed and continue for twenty years, until Lew's suicide note, which was as much to Philip as to anyone. They often sent poems back and forth, together with generous support for one another's work, though this included criticism. Lew wrote once of a title Philip proposed, "Don't you think that goes too far? I find myself wincing, as you did when I announced the title to my Reno story." Philip was infallibly gentle with Lew, knowing him to be self-critical to the point of debilitation. Lew would "carry a poem around in his head" for a long time, Philip told a class. "He would say, 'Hey I got a new poem, want to hear it?'" "Sure," Philip would tell him, and then after, "That's great, Lewie, you ought to write that down." "Aw, I dunno." The same "Aw, I dunno" would repeat itself with the typing up of a poem, the collecting, arranging, and eventual publishing of the poem. With his forceful and charming speech, Lew was not too shy to perform his works—he regarded the written versions to be like musical scores—but even after he'd had something come out in a magazine or broadside to general acclaim, he'd slough it off with, "Aw, it's no good."[36] Lew told Don Allen how "Whalen used to say, 'There you go Welch, flaying yourself again.'"[37]

One tires, in reading Welch's letters, of his fondness for the Pronouncement, the Discovery, the Proclamation, when invariably a few letters later, his views, plans, domestic or romantic situations have shifted, often dramatically. What did not shift was his view of Philip as the best poet of his time. Beginning with the imaginary "Poet Laureate" of Reed, Lew wrote in letter after letter how Philip's work was the best in whatever journal was newest—*Evergreen* or *Chicago Review,* for example. Lew wrote this kind of praise to other people—"He will always be the master to me, having a perfect sense of what our generation, and the other, is about"[38]—and he wrote it directly to Philip: "I still think you're the best poet of them all. You have the curious ability to make one think that a mind has been slowed down, or speeded up, until perception is going at the exact pace of things."[39] From time to time, Lew asked Philip explicitly for help, sending him a batch of poems together with a list of questions: "Is the ending as bad as I think it is? Does number 2 work?"[40]

Though less wont to gush in print, Philip also held Lew and his work in highest regard. One proof is his inclusion of Welch in a trio—together with Hart Crane and Wallace Stevens—as subjects of a thirteen-class course at Naropa. He gave no reason for this grouping but noted in the talks various similarities—how all three wrestled with the best diction for their thoughts, how they worked all their lives toward a fitting form on the page, how all three drank heavily (though Stevens did so in a contained way), how they were all three part of a more-or-less unconscious lineage of American poetry. Very likely Philip chose the three poets simply to broaden his students' minds: in 1980—only nine years after his disappearance—even Lew's recent body of work seemed to have fallen from the students' view.

Lew and Philip are often grouped with Gary Snyder as the Northwest branch of the Beats or of the San Francisco Renaissance. Lew's and Philip's works read differently, but their literary education, the music they listened to, paintings they looked at, contemporaries with whom they bantered—these were very similar. Like Gary, Lew and Philip took up Buddhist meditation early on, and aspects of the cultures that had nurtured it—wisdom traditions in India, China, and Japan—flowed into their minds as welcome enrichment. With varying degrees of formality, they came to regard themselves as Buddhists. For a period in 1956, after Gary had gone to Japan, Lew captained the Marin-an zendo/shack in Mill Valley. When neither Albert Saijo nor Philip could be there, Lew would open up, light the shrine, and lead meditation for those who came to practice. More than once he kept the rounds of sitting and walking meditation alone. During these days, Lew's engagement with Zen was, as Philip's was, physical and practical.

Lew stated as clearly (and passionately) as anyone that the job of a poet was to express mind: "We want the exact transmission of Mind."[41] He frequently capitalized the word, emphasizing that he, like Philip, understood mind to be very large indeed, transcending personality or possession. Lew's relationship to it was darker than Philip's.[42] The depressant effect of long-term drinking surely played a role, but even in drier times, Lew appeared to regard his mind as something suspect—to be explained, to be analyzed psychiatrically for problems, to be fixed; or if that were not possible, his mind was at least to be taken alone on a weeks-long trail for fresh air, or for a hermit spell in a cabin in the woods, or for numbing work in a boat on the sea. While he continued to deify Mind and to rail about the necessity of expressing it, Lew's own thoughts obviously tormented him. Philip understood this about his friend and rued it but seemed no more able than any of the many other people who loved Lew Welch—everybody loved Lewie—to effect relief. What Philip did do, in life and beyond, was to offer his companionship and his conversation. Betimes in teaching his work, Philip would break off and address him directly: "Don't listen, now, Lewie, in heaven or wherever you are, but *I* think that this is the poem right here" or "Well, what do you expect if you walk off into the woods alone with a gun?"[43]

Lew, Philip, and Gary were all profoundly unhappy with the military-religio-materialist thinking that ran America in the early part of their lives, though they complained about it differently. Gary seemed able to get work, keep it, and make ends meet; perhaps because he could literally afford to, Gary took a longer view of the problems, describing them in anthropologic, ecologic, and even geologic terms. Not so Lew and Philip: possessed by want, their critiques sounded shriller and were more focused on the near term. In

"Mozart's Watch," a trenchant essay Lew wrote for the *San Francisco Chronicle* to advertise a reading all three would give together, he laid out what he called "the basic con" leading to the nonpayment of artists. To promote this same reading, the three poets also recorded a conversation for KPFA radio, in which they inveighed lustily, variously, and intelligently against the contemporary lack of support for poets. In so doing, they also delineated the role(s) of a poet.

A crucial step for Philip and Lew[44] had been to admit—to themselves first—that they *were* poets, that it was a job: "carpenter" was their favorite comparison. Beyond that, they had individual purposes. Philip proclaimed that poetry produced delight, relief, intoxication (in the sense of a high), and that was enough. In the panel discussion, Lew only sketched his ideas of the poet's role: to express national grief, for example; or to "advise the Prince." But the question interested him. He came back to it repeatedly in essays and talks, taking a rather windswept, heroic stance and speaking of the "tribe," its "din," and how the poet's job was to imbibe that fully and using native words to express Mind with great exactness. Any shortcut or fakery—posing as a poet—came under his harsh criticism. "Unless you mean . . . to use this speech, your own speech, the language of your mother & father and your friends, the primary tool of all your actions toward all your wants & needs, to use this speech as a weapon, tool, a singer's voice, the means to total sharing of all your only Mind, unless you mean to do that, then to try to be a poet is a blasphemy."[45]

Philip, after flirting with it for years, finally had the role and title of "teacher" thrust upon him by his Zen teacher, Richard Baker. Lew daringly claimed it. The final two of five books assembled from his decades of writing show Lew taking a more didactic tone. One of his literary personae—the Red Monk—here proposes riddles and asserts that each has only one correct answer. Lew also offers a series of "Courses"—who but a teacher could offer courses? These pithy takes on standard university listings mean to puncture the academy's inflated sense of worth with humor and at the same time summarize each discipline's central questions. For example:

> THEOLOGY
> Guard the Mysteries!
> Constantly reveal them!

If not everyone regarded Lew Welch as a teacher—a wisdom holder of sorts—Philip Whalen did. During a public talk at Zen Center in the late 1970s, Philip came into the Buddha Hall, performed his bows before the shrine, seated himself, and began to speak about the Four Unlimited States of Mind. He ran through the standard definitions in about fifteen minutes, pointing out that really what counted was whether you could put them into practice. Lectures usually run forty minutes to an hour. Suddenly Philip announced, "I'm going to tell you what I really want to talk about: Lewie. Lewis Barrett Welch. He was my friend." Philip then gave a close account of Lew's background and their friendship. He discussed Lew's disappearance in 1971—"Lewie, you shouldn't have done that"—and speculated that perhaps Lew was off in Florida somewhere selling insurance and would turn up . . . but that more probably he was dead. He concluded the talk by carefully, and with great feeling, reading Welch's "Song of the Turkey Buzzard," which can be seen as his suicide note. As Philip read, the room was very still; many were in tears. When he finished, he said, "I thought I could read this here, in this Buddha Hall, because it is one man's truth, his Dharma, and so I felt justified in presenting it to you."

Philip's final estimation of Lew retains the lifelong admiration but reverses the precedence of poetry and poets. Lying in the Zen Center Hospice, Philip remarked to his close friend Dr. Richard Levine (also part of his healthcare team) that he thought, of his contemporaries, Lew's work would endure the longest.

"For all the good it'll do him," countered Rick, thinking of Lew's painful struggles with drink and his disappointing end. Philip smiled sweetly—Rick had rather feared an outburst—and said, "It's not *for* him. It's for art."

TEN

Solvitur Ambulando

1959–1971

This biography started by describing five friendships. The subsequent chapters—early family life, education, military service, and college—also emerged around friendships, and it began to be clear that Philip's personal connections *were* the story. The point of the following two chapters is to carry the book to the next friendship—the one with Richard Baker—which took real root during Philip's second stay in Japan. That relationship more than anything else determined the course of Philip's last thirty-five years, and it requires a sustained look. Many of the signal events in Philip's life have already found a place in the earlier accounts of poets' sodality, but some highlights want telling. This continues as an asynchronous mixture of affection and event. Because it features a swirl of poets, painters, peaks, parks, printers, and publishers in Philip's world from, roughly, 1959 to 1971, some boldface signposts appear.

THE FIRST BOOK OR TWO; DON ALLEN

Philip had a hard time getting his first book published, not because no one was interested but because the interest came in option-blocking knots. In mid-1958, as editors moved work by Beat writers from magazines to book form, Donald Allen (*Evergreen Review,* Grove Press) solicited a manuscript from Philip. Grove still had Philip's things from *Evergreen Review,*[1] but Philip sent Don Allen a "full book of poems," though noting to Ginsberg, "I have no hopes about that at all; I've had the routine before: 'We are thinking of considering the possibility of maybe printing your things, &c, &c.'"[2]

Indeed, he heard nothing back for weeks, then months. Immediately after Philip sent his book to Grove, Leroi Jones (later Amiri Baraka) wrote, wanting a book for Totem/Corinth. Thus Philip had two offers. Then Grove complicated things, airing the possibility of a twofer book of work by Philip and Gary Snyder, and perhaps a threefer, including Ginsberg. Meredith Weatherby of Tuttle asked about a limited anthology of work from Whalen, Snyder, Ginsberg, and Kerouac, and James Laughlin of New Directions also got in touch about a small anthology. Philip told the other poets he felt Grove had a first option but added, "I guess all I can do is stall until Grove decides what they want to do? Batshit."[3]

Philip was galled by the insouciant lack of communication and the high lifestyles of New York publishers, especially contrasted with his own penury. He thought he understood why Don Allen was taking so long to respond and wrote to Ginsberg,

> He just don't want to publish my stuff & he doesn't want to say so just this moment. He can't very well publish a whole book of poems by somebody completely unknown & expect people to buy it. . . .
>
> I imagine Don is afraid he doesn't "understand" my stuff, is afraid he is being imposed upon—"they aren't *really* poems, etc . . . & public interest in Zen, 'beatniks' &c is dying out—who wants another sample, &c." I still say he don't like the poems, new, old or otherwise, for all these reasons, plus their occasional "ugliness."

All but one of the options melted away, and in October 1959—a year after first contacting him—Leroi Jones compounded with Philip to publish a book of poems. The following year, backed by the Wilentz brothers of Corinth Books, Totem brought out *Like I Say*.

While he waited, ignorant of and frustrated by New York negotiations over his manuscript—if they were taking place—Philip kept writing. Three months before settling with Leroi Jones, he decided to give a collection of his newest work to friend and printer Dave Haselwood. To help raise money for the publication, Philip took part in a benefit, Mad Monster Mammoth Poets Reading, on 29 August 1959. Artists Robert LaVigne and Bruce Connor created "great banners, floats, and decorations, for a monster procession down Grant St. to Broadway Garibaldi Hall."[4] Costumed themselves, the painters led "an immense crowd"[5] to the reading, where sufficient money was raised for Auerhahn Press to complete the printing of older projects and to begin Philip's book.[6]

"Book getting done fast," Philip wrote to Ginsberg, inscribing the letter on rejected page proofs. He lived only a ten-minute walk from Haselwood's press but reported of his frequent visits, "I feel a long way off from those poems, they don't hardly exist for me no more, a strange feeling looking at them in print. . . . I feel like I haven't yet commenced to say what I REALLY mean."[7]

Watching the beautiful pages accumulate at Auerhahn Press, Philip meanwhile sent off "a mass of revision" to Leroi Jones and wrote to Gary, "It's a funny feeling having two books gone out of the way. . . . I feel like writing lots more, & at the same time, very dissatisfied with what I've done so far."[8] This feeling—at least the second, dissatisfied half of it—never really left Philip. Still, by June 1960 he could note in his journal, "*Memoirs [of an Interglacial Age]* published on 22 March. *Like I Say* published late May. Eight poems reprinted in *The New American Poetry 1945–60*." As far as print went, Philip had arrived.

When Don Allen moved to San Francisco's Pacific Heights neighborhood in 1960, he would have Philip over for drinks, meals, and little parties he hosted. Quietly but clearly gay, Don maintained friendly relations with Philip, but he also maintained critical reserve toward Philip's writing. He would always look at it but did not shy from rejecting it for publication, or—and this stung Philip—from commenting on it. Possibly by way of retaliation, Philip observed to Allen Ginsberg, whom he could trust not to misunderstand homosexual joking, that "Don Allen has dyed his hair a fruity chestnut brown." He called him "Dong Allen" in a number of letters and then gossiped that Don was "lurking in Golden Gate Park bushes after young Negro delinquents." To be fair, Philip applied this near-libel also to himself, telling Ginsberg in a lonely moment that he too would need to go lurk in the bushes to find suitable company.

Beginning in the early 1970s, though, Don Allen did bring out a series of Philip's works: six books of poems and two books of interviews. Philip usually received a three-hundred-dollar advance and some small royalties later. Beyond warming to Philip's work, Don Allen extended practical friendship. He was unnecessarily at the airport to help pick him up from Japan when Philip flew back a second time; he bought him a "stupendous" lunch in Chinatown before driving him an hour north to Bolinas, where Philip was to live. Philip stayed in a number of houses there during the second half of 1971, sometimes renting, sometimes just staying. Finally he lived with Don Allen in a small house, an arrangement that strained them both.

"First walking trip in the Sierra . . . " This line appears under the year 1957 in a "Short Chronology" Philip wrote about himself.[9] The chronology lists the famous names, big events, miserable jobs, varying residences, awards, grants, and publications, so this one line startles: it sits there flatly neutral, seeming to give equal weight to a hike as to the Six Gallery reading, or publication of Philip's first book, or his ordination as a monk. Philip mentions only this one Sierra trek, though he went on several, keeping a separate notebook for them through the years. Change of scenery, long views, fresh air, wild-flowers, exercise—Philip's reasons for going included these. Against them, one could list the hassles and mishaps of transportation—the mountains he wanted to walk in were two hundred miles east of San Francisco, the cars his friends had were old, the expeditions were underfunded. There were vagaries of wind and weather, the lugging of provisions, thin air at altitude, the proximity of bears and rattlesnakes, the tormenting presence of mosquitos. But these privations and the reduction of activity to essential acts of creating shelter, cooking food, and putting one foot in front of another were the goal. Not anti-intellectual exactly: Philip carried some reading, usually a one-volume Shakespeare or Chaucer, and he wrote a diary; but the writing was minor in the face of miles of granite, snow, pine, and juniper.

> Here, like the summers I worked on the Skagit, I am conscious of little more than the absolute present. I feel free of the past & from myself. There is a continuous roar of water & a slight breeze, & I breathe & digest food noisily but "I" has temporarily stopped his usual noisy clamor, feelings of irritation, frustration, ambition, remorse, &c. The view of mountains, the immediate trees & water, & at night the stars—all can be looked at for any length of time & enjoyed as themselves. They require nothing—& I feel that I require noth-ing either. I've been taught that they are beautiful, so I consider them so—but for me, they are useful: they destroy "ME," & cut me loose to drift, high as a kite "high on mountains & poetry," like Snyder wrote in his book.[10]

The hikes also helped with integration, or at least aeration, of Philip's customary city-life reading, which usually included five or six books concur-rently, for hours each day. He went to the mountains partly to reverse the proportion of physical exertion to mental absorption. The journal excerpts (from a few years later, but typical) show the style of his reading, as well as some of his feelings about it.

I'm reading a translation of selected letters of Rilke. I read a translation of
SONNETS TO ORPHEUS & AMERICAN INDIAN PROSE &
POETRY & re-read the introductory materials & the first chapter of
NIGGER OF THE NARCISSUS, & re-read KING JESUS & re-read the
essays on Jarry in THE BANQUET YEARS and the first one of the
INDIAN TALES OF Jaime De Angulo and a long essay on the "lost poems"
of WCW & the poems themselves {New Directions 16} AND I continue
reading MORTE D'ARTHUR and the translation of THE LOTUS
SUTRA and re-read the "Introduction" to MAGISTER LUDI. I read
THE RIEVERS without much excitement. I re-read bits from THE
ARABIAN NIGHTS, bits of Baudelaire, Apollinaire, Mallarmé, Jarry. I
read all through this notebook—a record of silliness & self-pity & self
indulgence.

I squandered shoals of money on books. . . . My eyes hurt. I feel worried &
guilty because I've been reading & spending & eating too much instead of
writing & thinking &c &c.[11]

Philip portrayed mountain landscapes in words, and he also drew peaks
and forests into his notebooks. He told of his companions on hikes, their
doings and moods, as well as his own. He gave his notebook generous
accounts of his changing physical states—hot, chilled, dirty, bathed, winded
and faint, or exuberant and strong. As ever, he kept a close record of his mind,
both the general tenor of it—its nearly subconscious emotional colors—and
its specific if temporary contents. This attention—this *mindfulness,* to use
the relevant word—makes the mountain outings spiritual as well as physical
exercises. Confirming this, Philip would sometimes practice meditation in
the official posture as his friends fished or explored side trails. He meditated
without an object other than his breath, and also contemplated the riddles of
Zen koans throughout the day. He admonished himself to a general, perva-
sive awareness: "What I came here for was to enjoy being here. Since getting
into the mountains a week ago, I've managed to be everyplace except HERE
11/12ths of the time. PAY ATTENTION!"[12] He laments, in a style familiar
to anyone finishing a retreat, the returning encroachments of duty and city
life, and notes a "general feeling of coming down, my mind grasping, trying
to keep the mountain feeling." Understanding that time in the mountains
gave him spiritual succor, Philip felt an apparent unease about saying this too
openly. He compared himself to perhaps the greatest hiker of California's
Sierra Nevada, writing, "[John] Muir puts me in the mountains again,
although he 'spiritualizes' or somewhat sentimentalizes them—are my own
mountain journals much better?"[13]

Philip experienced the first half of the 1960s as lean; he used the word *scuffling* to describe them, implying confusion, disorganization, altercation, inconclusion. True, in 1960 he'd gone on a second East Coast reading tour[14] and sold many books. He made good connections at both Harvard and Yale, and laid down recordings for both their audio archives. Most pleasing, he'd been able to visit the Gertrude Stein manuscript collection at Yale, followed by dinner discussions about her work with, among others, critic Donald Gallup. His five weeks on the road left him three hundred dollars richer. He paid back rent to his roommate, "gave some away to the deserving poor," and had fifty dollars left in his pocket. This, he imagines in writing to Gary Snyder, will do: "The roof and grub situation is temporarily under control."[15]

Soon, of course, he was broke again, debating inwardly how long he could dine with friends at their houses before ruining the relationships. Philip even babysat for a number of couples—including Don and Martha Carpenter and Richard and Suzanne Duerden, in exchange for meals and a bit of cash. A number of his poems from the early sixties have hunger as their theme or as lowering background. He sold off parts of his library but found himself buying more books before he was out of the shop. Finally strains would mount, and Philip would return to the post office for work he hated, there to "make $80 a week—in return for $80,000 worth of bother, & vexation. . . . That 4 hour stretch at the Post Office seems to occupy the whole day; the morning must be planned & scheduled in order to accomplish various chores before going to work. Then the job itself, its boredoms, worries, imaginary fears, then the confusion of supper & of social blather afterwards, breaking out of that into reading, letter writing, bath & NOTHING."[16]

He knew that to get through these periods, he would shut down mentally, and so warns himself, "I must contrive how to keep alert instead of trying to play dead for eight hours every day."[17] He continued alternating desperate poverty with stupefying work for some years. Whenever he did run across money—in early 1961, for example, the Poet's Foundation gave him an unexpected five hundred dollars—he would immediately quit his job, spend a big chunk of the money on books and other indulgences (including, with this grant, a piano), and then be back to begging meals. His journals of this period reveal that his teeth required attention; his glasses needed serious repair; and his wardrobe, such as it was, required amendment—he wished for a sturdy pair of pants and shoes without holes. But as long as he could, he delayed these practicalities and attempted to ward off money worries by telling himself they were unimportant, that anxiety was a bad habit. He preferred to walk in the park, to read there, to note the changes in flora and fauna and their effects on him—all this in service of what was important: composition.

And compose he did: an extensive, revealing journal, a vigorous correspondence, and a great deal of poetry. Philip often said in these years that poems "arrived." He wrote considerably more poems in the scuffling five years from 1960 to 1965 than in the preceding fifteen years—from the time he'd begun saving his work—and more than in the twenty-three years that followed until his last dated poems. He also accomplished something during this span that he'd tried and failed to do for twenty years: he wrote a complete novel.[18]

The knowledge that he suddenly had a book in him, that he knew clearly its structure—the size and shape and weight of its parts—dawned during a penniless walk in the redwoods of Mill Valley on the way home from the library to Albert Saijo's house, where he was living and dining for free. Back in his room, Philip cleaned the place and performed other rituals to honor the book's arrival. He rang a bell and sounded clappers he had from the Tantric Japanese Buddhist tradition. The music was intended to magnetize helpful energies and fend off obstructing ones. He recited a Buddhist sutra as well as a *dharani* (the nearest translation would be "spell"); he lit candles and offered incense and recited the Four Vows;[19] he dedicated the merit of all this to the enlightenment of all beings. Beyond these initial devotions, Philip prayed during the four months it took him to write the book. He did not pray to the Christian God; he prayed all over the place—to the elements, plants, animals, the Greek gods, other writers: "Eagle, mimosa, juncos & sunshine, be my help." "I MUST WRITE THIS BOOK, {THIS PRAYER TO PLUTUS, GOD OF RICHES}." "Praise the Muse! O Wyndham Lewis help me! O RARE BEN JONSON!"[20]

In addition to prayer, Philip took the occasional dexamyl,[21] if he could get one, to help things along. Like a hen on eggs or any animal guarding a young brood, he felt himself to be fierce and watchful—"in a continuous low-grade fury"—one that sometimes erupted into higher grades: "This afternoon my clipboard fell off the radio into a cup of tea, not all of which spilled on the floor; enough of it fell on my ms. to smear it & the rest got involved with a hundred sheets of good typing paper on the clipboard. I flew into a rage & burned all that blank paper." Having drinks with friends another evening he came home "by about 10:30 & in a horrible rage I broke 2 dishes, bent 2 cook-pots & kicked a hole in Albert's kitchen wall. Today I feel awful."[22]

Fits of temper plagued Philip all his life but were surely heightened by the pressure of working on something precious and fragile. Most of his problems arose not in the writing itself—"I didn't have to exert myself to do this; it all came fairly much when and as I needed it"—but in securing the time and place to do the work. As broke as he'd ever been, he yet knew that to look away from the novel, to go to a day job, would derail him. He put it to his journal that he needed forty more pages but couldn't afford them. The drive of the novel also had to survive a house move, as Albert Saijo also ran into financial woe and prepared to sell his place. He took Philip and his possessions back to San Francisco and deposited him back in a room at 123 Beaver Street, where he'd picked him up half a year earlier. With bad bronchitis and disoriented by the swift change of scene, Philip nevertheless issued a brisk command to himself—"I must remember that I'm trying to write a novel"—and continued, fundamentally undeterred.

As soon as he finished it, Philip showed the book around—first to friends, then to editors and publishers, and he tabulated the results in a graph. Opinion ran divided among the friends, but among the publishers, less so. He recorded one particularly sour response from Little Brown, who said the manuscript had "two critical flaws: The two main characters are profoundly unattractive" and "the narrative line is inert." Philip believed in his book, though; acknowledging it was perhaps not the greatest novel in English, he felt it contained much good material. When it appeared some years later, readers and the one traceable review agreed with him.[23] The hard words, though, and criticism—about this and other projects—hurt Philip, despite years of practice with the rejection that all writers seem to endure. He allowed in his journal that "I'm in despair & have feelings of failure & castration & anger at having all my little dreams shattered & broke & slithering down the black enameled metal slide."[24] Knowing such sensitivity to be impractical in his trade, Philip imagined how he might otherwise manifest. He wrote to Gary, "Now would be a good time to take up pipe-organ lessons so I could get a job playing the mighty Wurlitzer down at the skating rink."[25] A bit later to Diane di Prima (oddly, with the same location for his fantasy), "I've committed suicide & have quit all writing & now I'm a 2nd-string figure skater, a chorus boy in the Ice Follies boo hoo."[26]

BEAVER STREET AND GOLDEN GATE PARK: VISIONS
AND BAD BEHAVIOR

The rooms at 123 Beaver Street belonged to a woman called Tommy Sales, with whom Philip had uneasy relations. Tommy might, for reasons unfathomable to him, abruptly insist on a new rental agreement, or a rearrangement of the rooms, or a change of roommates. Philip's flatmates included, one at a time, Lew Welch, Richard Brautigan, John Montgomery, and David Kherdian; Philip managed to stay basically rent-free, taking considerable time and trouble to keep Tommy appeased. He thought of this, his longest-term residence since college, as "the Beaver St. period."[27] He found a scenic path over the steep chert hill of Beaver Street (as he'd done with his previous flat on Twenty-Fourth Street) down into the reclaimed and forested sand dunes of Golden Gate Park. He generally walked the length of the park to the ocean, where, if he had funds, he would refresh himself with a coffee and a piece of pie before heading back. He did this regularly: a book of poems drawn from the habit is titled *Every Day* and is respectfully dedicated to John McLaren, designer and builder of the park. As with his mountain perambulations, these park walks had overt spiritual meaning for Philip. He used these walks to commune or merge with nature. He got out into the elements and restored to himself the curative feeling of being made of them. He held conversation with them in various forms, as on the day when, having arrived at the shore, he "washed my hands & saluted the ocean, the sun, the Mountain." The same ritual appears, more purposively, in a poem:

> *I don't return to the trees until I've washed*
> *in the ocean, invoked its help*
> *I want its power in my writing hands*
> *the absolute freedom of action*
> *my own mystery and weight carrying*
> *independent living beings with/ in/ is*
> *we*
> *this* [28]

He often visited a tree he thought of as a healer—one he went to in need and into the limbs of which he climbed one day. His journal entry from ten feet above the ground, atop a thick branch of black pine, overhanging a mallard lake off Central Drive, chiefly worries about how he will get down. A bit

FIGURE 15. Philip Whalen practicing calligraphy, 1965. Photo © Larry Keenan.

later, the pages tell that he managed it more easily and gracefully than he'd thought possible, only slightly cramped in one thigh and scuffed in the shoes. Another time a "cypress tree tells me, 'You dropped your scarf.' I find it beside the lake."[29]

One late September day in 1963, Philip had what he called

> raptures and visions in the park, of some Indian KAMA deity, his laughing face & tall gold crown, the red rouge on his palms, sometimes I saw the rest of his body—jeweled rings on fingers, armlets &c gold and jewels. The mother, next, blue—sometimes white, a memory of the Kali statue in the DEVI movie—but at her most "real" or positive, she is blue. I am sliced to pieces by jewel knife/wires in space—ecstasy & calm—almost tears—recall picture of Artaud in ecstasy, Sri Ramakrishna et alia—feeling as of being "high"; but like a free-floating orgasm—an orgasm centered in chest, neck & head, rather than in sexual organs, although I was conscious of my body, I was free from it & free from this piece of space/time.[30]

Parallel to these private spiritual highs, though, and in the same season, Philip sank to lows of public comportment. In two recorded instances, his trouble stemmed from drinking too much. He didn't have the money to develop a drinking habit, but he loved beer and he loved gin, and both appear fondly in his works. If someone else was buying, Philip could and did drink copiously of whatever was offered. At a literary awards banquet sponsored by men's clothier Roos-Atkins in October, Philip got into his cups. He'd begun early, meeting Allen Ginsberg "for cocktails and champagne," then going with other friends to the dinner. Gossip columnist Herb Caen reported in the *San Francisco Chronicle* how San Francisco's World Trade Center "was jammed with literary lions,"[31] mentioning Ginsberg, Rexroth, and novelists Herb Gold and Nelson Algren. Philip cites all these in his journal, adding Ken Kesey, Evan Connell, Neal Cassady, Grover Sales, and Calvin Kentfield, as well as the honoree of the evening, Thomas Williams, who would go on to win the National Book Award ten years later.

Tongue loosened, Philip heckled the head table to the point that Mr. Williams asked others seated there if he should "belt him one." A company executive, in Philip's words, "then took me by the arm and hauled me out the door, telling me the while that I was rude and a son-of-a-bitch. At the door he kicked me across the buttocks." Straightening himself to go, Philip wrote how Ginsberg then emerged, "screaming at me to forgive the man and come back." Other writers gathered, and after some moments' confusion, all went back in, unremarked and uncontested. The incident humiliated Philip privately for his loss of decorum, and it required him to spend many hours explaining to friends what really happened. Nor can it have been pleasant to appear in Caen's objurgatory column as "Beat poet, tastefully attired in blue jeans and tennis shoes." Of the numerous quips Caen made and cited, Rexroth's was best; he warned executives against ejecting Philip by predicting the next day's leader: "Babbitt Boots Beat." Less than six weeks later, however, after a reading "with Lew & Mike & Allen & Andy Hoyem & Dave Meltzer," Philip lamented to his journal that he'd gotten very drunk and been arrested, together with the painter Tom Field. They spent the night in jail.

THE LONGSHOREMAN'S HALL READING; DON CARPENTER

Group readings of the kind from which Philip didn't make it home that night took place with some regularity in San Francisco in the 1960s. Novelist Don Carpenter reminisced about a reading he organized in 1964; he proposed to "do all the work and have the poets keep the money," partly to celebrate Gary Snyder's return from Japan, Lew Welch's descent from his cabin in the Trinity Alps, and Philip's example of the urban poet's life.[32] Partly as well, Carpenter exerted himself in reparation for an earlier reading he'd hosted in Portland in 1958. That time, he'd offered his basement space to Gary and Philip, and "it had been awful, except for the poetry." Apart from the broken window, trampled flowers, and hot, cramped space, they'd collected only $1.75 from the entire crowd. So economics surrounded this event. Publicity for it—Lew Welch's published deprecation against the nonpayment of artists, "Mozart's Watch," as well the KPFA panel discussion among the three poets[33]—circled around a poet's living or the lack of it. Don Carpenter's own essay was largely about money: the six-hundred-seat Longshoreman's Hall cost seventy-five dollars to rent; admission would be one dollar. Carpenter wrote the checks. Because it was still unusual to connect poetry and money, at the reading everyone forgot they would need to post ticket takers. Carpenter estimated they lost hundreds of dollars this way, despite his plea from the stage for the early arrivals to go back out and pay. With a crowd of eight hundred, though, they made out all right, more than covering their expenses, including a blow-out after-reading party at Tosca's. The poets came away with one hundred dollars cash each. In the lobby, Don Allen ran a profitable side business, having commissioned broadsides from each poet in their own calligraphic hand. The broadsides sold well that night and went on to become expensive collectibles.

THE VANCOUVER POETRY CONFERENCE

On 27 July 1963, Philip took a flight to Vancouver (paid by funds wired from Robert Creeley and Allen Ginsberg) to participate in a University of British Columbia Poetry Conference. The Vancouver conference—a three-week credit course at the university—brought together, in Robert Creeley's words, "for the first time a decisive company of then-disregarded poets, such as Denise Levertov, Charles Olson, Allen Ginsberg, Robert Duncan, Philip Whalen and myself, together with yet unrecognized younger poets of that time, Michael Palmer, Clark Coolidge and many more."[34] The mixture of readings, panels, workshops, and lectures seemed to Philip "very scary and official—terribly serious," causing him to feel continuously out of place. He wrote a number of journal entries and letters attempting to absorb, or to psychically place, the difficult time he had with other poets. Shaken by an automobile accident involving driving companions for his trip home, while waiting for one of them to be released from the hospital, Philip listed other reasons for feeling sad: "That I've been dropped by the Creeley family, that an uneasy truce has been settled with Olson ... Duncan pretending I don't exist, along with Denise Levertov and Margaret Avison who are of the same persuasion ... Allen alternately attacking and praising me."[35] In this same entry, though, Philip broadens the perspective and tries seeing it as "an excitement & a warring & a love feast among mountains & straits & rivers & islands," and praises the rich flora and fauna of Vancouver, as well as the good food and drink the poets enjoyed. Olson, the Creeleys, Ginsberg, Robert Duncan, and Philip were all living together in the home of conference organizer Warren Tallman and his wife, Ellen. It is easy to imagine tensions and paranoia arising among six (counting Bobbie Creeley) ambitious, intelligent, impoverished poets, some of them very tightly wound, living and teaching together for weeks on end. The single recording[36] of a panel discussion including Philip has everyone saying they are just continuing the conversation they'd begun earlier at home. The reunited Black Mountain faculty dominate it, Creeley alone exhibiting any spaciousness in his remarks; the other two—Duncan and Olson—pontificate loudly and rapidly, often across each other, so that even renowned talker Allen Ginsberg has trouble getting in a word. Philip is seldom heard at all and, like Creeley, is poorly recorded. The tape booms episodically with fists hitting the table, and the intensity of the event is palpable, but the discussion wanders around no clear (to this listener) topic, other than "what is it we are doing?"

Arriving back in San Francisco, Philip continued reconstructing the conference. "We were able to see each other & talk together after years of physical separation, and there were certain reconciliations & certain discussions & certain new disagreements; however we parted amiably. . . . So after all I am pleased, I feel myself changed, renewed, temporarily freed from a lot of the tiny obsessions that were troubling me before I went away."[37] This positivity may have arisen from his having swum every day in Vancouver off a secluded beach below the college, having eaten well and sufficiently for those weeks, and having enjoyed a restorative visit with Lloyd Reynolds on the drive home. For years, though, Philip worried the Olson story. In Vancouver Olson, in a mood, called Philip a vegetable—"Whalen is a great big vegetable." Philip told a class in 1977, "Even though that day Olson was mad at me, he later told me that I was undeniably marvelous. So we made up our quarrel." But he admitted, "I don't know what to do about Charles. He was very bright, and very *opinionated*. He had a very heavy style some days, a very heavy way of coming on. I used to scrap with him about it. Sometimes it was fun and sometimes it was embarrassing."[38]

NORTHWEST REVIEW SCANDAL; COYOTE'S JOURNAL

The most consequential connection for Philip at the Vancouver conference was not with any of the presenters but with a student, the only nonpoet admitted to the course—one Edward Van Aelstyn, who'd come from the University of Oregon as the new editor of the *Northwest Review (NWR)*. Before a year had passed, Philip's work in the pages of that magazine provoked a scandal, resulting in sustained public and private protest, suspension of publication of the *Northwest Review,* and the firing of its editors.

Begun in 1957 as a student-run journal, *NWR* was generally seen in 1962 as a sedate magazine devoted to poetry and other writing from the Pacific Northwest.[39] Taking the editorship, Van Aelstyn continued the established direction, but especially after the Vancouver conference, he began to solicit work from a wider geographical and aesthetic range. Possessed of an excellent academic record, copious energy, and enviable spine, Van Aelstyn soon lined up work for the publication from all the presenters at the Vancouver conference, as well as from Michael McClure, Gary Snyder, Ron Loewinsohn, Margaret Randall, J. Miles, Ed Dorn, and Charles Bukowski. By 1964, the journal had become a leading literary voice. But in January, it dawned on Oregonians that in *NWR*, a portion of their tax money had gone to publish poems lashing out at organized religion, an extended interview with Fidel Castro along with pictures of postrevolutionary Cuba, and an infamous radio play by Antonin Artaud—*To Have Done with the Judgment of God*.[40] The Cuban material appeared on the diplomatic heels of the missile crisis of 1962 and the failed Bay of Pigs invasion the year before that. These may have been provocative, but what really inflamed local fury were Philip Whalen's poems. The ones singled out for attack by the *National Eagle,* a right-wing Portland paper spearheading the protest, do not contain any swear words beyond *ass.* The general counsel's office of the U.S. Post Office cleared the whole magazine of obscenity or of being in violation of any existing laws. But Whalen's work poked at one of the Right's most tender spots— their religion. It wasn't the word *ass* that caused problems; it was that he juxtaposed it with the word *God's.* From the *National Eagle's* front page excerpt:

2 thousand years of work yourself to death
building God a house
tending God's ducks & pigs
killing God's enemies
kissing God's ass[41]

Reaction to the issue flowed back in two streams: praise, mostly from the literary community, and virulent attack from social conservatives. Holding university president Arthur Flemming responsible (only marginally more so than Oregon's liberal governor, Mark O. Hatfield), protesters deluged public offices with angry letters, petitions, and a stream of articles in the *National Eagle*. They demanded Flemming's resignation. "END MAD SEX DOPE MENACE," wrote Philip to Allen Ginsberg,[42] reporting on the excitement. "SEX DEVIATIONISM HORROR DOPE SCENE DEPRAVED YOUTH &C &C GODLESS UNIVERSITY COMMUNIST ATHEIST PLOT AT TAXPAYERS' EXPENSE." Philip's letter captures the *National Eagle*'s fondness for running lines of upper-case type, but his take on their message is no parody and hardly an exaggeration. He observes to Allen that "poetry is on the scene in Oregon. Who could ever have believed or expected it?" "On the scene" says it politely: President Flemming endured two summonses from the Oregon state legislature "to explain use or misuse of public funds," and professors from the English and journalism schools were made to submit briefs on the topic. Finally, President Flemming suspended publication of the magazine and fired the staff.

They reacted as any group of hot young editors would: they absconded with the galleys and manuscripts, they copied the magazine's mailing list, and three months after the university left them dangling, editors Van Aelstyn and Will Wroth, together with the new poetry editor Jim Koller,[43] put out *Coyote's Journal*. The cover proudly announced that it was from "the former editors of the *Northwest Review*." For those who'd been drawn into the struggle even as spectators, *Coyote's Journal* was a welcome sign of indomitability; beyond that, the content of the magazine reflected the editors' forward tastes. It attracted praise on both counts and continued for the next ten years as a pivotal outlet for new and experimental writing.[44]

Coyote's editors planned from the outset to publish books as well as the journal. Coyote Books' first venture was given over to Philip Whalen's poetry—*Every Day,* a handsome yellow paperback of fifty-three pages, the cover written in his calligraphy. A first edition of five hundred copies sold out quickly, as did a second edition printed a year later. In 1966, Coyote Books brought out a collection of Philip's graphical works—drawings and calligraphy and poetry he modestly termed "doodles" and immodestly titled *Highgrade*. A year later, in 1967, Coyote published Philip's novel, now titled *You Didn't Even Try*.

It is ironic that Philip was attacked for godlessness, as we have seen him to be a deeply religious person. A decade after the *NWR* incident, he would be ordained as a priest. In writing from every period of his life, Whalen grappled with spirituality, and he engaged it with all his resources: memory, logical analysis, practical (and impractical) experience, conversation, correspondence, and scholarship. In the poems published in the *NWR*, he quoted the King James Bible chapter and verse, cited the Upanishads, reached facilely into Greek, Roman, and Egyptian mythology; beyond these, he was at ease with the histories of Chinese and Japanese Zen ancestors, and with Mahayana Buddhism generally, such as it could be known in English in the 1960s.

Personal mystic experience colored all of Philip's writing. For one thing, he conducted an ongoing, personable conversation with the Muse, far beyond the standard conceits of that form: a reader cannot help feeling Philip was really talking with her, and she with him. One of the praises he made in this same period begins,

> O Goddess I call on you constantly
> People laugh when I speak of you
> They don't see you beside me,
> I'm young again when you appear
>
> "It stands to reason," people say,
> But I mean Holy Wisdom
> Buddha-mother Tara
> Bringing poems as I asked

The poem continues, impassioned, until concluding, "The poems and the writing all are yours."[45]

A number of Philip's poems record overpowering epiphanies and theophanies, close encounters with the gods. Being open to this range of experience posed artistic riddles, and it could make life inconvenient. Euphoria, for example, was not easy: "I have trouble displaying, expressing that sensation, it drives me to dance & laugh, to write, draw, sing, caper, gesticulate wildly. This seems to frighten many of the people who happen to see me hopping and giggling.... For several minutes at a time I become a glowing crystal, emitting rays of multicolored light."[46] Whatever else Philip Whalen was, he certainly was not a Christian God-fearing, clean-living, married, wage-earning taxpayer with kids in the house and cars in the garage. The *National Eagle* correctly identified Whalen as a smart young Oregonian gone off the rails. His work rudely challenged their society and good order.

It appears the attack against the *NWR* brought about—almost as if they were elements in an energy-producing chemical reaction—what everyone wanted: Philip came away with a regular publisher; editors Van Aelstyn, Koller, and Wroth came away with *Coyote,* a much stronger publication than the *NWR;* folks associated with the *National Eagle* got to flex muscles and push people around; and the University of Oregon, after suitable pause, resumed publication of the *Northwest Review,* printing work by exactly the same writers they had in the pre–Van Aelstyn years.

ELEVEN

Japan, Bolinas, Japan, Bolinas

1965–1971

Philip spent 10 and 11 November 1965 being filmed for a series on poetry by National Educational Television.[1] The original episode featured both Philip and Gary Snyder, and it exists now only in film archives. Ten years after it was shot, however, outtakes were re-edited into a half-hour short focused on Philip. Brief opening clips show him (soundlessly) climbing stairs in a windy fog at the Palace of the Legion of Honor, walking and pointing along the coast and out to sea. The rest of the film has sound and takes place in Philip's rooms at 123 Beaver Street. The filmmakers seem at pains to make poetry visually interesting. Thus Philip stands in a corner of his room, reading a work about being in a room in the city and thinking about mountains, and on walls to his immediate right and left are elevation maps of mountains. The camera creeps over his shoulder in another sequence, as he guides the viewer through the distinct sections of a calligraphic doodle. One chatty scene has him playing with scientific toys—a magnetic space wheel and a plastic cube housing smaller plastic cubes with a metal ball rolling among them. He remarks that this one reminds him of American involvement in Vietnam, which he strongly opposes. As Philip answers the interviewer's[2] questions, the camera trails around the room, showing hundreds of clothbound books closely shelved and neatly stacked. It lingers on Chinese landscapes pinned to a smallish wall. Polished rocks, crystals, and writing materials decorate his desk; a pile of bound sheet music sits below it.

Philip wears simple clothes in the shoot—work shirt under a sweater zippered over his belly. Mostly the camera rests on his face. At forty-two, Philip wore his lustrous hair long, parted and combed to the left. His beard and mustache were neatly groomed. Had the film been in color, they would have shone dark red. His pale eyes moved behind round, thick glasses. His is a sober visage yet mobile, twinkling with humor and strong opinion. His movements, as well as his posture at rest, convey strength housed in a large frame. He reads his works vigorously, answers questions softly.

Though they are largely off camera, Philip responds about the Buddhist icons and shrine arrangements around his place, saying that they are mnemonics—reminders of the magic of the phenomenal world. He adds that with life being so distracting, reminders are helpful. Then almost casually, hidden in vernacular, he points out that the senses—to which the incense, candle flame, food, drink, and pictures appeal—are mind, and thus of the nature of wisdom. The statues simply portray wisdom in idealized, fully developed form. He'd written this idea—and not for the first time—in a poem weeks earlier:

> This bronze Tara this bronze lady
> Represents that Lady of Heaven I now invoke,
> That idea of wisdom that saves more than itself or me . . .
> She also appears as a song, a diagram,
> As a pile of metal images in the market, Kathmandu

The poem ends, however, with a solemn observation about the difficulties of stabilizing this view: *"We seldom treat ourselves right."*[3]

. . .

The boat trip that took him to Japan began well enough on 24 February 1966, with Philip being celebrated by friends in a champagne send-off on the deck of the *SS Cleveland*. As the boat made its way past the lit-up city and under the bridges of San Francisco Bay, Philip "clutched a 2-lb. bag of uncooked popcorn to my palpitating wheezy chest . . . half mad with excitement and delight." Very soon, less pleasant realities of the voyage emerged: his bed down in "steerage class" sat in a long, hot dormitory. An aisle ran "18 inches wide between iron double-decker bunks fitted with sleazy, dusty, jackoff curtains & a feeble reading light," and the air had been "gathered and bottled from inside a large mohair sofa manufactured in 1907."[4] Philip called the food indescribably bad but described it often, terming one lunch "another triumph of the poisoner's art." Meals were taken in a gloomy dining room "located just below the water line. The steward who served our table had a dreadful cold all during the trip; at mealtimes he was miserable, poor man, coughing and sneezing down the backs of our respective necks, supporting himself by hanging on to my chair while I was eating." Philip's companions at table included "Hans Lufthansa," "Gus Green," and "Eleonora Cucamonga," as well as someone he did not nickname, calling him only "the long pink boy," a youth who liked to stand around naked in the dorm. Two weeks after setting out, the *Cleveland* made land at Yokohama. During the unloading, Philip went for a day and a night up to Tokyo, which impressed him as "more stylish and lively and exciting than New York or San Francisco." He then collected his luggage, shipped it to Kyoto, and took train and taxi to Gary Snyder's doorstep, where we have seen him earlier.[5]

Philip lived in Kyoto twice: from March 1966 to November 1967, then again from the end of March 1969 to mid-June 1971. He spent time with varying sets of people during these nearly three years, and he lived in several locations, but he conducted his affairs and apportioned his time in a very consistent pattern throughout. It is largely possible to treat the two stays together, as one period.

The job that freed Philip from his San Francisco poverty and anxiety was teaching English at the Kyoto YMCA. It required little of him—ten hours per week divided into three classes—and it absorbed a minimum of his interest. "The students . . . are very dull & impervious. To me it's just a job, I go & deliver the lessons & answer questions & make explanations. Usually the students don't ask—in Japanese schools, students are supposed to *listen* to the teacher & believe what he says, whatever that might be."[6] Philip established quarters in town[7]—minuscule for him but large by Japanese standards—comprising two rooms with a "closet-sized kitchen" and egress independent of the main house, behind which he was situated.

He used his free time to explore and came away from Kyoto's shrines and temples very moved. "The effect is partly produced by the size & shapes & materials of the architecture—& partly by the fact that they're built in places which, to my sensibilities, possess a strong GENIUS. Theoretically the shrines were established first & then the Shinto priests held special services designed to invite specific gods to take up residence in them. Whatever the true order of events, these great PLACES give the impression of being inhabited." He finds several of them also to contain "violence, terribilita. . . . Being empty, they are truly frightening. There really is an Okami-sama in each one—there couldn't possibly be anything else."[8] This contrasts with Buddhist temples, which for him "radiate calm & disinterested benevolence, i.e. compassion, and an atmosphere where one can sit quietly and learn, understand, quit fussing & fidgeting."

He filled his journal and letters with purely descriptive praise of the beauty and power of physical Japan, the jumbled and chaotic as well as the austere. He admired this kind of writing and enjoyed doing it. Making an acquaintance with Japan gave him rich material.

A great fair is held on the 25th of each month under the trees of the main avenues of the Kitano shrine, a noisy & marvelous occasion to go in search of treasure & strange foods—cloth, kimonos, crockery, second-hand statues and censors and saws, hot octopus fritters 'as you like it' {a kind of Japanese TACO or BURRITO} flowers, magic charms, your future delivered to you from a tiny Shinto shrine by a trained prophetic bird, balloons, young live crabs, umbrellas, cotton candy, tea, dried lizards, toads & snakes & other magic medicines. The red-skirted temple virgins perform dances & scatter a jingle over you from a purifying rattle if you pay a small fee.[9]

There may be a relation between the pleasure in pure description he showed and the writing materials he used. As soon as he gets to Kyoto, he abandons the lined, pocket-size journal books, gray lead pencil, and cramped hand in favor of blank books of unfamiliar papers sewn and bound in Japanese formats. He begins to write his journal in ink with an edged pen. He discovers colored pens in the stationery stores, and these turn him on extremely. On the first page of a book-length poem set in Kyoto, *Scenes of Life at the Capital,* he exhorts himself, "Loosen up. Festoon."[10]

Kyoto's weather sometimes oppressed its inhabitants: the rainy season was very wet and difficult, and summer was damp and hot. "I shall want to return here where it is quiet," Philip wrote to Allen Ginsberg, imagining places he might visit, "but *not* for the summer weather . . . climate is MONSTROUS and all the bugs that aren't biting you are singing a deafening anthem, day & night, & there's little sleep possible."[11] Against the damp, cold winter, Philip bought a second kerosene heater for his room. He owed his survival to these heaters, he told a friend, and to an electric blanket, and to "breathing 40 or 50 times a minute."[12]

Presented with so many new sights, sounds, tastes, touches, and fragrances, Philip had to possess a certain number of them. His tremendous intellectual dressage was not much service in the sense realms; here he had trouble even finding the reins, much less pulling on them. He called his purchases "plunder," though they weren't all for himself. He bought many things for friends abroad: this specific camera with carrying case for a woman who'd done him favors back home; those religious musical instruments and esoterica for

FIGURE 16. Whalen (front) at the summit of Mount Tamalpais during Buddha's birthday circumambulation, 1968. Photo courtesy of Gary Snyder.

Ginsberg; pictures and statues and the odd item of clothing for himself. He made sure he was supplied with every sort of local Tantric or shamanic implement. A picture of Philip on a Mount Tam hike post-Japan shows him bandoliered with strings of beads, holding a ritual bell with one hand and a "Shingon jingle stick" with the other. Beside him sits a small Tantric hand drum—a *damaru*—and a large conch with a mouthpiece. Philip bought himself yet another electric keyboard, this one with headphones, so he could practice his Bach at home without disturbing his neighbors or the serenity of the mossy rock garden out the sliding door. "I get J.S. Bach into both ears at once & my brains are now growing a long curly wig & a lace jabot & velvet waistcoat.... O rare delight! All sentient beans should know such sublimities."[13]

With a steady income and free time, Philip was able to attend Kabuki shows, which he found "a gas,"[14] and Noh, which transported him:

> The extraordinary controlled "forced" sound of NO singing, & the cries of the drummers {yeoh!} {and in the case of the horizontal drum YEE-OW!—a skip from the initial note to an impossible falsetto howl—but the drummer was able to produce that impossibility ACCURATELY every time he had to do it.} this music is absolutely other-worldly—as is the whole effect of a NO performance. It just calmly comes on & says "Here's this NO universe, which has always been here, & since it isn't going anywhere, it will always be where it is . . . temporarily here now." Its existence gives the best imitation I've seen of a completely self-contained reality.[15]

He tried repeatedy, as here, to analyze the music with Western vocabulary and discussed this, as well as classical Indian music, with concert pianist and Zen teacher Walter Nowick, who was finishing his own training in Japan.

Philip's tiny kitchen pushed him out into restaurants for nearly all his meals, a not entirely pleasant experience. He was able to write, regularly and pleasurably, in small coffee shops, where he was supplied with small cups of fresh coffee—a stream of these—and "things to nibble the while"; but lunches and dinners could be more difficult. More than once Philip received stern correction from a waiter or manager, and though these humiliated him, he could never discover his mistake. Had he come too late? Had he ordered the wrong dish, something out of season or otherwise inappropriate? Were the lectures simply anti-*gaijin* prejudice? Without speaking Japanese, he could only make his excuses and leave. Whatever might have been his paranoias— he called them so in his journal—about being an out-of-place foreigner, other views existed. Kenneth Rexroth, writing in the *New York Times,* reported, "When Philip Whalen, in his red whiskers, looking like a happy Ainu bear-god walks down Omiya-dori in Kyoto's weavers' quarters, every face lights up with that old-time Buddhist joy. . . . I have in fact seen Philip ambling past the market stalls and running into a march of demonstrating strikers, and everyone smiled and waved and he waved back."[16]

As much as Japan aroused Philip, it also tormented him. He'd built his life around a relationship to language and operated at a very high level of English. In Japan, every schoolchild could draw, speak, and write the local language more fluently than he could. This complicated the most mundane acts, including daily travel. He kept schedules in his journal of the time it took him to go to the public bath and come home, to go for dinner and come back, to get to a friend's house, to shop. Unable to dash off a note, he was often waiting for the laundry man or the postman. Buying the camera for his friend meant several visits to a store across town, spread over weeks, with embarrassed attempts at conversation. Getting to the Bank of America required a train ride as well as a taxi, and travel was the easy part. Philip's need to simply cash an American check collided with Japanese customs that wielded signatures, verifications of employment, documentation of residence, and so on in baffling ways, ways that did not conduce to or welcome small-scale American business. Philip was not alone among foreign nationals in experiencing this.

On one banking expedition with Richard Baker, newly in Japan, Philip short-circuited the system. They'd gone to a bank so that Baker could open an account and Philip could get cash. Philip's papers were accepted with a bow, scrutinized, passed to a colleague for further examination, then taken upstairs to management, and finally brought back to the counter, where it was softly explained that they were lacking and that disbursal of funds would be impossible. Having scrapped for money all his life, now having in hand what he'd been told were reasonable papers, yet being denied the actual money, Philip lost it. "But I want my money," he said. "I want my money." He repeated this more loudly, turning heads both at his English and his volume. "I WANT MY MONEY!!! I WANT MY MONEY!!!" he shouted repeatedly, no doubt gesturing to clarify his meaning. While Baker tried in vain to soothe him, mortified bank employees finally gave Philip his money.

He kept up vigorous correspondence with all his friends during his time in Kyoto, but Philip wrote with increasing frequency to two people in particular—Jim Koller and Don Carpenter. Koller had been—together with Coyote Books partners Bill and Zoe Brown—Philip's regular publisher for some years. Coyote brought out *Every Day* in 1965, the doodle book *Highgrade* in 1966, and the novel *You Didn't Even Try* in 1967. Comity developed between Philip and the entire Coyote crew, but the voluminous correspondence with Koller reveals how much Philip admired his poetry and his energy, and how grateful he was for the many practical favors Jim Koller did him. Reserved to the point of taciturnity, Koller had a penetrating presence; when he did, or said, or wrote something, it struck the point. Philip signed one letter to Gary Snyder as "written in Jim Koller's truck, going across the Bay Bridge." It is difficult to think of another of Philip's friends who might have left him space to write a letter in a truck, that truck surely carrying Philip and his possessions on an errand.

Philip knew Don Carpenter from his Portland days, as we have seen. Carpenter wrote hard-boiled novels and screenplays, and while he generally received very good reviews, only his first novel—*Hard Rain Falling*—had commercial success. Philip once wondered for pages in his journal how Carpenter could punch out such swift, clean prose. He compared Carpenter's upbringing, his physical stature, work habits, drinking habits, and marital status with other successful writers and with himself. He thought Don Carpenter would have made a tough cop. Philip stored boxes of his library in Carpenter's garage, and he also accepted money from him. Whether the money was loaned or given outright, Philip felt unsure; this naturally led to real and imagined frictions.

Carpenter, flush with the publication of *Hard Rain,* ate a boozy New York lunch with Harcourt, Brace, & World (HBW) president William Jovanovich. They hatched a plan for bringing to market at least three large books of the new poetry, to test the American appetite for it; these would be individuals' works, not anthologies. Names batted around included Ron Loewinsohn, Jack Spicer, Michael McClure, and Philip Whalen. Carpenter was deputized as West Coast poetry rep for HBW, and at another well-lubricated meal, Carpenter and Koller conspired to include in the volume all of Philip's poetry to date. Three somewhat slender books of his poetry had been published, as well as the doodle text. On the unpublished side, Philip had completed a short illustrated fable—*The Invention of the Letter*—which was still with the publisher, Irving Rosenthal. A large manuscript, *Brain Candy,* had been in production for several years but had not appeared, and Coyote Books itself was sitting on a number of Whalen collections, awaiting funding. The names and boundaries of all these slipped obscurely, but in sum Philip had ready many more unpublished poems than published ones. A "collected" volume would suddenly more than double his works in print.

Sorting and weeding the collections, amending and editing individual poems, understanding the terms of the publishing deal, arranging the permissions—such detailed work was more than he felt he could accomplish with thin air letters from Japan. He knew as well that he simply needed a break from Japan. "I want away from here. Maybe I will come home Sunday—simply throw the contents of these rooms onto the trash pile & start swimming East. I doubt that we can settle all this simply by exchanging a series of letters; I'd sure like to talk to you boys about what it is you're tryna do, what it is that's happening."[17]

In this letter, Philip lists his worries for four handwritten pages, among them that HBW would complain about the swear words; that they would force release forms on him each time he mentions a living person; that he and

Coyote would be ill treated financially by the big New York publisher; that the "message of his work" would be lost on most of the readership; that he would need real money if he were "to sell out all my work & all my friends in one fell swoop, not to mention the indignity of openly appearing to be a member of the Establishment, being published by HBW." He concluded by telling Koller, "You find out more details. If you figure we get away with only a slightly abraded ass-hole, maybe we should go ahead cautiously & with a large can of Vaseline. But FIRST I want to hear about the details, and the MONEY."

Torn about leaving, fearing Gary's contumely for quitting a job he'd arranged, Philip nevertheless closed out his first Kyoto sojourn, booked passage on a boat back to California, and, by the last day of November 1967, was living with the Browns on the Bolinas mesa. The work that had seemed so imposing from afar went quickly in collaboration with Koller and Brown, and by late December—not a month after he'd arrived—the manuscript was nearly ready. This left him at loose ends, a state he'd scented from the boat: "Fright about what America will be like. How shall I live and where.... Naturally I've begun developing a grand fit of the anxious." Despite trying "to decide to make it interesting & useful & enlightening, instead of continuing all this bleak noise,"[18] Philip was very soon camping with friends in San Francisco and holding only the slimmest prospects for employment as a teacher. He wailed to Ginsberg about "the lunacy of staying at other people's houses, involvement in family disorders and dissipations and teensy-weensy nerve-gnaw slobber and rat-shit."[19] He found San Francisco boring and felt the city had become dangerous, with many more criminals than before and a brutal police force. A solution arose when Philip moved to Stinson Beach and began living in a space he called variously a mother-in-law apartment, cabin, garage, shed, or the chauffeur's quarters. It sat on rural property owned by the Rick Duerden family. Here we shall leave him for a while, in a place where he had the solitude and quiet he needed, where he was not too far from a telephone and post office, where he could swim and hike to exhaustion, and where, if Jim Koller or Don Carpenter or Richard Duerden would just swing by in a truck, he could get groceries or a ride to the city for errands.

A tug-of-war had begun with HBW over typical publishing issues—timing, page proofs, permissions, and design—on the big book Philip was then calling *A Lick & a Promise*. (A casual remark from Bill Brown pointed him to the line "on bear's head,"[20] and Philip chose that as a title instead. Brown, horrified, remonstrated with him the next day that he'd only been joking, but it was too late.) Koller ran interference for Philip on the publishing quarrels, handling as much work and as many decisions as he could. But waiting for HBW to respond as "next week" stretched into "next month," then "after the summer holidays," there was little Koller or Don Carpenter could do.

Another vexing issue obstructed the collection. Philip had given a manuscript to Poets Press, under the direction of Diane di Prima in February 1965. He admired Diane's writing, her personality, and her complicated lifestyle, and he was pleased with the prospect of a new book. *Brain Candy* would present at least fifty-five new poems and was to appear almost immediately, in April. There was no contract. April came and went, as did May, June, and the other months of 1965. All the months of 1966 came and went. Philip and Diane corresponded regularly, and when problems arose for Poets Press, Philip suggested that Diane could just send the manuscript back and not worry about it. Some months later, he was more definite: he wrote that Coyote could publish *Brain Candy,* and that he didn't like having his work "hung up." In mid-1966, she sent Philip proofs for the layout; he corrected and returned them, telling her in the same mail about the HBW book and adding that he hoped she would not be mad. Perhaps neither of them understood the exclusivity that came along with the HBW collection, because Diane continued to report progress—negatives had been shot and were at the printers, instructions had already been given to the bindery—but then would fall silent and show him nothing. Finally in mid-1967, Philip lost patience. "As far as I'm concerned, Poets Press no longer exists," he wrote to Koller. "The sooner a Coyote Press edition of *Brain Candy* can be produced, the happier I should be." By this point, Coyote Press—that is, Jim Koller—was coproducing the big book with HBW. *Brain Candy* would first appear there.

Diane reacted angrily: she felt betrayed, sold out to "the Big Press," and she literally trashed the pasted-up boards—typesetting, original calligraphy, and all—in an act she lamented but justified in a poem thirty-five years later.[21] At the time, Philip asked Allen Ginsberg to intercede and "smooth the waters" with Diane, and from 1968 on, the waters appeared to have been smoothed. Philip and Diane lived only several houses removed from the Zen Center and from each other during the 1970s and early '80s. They appeared at ease, even affectionate, whenever they met in San Francisco or during summer stays at Naropa, and they maintained high regard for one another's work. They read together occasionally. Diane and friends would take Philip to lunch during his abbacy at Hartford Street, and when he took to bed in hospital and then hospice, Diane was among his regular visitors. The old hurt, the unfinished business, seemed to flare anew in the poem—"I Threw It Out"—that Diane contributed to Philip's Festschrift. In it, she recounts her side of the publishing incident. So many acts of kindness and mutual support had taken place by then that the choice was startling.

Philip received his first hardcover copy of *On Bear's Head* when he was back in Japan, on 12 May 1969, a year behind schedule. The price—incredibly and artificially boosted to $17.50—provoked outrage: it required even the well-off to think twice before buying the book, and it made it virtually inaccessible to poets. Philip would talk about having a worldwide audience of two or three readers, but in truth, people reading modern poetry often read him; they wanted to see his new work and own the collection. The New York poetry community mounted a protest, partially if not wholly organized by Anne Waldman, whose ability to manipulate power was remarkable even then. Artist George Schneeman ran up tasteful posters proclaiming, "$17.50 SUCKS"; a petition, to which New York City's Mayor Lindsay somehow became one of the hundreds of signers, arose; and on the day of publication, a picket line formed in front of the bookstore at HBW premises. Someone "liberated" a copy of *On Bear's Head,* and HBW called the police. A tactical unit arrived in riot gear and stood menacingly while poets Bill Berkson and Michael Brownstein presented the petition and spoke with HBW staff. The situation eventually defused without incident or injury; the poets kept their stolen book and felt perhaps they'd been vindicated when, some months later, the paperback edition appeared for a very reasonable $3.95.

News of the protest amused Philip, who had his own problems with the book. The price of the hardback had been an embarrassment, confirming his view that "what New York seems to offer is a big set of shiny white teeth & great big claws, the better to grab & devour anything and everything & turn it all into shit."[22] In a romantic mood while first looking at the book, Philip found the cover to be "infinitely sexy, all swathed in purple and crimson like a Cardinal Archbishop.... The pages don't have enough margin; contrari-wise, the print is clear & there's space between the lines."[23] The very next night, though, he saw it as "very low quality pasteboard, with dusty plastic flowers, painting poster colors on window glass, a dumb tiger, a view of Venice, all in vibrant neon paint on black velvet ... a great disappointment. Total failure on every level. *Now* what am I going to do.... I've already apolo-gized enough, not only in the text of the poems themselves, but also in the preface to the book. The only answer is 'Please make yourself into a better poet—a better writer in every form—even if it's only a matter of notes to the milkman, postcards to friends, or this journal.'"

Reviews appeared. The *San Francisco Chronicle* ran Lew Welch's piece—a rave, but an insightful, cleanly written one that ended with him stomping his boots on the high price, pained at how it contradicted Philip's life and principles. Kenneth Rexroth's chattier piece in the *New York Times* dealt with the humor, the apparent nonchalance and ease that characterized, for Rexroth, Philip's wisdom. *On Bear's Head* was short-listed for the National Book Award in Poetry for 1970. Other finalists that year were Robert Lowell, Elizabeth Bishop, Daniel Berrigan, and Lawrence Ferlinghetti. Ms. Bishop won, for *The Complete Poems*.

"One asks oneself why it is that one was so incredibly stupid and thoughtless as to leave Kyoto."[24] Philip typed this sentence as a paragraph in a letter to Allen Ginsberg. He then circled it with black marker and drew an arrow to the words *ONCE, EVERY DAY.* Suspended in Stinson Beach with time to walk and swim and write but little else, he began plotting his return to Japan. He undertook this with resolve, writing to embassies about visas, writing to the YMCA about having the job back, writing to every moneyed friend he had about money, and resigning himself to selling old manuscripts and letters and many pounds of his library to raise funds. He fretted that in doing so he made everyone mad, and he listed them out in his journal along with his imagined offenses. Some of it may have been true: at least Carpenter launched an "incisive and prolonged attack" one day, though it seems not to have damaged their friendship much.

Embarrassing as this about-face no doubt was, it triggered a shift in Philip's view of himself. He began to think more clearly about how he could make a living and, realizing he could not, to whom he might turn for patronage. Usual sources of support for writers seemed played out: the Guggenheim Foundation, the Rockefeller, the American Academy in Rome, the Berlin Literarisches Colloquium—none of these had offered aid. From California's university system, where many writers took refuge, he had only a faint possibility of part-time freelance teaching, and that in the extension program. So he looked elsewhere. "I can see the possible total satisfaction & pleasure of becoming a member of the Zenshinji community, for example," he wrote in his journal. "I should really commit myself to living in some conventional religious manner here, or to life in Japan—really making a new way in that place by totally accepting the old."[25] As part of this, he made two trips into the Sierra Nevada to look at land collectively bought there by friends, including Claude Dalenberg, Richard Baker, Allen Ginsberg, and Gary Snyder, who lives on it to this day. Philip went to see if the place might be a solution to his residence problem. It wasn't, though he much enjoyed the fresh air and feeling of the landscape. Richard Baker went because he was earnestly practicing Zen under Shunryu Suzuki Roshi, and was looking for land on which to establish a monastery. The Sierra outing began with morning meditation at Sokoji, Suzuki's temple in San Francisco, and it marked the first of three times Philip had any contact with the teacher who would become his spiritual grandfather.

From where he languished—homeless, jobless, without prospects—the community growing up around Suzuki must have looked attractive. But neither this first time nor the second time he meditated at Sokoji did he feel much. After meditation, "Suzuki-roshi was in his little office and I bowed to him and went through one door and out the other and nothing happened."[26] The third time, though, something happened. After Sunday breakfast with Gary and Masa Snyder, the men went over to hear Suzuki lecture. "We sat there near the back and could hear okay, and he was lecturing on Sun-Faced Buddha, Moon-Faced Buddha. I thought it was very wonderful. Hearing that lecture made me feel I'd made a big horrible gaff by not hanging around over there and talking to him."[27]

By now, though, he'd committed himself to return to Japan, and much had lined up to make it possible—the job was still there, as well as a place to land and be for a few days. First he would have to vacate Stinson Beach and stay somewhere else until he could leave. "I shall try to find a large room and bath somewhere in San Francisco," he wrote, and against the city's dangers "to buy a bullet-proof vest. If you hear anything about tiny cheap apartments, please let me know. Also, bargains in steel helmets, gas masks & a steel cup jock."[28] Bay Area hiking columnist Margot Patterson Doss lent Philip her family's summer house in Bolinas until he could travel, while book dealer Peter Howard took a large swath of his library on consignment. Thus Philip was able to land in Japan on 30 March 1969, noting proudly in his journal that it was "just a trifle short of six months after deciding to come back." He set his bags down for the first nights in the same house he had stayed in the first time; now, though, the Baker family lived there—Richard, his wife Virginia, and their very young daughter Sally—rather than Gary Snyder. Philip had been away sixteen months.

He immediately wrote to friends that he felt "1000% better than in California... very happy & subliminally fed, metaphysically zapped," adding that he "can't quite figure this out."[29] Trying to figure it out, though, occupied him. He detected "here in Kyoto, a tradition of discipline, training, & study. The vibes which were set up by generations of bodhisattvas, teachers, artists, monks, students, even musicians & dancers & craft workers in lacquer, silk, metal, wood and gardens... not to forget the poets & novelists & diarists... these benign influences & good examples all around me make me feel at once grateful & ambitious. I feel free to work hard, at my own pace, in my own manner."[30] The atmosphere in Kyoto—in which the ancient traditions of the crafts, and the disciplines of the arts mingled with them, were aligned with character development—inspired him. In a dark moment of California despair, he thought back to this and roused himself to "practice refusing to transmit injuries, bad news, unhappiness, illness &c—receive and quietly digest, dispose of it: BREAK THE CHAIN or transmute it—as, for example, the Lady Ukifune in GENJI {at the very end of the book.} I'm happy I burnt incense & recited sutras at Murasaki's tomb—& offered a chrysanthemum too. *This* i.e. the experiencing of this feeling, is what is meant by VALUE, CONNECTION, RECOGNITION, JOY, MEANING, LIFE, UNDERSTANDING &C."[31]

He knew Japan would require him again to "find patience & strength of nerves in order to teach & to live with Japanese people—& at last, patience & perseverance to work with the language." Trying to hear and use new words can of course support a writer; being sent to the dictionary, discovering the history of the language and patterns of its use, being forced into respect for, and seduced into play with, new phrases enriches anyone whose stock in trade is words. On his laziest days Philip had not just to use speech but to work at it. Reflecting this industry, his Japanese years were productive literarily. He wrote a second novel sitting in Kyoto's coffee shops;[32] he wrote a book-length poem[33] and many dozens of other poems of varying length; he produced two illustrated fables[34]—a mock-moral instruction for children and a homoerotic piece of pornography, commissioned by the publisher; he hand-wrote or typed hundreds of letters, and he wrote journals from which he mined poems for years after.

As he settled back into Japanese life, Philip renewed his free-time tourism, but less naively.

This passion of mine for temples—what's all that about?... I'm afraid that it is mere "aestheticism"... snobbery... sentimentality. I know perfectly well that these places, gardens, pictures & statues are only traces of something real which has already left town, already gone by, viz. the energy & inventive powers of generations of artists & craftsmen. Some of them were concerned personally with Buddhism.... Sesshu was a priest & so were many others ... & that particular concern is supposed to have a lot to do with the appearance of these places & scrolls, & so I ramble aimlessly instead of looking at the original question, "How come I like it?" I suppose I might go to one & watch myself, rather than repeat all these abstract speculations.[35]

It is exactly here that Philip begins to shift from what Gary Snyder called the "seductive cultural fascinations of old Japan" to actually "hearing the message of the big Buddhist temples."[36] For the architecture, gardens, scrolls, and sculptures did all encode messages, as any culture's do. Japan had been weaving the teachings of Buddhism into its every corner for thirteen centuries. A student of the translated texts and a steady, if imperfect, practitioner of the central meditation, Philip could read or decode them. This came simply at first; a little poem titled "They Are Gold,"[37] for example, points out how the Buddhas and bodhisattvas being this color corresponds to our valuing their work. More shocking imagery called forth more assurance. "Motives, those energies: which are demons. Their line is 'I want; I am going to have!' which is also expressed in the long fangs and heavy claws. Clinging, unquenchable fire, that's the substance of their bodies. I don't speak metaphorically—their 'flesh' is that stuff which is endless brainless torment."[38]

Finally, Philip experienced the messages of Japan's Buddhism delivering themselves to him unbidden, with an overwhelming power. Two instances stand out. The first broadsided him with a blatant expression of emptiness. Walking on the street one day toward Hyakumon Ben University, he was "trying to repeat the Hannya Shingyo [the Heart Sutra] from memory. The act of memory—or the magic vibrations of the sutra itself—smash the real world. The surrounding trees and mountains pass Kyodai [Kyoto University] kids and professors, empty, all walking at an angle to this reality which I'm trying to remember."[39] It goes by quickly in this journal entry, but it also went into a poem, and Philip remarked it in later years, attributing his ordination and monk's life to the incident—the manifest power of emptiness condensed in the sutra and his almost idle attempt to recite it. That he was memorizing a sutra at all, that he was trying to remember a particular reality, imply his deep familiarity with Buddhism. Indeed, we've seen that he'd first read Zen texts nearly twenty years earlier and had tried since then to meditate. But the next message that hit him—and it hit him as he traversed the same part of Kyoto—convinced him he would need to take it much more seriously.

> I was sitting on my own. I went one day over to a coffee shop near Kyodai and stopped off at the Hyakuman Jinja near Imadagawadori [a street]. I went up to look at the famous Buddha in the small hall by the gate—this Buddha was supposed to be carved in heaven. I looked in there, bowed, put a penny in the box and started circumambulating the building. I looked out to the North and the sun was shining nicely in that little graveyard. I thought, "Oh my goodness, I'm getting old and that's where I'm going to be one of these times. I'd better shape up about this Buddhism business." I saw how things looked and how I looked and I started to cry. I was walking around and around the building, crying. Then I walked off to the coffee shop and wrote in my notebook having coffee and croissant; I told myself that what I've got to do is find a teacher and be a monk. I had to do this thing though I had no idea what that meant.[40]

Until then, Philip had practiced zazen almost exclusively alone, despite having several Western friends studying at Zen temples. He went to sit with Richard Baker once, but most mornings he simply got up and did it at home, "no matter how late, no matter how drunk" he'd gone to bed. He sat at his own time, and he experimented with form, as when he went through a phase of meditating naked; to protect himself from the morning's chill, he would wrap himself in a sheet, wearing it like the *okesa* (outer monk's robe) he would properly don a few years later. Similar to the historical Buddha Gautama, the impact of inevitable death urged Philip to sobriety in his practice, and much like the Buddha, he now sought instruction. Philip approached his friend Irmgard Schloegel[41] and asked about sitting with her. She responded by arranging an interview with a teacher she knew and respected. Thus in late May 1969, with Irmgard translating, Philip had his first Zen interview; he spoke with the head monk at Daitoku-ji, a man called Daishu-in-san.[42]

> In his presence I felt the strangest combinations of feelings: great impatience, great fear, annoyance, shame—all these combined with a sense of great excitement and exhilaration. The temple, the celebrated lake were beautiful, but being with Daishu-in San, the beauty & interest & history all disappear: the man is more important than the place. . . . I felt, as we were walking along outside the temple grounds that I'd been in a lion's den & escaped alive . . . but only that: escaped into, slid back into a smaller, softer, looser, vaguer life, a low-quality paradise. I had seen Manjushri & his lion, all surrounded by

those wisdom-flames & raging impotent demons: absolute stillness, absolute self-control in the midst of tremendous chaos, turbulence & catastrophe.[43]

It may be that Philip experienced reflexive contraction after these openings. In the course of social relations in following years, he met with other Japanese Zen masters: he attended a luncheon in May 1971 at which Yamada Mumon Roshi, abbot of Myoshinji, was present; he visited Antaiji with friends to pay respects to Uchiyama Kosho Roshi; and in his journal he mentions Morimoto Roshi. But he appears not to have had further interviews with Daishu-in-san, or with any teacher. In a journal entry from six weeks after the interview, he mused again on the relative importance of man and temple: "He [Daishu-in-san] happens, temporarily, to be living at the Daishu-in but there's no connection between him & the place except the same name," and then apropos of nothing else obvious, Philip adds: "Don't tell me what to do."

Nor did Philip align with a temple or undertake group practice, as he confessed decades later: "She [Irmgard] said now you can come here and sit. I said 'I can't do that. I can't speak Japanese—I can't do it.' She said, 'You big dummy, all you have to do is come sit. It'll probably be hot and uncomfortable, and there will be lots of bugs but just do the sitting.' And I said, 'waa! waa! urah! urah!' and she got mad. So that was the second time I missed the boat."[44]

Philip kept sidling up to formal Buddhist practice, though, sitting each morning, reciting sutras, and thinking about Zen. He filled pages of his diary observing the intertwined evolution of Japanese culture—especially upper-class culture—and Buddhism. He also kept before him the deeper disturbance. "Today I walked out for fresh air & sunshine, all the way to Black Coffee shop at Hakubaicho, where I sit to write this & try to keep from thoughts of dying. Before I left the house it was a question of walking or going to bed & phoning for the pompes funebres operators to haul me away."[45]

Philip's knew his visa would expire in March 1971, and he had intelligence—rumor, really—that the YMCA might not keep on its foreign teachers. He continued to "fret & pine & go on expensive little excursions to historical beauty spots & gourmandising," adding, "I think I've sucked up the final drop of goody out of certain bits of the scene here, but [am] conscious of certain other big juicy chunks of it which my thirsty & trembling proboscis will never attain."[46]

When the YMCA did drop his job and his visa with it, Philip exerted himself to get an extension. He was proud not to have taken this change lying down, but it came to naught: he was forced to pack up possessions and send them east; he was forced to give up his good flat, forced by his boat's repeated delays to book a costly flight to the States, and forced at the last minute by the airline to leave behind one of his overfull suitcases. Predictably, he fell into a "swoon of hysteria," with "all [his] nerves frying," but with help from the Bakers, he made it. The Baker family drove him to the airport; the Baker family took care of his second bag, and shipped it to him. And six months later, the Baker family would visit Philip where he'd landed in Bolinas and make him an offer that would change the ground of his life.

TWELVE

New Years

WHALEN AND BAKER, ZEN CENTER

When Richard and Virginia Baker drove up to Bolinas to see Philip on New Year's Day 1972, Suzuki Roshi had not yet been dead a full month. Community members of Zen Center—located since late 1969 well outside Japantown—were grieving the loss. Even then, Suzuki Roshi was acknowledged as a spiritual teacher whose presence had fundamentally shifted Buddhism in America and helped anchor it. Much of Suzuki's broader impact came from publication of *Zen Mind, Beginner's Mind,* a collection of talks edited and arranged initially by Trudy Dixon, then again by Richard Baker. Although the teachings came from Suzuki, the book in its final form was a mélange of Baker's making.

With Suzuki Roshi gone, the spiritual and administrative leadership of Zen Center now rested in the hands of a Westerner, the strong-headed, energetic, talented Richard Baker. Devoted to the marrow of his bones to Suzuki Roshi, Baker was remarkably different from him in many ways. Suzuki was short, something over five feet tall, while Baker stood 6'4"; healthy, Suzuki had seemed to radiate sunny warmth from his beautiful smile to his broken but sensitive fingers. With a stubble, Baker, already pale, could appear positively ashen, and though he was friendly, with a good sense of humor, he often looked worried or irritated.

If the Zen Center scene was thus newly inchoate, Philip's situation was no better. He'd arrived back in America in June 1971, wanting "quiet mopery in Bolinas with notebook and pen"[1] and, after returning from a poetry festival in Michigan, busied himself sorting his things, extracting poems from his notebooks, and sidestepping the "huge buzzing social scene."[2] "18 June 71 . . . removed to the basement of Miriam Weber's house. . . . Today Creeley came to sit for Joe Brainard, who is living in the main part of this place. Then

Bobbie Creeley arrived with Diane DiPrima and Jim. Michael Palmer & group of four or five turned up, then Lampe, John Doss & Irving Doyle. Joanne arrived. Bill Berkson. Brautigan. Ebbe Borregaard. Later still, David Meltzer and Tom Clark came to tea. Joanne & I both exhausted from entertaining & being entertained."

That he now figured as a treasured elder among the many Bolinas writers did not immunize Philip from more junior diversions, which included getting high regularly on pot, LSD, and other psychedelia. Pleasurable notice of these appears in his journals, letters, and poems, but as his friend wrote, Philip "one day on acid, sternly informed me, 'Thomas Clark, poetry will never get written this way!'"[3] Nor under these circumstances did Philip come much farther with Zen.

At first he lived a floor below artist Joe Brainard. They respected each other's commitment to work and left one another largely in peace, though Joe did sit for a sketch by Philip, which Joe preserved. He noted in his own journal that Philip "reminds me a bit of Santa Claus. And Buddha. (somewhere in between the two) And I suspect he's very wise but that either he doesn't know it, or else he doesn't value it much. (The only two ways I find 'wisdom' tolerable) At any rate—I really do like him a lot."[4] Brainard was one of the "second-generation" New York school of poets in Bolinas for the season; Anne Waldman, Alice Notley, and Ted Berrigan also lived there in the second half of 1971, and these three connections in particular grew beyond mutual admiration to become enduring friendships.

Soon the arrangements changed, and Philip began sharing a house with Don Allen. Very likely he'd just run out of rent money. Pay from the Michigan poetry festival and from readings in Oregon and New Mexico would not have supported him long. Royalties only trickled in. "I really got into a dreadful mess in order to get here. Sent all my books & toys & games via ship at Ruinous expense, & spent all the rest of life savings on airplane ticket. I don't quite know how I will pay the shipping agent in San Francisco for customs brokerage &c but must find the money someplace, under some tree." It was either that or "sell my beauty & charm & toenails in order to live for the next 3 minutes."[5] Buried treasure eluded him, and the market for toenails was slow.

Additionally, Philip's possessions had come to occupy his time: there were protracted and expensive dealings with customs; things needed sorting— many were fragile—and repacking and storing with each move. Functionally homeless again, this required his attention. One poem from the period—

"October 1st"—simply lists out twenty possessions, then goes through the inventory again, commenting.

Don Allen had his own Bolinas house. At this point, he'd worked with Philip for fifteen years as an editor; with the recent publication of *Severance Pay* and *Scenes of Life at the Capital*—two of Philip's works from Japan—Don had become Philip's main publisher.[6] He took Philip in, then he regretted it. "Don was a very proper bachelor," noted Joanne Kyger. His small place was elegantly appointed with rugs, lamps, and a pair of wingback chairs. Philip possessed his own elegance, but their styles clashed. Philip apparently put his toothbrush in the wrong place in the bathroom, and there *was* only one bathroom. While Don sat with a drink, quietly reading in one of the chairs, Philip occupied the other, and chomped his daily popcorn—salted, buttered, and turned from the pot into a brown paper grocery bag. Whenever Don spoke with Richard Baker,[7] he complained about Philip: there was no space in the house; doubling the population had put strain on the septic system. Relations between the two men, though constant and enduring, had always been edgy; now they were driving each other crazy. Don didn't want to kick Philip out, he said, but. . . . Baker saw that as the new abbot of Zen Center, he was in a position to help, and so on New Year's Day he invited Philip to move into Zen Center. Six weeks later, Philip, with his books, boxes, toys, and electric organ, moved to 300 Page Street. He had unwittingly leapfrogged the waiting list and been installed in a choice single room on the inner courtyard. Baker had taken it upon himself to invite him, he said, citing Philip's background ancestral role in American Zen.[8] This minor display of Baker's complete authority caused some "gossipy dissonance," and it embarrassed Philip to learn he'd cut in line, but any discontent blew over quickly as people got to know him.

When the front door of Zen Center closed behind him, it must have seemed to friends and acquaintances that that was that: Philip was put away, like a jar in a cupboard or a big roasting bird in the oven. At Zen Center it quickly felt like he'd always been there. Richard Baker appeared to have simply dropped the puzzle piece called Philip Whalen into a strangely shaped space called Zen Center and found a fit. Philip's Zen career—a fair word, considering Snyder's quip that Philip had "at last found a job!"—ran variously. There were definite phases, distinct locations, signal turning points. These all had to do with Richard Baker.

To begin, the two men recalled the conditions for Zen Center residence slightly differently. Baker said that for Philip there were none; Philip could just be there and wouldn't have to do anything at all. Philip reported he'd been told to "attend zazen, take your meals in the dining room, and do a daily chore."⁹ None of these would have strained him much, least of all the chore. Zen Center's schedule, though, had a great deal more zazen built into it than the amorphous daily sit he'd been used to. The first sitting began at five in the morning (students needed to be seated by 4:57) and ran for forty minutes. This was followed by ten minutes of very slow walking meditation and another forty-minute sit. The assembly would then depart the basement zendo in a ritual pattern, climb to the first floor, and regather in the Buddha Hall for twenty minutes of bowing and chanting, mostly in Japanese. The morning events were announced and timed with traditional Japanese temple instruments. Handbells trilled, large and small gongs sounded, drums boomed, blocks of wood clacked. It was difficult to sleep through the music, though not impossible. Breakfast was collected from a steam-table serving area adjacent to the kitchen and taken, in silence, in the dining room next to it. Thus at 7:45 Philip, who consistently attended all of these devotions, would be looking at a day in San Francisco's Western Addition, a dangerous neighborhood at the time. He had his chore to accomplish, either morning or afternoon, while other residents often did more extended work—meal preparation, building maintenance and renovation. (Readers will perhaps forgive the continuing elaboration of the schedule when they realize that Philip followed something very close to this for the final thirty years of his life.)

A short service of bowing and sutra recitation took place midday, followed by lunch in the dining room, for which silence was generally not required. Meditators assembled again for a 5:30 afternoon sitting, the most popular of the day, then climbed up again to the Buddha Hall for more prostrations and chants. The first several minutes of dinner took place in silence, but upon signal, gentle conversation might begin. The zendo altar was lit again, and a block of wood was struck in the pattern alerting the interested that meditation would start at 8:30 P.M. Philip usually declined the invitation. "Since I've been here, I've been on this loony schedule. So I can't go around very much, and my head is all bent."¹⁰ Philip apologized humorously with these words to poet Aram Saroyan and then gave him a poet-to-poet definition of zazen: "To do zazen, you sit, that's all. You have to put your feet up in your lap—you sit on this little round cushion—and you try to think the unthinkable, like Suzuki Roshi said, or try to just sit there without letting the thoughts that you do have scare you, or drag you, or do anything more than just go by, sort of let them all go. . . . [You] don't hang on—just sort of let it go—and try to sit straight, try to keep your back straight, and try to breathe smoothly, and try not to go to sleep."

Increased hours of meditation may have given Philip the feeling of having a bent head, but more challenging for him were the implications of taking his meals in the dining room. He had not lived a regimented communal life since his army days, and in the interim he'd very often lived alone. In fact, he often compared Zen Center to the U.S. Army, not intending it as a compliment. Philip entered Zen Center when he was forty-eight; he was fifteen to twenty-five years older than all but a handful of the other fifty-plus residents and the dozens more who lived nearby. Mostly white, mostly with some college, not poor—living at Zen Center cost money—the "kids," as he called them, crowded him as they zoomed around accomplishing tasks in the building or heading off for school or jobs in town.

"I have tried very hard to believe in the real existence of other persons," he wrote in his journal at Zen Center. "Perhaps I've succeeded too well, since I often feel imposed upon?"[11] He spent time shut up in his room reading, writing, or playing music through headphones, but he also for no reason regularly positioned himself—large and round, with white hair and beard not quite unkempt—at the reception desk in Zen Center's front hall. He also began to use the first person plural: "Here we are very serious & full of vegetables & mush & gomashio."[12]

"Here we spend much of every morning looking for each other, 'Where is Richard. Have you seen Janet, which way did Steven go, where is David.' Searching, 'Go find Angie or Jane. Alice might know. Ask Reb. Tell Katherine.' The disconnected communion of the saints. 'Where is Dick, I mean Baker Roshi. Please ask Pat about it.'"[13] Other times he could be found kneeling at the low table in the Flop Room (the name was later upgraded by administrative order) reading one of the house newspapers or sitting in the small annex kitchen with a coffee and, on lucky days, a toast or other snack. He would generally be talking, theatrically, to whoever else was present, or to the newspaper itself if no one was. He might be humming or singing. He did not go in for the hushed tones, clipped sentences, or imitations of Japanese English many house residents used. In short, Philip was fat where most everyone else was trim, loud where everyone else was quiet, loosely hirsute where many wore shaved heads or closely cropped hair; he was older, crazier, funnier, and with much more experience of Japan.

So passed his first months at Zen Center. It was not at all clear to him that he would stay, much less that he would live connected to Zen Center for the rest of his life. In April, he wrote to Jim Koller about staying "a few more months," but when those months were up, Philip went not back out to the broader society—not a jot away from steady room and board at Zen Center—but more deeply in. As autumn began, he sat with a selection of his possessions in a truck heading to Tassajara, Zen Center's monastery at the bottom of a steep valley, at the end of a long dirt road, in the middle of Los Padres National Forest. The decision to enter the monastery and to follow the rigorous schedule there for the next three months had been taken in discussion with Richard Baker. It is crucial to note that right here—during Philip's first months at Zen Center—the nature of his friendship with Baker radically, formally, and surprisingly shifted. Philip took Baker as his Zen teacher. He used the forms of respect belonging to that relationship, as well as the titles. He might call him "Dick" or "the boss" in conversation with other students, but Philip now directly addressed the younger man he'd known for a dozen years with the honorific *roshi*.[14] Whenever Philip went for a practice interview, he, like everyone else, prostrated to the floor three times in front of Baker before sitting nearly knee to knee with him and beginning to talk. "I was surprised!" Baker averred in a fond, humorous memory.

> He would come to dokusan, and I took it with a grain of salt! We had to go through this formal thing. I'm now sitting there in dokusan and he's bowing, and I'm thinking "What is my companion—not friend at this point, but companion—what is my dharma companion bowing to me for?" But we agreed that this was the game we were going to play. He continued to come, and it developed into a real relationship. And he took it seriously. He related to me—and to his practice—and he talked about his practice to me, in a real way. It just kept developing.[15]

Others who'd known Suzuki Roshi or who'd experienced the heavier-handed sides of Baker may have wrestled with issues of his authority, but Philip saw it straightforwardly. "I didn't ask why Richard was head of the place. It was simple. It was his. The old man had handed it to him. I didn't expect anything of him. Baker couldn't disappoint me. He had it from Suzuki-roshi. Isn't that why he and I were both there?"[16]

Though Baker termed their connection "the game we decided to play," both he and Philip understood its seriousness. No relationship cuts more deeply or affects the course of life more profoundly than master and disciple working together in a spiritual context. As intimate as any love affair, often expressed in the vocabulary of parentage, both parties eventually bring everything they have to it, of necessity exposing themselves completely. It doesn't usually start out that way, of course.

Philip and Richard had become acquaintances as part of one circle around Don Allen and another around John and Margot Doss. Earlier, though, dating from his days at Grove in the mid-1950s in New York, Baker had admired Philip's poetry and told Don Allen that Philip's "language is on my mind more than that of any other poet." In the essay where he mentions this, Baker explains that "I was searching for Zen and for a language."[17] Why? "My experience—of the world, other people, and so forth—was not congruent with the usual way the world is described or viewed, the way most people describe it. So I was trying to find some way to speak that allowed me to express myself. I never tried much to write poems or anything, because it was mostly an internal process—looking for words that seemed to fit my experience or would lead my experience. And I had the feeling that Philip was doing that; I found something like that in Philip's writings."[18] It was not just that Philip worked to match his language to his own unusual experience, or that—like Ezra Pound, it seemed to Baker— Philip treated words as solid objects and juxtaposed them creatively; there was also a slant, a retiring slant. "Until we went to Japan, we had a friendship based not on spending time together but on a continuous recognition of each other, as having similar interest in the world or a similar feel for the world. . . . For me, the American muses were definitely out to lunch, and I really didn't want to be a part of the society, or this world, even. Perhaps I shared something like that with Philip." Baker distinguished this from what he shared with other poets: "Gary [Snyder] and I might do things in the world together—environmental, antinuclear—things that might affect the world. With Philip, the side of me that was similar was of pulling away from the world, not getting too involved with the world. Stepping out of this world."

When in 1970 they found themselves both in Kyoto, they began to see much more of one another, the way ex-pats, especially two very un-Japanese-looking ex-pats—Baker a tower and Whalen a tank—might do in foreign surroundings. The Baker family profited from Philip's passion for temples, and he profited, if that is the word, from their car, which he termed a monster. Philip's journal gives the flavor:

Left yesterday with RD Baker family & Dick's brother-in-law, Lambert Brackett, for Eiheiji. Car died in or near Hikone but recovered. Arrived late in Monzen village, too late to stay at Eiheiji, too late for supper in hotel where we dined on sake, beer, candy, mikan, roasted peas & beans & trash. Bath and sleep. Arise at 4:40 AM for ceremony at Eiheiji. Earthquake during ceremony in the hatto. After breakfast, push car for long time in heavy snow. At last return trip begins. Car dies somewhere outside Fukui city. Recovers. Minor repairs. Return to hotel where Richard had left his jewelry. Start home again. Flat tire above Tsunga Bay. Repair. Food. A few miles later, something hit windshield & exploded small hole in it, after which windshield cracked uniformly all over until it was impossible—night now—to see through it. Left car with cops in Tsuruga City & took train to Kyoto & so home via taxi. Whew, and vast expense.[19]

They also had fun, no matter that Philip might be late or that the Bakers might find him at home unresponsive, sweating and playing Bach through the headphones, wearing only his underpants. On would go the clothes and off they'd be to adventure. In the parking lot at Entsuji one day, as the Baker family got out of the car and arranged themselves, a huge thunderclap rocked everyone. Philip immediately and loudly addressed the heavens: "Okay! All right! I promise never to play with my wee-wee again!" At the theater another evening with the Bakers, Philip felt he could no longer endure the performance. To make his way down the long, scandalized row of viewers, he rose to his tiptoes, extended his arms, and slid his bulk along sideways, swooping and intoning, "Butterfly, butterfly, flap, flap! Butterfly, butterfly, flap flap!" Yet another outing found the group overnighting in the guesthouse of a Shingon temple on Koya-san. Having come somehow into possession of two magnums of sake, Philip gave them to the host monk so they could be served along with the many courses of the evening meal, which they were taking in their rooms. When the shoji doors slid open, several trays were slid in, each tray holding only heated ceramic flasks of sake—the entire contents of the two magnums—to start the meal. Surprised but undaunted, the group set to drinking, and soon natural conviviality merged into humorous, even raucous casualness. Hearing dinner server monks coming along the planks, Philip suddenly barked, "STRAIGHTEN UP!" All three adults, without thinking, temporarily did.

These and other expeditions gave Philip and Richard ample time and suggestive settings in which to discuss Buddhism. Though he'd been sitting a decade longer than Richard, Philip thought of himself as a poet and novelist with a meditation habit. Richard, though, was a man who had by now given his life over to Zen. He was in Japan at the request of Suzuki Roshi, to absorb what he could of cultural background, to spend some time in traditional monasteries—and to do all this in preparation for succeeding Suzuki Roshi as abbot of Zen Center, a plan Suzuki confided in Baker as early as 1967. Richard Baker was not the only Westerner Philip knew who'd dedicated his or her life to Zen; Walter Nowick, Irmgard Schloegel, and Gary Snyder had also done this, but as Philip's second sojourn in Japan continued, Baker became the most intimate. In April 1971, a character called "Fast Talking Buddha" appears in Philip's journal; several pages go by before it emerges that the FTB (as Philip often wrote it) is Baker. Philip observed the FTB closely and not uncritically. Philip sometimes painted Baker's manners as insensitive—continuing to speak broken Japanese, for example, to salespeople who were able and wanted to converse in English; taking a long time to buy something and asking many questions, only to make a very small purchase; relating to others with a general sense of busyness and speed; and having a tendency to complain. These harsh remarks are no more than the chiding Philip would (and did) give himself. The point is that of the many things Philip could be attending to, listening to, and writing about, he told his journal about Richard Baker, who had come to matter. Baker had been given the status of Buddha in Philip's inner pantheon, even if he was a fast-talking one.

"If you were to ask me if I were Philip's teacher, I would never say that. We had a relationship, that's all." In interview, Baker curiously but repeatedly declines being labeled as Philip's teacher, though he does admit that he was "technically and formally Philip's teacher … though I never thought of myself that way—I was always amazed that *he* thought of me that way." When speaking, Baker preferred to construct an extended metaphor for their relations, with Buddhism as water and he and Philip as swimmers: before Japan, they'd shared an interest in the water; this deepened in Japan, and when Philip came to Zen Center, Baker coached him, showed him something about swimming. Later, they'd just swum along together. "If you say I was his teacher, that's less than what it was." In print, however, Baker was perfectly capable of simply stating, "Philip Whalen, Zenshin Ryufu, is my teacher, and I am his teacher. We have shared these roles."[20] From Philip's side, Baker completely and thoroughly fulfilled the role of teacher.

Early in his Zen Center days, Philip told poet Alice Notley that he was "trying to do the Buddhism right." Whatever meanings he may have coded into this phrase, it certainly included the Buddha's original structure. To be a disciple, one went for refuge to the Three Jewels: the Buddha as teacher and example; the dharma as the body of the teachings, canonical and spontaneous; and the sangha, the community of fellow practitioners. Philip had not yet gone through this most ancient of all Buddhist ceremonies, but he'd long before adopted the Buddhist dharma as a tool for understanding the world. With the "kids" at Zen Center, he'd joined the sangha, and in Baker, he'd found his Buddha.

Before he went to Tassajara, Philip got away to the mountains for a visit with Gary, and then for a long hike accompanied by a Zen student named Eric Larson. Wondering at first in his journal "if I am the only nearsighted intellectual who likes to walk into remote parts of the woods, swim or wade a while then jump about on rocks & grass," Philip went on to record what he termed

> dreams of magnificence all through the night—Trungpa Tulku Rinpoche, in midst of large quasi-ceremonial occasion is in prophetic phrenzy. He sees me & says that although I am Richard's son & successor, he will give me a special initiation later—I must meet him at (—) in Sikkhim a year from now. And it is in the valley of (—) in Sikkhim where my "true robe" is kept in a gompa, & where I could go & get it if I wanted it, but it was scarcely a matter worth bothering about. It seemed quite possible that I would find a way to get to Sikkhim, & that Richard would probably go, also. I must write to Allen & find out what was he up to last night, as some kind of communication {"Hello & how are you?"} was coming from him.
>
> Part of Trungpa's oration to me was about being free from the past, about conversion of old karma energy into immediate wise action &c. Anyway, the spirit of the Rinpoche was roused & roaring. This material was repeated obsessively.
>
> There were also instructions in the shape of images of fish & fowl bodies being cut up—we ought not to eat meat. Vivid recall of how the knife goes through gristle & fine bones when cutting up a chicken. On the one hand it is a simple mechanical operation; on the other, it shouldn't take place at all. Still, I would vastly enjoy a chicken dinner right now.[21]

It bears noting that Philip had never met Trungpa Rinpoche, though he'd certainly heard of him. It is also odd that he would interpret the dream cutting as a prohibition against eating meat. He knew that Tantric imagery is replete with weapons for cutting, though the objects to be cut are one's delusions. Philip never gave up eating chicken or fish; neither did he ever stop listing (for himself) oughts and ought-nots.

In August of that same summer, Philip pushed himself through another journey, this one entirely within the confines of Zen Center: he completed his first *sesshin*.[22] These seven-day all-day meditation retreats occurred once every two months. Periods of zazen—separated by short stretches of walking meditation—usually ran forty minutes, and there were many of them: two before breakfast, four between breakfast and lunch, interrupted by a brief tea served to students in their places, at least two more periods before dinner, and two after dinner. Meals were taken in meditation posture in the zendo, and they were vegetarian (as all were at Zen Center), swift, and silent except for liturgical recitation. Indeed, the entire *sesshin* theoretically proceeded in silence. Necessary chores were done after lunch, and a talk was given each day, also in the afternoon. The schedule demanded a great deal of everyone. Inevitable fatigue and physical pain—knees, back, shoulders, neck—were discussed as integral to the practice, not as problems.

"I couldn't, wouldn't follow all the rules," Philip confessed. "I kept seeing what I thought of as fake aspects of the scene. I didn't have so direct a sense of empathy with the group, or as much of communal spirit. The last 2 periods of zazen were fairly persuasive. In general the experience is still very strange & exciting & intriguing, & I've been feeling very happy & free & decisive about everything. I keep telling myself that I'll probably feel 'down' from this temporary exaltation, after a few more days have passed. Eventually, one learns to stay 'up.' {or 'don't come down,' Roshi says.}"[23]

Baker said that the tradition in his lineage—the Dongshan lineage—was to leave students alone. Opportunities, pitfalls, direction—the student must see these for themselves. They might decide things in consultation with their teacher, but impetus must come from the student. Thus it was Philip who proposed doing the *sesshin,* Philip who asked about living at Tassajara, and even before the summer was over, it was Philip who requested ordination. Whatever Baker felt about his rapid embrace of Zen life, he supported Philip's choices.

When he finally got there, Philip's early impressions of Tassajara and its inhabitants were not promising, as a sample of journal entries shows:

Boiling hot & flies. No mountains to speak of. Lots of dust. Dry in spite of creek & the hot sulphur spring—perpetual smell of egg/fart. Rural California—where there is piped water & where there are flush toilets & propane gas stoves; I find it hard to think of life here as being "primitive" or "far away in the mountains" as it is represented.

Do the creep vibes here come from the same kind of source as the creep vibes in Page St.—a nucleus of 3 or 4 ladies with large voices & very clear enunciation helped on by a little cluster of crypto-faggot masochist rule-book players?

Hot & buggy sitting, gnats & sweat. Heat becomes quite unusual just before sundown. A heavy chill sets in at about 3 AM & STAYS til sunrise.

Boredom. anguish, hysteria {deeply contained} & aggressiveness {"ill temper" "crotchety" &c.} Too much like the Boy Scout camp I never went to because my family was poor? Too many rich kids here?

I guess it is simply good management to leave the running of things to small, neat, worried people—& heavy monotonous drudgery to the strong & simple minded {e.g. the kitchen}. the contemplative imaginative type—where does he belong . . . is he "out" again, just as he is in regular society . . . & obliged to save himself however he can from the natterings of the busy & the grumbling of the dull? {cut corners, steal time, break rules}

Tassajara suffers from its borrowed style—& wants "tone"—Americans early in the morning are a college dorm, the Army or a lumber camp.[24]

Some grumpiness in these entries can be forgiven, considering the conditions under which they were written. Philip had climbed out of the Volkswagen in which he'd ridden the last fourteen steep, sometimes cliff-hanging, miles on 13 September 1972, breathed the nasty smell of the mineral baths, and was next morning immured on his seat in the zendo. All new entrants to the monastery sat through this testing/hazing ritual, called *tangaryo,* in Japanese. They followed the usual schedule of two morning zazen periods and two in the evening, and they ate meals with everyone in the zendo; but when the others went off to monastery jobs, maintenance, or study, Philip and other first-timers returned to their cushions and just sat there: no walking meditation, no tea break, no moving, no nothing (apart from bathroom visits) for hours at a time, five to ten days in a row. It is rumored that during stretches lacking any stick-carrying hall monitor, Philip passed lemon drops and Lifesavers down the row.

During a Tassajara practice period,[25] time revolved around a heavy nonoptional schedule of zazen, study, work, and a daily bath in the famed hot springs. Weekly ceremonies punctuated the routine: calendar dates ending in 4 and 9 were locally termed "day off," because there was only one period of zazen morning and evening with an unscheduled day in between. Students used these to do laundry, room cleaning, and, for the ordained, head shaving. Materials for a bag lunch were set out, and students attacked the tables immediately after their study hall. Dinner was in the dining room, at tables with silverware. Days numbered with 3 and 8 were for communal cleaning; talks from the abbot took place on 2, 5, and 7 days. Students awaited with covetous delight the delivery, every ten days or so, of the five items they'd been allowed to order from town: salted pretzels and peanut butter in Philip's case, also (illegally) sardines, as well as toiletries.

As his forty-ninth birthday came and went, Philip felt tired, unsettled, trapped, and crowded. "I keep thinking I must get away from this organization—for one thing, I don't have the physical stamina to keep up with these children—& I want 'away' from them—they are dull, middle-class &c. I must go think & read & write & consider—somewhere away from their rules & schedules . . . "

"Why don't I have more patience with children—& more patience with my own middle aged grumbling & creaks? & where is 'out'—who, among my sometimes friends, would receive me if I were to phone X, Y or Z & say, 'I need a bed, temporarily.' Who would say 'Where are you phoning from—stay there until I drive over & pick you up—5 minutes.' Poor little me!!"[26]

The somber, relentless forms of monastic life and the many daily hours of group meditation had begun corroding whatever internal structures and beliefs composed Philip's "personality," leaving him not very much. Finally he wrote, "I keep wondering when & how I might kill myself. It makes me nervous to live with this group of children, acting out somebody else's theory. There's no job, home or place for me 'outside'—only 'begging & borrowing.' I keep saying that I have lots of work {i.e. lots of writing & drawing & music practice & reading & studying} to do. I still don't know how I can live—how to get food & lodging & books & musical instruments—so I think I must die—die of pique & frustration & self-pity & regret—die of silliness."

Silly or not, these suicidal thoughts persisted for three days running: "One contemplates the entry & path of the knife blade, the bullet—sensations of suffocation or strangling or the action of poison—jolt as one hits ground at the bottom of cliff, pavement in front of Empire State Building, water under Golden Gate Bridge—whack and grind of train, truck or the wheels &c.—& all this in addition to paranoiac fantasies of being murdered in any number of fancy ways for any number of reasons—of death by 'natural' causes, whether disease or old age &c. &c. &c. So what."

Tassajara lay literally at the end of the road. The psychologically equivalent feeling was compounded with the phrase "Nobody in, nobody out," bandied between students. Not strictly true—Richard Baker came and went as the duties of abbotship dictated, and the town-trippers—but it was very exceptional for a student to depart. Philip, however, had long been committed to a series of readings in Chicago. He had Baker's permission to fulfill this, and so he arrived there on 11 November, where Ted Berrigan collected him and took him to the apartment he shared with Alice Notley. Eleven years younger than Philip, in awe of his poems and especially of their formal and structural "breakthroughs," Ted himself would soon go on to be one of the central poets in the New York school anchored in the Lower East Side. Alice Notley, in turn eleven years younger than Ted, would be another one. They were early in their life together, a marriage that would last until Ted's death in 1983, producing two sons, a vibrant salon, and much brilliant poetry.

Philip felt immediately at ease with these two extraordinary artists—he repeatedly referred to Alice as a genius—who lived as he had done, undaunted by the poverty inflicted on poets; who had read and digested the canon of English literature; who continued to read that, as well as new work, and to take pleasure and relief in reading modern "trash." They fed and housed Philip for the week—he'd arrived with three dollars in his pocket—and they escorted him to his readings and to Chicago's great museums. Philip and Alice also fell in love, platonically, during long talks at the kitchen table, cookbooks spread open. Ted minded "not a bit," according to Alice. "He was also in love with Philip." When he'd been paid, Philip bought ingredients and cooked them all a massive "graveyard stew"—the antisadness dish of poached eggs in milk and cream he'd written about to Joanne Kyger. Thus fortified, enriched, loved, and admired, Philip made his way back to Tassajara and sat out the practice period, including the very demanding *rohatsu sesshin* in the bleak, cold days of December.[27]

His question from the *Shosan* ceremony—one of the final rituals of a practice period—made a deep impression on those who heard it. During this ceremony, students would rise one by one from their seats, proceed to the back of the zendo, and from across the hall, pose a question to the abbot. The distance requires that they raise their voice; tradition requires they ask a real question, something they were working on, something that exposes them. Philip, shaking and in tears, demanded to know, "Why am I the only one afraid to die?!" Richard Baker calmly surveyed his friend and said, "You have twenty years to practice Buddhism."[28] Philip outlived this by ten.

THIRTEEN

An Order to Love

ORDINATION

The job Philip did during Tassajara work periods was in the library. He'd been assigned the light work because he was old and fat and knowledgeable about books, but also because it afforded him time to sew his formal outer robe—his *okesa*—for the ordination. This garment, modeled after Shakyamuni Buddha's own patch-robe, required many hours of hand stitching from ordainees. Simple rectangles—representing rags from the Indian tradition, rags that were scavenged from horrible sources and then washed and purified—were joined into panels; the panels were joined and hemmed around three times until the final product measured something like seven feet by four. A short mantra—Japanese for "I take refuge in the Buddha"—accompanied each of the thousands of stitches. Ordination also meant having hand sewn a smaller robe, a *rakusu,* for more informal wear, silk-lined envelopes for both robes, and a bowing mat, so that nothing ever touched the ground. Precise, slow, boring work, hard on the eyes; even though he started late, Philip accomplished it, all but the *rakusu,* which involved very fussy sewing indeed. That he did later.

"I hope that you & Allen G can come to the ceremony," Philip had written to Gary before leaving for Tassajara. "Especially you, since I am so much obliged to you for teaching me & helping me find good Buddha friends."[1] Planned for December in the monastery, the ordination for Philip and seven others took place 3 February 1973 in the city center. Allen couldn't make it at all, and serious illness forced Gary to pull out at the last minute. Happily for the record, Philip sent Allen a copy of the ceremony liturgy, "painfully translated out of the Oriental Tongues by Suzuki Roshi & cut & rearranged by Baker Roshi." Philip added extensive marginalia to the seven typed pages: translations of vocabulary and explanations of the action implied by the brief instructions. This included six drawings showing the construction and comportment of the hand-sewn robes. (Attention given to this, both by Philip and the present author, reflects the centuries-old tradition of transmitting Zen lineage not with a text, as in other lineages, but with presentation of the robe and bowl.) The long letter accompanying the ceremony script contains a number of Chinese characters in Philip's best handwriting, as well as this: "Our heads are shaved & we have taken sundry vows & we wear Buddha's robe & technically we are supposed to be unmarried & homeless & begging for our daily food." Philip knew that Baker was married, that several senior priests at Zen Center were, that Suzuki Roshi had been. He'd seen married priests in Japan. Thus it is not clear what "technically unmarried" meant, or after which tradition Zen Center ordainees were to model themselves—Chinese? Indian? training monastery? Japanese? He lived out his days among married Zen priests, but Philip retained his conservative view on the matter. This cuts to the heart of how even to name such a person as himself. His letter continues, "Dick is now officially my teacher & and I am his disciple. Sino/Japanese expression for 'monk' is *unsui* {Jap} or *yün shui* {Chin} [Philip also draws the characters] 'clouds and water' . . . wandering priest. We shut ourselves in monastery at Tassajara for limited times only, not forever—we chant but don't pray, really."[2] When he wrote to Gary, he included none of this, as Gary had gone through his own ordination in Japan in 1956. Philip did, though, send him the characters for his new name—Dai Shin Ryu Fu—which he translated "Big Heart Dragon Wind." Later Baker changed the "Dai" to Zen."

On the matter of his now being Philip's teacher, the ceremony dramatized this. In front of the audience, Philip knelt (as in turn each disciple did) and raised his hands palm-to-palm in front of his face. Baker Roshi stood above, straight razor in his hand. Referring to the dime-size patch of hair on the otherwise shaven head, Roshi said:

> "THIS LAST HAIR IS CALLED THE SHURA.
> ONLY A BUDDHA CAN CUT IT OFF!
> NOW I WILL CUT IT OFF!
> DO YOU ALLOW ME TO CUT IT OFF?"
> EACH DISCIPLE: "YES!"[3]

The ordination mixes letting go of old things and receiving new ones. Called *tokudo* (literally, "home departure"), it means leaving "this drifting wandering life" and taking the path of nirvana. For this new life, ordainees are supplied with new clothes and bowls, new names, and a new family lineage; but before this can happen, they must clear away the old. In Buddha's time, new sangha members would, after the ceremony, literally walk away from their homes and families forever. In 1973, they symbolized this with a prostration to any family members present. On the new path, they would need to travel very lightly. As their heads were being shaved, Philip's group recited:

> WITHIN THE KARMA OF PAST, PRESENT & FUTURE
> O THE TIES OF AFFECTION ARE HARD TO BREAK
> BUT BEYOND THE THREE WORLDS OF KARMA
> IS THE REALM OF TRUE COMPASSION.

Even with no family present, Philip had "ties of affection" aplenty. In case anyone missed it the first time, the Roshi specified:

> SHAVING YOUR HEAD AND AGAIN SHAVING YOUR HEAD
> YOU ARE CUTTING YOUR ATTACHMENTS.

and the disciples responded:

> FREED FROM KARMA AND WORLDLY ATTACHMENTS
> FREED FROM FORM & COLOR, EVERYTHING IS CHANGED
> EXCEPT MY DESIRE TO LIVE IN TRUTH
> AND SAVE ALL BEINGS.

Cutting off all the hair on a person's head and face—particularly if there was a lot of it, particularly if it was coppery red turning dignified white—will leave them looking different. Philip looked like a plucked bird. His skull's roundness accentuated the rest of his roundness. His eyes appeared to protrude. Alice Notley rued the bald look, recalling how "a lot of his beauty had been located in his hair." She reported that Joanne too had been "decidedly snippy" about it. As a measure to help reduce attachments, tonsure seemed to be working, but the text contained a second section spelling out behavior for the new monks and nuns. Orders came in the form of refuges, vows, and precepts—both "pure" and "prohibitory." Though in English one "takes" such vows, their overwhelming message is to release, renounce, let go, and restrain. The prohibitory precepts restrict acts of body, speech, and mind, both explicitly and subtly. They were not, however, like the Ten Commandments, which they vaguely resemble, placed front and center. In fact, they were rarely taught; in Suzuki Roshi's lineage at least, ethical conduct was supposed to arise from meditation; from relaxing the tight weave of self-centered thoughts; from sustained contact with deeper, calmer, more benevolent and illuminative aspects of mind. Experiences on the cushion were supplemented by encounters with the teacher. However it worked, Philip reined himself in noticeably. At meals out, and at parties from then on, he drank very moderately. In social situations with old friends, if other intoxicants were around, he refrained. Explosions of temper—"tantrums," he called them—and eating binges still plagued him occasionally, but almost to the letter, he continued to try to "do the Buddhism right."

He also stopped doing something else: "What disappointed me is that he basically stopped writing poetry when he started to practice," said Baker. "He wrote poems—at Tassajara, or in the city, I know—but really, he kind of stopped writing." Philip wrote eight poems in his first year at Zen Center, eight more his second year, fifteen the year after that, nine the year after that, and eight the year after that. By 1978–79, he was writing more freely again, but no more long works, nothing over two pages, none with his earlier drive and desperation. These poems were more reflective, quizzical, quieter. They remained incisive and humorous, perhaps even wiser for their brevity. Those who followed Philip's work suggested a variety of reasons for his slowdown: he had gotten older, and many artists quiet down with age and maturity; he stopped keeping up with new writing; he shifted his study and reflection from literature to Buddhism—his journal testifies to this; his eyes worsened, impeding his reading and reducing for him the pleasures of writing and drawing with pen and ink; his writing "habit" relaxed its grip; something in the hours of meditation and study, and the saturated schedule of communal life, answered his needs.

Philip came at the question himself, repeatedly: "I wish I were writing a long complicated something but I am either too tired or too busy to do any writing—hard enough to write letters &c."[4] "I tell myself that the organization bores me—the rules & the people. What I'm doing is boring myself. I really mean that I want to work. Yesterday I could see things for a minute: i.e. see clearly &/or 'poetically' just how, walking along Oak Street making all these decisions I picked up on geranium & pelargonium leaves, their different shapes & colors; pansy faces of Martha Washington flowers, brings all up to date."[5] Wondering to Allen Ginsberg about what he would write next, Philip said, "The schedule and noise at the Zen Center building are so loud I can't find out while I'm there."[6] And after more than eighteen months at Zen Center, he told Jim Koller,

I am endlessly "busy" & can scarcely get my head together to write a letter, much less anything like poems. . . . My plans are to stay here & try to write something interesting, but so far I haven't had time to write anything. I maunder & dote. I also plan to find lots of money & run away to someplace quiet. Life in this quarter is dirty & dangerous. Shall I survive the race war &c &c. My leg hurts, I broke cartilage or ligaments or something in my right knee by falling a couple times in February. My teeth and eyes are going funny. I grow fatter every day.[7]

Despite these personal difficulties, Philip did stay at Zen Center; despite largely empty days, he wrote very little. Perhaps this adds up to Baker's insight that Philip fundamentally changed his identity—as indeed the ordination text states—in his case from a poet with a meditation habit to a monk who wrote occasional verse.

"JISHA to Baker Roshi," Philip told his journal on 9 March 1973, meaning that he now held the position of ceremonial attendant to the abbot. When the abbot entered Zen Center several minutes before 5 A.M., the *jisha* would meet him in his quarters. Philip (or another *jisha*—Baker Roshi used several) would accompany him on his rounds to the temple's shrines, carrying the incense stick to be offered at each and sounding the instruments that signaled their progress. The *jisha* would approach the final shrine in the zendo with the abbot, give him the last piece of incense, and take his seat next to the abbot's place. If Baker was staying for zazen, Philip would stay too; if Baker was retiring to his interview room, Philip would accompany him and manage the list. During the morning service in the Buddha Hall, Philip would need to meet Baker at the altar as each chant began and have prepared the proper incense. After nine prostrations, service was recited kneeling, sitting on one's heels. The *jisha,* though, would need to pop to his or her feet several times, briskly move forward to the shrine, and perform the arrangements. After all the recitations and the concluding bows, Philip would then trail Baker out of the Buddha Hall and on to other devotions. If, after these, Baker continued interviews, Philip remained on duty.

Despite pressured, claustrophobic moments at the altar, despite the discomforts of feeling oneself to be on stage, despite early duties and uncertain conclusions, the job was considered an honor. Philip had it barely a year after arriving, signaling very rapid "progress." In fact, in his first year, Philip had lived in a coveted single room, had had the time and funds for several *sesshins,* had attended a practice period at Tassajara, and had been ordained. Had it been anyone else, this could have provoked real resentment; everyone at Zen Center was in a tradition of selfless enlightenment, but everyone also watched remarkably closely who held which position, who had which rank, who had been practicing where and for how long. Little jealousies burned. Philip escaped such resentment mostly by being tremendously funny, smart, mischievous, and unholy. Even his grumpiness was forgiven. Moreover, he was not very good at being a Zen student, and he made no effort to hide his difficulties. The bowls and cloths for meals—the *oryoki*—were operated with great speed and precision; these flummoxed him. Weeks into his first Tassajara sojourn, he told his journal that he was *almost* able to use them correctly. With ordination, he received a new set of black lacquer bowls, more numerous, more complex, highly polished, and much more slippery than ceramic. When one of these bowls skittered off the meal board and onto the floor at Zen Center, he let out a yell as he lunged for it, breaking the silence with the cry of a foot soldier gored on a pike. Everyone was supposed to sit silently as the head server collected the bowl, took it out, washed it, and returned it to a red-faced Philip, who had had to remain with hands raised palm-to-palm during this delay.

The bowls were minor compared to the robes—many rules governed their wearing, folding, and storage. Baker once described Japanese Buddhism as a "cloth event." Philip had never been strong sartorially, but now he was obliged to work with robes. Their several layers were supposed to sit just so and to be crossed and tied so that each showed the right amount. Sleeves hung fully three feet below a horizontally extended arm; steps were circumscribed by the hang of the ankle-length under-robe. Any haste or lapse in mindfulness of the garment extension of one's body could result in a snag, tear, trip, or tumble. With a substantial and expanding body, Philip had perhaps more than his share of these new-monk trials, and he was rarely quiet about it. Particularly the *okesa*—the most formal robe, the one that had taken him months to sew—presented difficulties. It could only be donned after placing it atop one's head and reciting verses of appreciation. In the 1973 Zen Center, this took place for the first time each morning, at the end of meditation. The *okesa* needed then to be unfurled and tied, tucked, and draped so that it hung properly over one shoulder, and over the other (at least three) layers of robes. In the dim zendo, one might not find the ties, one might join them improperly, one might get hold of the wrong corner and tuck it where it ought not be tucked, one might literally tie oneself in knots. An unspoken race took place each morning among the ordained not to be the last. But regularly, as everyone else in the room stood, clearing their throats, smoothing out wrinkles, waiting for feeling to return to feet and legs, Philip would still be sitting at his place, muted curses and hisses, like the spitting of a cornered cat, emanating from him as he labored with his *okesa*. He of course gained familiarity with robes, even a certain pride about wearing them, but as poet and Zen teacher Norman Fischer observed, "Any small distance—down the stairs, from his cabin to the zendo, or whatever, was an opportunity for disaster." The combination of robes, heavy, steaming pots of food with ladles extending, *oryoki* bowls perched on a meal board about eight inches wide, and the peculiar, inherited Zen demand for speed, formed the challenge of each meal at the monastery.

> Today I am SOKU, butler/headwaiter three times today
> Today Elemental Powers gnomes and gremlins catch
> Heels and jog elbows. Conspicuous minor hysteria.[8]

That poem continues, further illustrating Philip's ceremonial weaknesses:

> Today I am supposed to be the DOAN (gong klonger)
> But I lost my temper during the morning service
> Lost all recollection of the schedule and my various duties
> Missed breakfast, God knows who played the Buddha drum
> While I was finding out who was Wangshi Sogaku
> In the wrong kind of Chinese transliteration.

"How did we ever let that happen?" wondered gardening writer Wendy Johnson, of Philip's turn on the team responsible for timing and ritual.[9] But the "we" Wendy meant—the average Zen student of the day—would have had little say in it. Like all of Philip's appointments at Zen Center, his service on the DOAN crew must have at least been known to Baker Roshi, if not initiated by him.

Philip's loud ineptitude at Zen skills more than endeared him to fellow students; it made room for them. A number echoed Norman Fischer when he said that he never would have been able to stay at Zen Center if everyone (except himself) "had done everything 'right.' Philip performed a valuable service." That, his heterodox views about Zen Center and its leadership, his hedonism, erudition, and scandalous humor attracted to him a loyal cadre of friends, who were often in his company.

As Baker worked skillfully and tirelessly to secure Zen Center's properties, extend its influence, and enter the marketplace with a number of shrewdly conceived, highly visible, and successful businesses, he seemed, or actually was, absent from Zen Center for extended periods. His attention was elsewhere, and the work meant as well that he moved with a different crowd. If any rift developed between the abbot and the student body as a result of this, Philip was perceived to be with the students. "Even though Philip was Dick's friend," noted author David Chadwick, "he was never part of the salon." This refers to an amorphous group—the "Invisible College" was a term Baker used for it—of creative, forward-thinking, powerful or about-to-be-powerful politicians, economists, architects, painters, chefs, scholars, poets, philosophers, theater people, activists, publishers, businessmen and women—"cultural movers and shakers" was another name for them—who circled in and around Zen Center in the 1970s and early 1980s. More accurately, they swirled around Richard and Virginia Baker, and sometimes Zen Center. Zen students would cook for gatherings of the Invisible College, set up the rooms, serve food, and clean up, but were only very exceptionally invited. Philip stayed apart from it, unless an evening's event was specifically poetical. He avoided such fanciness from personal preference as much as anything else but was not much bothered by the time and enthusiasm Baker focused on it. Philip saw it as part of the abbot's traditional duties, to make available a temple's reputed calm and Buddhism's undeniable wisdom to leaders in need. Chinese and Japanese temples had done this for centuries and had enjoyed various kinds of governmental support. Patronage may or may not have figured into Baker's activity, but he knew that friends in high places could help Zen Center. Philip was at Zen Center from necessity and to be a monk. He had seen Baker in New York, San Francisco, and Kyoto, and took a bemused attitude toward the salon activity, as long as it did not crowd him personally. And though students may have felt he belonged, proletariat-like, to their number, he urged them to respect Baker's work. "Don't mess with the magic!" he said on more than one occasion.

Philip lived on a stipend from Zen Center and in housing paid for by them for twelve years, until August 1984. He alternated time in San Francisco with practice periods at Tassajara, completing ten of these in all. For several weeks during most summers, he taught at Naropa, in Boulder, but he also endured a summer guest season at Tassajara, during which students traditionally moved into even more provisional housing than the uninsulated, cold-water, clapboard cabins in which they passed the winters, so that these spaces could be rented out at resort prices to the well-heeled. Philip did not work in the kitchen to prepare the sixty-odd gourmet breakfasts and dinners for the guests (they packed their own lunches); or in the dining room serving and clearing the meals, or on the cabin-cleaning crew, or in the extensive gardens, or in any aspect of transportation or maintenance. He did don his robes every afternoon in the baking heat and offer meditation instruction to any who wished it. He gave a Zen talk every few evenings, but mostly he just chatted sociably with guests—and with students as well, if they could spare the time. These latter he rather consoled, as the grinding labor and obvious (if temporary) second-class citizenship at their monastery frustrated them.

The brief and broad-stroke descriptions of the previous pages must stand for Philip's twelve years at Zen Center. Describing a dozen years of a monk's life compares to describing a person in meditation: where they sit, what they wear, their posture, the instructions they've been given—these can be told; their silence or recitation can be reported. But the real work Philip did—on himself and with his teacher—remains largely invisible. Possibly it can be inferred. Before departing this Zen Center period, two highlights require mention: Philip's tenure in 1975 as head monk *(shuso)* for a practice period at Tassajara, and his year as resident teacher at a satellite zendo in San Francisco.

SHUSO, AUTUMN 1975

Part of Philip's duties as head monk was to give formal Zen talks from the raised platform, in meditation posture, to forty or so other students, also sitting in robes, theoretically in meditation. These talks had to be given every ten days, a demand that could petrify shusos without experience in public speaking. Philip relied on familiar material. Poet Jane Hirshfield reported, "When he wasn't the shuso, we had long talks on literature during study hall. When he was shuso, we had long talks on literature in the zendo." This is not to imply that his talks were not "Zen" or "Buddhist"; they surely were. But part of the shuso's job is to tell the other practitioners how he or she got to that particular seat—where he or she was coming from. Philip was coming from literature as much as anywhere else. His forty-five years of heavy reading and his quarter-century of writing meant that the illustrations and examples for his "religious" points could hardly be other than literary. It *was* unusual locution, though, in the abrupt, abbreviated, coded style of Zen speech. It also took lots of time. His lectures in the zendo were (to some) excruciatingly long. The whole practice period felt long and slow, and his shuso ceremony was the longest ever, requiring an intermission.

This event is held late each practice period (ango) and showcases the Zen method of "dharma combat," during which the shuso, holding a fan and a staff (shakujo),[10] sits for questioning from each of the participants in the ango and from any past shuso who cares to attend. Unlike the questions for the abbot, these are directed with force at a shuso's mind; they are meant to test, and have been compared to arrows or sword thrusts. The shuso bangs the staff down on a wooden disc, and directly a student shouts, "Shuso!" to preface the question. Tassajara tradition was for the shuso to respond immediately; parries were brief, nondiscursive, possibly humorous. Philip's were long and slow. Such a ceremony is supposed to be beyond good and bad, despite the impossibly dualistic setup. It is meant to call forth Buddhist dharma and then be over, gone. Philip was capable of public disputation; he'd shown this when jostling Olson in 1957; he'd read the brusque Zen encounters for decades, and he'd participated in several shuso ceremonies as a student. He knew the drill but chose to do something different, boycotting what Trungpa Rinpoche called "the militancy of American Zen."[11] It may have been for Philip another "fake aspect of the scene." Contemporary accounts tell of him working with people's questions, dancing along with them but perhaps being shy, unwilling to slam down the staff. In any case, his ceremony was so unorthodox, so uncomfortable, that it received only the faintest formal praise. In an interview years later, poet David Meltzer noted the sporting aspect of the ceremony and asked Philip if it was possible to strike out. "Oh yeah, I struck out. A guy called Bob asked me some question or another, and I had no idea what the answer was or if there was an answer. I didn't know. I think that in a regular place they would have thrown your ass out."[12] Disconcerting as Bob's question may have been, Philip answered forty-seven questions. The group portrait after shows a warm smile on Richard Baker's face; it shows a nearly incandescent grin on Philip's.

After being the first person to rise for each of the ninety days—around 3:00 A.M.—after running all over the monastery to ring the wake-up bell and leading meditation and service if the abbot was not there, shusos had many other duties. They are supposed to clean the toilets, for one, the idea being that as one rises in the religious hierarchy, one can do lower and lower work with equanimity. The shuso also begins to give individual practice instruction to students. This instruction is nowhere near as formal as interviews with the abbot, but it is not casual. It does guide a person along the path. For Philip, such instruction signified further responsibility and, together with the lectures, the first steps toward becoming a fully fledged Zen teacher. Thus

FIGURE 17. Philip Whalen and Richard Baker Roshi at Tassajara, following Whalen's Hossenshiki (head monk ceremony), November 1975. Photo by Ted Howell.

only three years after beginning temple life, his way forward seemed marked out. The *ango* itself was regarded as a second-level ordination. Philip went through it earlier than strict seniority might suggest he would, and those who observed this put forth various reasons: he was older; he was not in great shape; he had some kind of seniority, being steeped in both Buddhism and Japanese culture; he had real Buddhist faith, the kind awakened by living for years among people who devotedly pray to Buddha, the kind of faith that propels a person along the path despite clumsiness of all kinds. In truth, the decision to appoint a shuso rested entirely with Richard Baker. Seniority and tradition counted, of course, but if Baker thought someone was ready, as he thought Philip was, if that person's living situation permitted it, as Philip's did, it was his call.

The tight regulations and long repetitions of Zen life allow for subtlety: after passing someone every day at the same part of the same path and making the same prescribed bow each time, if one varies it, even slightly, the other notices. Little shifts communicate a great deal. Through centuries, Zen has used this heightened field of awareness to convey Buddhist meaning, especially the teaching of nowness. Philip's sense of theatricality fit perfectly here, and like many lineage teachers before him, he used it. A gesture, a tossed-off word, a little sign, not necessarily in the zendo or interview room but rather, traditionally, outside them—this is where Zen lives. This is how it has been taught and transmitted. Philip might have been long-winded in lecture, he might have been formal in interview, but he could still get his point across in this other language.

Very often, his point was that people, including himself, should cheer up.[13] Early on, he burst into Rick Levine's room—not bothering to knock— and shouted at his reclining, reading, younger friend: "*You don't belong in a monastery! You're too young to be in a monastery! Monasteries are for fat old men like me! You should read the classics! You should be going to bars, getting drunk for three days! Setting you hair on fire! Listening to the way people talk!*"[14]

Meals at the monastery provided him with a stage. For these, students sat at their places, but instead of facing the wall, as they did in zazen, they faced one another across a central aisle, about as wide and long as a bowling lane. Four rows of students, two aisles, meals conducted in silence and stillness, spiced with anticipation of pleasure, satiety, or at least a change of activity. Down the aisle comes Philip unexpectedly, all out of meal ritual. He jitterbugs and sings scat under his breath, up the aisle and then back, before melting into the group of other servers, as if it never happened. It was not supposed to have happened. No one was supposed to have reacted. When he carried a teapot of hot water to serve, holding it in front of his face, elbows out as prescribed, instead of gliding smoothly forward with the other servers, he might mince along in the tiniest, choppiest steps possible, an idiot grin on his face.[15] He might do his best imitation of a sugarplum fairy.

Another kind of story students who practiced with Philip tell—everyone has Philip stories—concerns his devotion to learning: to knowing or at least discovering where you are historically; what had happened; what were the traditions and institutions and the changes in those that had led to here. It did not always run smooth or quick. "Philip," began Rick Levine one day in the steam room, judging it to be a relaxed moment. "What did Williams mean by 'No ideas but in things?'" "He meant," said Philip, considering, "he was trying to say . . . it's that . . . *O why do people ask me these things? How the fuck should I know? He meant he liked to sleep with his patients, that's what he meant!!*" And at that he stood and slammed out of the steam room. A few years later, when they were back in the city, neighbors in the same apartment building, Philip knocked at Rick's door and without explanation handed him a copy of Blake's works. Rick later saw that Philip had marked every reference to the phrase "the minute particular," giving him a several-years-delayed answer.

"He really did listen to you," remarked Laura Burges. "He paid attention. He got you." This same person, however, did not enjoy Philip's talks. She loved the classical English literature he taught, and she recognized that Philip was one of the most learned, eloquent persons she would ever meet. But she found the way he read things aloud—in a monotone—to be so annoying that she requested of the abbot that she might be excused from attending. Baker acknowledged her complaint but pointed out that Philip had given his life to literature, and the books he was teaching were of such value to him that if he were to read them with his real feelings, "he would probably burst into flames."

Having stood for questions during the shuso ceremony, Philip had a chance to ask his own during the *shosan* ceremony with the abbot. As head monk, Philip went last. Again in high emotion, he shouted out, "Why is everyone and everything enlightened but me?" Thirty-plus years after this brief moment, it still moved Jane Hirshfield, who was there to see it. "*That* is what stuck for me—its rawness, its truthfulness, its humility. . . . You have to know a lot to ask that question."

"Our real life is in other persons, is in our relationship with them. That's where our real reality is, when push comes to shove," Philip told a Naropa class in 1977.[16] He'd just finished reading aloud to them the final pages of Virginia Woolf's *The Waves* and was explicating Bernard.

> And we don't like that, because we like to be alone; we like to indulge our fantasies, and to have a pleasant, quiet, uncomplicated life, to enjoy the beauties of nature and pleasures of human art and so forth. But we're stuck at this point—where we exist outside ourselves, and that outside is coming to get us. On the one hand, we think of that outside that's coming after us in the shape of death, but at the same time, that's where our real life is—in those other persons, and things. And we ourselves are a changing conglomeration of all sorts of ideas and feelings, which lift and heave and whatnot, like the ocean. So it's all a big funny illusion, a big funny mistake; and yet, if we're aware enough of these things, we can *meet* death, or we can meet disappointment, and not be crushed by it, by reality. The ugliness of an empty restaurant becomes a place we can use.

It took him less than a minute to speak this. It seemed—though it was hard to tell—as though he were speaking about far more than Woolf's character

Bernard. The remarks startled the class, so when Philip called for questions, the first one went directly to this. He replied,

> We say, "People bother me. I'm getting along just fine and then this other person bothers me, and keeps me from doing what I want to do. . . . Why are those people starting all those wars, messing up my life? Why are they burning the house down next door . . . ?" What are you going to do about other people and their problems? What are you going to do about the fact that there are all sorts of people wandering around starving and killing each other, having a terrible life. What is our relationship to all that? And eventually, I think you'll find out that the connection is that they are you. That's who you really are, is all those other people. You are not simply the person you customarily imagine yourself to be. You are all those other people. That's what I mean.

But he meant even more than that. Philip meant that in his work as a newish teacher of Buddhism, a formal species of bodhisattva, this was a hard perspective, and that he was trying to hold it. "Your own preferences, your own wishes, the things you reject and so on, are not so important. It's a very difficult problem, but if you can see it that way, it helps a lot. You can see that those other people are your real existence."

SOUTH RIDGE ZENDO, SHOGAKU-AN

By 1981, Philip and everyone else had noticed a population problem at Zen Center. He wrote to Gary, "The Beginner's Mind is unbelievably jammed with earnest seekers of the way out. All authorities on the subject assure me that zen was a fad of the '50's and 60's; I can't guess what these new customers imagine they are doing."[17] Baker Roshi noticed the crowding too and saw a solution to at least two of his problems in a satellite temple. "I thought some of these people wouldn't have to come across town to sit—they could go to a local place. And I thought it would be a good way for senior people to have some experience teaching and to see, 'Can you make a group?' One of the measures of being a roshi, or teacher, is if people spontaneously recognize you. . . . So the first experiment was Philip. To create the opportunity where people could have some experience of being a teacher on their own. I wanted to give Philip the chance to do it."[18]

The house in which Philip was installed that August for his experiment sat halfway up a hill in a very quiet residential area of little houses, out beyond the Church Street trolley terminus. Baker Roshi had spent hours driving around—sometimes with Philip, sometimes without—looking for a suitable place. Philip called it the South Ridge Zendo since the hill rose near the bottom edge of the city. The usable space comprised two levels—a main floor of four small rooms, plus a kitchen and bathroom, and below, a renovated basement. The house perched above the corner of Fairmount and Chenery Streets, so that the sidewalk running down Chenery directly bordered the basement. Sitters inside heard and felt people walk by a few feet away, on the other side of the wall. Thick brown shag carpet in the basement zendo contributed to a pleasant if soporific atmosphere. Philip said that the upstairs, with its large windows and blond flooring, had a lot of ghosts, though he didn't seem much bothered. More vexing were the many blocks that lay between his house and the nearest grocery store or Laundromat. A wash took all morning; so did shopping. Zen friends and other sitters, some of whom— like Leslie Scalapino or Nancy Davis—came from the poetry scenes, would pitch in with transport and errands, but Philip was largely isolated on the South Ridge. Baker continued to monitor Philip's situation there, but primarily he left him alone—that was the point.

"It is an affiliate of Zen Center, which pays the rent," Philip wrote to Gary. "I'm supposed to be here by myself for a couple of months & see whether people will come here to sit with me—'new part of my practice &c.' Later a couple or so will come from Zen Center to live here & help."[19]

After morning practice, Philip would offer tea and polite conversation upstairs. He'd then breakfast, peel the candles, sift incense ash, and run a vacuum around the place. Diane di Prima, Michael or Joanna McClure, or possibly others of his friends would occasionally collect him for lunch. Afternoon zazen was at 5:30 P.M., after which was dinner and an early bed.

"My first day one student appeared for the 2 morning periods, & three showed up for the 5:30 PM sitting. Sometimes nobody comes, sometimes there are 7—on those large occasions people have driven over from Page St to dig the scene here. I must do the chanting 3 times a day, whether anyone sits with me or not. Zazen also happens Saturday AM, but not Saturday PM, nor on Sunday. On Sunday I must chant morning & evening."[20]

"I must" is interesting, because the place and its schedule were his to run; it was, after all, an experiment. His sense of responsibility went beyond answering to Zen Center or Baker for a schedule. He once told poet Miriam Sagan, "The world is in such bad shape that no one should stop doing what they're doing—like ringing the bell—because we don't know what's keeping it going."[21]

In November, he reported to this author another angle on the theme.

"I went really crazy yesterday morning."

"You did? What happened?"

"I can't explain it. I just flipped totally out."

"What did you do?"

"Well sir, yesterday morning I was sitting down there in the zendo, and I had my little time thing, you know, and I looked down at it and it said 5:30. So I said to myself, "Oh 5:30! Whang! Bang!" Here Philip gestured wildly with his arm, like someone chopping wood with a hatchet. The gesture of hitting a bell in the zendo has more the feeling of a golf putt or pool shot.

"And then immediately I realized what had happened and thought 'Oh shit, now I've set the *machina universalis* all askew and . . . '"

"You hit the bell at 5:30 instead of 5:40, right?"

"Yeah, and so we get up and do the *kinghing [kinhin]* for ten minutes and then I sort of explained or apologized or something."

"You mean you told everybody what had happened?"

"Well, sort of. And then, you know, I thought it would be one of those usual days when nothing happens. But the next thing is, in come Teah and Katherine and Darlene, and god knows who else for the second period."

"And you guys are all already sitting again?"

"Right."

"And so they wonder why they're late?"

"Right."

"And how come they have to sit so long?"

"So short."

"What do you mean? You mean you just sat a regular forty-minute period? You didn't stretch it out to get done at the usual 6:30?"

"No man. We just sat forty minutes and I had to get up and apologize all over again."

Whether from a view of keeping universal forces appeased or from a plainer sense of duty, Philip sat. He sat alone sometimes at South Ridge, and again in Santa Fe, and later again at Hartford Street. When questioned, he told poetry students at Naropa,

If you sit long enough, you find yourself going through a great many changes—this is interesting enough so that you don't stop. You either do or don't feel that it's necessary to sit. This is hard to talk about, in any sensible way.

It's my way of handling the condition . . . what the world is like. That's how I can approach it—rather than taking a gun and killing everybody in Washington, DC, or blowing up Bank of America, or any of these other righteous things I might do. But I'm not doing that. I'm coming at it backward for a change, and seeing how to do it some other way. The problem of human suffering is very vivid to me, very great. I have trouble with it, and so part of the thing you do about suffering is, you join it. You accept it. You suffer. And this helps, to some degree, to handle the thing. It may not have any giant, earth-shaking effects, but it makes you feel better. . . .

If you sit for some time—for several years—you change. You either feel like you have to go on sitting or not. If you don't, it's all right. If you do it's all right. Nothing will happen. Nothing seems to happen—except that you change. You get different angles on things. You see different things, in different ways. And you observe yourself becoming . . . you find yourself doing things in a way you hadn't thought of before . . . you observe yourself in different ways. As I said, it's difficult to speak about.[22]

Despite the house's placement in what seemed then to be an energetically dead part of the city, Philip was slowly attracting a group of four or five regular practitioners, especially in the afternoons. It is a wonder anyone came, since there hadn't been any advertisement or public announcement, no blinking neon arrows on the house—"Zen Teacher Here"—or even any characters brushed over a board and hung out on the gate. Zen Center itself had started slowly under Suzuki Roshi in the midst of Japantown. South Ridge—or as Philip called it in formal moments, Shogaku-an—in the middle of nowhere, seemed to be going all right in its quiet way. But seven months in, Philip wrote to Gary, "Now the greater wheels in Zen Center want to get some kind of building in the Cole Valley neighborhood—up the hill from our Bakery & Alaya Stitchery. It appears that it will cost too much to buy 65 Fairmount St & 'ZC already has a commitment to the Cole Valley neighborhood, &c' So unless the Hojo decides that he wants it 'irregardless' of the impossibility, I'll probably be gone from here by autumn." Philip was indeed back in Tassajara by the end of September, but as his letter to Gary continues, "There are photographs of it [South Ridge Zendo] & a written record—& the great feeling of actually working here with people remains."[23]

FOURTEEN

Rope of Sand

SANTA FE AND DHARMA TRANSMISSION

The scandal that erupted in April 1983 at Zen Center tore the sangha apart. Before the year was out, Richard Baker had resigned his abbotship, and by mid-1984, he'd left San Francisco to set up house and temple in Santa Fe, New Mexico. The story of the gathering background conditions at Zen Center, the precipitating events, and the extraordinarily painful, damaging, and prolonged schism ran in local newspapers and magazines at the time. The trigger was that Baker had a dalliance—an afternoon—with a woman who was alas both his student and the wife of his best friend at the time. This was not, it would emerge, his only extramarital relationship, or the only one he had with a student, but this one ignited a blast of discontent and led to public examination of issues running from the grand—teacher-student relations and power dynamics in Asian Buddhist traditions—to the line items of financial audits. Chapters in several books in the following years (including one by this author)[1] told the story in more depth, and finally in 2001, Michael Downing published an entire book on it. *Shoes Outside the Door* seemed to those who'd been there to have gotten some things right, to have gotten other things wrong, to have left out some balancing material, but in any case to have been so exhaustive as to obviate the need for further writing about the mess. This biography, then, will not attempt to treat the Zen Center crisis of 1983, except to note its effects on Philip. The first effect was that life there became untenable for those, like Philip, who aligned themselves variously with Baker.

> Everything here remains in a gluey mess, all undecided & unresolvable, maybe. It is very hard to remain calm & wise; all I can do is stay here as long as Dick keeps coming back & intends to stay connected with Zen Center

(although the Board of Directors has been trying very hard to get rid of him.) He officially resigned on 20 December as Abbot & Chief Priest, with the intention of helping to simplify everything. The Board keeps dithering & twiddling & can't seem to talk with Dick & Dick says it is a question of there being two kinds of reality unable to get together. (It is to be understood that the Board's "reality" is something remote from fact or actuality.) Meanwhile, he has been meeting weekly with 4 of us to work on koan from SHOYOROKU— an unusual but interesting way to spend time with him. He seems to enjoy talking about Buddhism as a relief from "politics." . . .

The real world gets realer as various patrons slowly (& with infinite regret) withdraw their financial support from under Zen Center. The Board may quite simply drive the whole works into the ground, before they're done. Mr PH & certain rich ladies in Tiburon either will or won't bring a lawsuit against Zen Center for misappropriation of funds &c. It seems that this is no more than bluster & threat, but the Board frets about it. Anyway, I hang on but suspect that it is a rope of sand, &c.[2]

The property on which Baker landed in Santa Fe held a *chöten*—a Tibetan stupa—a magical building dedicated, in this case, to the cessation of all hostilities.[3] A courtyard surrounded the stupa, and on one end of it sat a temple/zendo—a room for meditation with small changing rooms to either side. At the other end of the courtyard was an entrance building with a library and small bath. About fifty yards up a slight rise from the stupa stood a split-level ranch house. Friend David Padwa had simply given Baker the temple; the house needed to be bought. With his typical mixture of fundraising acumen and useful connections, Baker managed this, and as soon as negotiations were settled, a small crew, including Philip, moved in. Meditation and chanting took place in the zendo; study, meals, and socializing were at the main house. There, Baker Roshi had a couple of rooms, Philip had a room, and across from his was a guest room, usually full of visitors. As Baker was very often gone, care of these would fall to Philip.

The group who migrated with Baker arrived within weeks of one another during August 1984. Writer Miriam Sagan came with her husband Robert Winson and lived in town. She described the scene as "a series of people who had all been hopelessly uprooted, and were somewhere neutral at best. No one had chosen this, no one desired it, it wasn't anyone's home, the age range was 30–60. It was a small, dislocated group of people who'd been through a trauma, however you want to see it. I think in cases also marital trauma, economic trauma, job loss. Although it seemed fairly functional from day to day, it was patched together with glue. Philip definitely experienced this. He was part of it and part of the problem and he suffered from it."[4] Miriam Bobkoff—one of the migrants, and soon Santa Fe's reference librarian—continues about Philip, "He was surrounded by dislocated people, and his own geographic dislocation was spectacular. He was 1,100 miles from Stockton or Grant, from all his literary friends, and from a bus system he understood. He was in a town he didn't like, in a house he hated, and he was stuck there. He was very definitely in exile."[5]

"I wish that we were nearer the ocean," Philip wrote. "As it is, we inhabit an ancient {Pennsylvania series} ocean bed. Dust instead of water. I sneeze. Miriam sneezes. Steve sneezes."[6] The dry climate abraded Philip's skin, and the thin air at altitude exacerbated his asthma. What was left of his vision was deteriorating, and he had grown very broad. He rose one morning well before zazen, as was his custom, to note in his journal, "Early. Fattened. Blinded. Besotted. Breathless. Speechless. I think the cat is sicker. My nerves are bad."[7] He did walk almost every afternoon with neighbor and friend Jack Loeffler, who loved the territory and knew it well. When Philip was out in it, he enjoyed the sky and light and landscape of New Mexico. Jack steadied Philip in slippery weather and provided a year-round second pair of eyes. They partook of other rituals as well, beginning early one morning when Philip simply marched over to the house where Jack lived with his wife, Katherine—a place even closer to the zendo than the main house—and knocked on the door:

> There stood Philip. He didn't say, "Hello Jack," or "How are you?" He said, "You got any meat?" So I invited him in. I cooked him an entire pound of sausage, and he ate the whole thing. We knew we were going to be friends. . . .
> At least half the time after zazen, he'd come by, we'd climb in my car and go down to a place called Little Chef, and eat red chili for breakfast. I'd get a red chili burrito, and he'd get huevos rancheros or whatever he fancied, but he had to have meat, because Dick wouldn't let meat in the house.[8]

Philip disliked the "pueblo" architecture all over town and felt that underneath it, Santa Fe was a deeply Midwestern town, but on matters culinary, he sided with locals. He wrote to Gary explaining how "Zentatsu Roshi [Baker] is enormously occupied with making a new restaurant which, theoretically will support our operation here. I have great doubts about the success of an expensive vegetarian restaurant in a town whose inhabitants customarily eat beef burritos and chili, or tripe or hominy or eggs & tortillas in chili at breakfast time, hamburgers for lunch and steak for supper."[9]

Jack joined the team that ferried Philip on errands—the "keep-Philip-happy" crew, as Miriam Sagan dubbed it. Others on it included her husband Robert, Steve Allen, and Miriam Bobkoff. (These women called each other "Mir S" and "Mir B," respectively, and were close friends.) All of them felt they did such errands all the time, and all of them enjoyed it, mostly. "I would call before leaving work to see if he needed something, and there was always something. One day carrots. The next day, onions." Here Mir B permits herself a brief complaint about Philip's inability to plan, before acknowledging that he "just came from a time where you shopped every day for what you needed that day." When he wasn't out for breakfast with Jack or having the "handburgers" or grilled beef with other friends at Mr. Steak, Philip had to cook for himself. He also saw to food for Baker Roshi, as well as, from time to time, any meals guests might have at the house.

A theme running through Philip's journals and letters from Santa Fe is his health: he notices many little issues, but his eyes and his weight concern him primarily. He admits that he'd completely missed seeing an approaching car as he made to cross the street, though he'd been careful of exactly that. Finally he receives a diagnosis of Schnabel's Cavernous Nerve Syndrome, which he says "looks like glaucoma, but ain't." It meant that reading would be pretty well shot, but his peripheral vision would let him get around. Doctors advised him to lose weight, and he tried. He'd gone on stringent diets before at Zen Center, once losing as much as seventy pounds. Predictably, he became even grumpier during these austerities, and equally predictably, whenever he stopped limiting himself to 1,000 calories per day, he'd swell up again. During diets in Santa Fe, his journal becomes only lists of mealtime ingredients and their caloric values. For pages on end, he writes of boiled eggs (he calls them "X"), "college cheese," salad, fruit. Either that or "I walked to the Casa Sena & pigged out while sitting in the garden on blue corn/green chili chicken enchilada, 2 dishes red wine, flan, coffee. I also devoured 5 soparpillas with great wads of honey."

Necessity scattered the group most days, but they gathered at specific times. "On Thursday night we watch Hill St BLUES which Miriam finds extremely depressing but addictive. Friday is MIAMI VICE; Miriam allows that she's in love with the boy who plays Sonny Crocket. Saturday evening is DR. WHO, which is endlessly extravagant and entertaining. The rest of the time we do zazen & study SHOYOROKU together. (Of course, in the *rest* of the rest of the time, Steve works in Sarah's restaurant & Miriam does 2 jobs downtown. . . . Miriam Sagan has finished her novel but the agent hasn't sold it yet.)"[10] What Philip did with the rest of the rest of *his* time was to stay in his room. With weakened eyes, reading and writing were much slower and more laborious. He kept a journal, and he wrote correspondence; poetry all but dried up. They lived what poet Robert Winson, riffing on the Japanese conceit, called "the floaty life," everyone needing to reinvent themselves. The ordained were not particularly looking for new careers. They floated or treaded water, feeling that whatever new shape they found would depend in some way upon Baker Roshi. Baker, though, was busy putting together his own (new) life, and this often took him to Asia, Europe, or the West Coast. It also became clear to him as the months rolled on that temple life in Santa Fe—while certainly preferable to the strife in San Francisco—was unlikely to blossom beyond what the smallish zendo could accommodate. The restaurant suffered the fate Philip had predicted (lack of a liquor license was a bigger problem than vegetarianism), and prospects for a functioning Zen temple looked better across the border, in Crestone, Colorado. There, the Lindisfarne Fellows had given Baker a piece of land with a few buildings on it. He had refused the gift a few years earlier but meant to keep it this time and develop it. Thus for the three-plus years Philip lived in Santa Fe, Baker's energy tilted more and more toward Colorado and Germany, and away from Santa Fe. No one, including Baker, could clearly see the way forward; they were all barely sure where they were at the time.

Scooped up and shaken, rolled like dice onto the table, they questioned almost everything they'd routinely done at the San Francisco Zen Center. Shall we chant sutras? Shall we wear robes? How often shall we sit? (They changed the schedule repeatedly.) What does Japanese tradition really offer North Americans? What do we call ourselves? Specifically, what is the meaning of ordination? Especially, what does it mean when several of the ordained are in conjugal relationships or looking for them? Philip told Gary of these deliberations, since he knew Gary had long wrestled with such issues. Philip said he could now only sit in robes, and that on the monk/priest/lay question, he found Thomas Merton's statement from his Asian journals to be useful: "The monk is a man who has attained, or is about to attain, or seeks to attain, full realization. He dwells in the center of society as one who has attained realization—he knows the score. Not that he has acquired unusual or esoteric information, but he has come to experience the ground of his own being in such a way that he knows the secret of liberation and can somehow or other communicate this to others."[11] When Merton wrote this, he was, as Philip was, out of his element and experiencing the openness and sharpened awareness that can accompany such dislocation. Merton's definition surely attracted Philip also for being unbound to Christianity—or to the Buddhism Merton was just then observing. Particularly the words "somehow or other communicate this to others" apply to Philip, who, for all his desire to do things classically and correctly, never did. His way of communicating Zen did not look like anyone else's. Those who loved him, hung out with him, practiced and studied under his guidance, would not for the most part call him their "Zen master." Every one of them *would* say, however, that Philip was teaching them something, that he was a master of something, and that they were getting it from him. Merton's open-ended words about "knowing the score" and "experiencing the ground of his own being" come very close. Perhaps the person who put this most succinctly was an anonymous stranger in Santa Fe, a young man who approached Philip as he stood in an army-navy surplus store, attired (as he often was) in an extra-large white T-shirt under his Buddhist *rakusu* and a Day-Glo orange sun hat. The young man addressed him, "Sir. I don't know exactly what you do, but I know it is *something* and I want to follow you."[12]

Mir S, who saw this encounter, said of her own relationship to Philip that she was "sort of afraid of him, but he was also unbelievably soothing to be around. I found him calming in some way. Like an animal. I just used to stand next to him, and he calmed me down. I think it was the bulk of his body, the bulk of his energy. He wasn't overstimulating. He was very sooth-ing." Philip could of course communicate in standard ways as well, as when he walked with Robert into their house and found Mir S sprawled on the floor weeping, distraught with delays and rejections of her novel. "Anyone else would have asked 'Why are you lying on the floor? What's wrong? Don't you want to get up?'" she recalled. Philip simply stepped over her into the room and slowly advised, "I wouldn't add alcohol to this if I were you."[13]

Though he was writing little new poetry, Philip did not ignore his oeuvre. He prevailed upon Jack Loeffler, who worked as an ethnomusicologist, to record him. Philip laid down hours of his poetry on tape, including the entirety of his Kyoto poem *Scenes of Life at the Capital*. He also recorded with Jack extended stretches of his prose and a number of biographical interviews.

At the Shoyoroku study seminars, Philip was a voluble and regular partici-
pant. Everyone who was there recalls how Philip would spring from his seat,
ignore Baker Roshi's protestations to stay, run (or at least shuffle) to his room,
fetch a book, and with his nose practically stuck in the gutter of the page,
read aloud a relevant passage.

Philip had moved to Santa Fe to continue his Zen training with Baker Roshi
and to complete the next step between them, the dharma transmission.
"'Transmission' means to receive and realize the Mind, spirit, and essential
teachings of your teacher and lineage," Baker put it in an introduction to a
book of Philip's more overtly Buddhist poems.[14] The trust required to
pass on a teaching lineage develops over years, and as early as 1979, Philip
began to keep an additional journal, at Baker's request, in preparation for
transmission. Like all materials connected to Zen transmission, the journal
is private, though Baker cited a few poems from it in his introduction. Part
of what can be told about an essentially secret process is that it involves vari-
ous kinds of handwriting. Baker Roshi distinguishes what this is from what
it is not:

This whole thing of *kiragami*—cut paper—is that what Zen tries to do is keep an oral tradition alive with written notes. But you never pass on the paper. If you were my disciple, I would tell you things; you'd write them down; I'd make sure they made sense; but I would never pass mine on to you, and you wouldn't pass yours on to the next person. It's a very strong tradition that the papers stay with the teacher, or they stay with the new disciple. But it's essentially an oral tradition, so they're not meant to be published or anything. They are just notes for an oral tradition.

Other kinds of writing figure into transmission, but Baker Roshi continues,

I went through the transmission more formally and completely with Philip than I have with anyone else—the only person comparable would be Issan—because we lived together in Santa Fe and could meet two or three times a week, for two or three hours a time, for a year.

It's not calligraphy, it's going through certain things—understanding. How do you understand certain things? What is the traditional understanding? What's my understanding? *Can you reproduce my understanding?* Once you can reproduce my understanding, then you're free to have your own understanding.

So I would present something, and he would present it back to me, and I'd have to say, "Well, you didn't understand it exactly as I do; as Suzuki-roshi did. Then we'd change it. When he gets it completely—exactly—as I understand it, so we have a mutual understanding, then I put my seal on it. So this process went on for a year, more than a year. We met like two days a week, like from two o'clock to five o'clock. We'd just sit and go through these things.[15]

Baker Roshi was also bringing others along in this way—Issan Dorsey and Steve Allen.

In the introduction cited above, Baker wrote, "During this time we completed the Transmission studies. Zenshin Ryufu (Zen Heart, Dragon Wind) Philip Whalen, truly entered the Mind of the Dongshan lineage and of Suzuki-roshi. On July, 1987, at Crestone Mountain Zen Center, we did the formal ceremonies and empowerments. Zenshin Ryufu is my first fully transmitted student in Suzuki-roshi's lineage. It was also the first Transmission Ceremony done at Crestone Monastery and thus a consecration of the monastery." A number of things are coded into this passage: that Baker used a very solemn tone, including curious capitalization, points to how important it was for him; that he described Philip as his "first fully transmitted student" meant that earlier extensive work on transmission done with Tenshin Reb Anderson during the Zen Center days was less than complete. (We shall return to this awkward point.) Finally, though it sounds as though the events at Crestone Monastery were the end of it, both Philip and Baker Roshi acknowledged at the time that there remained formal work to do. They clearly agreed about what had happened between them from 23 to 30 July, and Philip made certain he also understood what the ceremonies did and did not empower him to do. "I can ordain students. I am certainly authorized to run a zendo. Roshi said that the *sammotsu* are my 'permission to teach.'" The rites themselves are extremely secret, and all Philip ever divulged to the public was that "it's a private ceremony, very elegant, very elaborate; it takes hours and hours and endless quantities of equipment. It's a huge affair that goes on for a week, culminating in all-night, all-day, all-night sessions and ceremonies, after which you are added to the list of patriarchs of the Zen school."[16]

What they did not finish, however, was the paperwork, the official written permissions to teach. Philip worried nearly obsessively about these, which was understandable in someone who'd spent a lifetime putting ink on paper. Baker felt, however—and he told Philip—these were "'details' that could be taken care of 'anytime.'"[17] Philip's concerns make the last section of his Santa Fe journal painful reading. He wants very much to be gone from Santa Fe, preferably by his birthday (20 October) but at least before another "Dakota-style" winter sets in. He has no firm plan, no destination but away. "Roshi keeps telling everyone that I'm leaving here or am practically gone—but he makes no move to finish the *sammotsu* and the *kirigami*. I don't see how I can go anywhere without those, nor how I can leave the zendo while both he & Miriam are away." Time to work on the papers is reserved, then it disappears; this happens repeatedly. Philip feels frustrated and helpless. He gets mad but berates himself for being so. "What a grand imagination I have. What a lack of charity & gratitude!" Soon, though, he tries to raise the issue again or to create situations to force it. He records Baker's responses: "'We can do it later, in San Francisco, where there is less distraction. We can do it after I come back from San Francisco' {i.e. 'I am *not innarrested* to do it. *Later. Much later.*'} So I must content myself to waiting. {& I can see him showing up in San Francisco to say 'How can you expect people to come to sit with you in THIS place?' and 'Oh I'll bring the seals &c next time . . .'} In this way our little war continues."[18]

It felt to Philip that indeed even the quality of their relations had soured. He writes of Baker Roshi being "very severe" with him in *dokusan,* being cool toward him generally, being in a snibbing mood for days at a time. Of a short trip together to Crestone, ostensibly to finish the papers, Philip reports,

"Aside from a short sermon on my faults & an exercise in paper-folding . . . nothing has been accomplished. The whole time has been occupied by 'meetings' and telephonings. He says if I leave Wednesday he'll write up everything Tuesday. I think that is my next move: airplane ticket for Wednesday." They discussed whether San Francisco would be a good place for Philip to go teach. Or rather not. They discussed *when* he should go *wherever* he would go. *Discuss* is one word; *dispute* might be another. Philip does finally book a ticket to San Francisco and lets this be known. The reader should not wonder at these jostlings. Having a hard time with one's teacher is typical of Zen lineage. From Philip's journals, he and Baker also sound like an old couple of some sort, heating up their discontents for a fight, a blowup to make parting easier. They both knew that soon they would, and must, separate.

Even in such a tense atmosphere, Philip resigned himself to dieting again, having grown, as he wrote, "fatter with every breath." He was also running through an anonymous grant he'd gotten months before from the Fund for Poetry and wanted to get back, if not to San Francisco then at least to California, where he could collect Social Security and Medi-Cal. "My problems remain the same: Roshi & money. & FAT."

Philip knew the dangers of "little wars" with the roshi from the cautionary example of Tenshin Reb Anderson. At Zen Center, Baker Roshi had, or had not (depending on when you heard it), completed dharma transmission with Reb Anderson. The schism that ripped Zen Center apart found Reb decisively aligned with the board—against Baker—thus severing their connection in a way that took some thirty years to heal. Even if Philip didn't have this painful story in mind (which he did),[19] Baker kept it before him. Philip records how, with the gash still fresh and stinging, Baker "again denounced Reb: 'Reb is NOT my Dharma heir. He doesn't act like a Dharma heir. We have never finished the transmission &c &c.'" This poignant entry continues, "Until I get those papers signed & sealed, I feel that I'm in the same position as Reb. The boss will tell everyone that I got mad & left Santa Fe without finishing 'the papers.'"[20] It seems unlikely that Baker would have done such a thing—the two situations were very different—but the possibility helped fray Philip's nerves.

Finally on 22 December—having made one exploratory trip to San Francisco and decided that whatever anyone said, he was going back there—Philip sat on the plane and described how Baker had sat up most of the night before finishing one set of necessary papers, and how he would deliver the others to him out west in a few days. This seems not to have happened. Two months later, Philip records having seen Baker Roshi at Hartford Street and says that there were "many reasons why he didn't bring the completed papers." Finally, in December a year later, in an apartment he shared with its principal tenant, Philip recorded the presentation of the papers from Baker. He notes what is complete and what is still not, though at this point the delays arise from Baker wanting to double-check certain ritual markings and the need to order materials from Japan. Philip sounds mollified but adds, "I'll believe in the project to finish . . . when it happens." His flatmate Britton Pyland recalls the evening and his distinct feeling that the transmission was in the soup:

> It was a corn chowder in a ten-gallon pot that Philip prepared for this dinner date. The time came and the soup was ready and we were ready and the guest is . . . coming. And the guest is . . . coming. So after about forty-five minutes of the guest still . . . coming, Philip decided to serve up the soup. I decided to wait. Philip has his soup, and about an hour and a half late, Baker Roshi arrives. A nice greeting with perhaps a bit of subterranean frostiness from Philip. So Baker Roshi sits down with me to enjoy the soup. I remember that Richard Baker said, "Philip always knows exactly what kind of soup I like!" It *was* truly a perfect winter soup—nothing fancy but with a salad and a chunk of bread, a glass of wine—a quite hearty meal. After the soup and a little bit of talk, they went off to Philip's room, where they completed, I think, some transmission papers and seals and chops. I remember red ink on Philip's hands afterwards. Then good-byes, and we all went on about ordinary life as if this miracle were just a passing event.[21]

With the luxury of perspective, one can see how very kind Richard Baker had been to Philip. Rising above the delayed meetings, the harsh or critical words, and being late for soup, a picture emerges of overwhelming generosity. One of Buddhism's many formulations about generosity says that you give material goods, you give the dharma, and you give the gift of fearlessness. Beginning in 1972, Richard Baker gave Philip a place to live, food to eat, and soon enough, robes to wear. Through public lecture and private interview, he taught him Zen Buddhism, culminating in the extensive, intimate transmission of his lineage's treasures. He pushed Philip to teach and ushered him into situations where he'd have to do so. By 1988 he'd finally given Philip all that he would need. Baker referred to him as Whalen Roshi, writing, "When the title 'Roshi' is given, it means this realization has matured and flowered in practice."[22] Philip understood all of this, and grouse though he might, engage in the "little wars" though he did, he was never really anything but loyal and grateful. He accepted the ineluctable truth that in every lineage, a disciple simply must deal with the teacher's personality. Teachers strive to perfect their personalities—Buddha was very good at it, Suzuki Roshi was good at it—but teachers are humans, and the best among them don't stoop to hide it.

There was something that Philip did not understand, however. Jack Loeffler recalled a last-minute chat with Baker about this. Perhaps because Jack was not a Zen student, perhaps because his friendship with Baker was older than it was with Philip, an opening occurred. "It was a poignant moment when Kath and I were taking Philip to the airport. Dick shed a tear, man, to lose Philip. He said, 'I don't know how I'm going to make it now.' Because he really relied on Philip. I don't think Philip ever understood the degree to which Dick relied on him as just this stable part of life." Jack continued, "I also remember Philip sitting there, a tear streaming down his cheek, saying 'I'll *never* be a bodhisattva!'"[23]

Pains have been taken in the previous pages to tell enough about an ultimately inexplicable meeting of minds so that a reader might understand what Philip was really doing for four or five years. But in respect of the power of Zen's long lineage and the ancient, intensely secret nature of transmission, material has been left out; this includes even avoiding cheapening certain names and terms through overuse. A curious reader can rest assured that such things are in any case self-secret: they mean nothing to someone unprepared to work with them. The same holds for Philip's entries—poetical and otherwise—in journals connected to the transmission. The ones that can be read in Baker's introduction sound completely consistent with the rest of Philip's writing. Baker knew what kind of poet Philip was, and he said of Philip's work, "There was a greater realization in his poems than there was in his practice. Some of his poems show the kind of insight and knowledge of the world that I call realization. He was able to find it in literature, but he wasn't able to find it in his life, until quite late in his practice. But it was there, in the background, and I could feel it there, and he could feel it there."[24] Assigning Philip a journal would have been, among other things, handing him a tool he already knew how to hold; it would have empowered Philip in cutting a channel to the lineage stream. Given the topic of these pages, it seems fitting to end, as indeed Baker ends his essay about Philip, with Philip's own poem.

Secret

The great secret books are available to all. There are copies in most libraries; they can be bought in cheap paper editions. However accessible, they are still secret books. The careless, the casual, the thoughtless reader will come away from them no wiser than he was before. The really secret books are dictated to me by my own ears and I write down what they say. (31 vii 65)

RSVP

HARTFORD STREET, DECLINE AND DEATH

Before leaving Santa Fe, Philip wrote to Gary,

> What I've done is something I decided on in Kyoto in spring of 1969—having absolutely no real or practical idea at the time as to what is a "monk"/ "unsui"/ teacher/priest or what was the life of such a creature. Anyhow, the Buddhism came & got me & carried me off. Now I feel like the lady in the story of O.; here I stand in my owl-suit, alone, hundreds of miles from home (whatever or wherever that is) completely befuddled. Of course there isn't any home & I'm just fine. Whether this adventure is good for anybody else I can't say; I feel good about it all.[1]

He decamped to a small but adequate flat on Sanchez Street in San Francisco, sharing the place with Britton Pyland, a Zen student with whom he had roomed during his first practice period at Tassajara sixteen years earlier. Both men were studious, private, bibliophilic. They amicably kept to their own rooms and schedules, Philip's starting early each morning and including frequent visits to Hartford Street Zen Center (HSZC). Once a week Philip and Brit rearranged their front room and hosted an open sitting, attended betimes by poets, artists, and a few students from Philip's South Ridge days. Philip continued dieting—boiled "X," "feesh"—in a sour mood. He felt isolated. He *was* isolated, to the point that "Michael [McClure] called to say that I am hiding: I must advertise myself, put up a neon sign, print business cards, phone everybody, let everybody know where I am & what are my office hours & my fee for consultations &c 'It's showbiz!' Like Roshi, he says that I'm always wearing the wrong clothes, I don't project the right IMAGE. So I feel quite set up by his concern & offers of help & by his good advice."[2]

Philip's journal entries read similarly to those from a disoriented period twenty-some years earlier: he visits the park, he visits friends, he worries about the larder and pocketbook; he now describes as well difficulties with losing his eyesight and aging generally. He also wrestles with ideas of his possible religious duties and career, to be carried out in a suitable location in an imaginary future. He did receive an invitation to live and teach in Mendocino, from one of his South Ridge students, Sharon Baranowska. Though it seemed impractical to him, her invitation cheered him. Renowned printer (and friend) Clifford Burke also angled for a situation for Philip farther north, in Port Townsend, Washington, where, in addition to an interest in Zen and Buddhism, there was a strong poetry scene. Finally, though, the need for Philip's presence mounted at HSZC, where founding abbot Issan Dorsey was overwhelmed.

Issan had worked on dharma transmission from Baker Roshi in parallel with Philip at Santa Fe. Before that, Issan and Philip had practiced at Zen Center and Tassajara, living and mixing as Zen advises sangha should, "like milk and water." Issan too had been markedly older than most other Zen students when he arrived, and had lived an exotic life beforehand, though a very different one from Philip's. Issan had pulled himself from the undertow of drug addiction, prostitution, and petty thievery, perfumed though this way of life had been at the end by the communes and high ideals of the hippie era. He caught the lifeline that Zen, and specifically Suzuki Roshi, threw his way, but began his Zen career addled. When Philip came to Zen Center a few years later, he and Issan recognized in each another the experience of—perhaps even the taste for—exotic states of mind. This, combined with dogged adherence to the forms of Zen Center life, left them crazy and sane in individual, compatible ways.

With his magnetic style, Issan had mentored a collection of gay men interested in Zen from their first days in the 1970s as a discussion group—the self-styled "Posture Queens"—to their property-owning status as the Hartford Street Zen Center in the mid-1980s. With Baker Roshi's encouragement, Issan left Santa Fe in 1986 to lead the Hartford Street group. Baker named the place Issanji—One Mountain Temple—and, with a formal Mountain Seat Ceremony, installed Issan as the founding abbot in 1989. The house sat very near the center of the Castro district—San Francisco's famous gay quarter—and was open to the joys and tragedies of that time and place. Issan, himself HIV-positive, began caring for sick, dying, disenfranchised young men in his sangha and all around it. He moved them into the temple. Very soon he mag-

FIGURE 19. Issan Dorsey and Philip Whalen in the San Francisco Zen Center courtyard, ca. 1982. Photo by Barbara Lubanski Wenger.

icked the purchase of the next-door house, cut out walls in both buildings to create an interior passageway, and moved dying people in there too. He forged what came to be Maitri Hospice seemingly out of nothing, though the legal, medical, financial, logistical, and personal problems that met him as he emerged each day from the zendo were considerable. Steve Allen moved from Santa Fe to assume most of the hospice operation. During his stay at Brit's, Philip had been leading classes and discussion groups at HSZC and providing experienced presence in the zendo for the monthly all-day sittings. It seemed obvious that he should move into the temple, but he had continued to receive mixed advice from Baker about this. Finally Philip recorded in his journal what Baker told him, solicitous that his two most senior students should have a clear working basis. "He was most concerned that I should understand Issan is the abbot at Hartford St & should be thought of as having received transmission. My position there will be that of Godō [head of training]. Issan will defer to me as an elder, but I must remember that he is abbot & teacher."[3] On 1 January 1989, Philip moved into a smallish, low-ceilinged mother-in-law suite in the basement of 61 Hartford Street.

It sounds ominous to move into a hospice, but Philip was not there to die, not yet. His new position did confront him with physical and emotional chaos. Temple and hospice bordered one another on the street; they had been joined in the middle by the (illegal) passageway, and Issan intentionally placed patients in both buildings. Putting the head of Zen training on the hospice side swirled the functions of the two houses completely, a concept that pleased Issan but almost no one else. The addition of three monks to the premises—Philip, Steve, and soon Shunko Jamvold—all of them with shaved heads, all of them often in voluminous black robes, unsettled some of the dying, their visitors, and caregivers. Additionally, Steve was married, and the intrusion of his wife, Angelique Farrow, as a resident in the proudly gay male demographic of the place chafed. From the perspective of resident Zen students, whatever coziness they might have created in their home had been invaded. Some had just been happy to live in the pretty Victorian house, one street over from the main drag, and keep, as they put it, "a pet zendo in the basement." Now, whenever they went out, they passed rooms housing dying men, ill with a disease to which they too were vulnerable. Their living room was full of people they didn't know; in their dining room sat frail, nauseous people in wheelchairs rolled up to the table; their kitchen, if not quite working at industrial scale, was overtaxed; their bathrooms served strangers. The confluence of hospice and temple seemed viable mostly in the compassionate mind of Issan Dorsey. The force of his belief sustained the place for a while, and his own decline seemed to highlight the need for a hands-on spiritual engagement with death. His own decline also rent the place with grief.

This, then, was Philip's home. The path from his rooms to the zendo was often cluttered with heaps of objects: bedpans, wheelchairs, cardboard boxes of supplies, or the clothes, books, knickknacks of the departed; their art. Philip could hardly see any of this as he made his way, in robes and with cane, up from his basement suite, through the passage between the buildings, across to the other set of stairs, and down to the zendo. Philip had come to HSZC while Issan was alive, and their relations remained mostly supportive and warmly fraternal. Privately, Philip termed the temple-hospice "Issan's Folly," and Issan once—also in private frustration at the enormity of his job and the diminishment of his energy—spat out in regard to Philip that "he's a great poet and everything, but he's also just a fat old man!"

On 1 September 1990, Issan passed the abbotship of the temple to Steve. Ceremonially, Issan descended from the Mountain Seat, and Steve climbed into it, remarking that sitting there felt like "being in a tornado in the eye of a hurricane." Five days later, Issan died. Steve lasted in the abbot's role for a year and a week, and it amazed his friends that he endured so long. The position was untenable; not only was he still running the hospice but Steve was now also trying to run the temple. Such places exist on donations and membership, and Steve—mild-mannered, literary, straight, and married—presented a very different picture to patrons than had Issan with his intuitive, flamboyant, gay style. Nor was it easy to gather much support locally, as the sangha, grieving Issan, became by turns dispirited, apathetic, disoriented, or angry. Thus financial worries compounded the existing stresses of temple-hospice life. Philip at least upheld the sitting schedule: he made it to the zendo each morning and afternoon, but even he admitted, "People were pulling in different directions. A lot of really heavy scenes were taking place between the people living here, working here, and sitting here. It was a very heavy scene."[4]

Given this, Steve did the obvious thing: he handed off both jobs and left town to recuperate and continue his studies with Baker Roshi, now in Colorado. Philip and Steve both said they wanted the ceremony transferring the abbot position to be as brief possible: "Do you?" "I do." "Thank you." "Good-bye." The actual event turned out to be marginally more elaborate, and during it, Philip made his enigmatic observation that the abbot's chair was still empty. Pressed to explain this in an interview, he pointed to the interpenetration of form (chair) and emptiness (abbot), Zen being attached to neither. "Also I was thinking of something from a Gertrude Stein book called *The World Is Round,* where this little girl climbs up a mountain and finds a chair."[5]

Philip's sexuality caused no issues: it seemed to most he'd retired from the field, and that when he'd been on it, he'd been gay enough. He patiently repeated that HSZC was not a gay zendo: it was a neighborhood zendo, open to anyone, located in a gay neighborhood. He regarded himself as the temple priest and kept his focus on the health of that institution. In formal and casual talks, Philip emphasized to the group what they *did* have—a zendo, in a temple, on a good piece of property, as well as a lineage, a resident teacher, and an opportunity—over what they did *not* have: Issan, enough money, or a steady, acceptable cook. By 1994, the indefatigable newsletter editor and temple historian Jennifer Birkett wrote, "The tornado phase of One Mountain Temple has calmed into a wind storm. Zenshin's constant presence has stabilized the community.... His natural, quirky, cantankerous presence is a relief after daily inner-urban shockwaves of the late 20th century."[6] Resident Brian O'Toole reflected, "I consider him a teacher, I see how much effort he puts into getting up in the morning, and coming to the zendo.

He has tremendous dedication to practice. I've been trying to keep up with him, but with my illness, I can't quite do it. He does it over and over, day after day.... It must be very hard to have as much physical distress as he does, and just do it anyway. He doesn't miss very much in the zendo."[7] Philip reported to his old friend Albert Saijo, "I'm still engaged in some manifestation of the Zen trip. Don't ask. Technically, I am the abbot of this temple, called Issanji.... Except for a few hours a day, the outfit is invisible, very much like me. Nevertheless, we must believe that it is all taking place in the Dharmakaya, 24 hours a day."[8]

These twenty-four hours sorted themselves into a regular pattern. After the early meditations and breakfast, the house often convened midmorning for a "second breakfast." Philip made it a point to be gone at lunchtime as often as he could. Temple residents and hospice patients took this meal together, and some at the table were loudly unable to keep food down. (Caring for young men dying of AIDS had been Issan's passion, not Philip's. He made friends and had students among the caregivers; he would readily speak with any of the sick if they wished and did whatever he could to help. However benevolent it was, though, Philip saw the hospice as an impossible complication to the temple.) Afternoon errands took him to the post office, the bank, and most regularly, the supermarket. He might dress in day robes or civvies; he carried a cane, sometimes whacking things more or less for the fun of it, and he walked slowly, pausing to open a Japanese folding change purse to any beggar who asked. His near-blindness meant that someone always went with him, and two well-written contemporary accounts exist of these outings.[9] "Walking around the neighborhood one notices how sharp Philip's listening is, how receptive ... how much he's always jamming with what's being said in the airs of the street. He laughs to himself, clucks, spins on vivid fragments he picks up and throws away, filtering everything like a vast sensitive Whale-n slipping through mists of krill, digesting."[10] Some months later, "Philip actually seems to be dieting.... He never says he simply has to lose weight; he says Sandor [Burstein, his doctor] is mad at him.... No bologna or steak today in the supermarket, but in front of the dairy case, Phil suddenly shouts, 'Fuck it! I'm gonna buy six or seven bags of junk food and sit down in the middle of my rug and eat 'em for dinner! Yeah!' An old Jewish grandpa chimes in, 'That's right!' and gives Phil the thumbs up, as he wheels past."[11]

Impious ejaculations like this one and bursts of outright anger continued to plague him. These were rarely, if ever, directed at any one person, and they lasted only a few minutes. They were loud enough, though, and powerful enough to dominate any scene. When they occurred at the temple, some students saw them as a teaching device and worked with them that way; others simply saw an old man losing his temper. Philip seldom apologized and never held on to them, but he did feel ashamed, as he told a Saturday morning assembly. "People at different times in my life have told me that I'm scary; but I don't make myself ridiculous and jump up and down to scare people. Usually I'm just scared and upset myself. It's difficult to get used to one's own failure to control one's temper." He went on to say that anger was just a temporary state of mind; it eventually dissolved and should not scare one.[12]

When he got back to the temple in the afternoon, Philip would generally have a nap, rising from it in time to dress and get to the living room by 4:30 P.M. Here he would sit magisterial, doing something between holding court and having office hours before zazen. In either case, he was open for conversation, and when any HSZC residents reflect on their experience of Philip as a teacher, they mention this hour rather than the Saturday lecture in the zendo, as the time and place they felt they learned from him. This was where he seemed best able to "somehow or other communicate" (in Merton's words), though the ostensible topics might be Lewis Carroll, Dogen-zenji, or the miracle of a bumblebee's flight. His entrances to the zendo, when that hour came, could be spectacular. One warm afternoon Philip's cane escaped his grasp and preceded him down the stairs. "*God fuck us all!*" rang from the top of the flight on the room full of men in shorts and tank tops facing the wall. One dim morning, Philip surprised a zendo pillar by walking into it during his circumambulation. He proceeded with stately pace until he reached the mat in front of the altar, where, as he unfolded his bowing cloth, he tossed aside his cane and bellowed, "God DAMN it!" startling the other sitter, before he continued otherwise unperturbed with his prostrations and the subsequent sitting. Philip caused Jennifer Birkett to wonder for a period of meditation whether he meant her or himself as they paused at the bottom of the stairs—she carrying his incense—so that he could announce to any in doubt about it, "Here Comes the Whore of Babylon!" Mostly, though, things in the zendo stayed quiet and boring, as they are supposed to seem when viewed from outside. Practitioners simply felt glad of Philip's presence there, whether he sat on a cushion or, as he grew older, stiffer, and more achy, on the abbot's chair.

During these years, he often fell seriously ill. First, in 1992, he succumbed to endocarditis, an infection he described as "all sorts of staph bugs tromping around on the heart valves." This put him in the hospital for weeks and required heart surgery a year later. "You know they kill you?" he told David Meltzer. "First of all they anesthetize you; then they refrigerate you and bring your body temperature down to some wonderfully low level where your life functions decline and fail, and then they get out their electricity and pop you with that and hook you up to a heart-lung machine and you don't breathe anymore and your heart isn't leaking anymore."[13] Philip's imagination of the operation was more connected to what he experienced after. Whether from the "gallons" of antibiotics or the painkillers, he often became disoriented during prolonged hospital stays. A mind stocked as fully as Philip's can produce powerful, frightening imagery. His nightmares horrified him, and his conduct in parallel universes stunned some of his visitors, as he related to them the scenes he was presently visiting. Sometimes these involved his visitors, as when he commanded Zen student Rick London to arrange things on a side table—Philip was perceiving it as a shrine—and to offer incense. When London had pantomimed this to satisfaction, they (mostly London) chanted sutras. Coming back the next day, London brought a sutra card, since he felt his chanting had been spotty. As small talk lulled, he asked Philip if he'd like to chant sutras. "Are you crazy?" came the reply. "Can't you see I'm sick in bed!?"[14] Philip eventually regained strength sufficient to continue his residence and abbot's duties at HSZC, though he admitted to feeling "pale." Shunko Jamvold—who helped look after Philip's papers, drove him to appointments, and the like—thought he never fully recovered; indeed infections seemed to chase around Philip's body until finally taking up residence in his spine.

. . .

During his five years as abbot, Philip's activity fell into four main divisions: teaching, conducting temple ceremony and ritual, attending to administration, and sorting out his literary life.

In addition to his regular presence in the zendo and his informal "office" hour, Philip delivered a Zen talk each Saturday, unless a guest lecturer had been invited. It's startling that only twenty or thirty short paragraphs remain from hundreds of his talks, considering how closely he'd tracked his thoughts, moods, and behavior during years of keeping a journal. He intended this.

"When I asked if his dharma talks were being recorded, he said they weren't," wrote Randy Roark. "When I said they should be, he argued that dharma talks were in the moment—to take them out of the moment would make them worse than irrelevant, it would make them misleading. I told him that truth was truth, and would become truth in the moment, whichever moment that was, if it were really truth. But he shook me off. Although I think he'd really be pleased if someone would make the effort."[15] The teaching fragments that survive do so only because Jennifer Birkett or another student thought to write up their notes immediately. Philip's position on this has precedence in Buddhist and Zen history, but many other great teachers—Shakyamuni Buddha, for example—have done otherwise, allowing, even encouraging, preservation of their teaching. Philip's tack may be partially explained by profound shyness or self-criticism. He kept extensive notes for the classes he taught through the years but only recorded about any zendo talk that one of them at Green Gulch had been "embarrassingly bad." Whatever his reasons, this reticence fits with Philip's general approach during the period, as can been seen from bickering with Randy Roark about poems from Jack Kerouac, then newly published.

> "No, don't read them to me!" Philip said. "I don't want to hear them!"
> I couldn't believe it. I said, " . . . you probably haven't heard these, they've just been published. You loved Kerouac and these are love poems to you. How can you possibly not want to hear them?"
> "No! There's no point to it. I don't want to look back, I don't want to remember the past. Those days are over and best forgotten. Kerouac's dead. Let him rest in peace. And let me rest in peace as well."[16]

When in light of building code and licensing requirements, it became clear that Maitri Hospice would need its own space, Philip roused attention to engineer the split. His purpose in helping uncouple the two institutions remained the protection and flourishing of the temple. When Maitri did find new space, Philip presided over the groundbreaking ceremony and gave a talk reminding listeners of Issan's original efforts: "There was a plague, and no one was paying attention, so he decided 'We must start taking care of people.'" Philip also used the occasion to discuss the karmic chains that follow on any (even compassionate) action, alerting the audience to their immediate responsibilities. "Causes are boiling away inside of ourselves. . . . I believe that all of us feel a pressure in ourselves to respond to the mess the world is in, an experience of mutual suffering with all beings. 'Other people' is us. And Buddhism is you—what you are doing now, and how you are affecting the feelings of other people."[17]

Very shortly after becoming abbot, Philip performed the first of numerous ordinations, both *jukai* and *tokudo*. *Jukai* signified that a person had accepted precepts, taken refuge, and become a Buddhist. During the ceremony the initiates received the small robe—the *rakusu*—they'd sewn, with their Buddhist name inscribed on silk lining the reverse. Philip composed these names, drawing on long tradition, and gave them both in romanized Japanese and in translation. Because there was no tonsure, no new bowls, no larger robe, this was colloquially called a "lay" ordination, and of course everyone would joke that they'd been "layed." Philip's own passage through these rites took place at the time of his full ordination, the *tokudo*. He also performed several of these, with the head-shaving, the *okesa,* and *oryoki*.

The names Philip recorded in the temple record—*The 10,000 Year Book*— names like Houn Tokuzan or Genzan Hokai (Dark Mountain Dharma Ocean) or Unzan Kakudo (Mountain Enlightenment Cloud Way)—would all too often appear a few pages later, with notices of that person's cremation, funeral, or ashes interment. It was a neighborhood zendo, and the neighborhood was suffering a plague. Philip described these ceremonies in connection with the death of one of his ordainees. He began with an overview:

According to Buddhist custom we kept his body several days so people could pay their respects ... then we held a funeral service for family and friends. Another ritual will be held 49 days later, when some of his ashes will be mixed with rice, water, and salt, and then buried. The Buddhist rituals around death and remembrance help us manage this transformation. The point is to create a feeling of completion, care, and attention to death. It has to do with detachment—not being hung up on life or death. Life doesn't last, and attachments are something to re-organize, and understand in a different way. Rituals provide complete involvement and disengagement simultane-ously. This works in with compassion, unobstructed caring, being in the situ-ation totally, but not stuck. Zazen is the detachment part—seeing how form and emptiness fully intertwine: no enlightenment without delusion, no birth without death. Practice is about realizing both worlds at once—the merging of difference and unity—and can help clarify the nature of suffering. ...

The Buddhist custom of sitting with the body is similar to an Irish wake. You can see in American literature the tradition of keeping the corpse

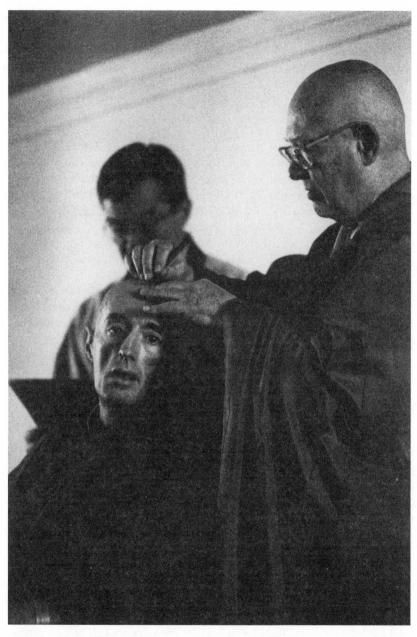

FIGURE 20. Whalen shaving a student's head as part of a *tokudo* ordination ceremony at Issanji, Hartford Street Zen Center, ca. 1993. Photographer unknown.

around, perhaps because relatives are scattered geographically and need time to get there to pay final respects. People are laid out in the parlor, it's called "lying in state." At HSZC we sit with practitioners after their death and would do it for others if asked.

He then went on to explain what stood behind the specific ceremonies:

The actual cremation is called The Gate of Relics. The body takes about 11 hours to burn and cool. A chant about relics is offered called the *Shirirai Mon,* and also the *Kanro Mon* or *Gate of Sweet Dew.* There is a story about Shakyamuni's cremation, where among the ashes and bones were what appeared to be little pellets of glass. In Japan they poke around the cremated remains of a person with noted spiritual development looking for these shirirai. If found, they are placed in a special reliquary and kept on an altar.

The funeral service is a rite of ordination. The ceremony begins with a procession. The box of ashes is wrapped in a white cloth sling and carried in around the neck of a priest, family member, or friend. Offerings of water, sweet tea, food, incense, flowers and lights are made. The ashes are moved about in the incense smoke to make them pure before being placed on the altar. At his funeral I recited the precepts and performed ordination for him again because he was my student. We chanted sutras. Then we invoked his presence and invited people to speak. The service is more for the living than for the one who died. It gives a chance for people to engage their anxiety about separation, and to let go of the grief and sadness. The point of these rituals is to reorganize and understand the transformation of death in a more detached way. . . . Zen is about living and dying. It is a way of living in the immediate present. At the same time, the immediate present must include death.[18]

The reader will understand, then, as perhaps Philip meant his listeners also to intuit, that these descriptions would apply soon enough to the same ceremonies carried out for him.

"My life is drawing to a close, and not a moment too soon!" he told Steve Silberman, eight years before it actually did. "Soon I shall be Zen Shin Flat Line, not worth the stealing." In tones only slightly more sober, he told the annual members' meeting that he was "running down like an old cuckoo clock," and from one of his hospital stays he called David Chadwick to announce that he was dying. "Philip, you've been saying you were dying for as long as I've known you!" "No, this time I'm really dying." But he was premature. In these latter years at the temple, Philip continued to study sutras and other scholarly literature of Buddhism, including Zen, depending on a series of readers for this, some of whom balked at the heavier material. He also heard a summary reprise of all his published poetry, for it was at this point that Philip's final editor, Michael Rothenberg, entered his life in a consequential way.

Rothenberg and his then-wife, Nancy Davis, had made Philip's acquaintance through an introduction from Joanne Kyger. Nancy became a regular sitter at South Ridge, and a friendship arose. Philip visited their bromeliad nursery in Pacifica; they came up to the city for lunches. When Philip returned from Santa Fe, they renewed the friendship, with Nancy and Michael inquiring how they could support Philip's literary life. Rothenberg was just then starting an online magazine—*Big Bridge*—and its maiden issue featured a chapbook of Philip's poems illustrated with Nancy's drawings. Rothenberg next worked up material from an envelope of Philip's unpublished poems. These ranged in date from 1971 to 1988. Philip had not suppressed them particularly, but for a variety of reasons they'd simply not made it into print. Involving Jim Koller's editorial eye and Clifford Burke's printing skills, the manuscript finally appeared in 1999 as *Some of These Days*.[19] It served also as Clifford's letterpress homage to Dave Haselwood, whose work on Philip's first book had set a bibliophilic high-water mark.

At this point, Rothenberg, struggling with discouragement after a rough sojourn in Nashville, asked Philip about producing a book of collected poems. Philip adamantly refused, never wanting such a thing to happen as long as he was alive. He also resisted Rothenberg's next suggestion—"selected poems"—with a long list of self-deprecation: no one will want to read it; no one will want to buy it; there are enough books already; he wasn't writing anymore. In the face of Rothenberg's persistence, Philip finally put it bluntly, "Why should I? Why do you want to do that?" Rothenberg answered in kind: "Because when I was in Nashville I had a terrible time, I'm totally a nervous wreck, and it would give me something to do, something that would be good for me to do." On that basis, Philip assented—"Like that!" as Rothenberg said, acknowledging,

> It was a great gift. A *great* gift. I started reading to him from his very first books. I read all of *On Bear's Head* and just went on. I'd read, then we'd eat, then I'd read. Sometimes it was yes, sometimes it was no; sometimes it was a debate.... We did it two or three times a week.... I was scared to death! There are an awful lot of words in there that I didn't know how to say, or what they meant. There were foreign words. I would stumble over things, which he

would correct in a gentle way. As I read, I became aware of how *amazing* he was. I knew he was really good, but I hadn't known how great.

Though Rothenberg resisted the pleasures of Zen meditation, he did reap spiritual benefits from the reading. "It put me in the moment. There wasn't a lot of room for my mind to wander. I had to be there, for it, at that moment, with him sitting there making *sure* I was there. I had to put aside any personal agenda I had—any neediness, or personal writer questions I might try to sneak in. I just knew not to do that, and I felt better for it. I grew for that. Everything in Nashville had been about making it. With Philip, it wasn't about 'making it.' It was about doing it."[20]

. . .

By the time of this work with Rothenberg, Philip had officially retired as abbot. In letters so shaky and misaligned they do not actually stay on the page, but stubbornly handwritten anyway—Philip recorded that as of 15 August 1996 he was resigning as abbot and leaving the zendo and temple affairs under the supervision of "the monk Shunko Enjo." He filled out the page and completed his entries in *The 10,000 Year Book* with two red seals. Dramatic as this might sound, Philip's life looked much the same. He sat in the zendo as much as his health allowed, and he continued giving talks, meeting people, and performing ceremonies. At some point, he'd moved from his subterranean suite up to the abbot's room, and he continued living there. The same circle of Zen friends who'd arranged for his residence, found the funding, filled out the forms, and worked with officials—a constellation chiefly dating back to his Tassajara days: Steve Allen, Shunko, Michael Wenger, Myphon Hunt, Rick Levine, but also including HSZC members David Bullock, Myo Lahey, Rick London, and David Prowler[21]—went on trying to cover Philip's physical needs. Rothenberg joined this group, though as a skeptical member. As Philip began moving in and out of hospitals and then hospices, Rothenberg felt the Zen community should band together more tightly, empty their pockets more completely, and take better care of the great poet in their midst. The Zen community—the really various members of it involved with Philip—tried their impressive best but were overwhelmed. Philip grew increasingly difficult as his body hurt him more and frustration with his blindness mounted.

Shunko oversaw temple affairs for a while but soon felt it necessary to continue his training in Japan. Leadership of the practice life fell to a committee, as the retired abbot now lay sick and weak in his room. Finally the board petitioned Baker Roshi for help, and one of his German students arrived directly, first for a three-month trial, then for an indefinite period. Tall, earnest, humble, and cheerful, Ottmar Engel made everyone, including Philip, feel good about his presence. Philip was not able to pass the temple succession to Engel—no ceremony took place—but the leadership was clearly seen to be in new, capable hands.

Very shortly after, Philip's health went into steep decline. He grew unintentionally thin, told people he was on the way out, and began giving away possessions. His care now demanded far more than the few temple residents could manage; thus even though Philip initially disliked the plan, he moved into a big, sunny room in the Zen Hospice Center, a Victorian house virtually across the street from Zen Center. Here, confounding expectations, Philip thrived. Poets young and old came to visit him; Zen friends who, for reasons of loyalty or necessity, had remained in the neighborhood came; HSZC and Maitri staff came, as did those from farther afield who just wanted to see and be with Philip before his death. Russell Smith and Joe Kanaster journeyed from Santa Fe for the purpose. Rothenberg was steadily there; Norman Fischer—Philip's literary executor—Leslie Scalapino, and Nancy Davis as well.

Laura Burges entered his room one afternoon to read to him and found Philip sitting calmly on his bed, either not noticing or not caring that he was naked as the day he was born. (She suggested a bathrobe.) Beyond chatting, listening to people read to him, and taking his meals, Philip showed no interest in other activities—not in being escorted around the floor to look at things, not in being helped in and out of the bathtub down the hall. He retained a sharp sense of humor, if darkening it toward noir. Talking with Rick London about tombstones, Philip mentioned that instead of "RIP" as an inscription, he found "RSVP" much more fitting, and wondered if it could be done in a tasteful neon. Postmortem, he said to others, he should like to be "laid upon a bed of frozen raspberries" before cremation; and when Rothenberg said he had something important to discuss—he had in mind the dispersal of Philip's ashes—Philip said, "Oh, something important! For that we should go into the parlor." Philip then said he'd like his ashes placed on Mount Hood. Ottmar Engel had entered the room (parlor) during this discussion and protested that some should go to Hartford Street. "Give the man some ashes!" Philip offered. Their business complete, he instructed them, "Now we should eat cobbler. That's what you do after such a talk."[22]

Philip had come to the hospice to die; the problem was that from January to August of 2001 he didn't. Regulations stipulated an eight-month stay; by then you had leave, dead or alive. Philip would say he "flunked" hospice, and he again resisted options floated his way: an apartment in the Zen Center neighborhood, with care provided, or near Hartford Street. For a few days he was moved into a pied-a-terre inside Zen Center, but he was so unhappy with this and made his feelings known so forcefully that it lasted only a few days. Finally, pleasing almost no one, Philip went into the hospice at Laguna Honda. An old hospital owned and operated by the city, its environment and services were naturally more institutional than he'd had. He was in an open ward. Visually and aurally, his visitors found the place less pleasant, though they continued undiscouraged to come. Zen Center employed Myphon Hunt—a trained nurse—to attend him part-time, but after biking many steep miles each day to get there, she had little to do. Rules prevented her from doing actual nursing, and Philip did not desire activity. He did not wish to be wheeled around the extensive grounds (he could not see); he did not wish to be lifted by machine into a bath, though he submitted to this, as well as to sessions with the person he termed his "physical terrorist." As before, he preferred to lie there—now in hospital gowns and a green wool hat—talking with friends and listening to their reading. He did prefer a better diet than the hospital offered, and friends obliged with take-out from favorite restaurants or dishes they'd prepared. He enjoyed these attentions, but Philip kept his eye on the end game. Asked, for example, if he'd like a milkshake, he said he'd rather have what they gave Socrates. He continued this playful manner as long as he could. Laura Burges closed the book she'd been reading him— Karen Armstrong's *Buddha*—and reflected on Philip's present mildness and acceptance, after a lifetime of magnificent complaint. "Do you think Buddhism has helped you with this?" she asked. After a considered pause, Philip replied, "Not really." And then, "You didn't think it was supposed to *help*, did you?"[23]

On 25 June 2002, midday, Philip slipped into a coma. Calls rocketed around the country as Rothenberg—painfully stranded in Florida with his own dying mother—got word from the hospice doctor that he didn't expect Philip to revive. He was taken off the ward and installed in more private space, the "dying room," as visitors flowed in all afternoon and evening. Everyone who could come by, did. By midnight, the crew was down to Shunko, a Zen Hospice volunteer named Maria Hirano, and Rick London. Most Buddhist traditions view death as a nuanced process, with various stages of dissolution and departure taking place before and after—sometimes days after—the lungs and heart cease. From this perspective, the "moment" of passing is less important than the atmosphere surrounding the whole transition. In any case, specific timing is unpredictable and can be drawn out, as Philip himself had remarked a few days before, crying, "My god, how long is this going to take?" This night Shunko, patient and experienced in such matters (having ministered similarly to Issan), went out around 2 A.M. to get some rest, leaving Rick London in the room holding Philip's hand and saying an occasional encouraging word. Sometime after 4 A.M., Rick was alerted by a definite and powerful change in the room. "I can only say there was an opening in the universe and love poured into the room, filling the room with love, Big Love. Since this didn't seem to have anything to do with me, I assume this was something between Philip and the universe. I was sort of a bystander." Around dawn, Philip took a last long breath, one that "sounded like a machine breaking," and stopped.[24] Shunko led Rick and Maria in chanting the Dai Hi Shin Dharani around Philip's body. Then Nancy Davis and Myphon arrived to help wash him and dress him in robes. By early afternoon Philip lay in state in his old room at the Zen Hospice Center, where visitors both reverent and irreverent, both silent and vocal, paid respects for the next three days.

Baker Roshi arrived shortly after Philip's medical death and conducted the cremation ceremony at the Woodlawn Cemetery in Colma, with an assembly of about fifty people.[25] Everyone recalling the event says something to the effect of "that was nice." At least the charged emotions from old Zen Center wounds seemed to have been temporarily pacified, in respect of the elemental ritual before them. Philip, now several days dead, lay in a cardboard box draped with a red velvet cloth for the chanting. Cloth and box top were removed before the corpse went into the ovens. "It's only Philip's body," said Baker. "The rest of him is in us. We cast off our body like an old pair of pants." Everyone then threw flowers and (indeed) raspberries into the box as it slid forward into the roaring flames. Jennifer Birkett thought, as the oven doors clanged shut, of Philip's teaching: "Be moved aside to who you are and what is really happening. In the life of Zen practice, you shouldn't come out alive."[26]

Two months later, a large crowd gathered for a giant Philip Whalen Memorial Reading. Organizers scheduled at least three hours for the event and involved twenty-five readers—among them Anne Waldman (who sang her offering), the McClures, Jane Hirshfield, David Meltzer, Diane di Prima, Leslie Scalapino, and Michael Rothenberg. Norman Fischer asserted that

Philip was "the best writer of his generation" to an audience that included many writers of that generation. Earlier, Irving Rosenthal had prodded event planners for permission to distribute free copies of Philip's graphic story, the pornographic piece called *Winning His Way: The Rise of Wm. Johnson*. Part of Philip's subtitle described the book as "A Diverting History"—rather too diverting for some tastes, it turned out, as a series of spirited phone calls resulted in denial of permission. Rosenthal instead passed out coupons that could be redeemed for a free copy of the book. He also wrote a lucid and charming account of the whole incident, publishing it as a pamphlet.[27].

Two days after the poets had their say (filling four CDs), on 1 September 2002, Green Gulch Farm hosted Philip's funeral, his "Crossing Over Ceremony." Still displeased with Zen Center after decades, Philip had not wanted the ceremony held in its locations, but Baker—who might have had his own reasons to want another location—told Philip it was the only space big enough to accommodate the crowd who would want to attend. "Oh, all right," Philip grumbled.[28]

The procession included Steve Allen carrying Philip's ashes slung around his neck, and Sozan Schellin—one of the monks Philip had ordained—carrying Philip's picture for the shrine. Among other things, Baker said, "He is in us, or you would not be here. Philip died well. This is his last teaching. Zenshin Ryufu—absorbed, transformed, mind & dragon wind, or breath. In his mother's lap. Accepting this moment." Norman Fischer, co-officiating, said, "In this world you lose your friends in the end. I haven't cried yet, but maybe I will burst into tears when I see nasturtiums."[29] As is traditional, the audience was invited to speak, and many passionate statements of gratitude poured forth, none more moving perhaps than Dave Haselwood's. An ordained Zen teacher himself now in a parallel lineage, Joko (Dave) found himself rising and telling the crowd what had just then become clear to him, which, if he said it, he hoped everyone would realize was true for them as well, in words that only occurred to him as he spoke them, "Philip Whalen has always been my teacher."[30]

POSTSCRIPT

At a table at Green Gulch Farm after the funeral, Baker Roshi, Michael Rothenberg, Norman Fischer, and others divided Philip's ashes according to his wishes, variously expressed. Some were interred under a rock, chosen and hauled from Tassajara by Peter Van der Steere and installed by him at Hartford Street Zen Center. Some were given to Velna Whalen, Philip's sister in San Diego. Some went to Richard Baker to be taken to Crestone Mountain Center. Some went to Mount Hood with Michael and Cosmos Rothenberg, Suzi Winson, and Nancy Davis, who performed a ceremony there. The group was led to an auspicious spot by Moshe Lensky, a friend of Philip's from Portland.

Before he died, Philip donated what he had of his archive to Poets in Need, a foundation whose title describes the intended recipients of its grants. The sale of his papers netted many tens of thousands of dollars. The journals, letters, and manuscripts went mostly to the University of California, Berkeley's Bancroft Library, where they were carefully processed by Dean Smith.

Myo Lahey, whom Philip called "Lord High Everything Else" during his own term as abbot, continued at Hartford Street (with stretches elsewhere) until his own Mountain Seat Ceremony in 2013, making him—after an interregnum of seventeen years—Issanji's fourth abbot.

Michael Rothenberg continued to faithfully edit and publish Philip's written works. Rothenberg and Suzi Winson assembled a Festschrift for Philip in 2004—*Continuous Flame*—and in 2007, Rothenberg brought out *The Collected Poems of Philip Whalen,* a massive, chronologically arranged, and extremely useful volume.

ACKNOWLEDGMENTS

"You know what's wrong with you?" my teacher began, turning his remarkable attention on me, enclosing us in it, as if we were not sitting in a lively, crowded booth with several other people in a lively, crowded brewery in a midsize town in France on a warm evening. Such a question leaves the devoted student few options. This information is exactly what you are supposed to want to hear from your teacher, regardless of the emotional color with which your evening, week, or month will be dyed by hearing it. I made some sort of response—possibly nonverbal—indicating how delighted I would be to know. Not that he was waiting.

"I was thinking about it," he said, looking into my eyes, tightening the focus around us in a way that eliminated any other time and place. "What's wrong with you is that you're not writing. You need to be writing. If you feel you can't do it with everything else that's going on, then I"—here he used a lengthy version of his name and one of his titles—"am now formally giving you this as a practice to do." Then he released me from his focus and turned back to the beery merriment of the gathering. He did this without hurry but somehow abruptly. With finality. There would be no explanation. He immersed himself so quickly and thoroughly in other conversations that it now seemed impossible our "exchange" had even taken place. But I knew it had, from the uneven breathing I felt, and from the mixture of shock and gratitude slowly branching from my heart out to my limbs. Thus it is to my teacher, the Kongma Sakyong of Shambhala, that I owe the first order of gratitude.

Buddhists say that everything comes about through causes and conditions. But the faithful also say that only the Buddha can understand karma completely; only he knows why each color is where it is on the peacock's fanned tail. Because I am far from that state of knowledge, I confess in advance there will be oversights and omissions, and I apologize for them.

Most sincere thanks to the following people for having lent a hand, an ear, an eye, books, or money; for having offered their time, spaces, rides, recommendations, introductions, company, and—connected to writing this book—sympathy: Keith Abbot, John Bailes (Zen heroics, airport heroics), Barbara Bash, Bill Berkson, Reed Bye, Carl Castro, David Chadwick (Cuke heroics), Paul Christensen, Maggie Colby, Peter Conradi, Andrew Cooper, Rick Cusick, Jordan Davis, Steve Dickison, Elsa Dorfman, Michael Downing, Susan Edmiston, Gaylon Ferguson, Carol Gallup, my son Kit Gallup, Barry Gifford, Natalie Goldberg, Maciej Goralski, Peter Hale, Catherine Hanson, Moh Hardin, Mark Hazell, Frances Herb, Amy Holloway, Carine Holties, Lorraine Husmann, Stefan Hyner, Carl Jerome, Debbie Johnson, Alastair Johnston, Albert Kaba, Paul Kahn, Denis Kelley, Mary Kiger, Lisa Knighton, Steven Kushner (Kush), Tessa Ladendorff, Lydia Linker, Valerie Lorig, Lewis MacAdams, Patrick MacMahon, Heike Makoschey-Weiss, Mimi Manning, Jerry Martien, Rebekka Martorano, Liza Matthews, Jane McClure, Linda and Henry McHenry, Palden McLennen, Michael McPherson, Baizan Lynn Menefee, Larry Mermelstein, Brad Miskell, Dave Moore, Gerard Nicosia, Pat Nolan, Fokke Obbema, Jenny O'Neill, Jim O'Neill, Kevin Opstedal, Josef Ortner, Eric Overmyer, Danny Parker, Rianne Pelleboer, Jonathan Raskin, Kevin Ring, Georgia Ringle, Randy Roark, Nina Rolle, Christine Rossini, Peter Schellin, John Sheehy, David Silva (photo hero; heroics generally), Dale Smith, Louise Steinman, Amanda and Fred Stimson, John Suiter, Lara Summerville (research heroics), Eugene Tashima, Mark Thorpe, Jeremy Thorton, Brian Unger,[1] Edward Van Aelstyn, Timothy Vos, John Whalen-Bridge, Carol Windfuhr, Suzi Winson, Laura E. Wright.

Profound thanks:

To the interviewees, including Kijun Steve Allen, Richard Baker, Stanworth Beckler, Rosemary Lapham Berleman, Miriam Bobkoff, Zoe and Maggie Brown, Clifford Burke, Ottmar Engel, Georgianna Greenwood, Joko Dave Haselwood, Myphon Hunt, Shunko Jamvold, Jim Koller, Joanne Kyger, Myo Lahey, Jack Loeffler, Rick London, Joanna McClure, Michael McClure, Alice Notley, Marc Olmstead, David Prowler, Brit Pyland, Irving Rosenthal, Michael Rothenberg, Miriam Sagan, Leslie Scalapino, Dale

Smith, Gary Snyder, Kazuaki Tanahashi, Tony Trigilio, Anne Waldman, Michael and Barbara Wenger, Velna Whalen.

To participants in a group interview of San Francisco Zen Center alumni, graciously hosted at Peter Rudnick and Wendy Johnson's house (apart from those already mentioned above): Alan Block, Edward Espe Brown, Laura Burges, Mary Cunov, Jane Hirshfield, Margot Koch, Susan Leslie, Richard Levine, Ted Marshall, Patrick McMahon, Sojun Mel Weitsman.

To participants in a group interview at Hartford Street Zen Center, including Tove Beatty, Jennifer Birkett, David Bullock, Myo Lahey, Rick London, Mimi Manning, Sozan Peter Schellin, Will Spriestsma.

To Philip's literary executor, Zoketsu Norman Fischer, assisted at times by Michael Rothenberg, Leslie Scalapino, Nancy Davis.

And deep thanks also to noble and knowledgeable librarians, including:

At Reed College, Marilyn Kierstead and Gay Walker; at Columbia University, Alexandra Bernet; at UC Davis, Daryl Morrison and John Skarstad; at the New York Public Library, Dr. Isaac Gewirtz.

At University of Connecticut, Melissa Watterworth; at the Bennett Library, Simon Fraser University, Tony Power; at Green Library, Stanford University, Polly Armstrong and Annette Keogh; at the Bancroft Special Collections, UC Berkeley, everyone, but especially Anthony Bliss, David Kessler, Crystal Miles, Erica Nordmeier, Dean Smith (who brilliantly processed the many shelf-feet of Whalen's papers), Susan Snyder, Baiba Strads.

At Naropa University Audio Archive, Joseph Conway, Tim Hawkins, Mark Kille, Jennifer Tobias.

At Indiana University Libraries Film Archive, Rachael Stoeltje.

And great thanks:

To Jeanne Field, for much-needed warm counsel, protection, and support.

To Reed Malcolm, a subtle, skillful editor, who provided the ways and means to write the book; "I'm your audience." Also at University of California Press, Rachel Berchten, Amy Boyer, Alex Dahne, Stacy Eisenstark, Kalicia Pivirotto.

To Elizabeth Berg, for copy editing the manuscript.

To Richard Levine. The book has had no better friend. Nor in this life, have I.

NOTES

PREFACE

1. Donald Allen, ed., *Off the Wall: Interviews with Philip Whalen* (Bolinas, CA: Four Seasons, 1978).

CHAPTER 1: REFLECTION IN FRIENDS

1. Snyder had his own shack, on Hillegass. Whalen also lived on his own, in an apartment he got from artist Will Petersen. Ginsberg's place was on Milvia; Kerouac spent three months there in 1955.

2. Author interview with Joanne Kyger, 15 June 2006.

3. "Since You Ask Me," in *On Bear's Head* (New York: Harcourt, Brace & World, 1969). The great printer and later Zen teacher Joko Dave Haselwood—for whom this text was composed as a press release in 1959—commented on it while watching a film of Whalen reading years later. As Whalen announced that he was not trying to inherit Dr. Johnson's mantle, Haselwood smiled, clucked his tongue at the TV, and retorted, "Oh yes you were!"

4. Gary Snyder, *The Gary Snyder Reader: Prose, Poetry, and Translations, 1952–1998* (New York: Counterpoint, 1999), xxii.

5. Allen Ginsberg, Naropa class on spontaneous poetics—part 1, August 6, 1976.

6. Author interview with Michael McClure, 18 March 2005.

7. Whalen to Ginsberg, 26 November 1958. Literally "enlightenment beings," bodhisattvas are the classical heroes and heroines of Buddhism's second turning, the Mahayana. They are famed for putting off their own enlightenment to help others along the path.

8. Author interview with Richard Baker Roshi, 6–7 October 2005.

"Banjo Eyes": Philip began a letter to Allen, "Dear Banjo Eyes" (24 March 1966).

1. John Suiter, *Poets on the Peaks: Gary Snyder, Philip Whalen, and Jack Kerouac in the North Cascades* (New York: Counterpoint, 2002), p. 144ff.

2. Anne Waldman interview with Whalen, in Allen, ed., *Off the Wall*, p. 20.

3. Among the main figures that night, Kerouac has written about the reading in fiction, McClure has written about it in memoir, and Ginsberg has written about it in memoir; Snyder and Whalen have been interviewed extensively and repeatedly about it, and much of this has been published. The many Ginsberg and Kerouac biographies describe the event (though not always agreeing on even the date), as does Kenneth Rexroth's biography. Most authoritatively and carefully, and in the greatest detail, John Suiter describes the reading in *Poets on the Peaks*.

4. Waldman interview with Whalen, in Allen, ed., *Off the Wall*, p. 26.

5. Ibid.

6. Gary Snyder, *The Real Work: Interviews and Talks, 1964–1979* (New York: New Directions, 1980), pp. 162, 163.

7. Whalen to Ginsberg, 9 March 1959.

8. Whalen to Ginsberg, 21 July 1956.

9. Carbon copy (signed) among Ginsberg letters to Whalen, 10 February 1968, Columbia University Libraries.

10. Ginsberg to Whalen, 12 February 1971, Columbia University Libraries, Special Collections.

11. Ginsberg to Whalen, 2 October, 1973, Columbia University Libraries.

12. Whalen to Ginsberg, undated (1968), Department of Special Collections, Stanford University Libraries.

13. Ginsberg to Whalen, 18 February 1956.

14. Whalen to Ginsberg, 26 July 1960, Department of Special Collections, Stanford University Libraries.

15. Whalen to Ginsberg, 21 July 1956.

16. Whalen to Ginsberg, undated, circa 1957.

17. Whalen to Ginsberg, 12 April 1958.

18. Whalen to Ginsberg, 3 November 1966, Department of Special Collections, Stanford University.

19. A year later, in 1971, Ginsberg wrote to Whalen, in pique over a book of Gregory Corso's, that he was thinking of retiring from the selection committee. Kenneth Rexroth had also supported Whalen's entry in 1970.

20. Whalen and Ginsberg had been exchanging this kind of information since 1966, when Allen urgently wrote to Japan to ask Philip—and Gary Snyder—how to chant the Heart Sutra in English. Ginsberg was planning to recite it at a concert, over what he called a rock drone to be provided by Sopworth Camel (the band).

After Whalen's ordination at Zen Center in 1972, he sent Allen not only a description of the ceremony but the actual liturgical text, annotated with his doodles, drawings, and musical notations. Some years later, responding to Ginsberg's interest, Philip sent along a list of the Indian, Chinese, and early Japanese lineage patriarchs, again with musical notation for proper lineage recitation.

21. The Hartford Street Zen Center rooms are not large. The large public memorial for Allen Ginsberg took place at Temple El Emmanual. Whalen attended.

22. E-mail to the author from Jennifer Birkett, 18 September 2008.

23. E-mail to the author from Britton Pyland, 25 September 2008.

24. Hartford Street Zen Center Newsletter, summer 1997. "Sawing on the limb" is described in "The Martyrdom of Two Pagans," one of the poems read at the Six Gallery.

CHAPTER 3: BUDDHA RED EARS

"Buddha Red Ears": "I did a lifelike portrait of Phil in pencil . . . 'Buddha Red Ears' is title, because the red flowers in the sun came into window and lit up his shell translucent ears bright red." Jack Kerouac, *Selected Letters, 1957–1969*, ed. Ann Charters (New York: Viking, 1999), p. 36.

1. Jack Kerouac, *Big Sur* (Harmondsworth: Penguin, 1992), pp. 104–5.

2. Ibid., p. 164.

3. Jack Kerouac, *Desolation Angels* (New York: Riverhead, 1995), p. 220. Mickey Cochrane and Hank Gowdy were two famous baseball catchers from the 1920s and 1930s.

4. Ibid., p. 220.

5. "In the Pressure Tank," Naropa University lectures, talk 1. Later in the series, Whalen opines that "them Irishmen is none too smart."

6. Whalen to Kerouac, undated (1956).

7. Kerouac, *Big Sur,* pp. 160–65.

8. Kerouac, *Selected Letters, 1957–1969*. Philip had a private theory that baroque music underlay the rhythms of his own poetry.

9. Ginsberg's description in "Howl," in *Howl and Other Poems* (San Francisco: City Lights, 1956).

10. Kerouac, *Desolation Angels*, p. 22.

11. Whalen journals, 13 March 1963, Bancroft Library, UC Berkeley.

12. Anne Waldman interview with Whalen, in Allen, ed., *Off the Wall*, p. 24.

13. Kerouac, *Desolation Angels*, p. 389.

14. Jack Kerouac, *Selected Letters 1940–1956*, ed. Ann Charters (Harmondsworth: Penguin 1996), p. 542.

15. Ibid., p. 531; Kerouac, *Selected Letters 1957–69*, p. 135.

16. Kerouac, *Selected Letters 1957–69*, p. 96.

17. Whalen to Kerouac, 16 January 1956.

18. It was this poem that Kerouac admired from the *Chicago Review*.

19. Truman Capote's snide remark that Kerouac's work wasn't writing, it was typewriting, can be found in Lawrence Grobel, *Conversations with Capote* (Cambridge, MA: Da Capo Press, 2000), p. 32.

20. Whalen to Kerouac, 9 January 1957.

21. Whalen to Kerouac, 7 June 1963.

22. Kerouac, *Selected Letters 1957–69*, p. 250.

23. Ibid., p. 280.

24. Philip Whalen, *Goofbook* (San Francisco: Big Bridge Press, 2001).

25. McClure, cited in *Jack's Book,* by Barry Gifford and Lawrence Lee (New York: St. Martin's Press, 1978), p. 220.

26. Whalen to Kerouac, April 1961.

27. Whalen, cited in *Jack's Book,* by Gifford and Lee, pp. 216–17.

28. "Against the Magic War," p. 83.

29. Whalen to Kerouac, 23 July 1957.

30. Lewis Ellingham and Kevin Killian, *Poet Be Like God: Jack Spicer and the San Francisco Renaissance* (Hanover, NH: University Press of New England, 1998), pp. 84–85.

31. Kerouac, *Big Sur,* p. 164.

32. "Against the Magic War," pp. 83, 84.

33. "2. Submissive to everything, open, listening": second in Kerouac's list of thirty essentials, from *Belief and Techniques for Modern Prose.* Jack Kerouac, "Essentials of Spontaneous Prose," in Ann Charters, ed., *The Portable Beat Reader* (New York: Viking, 1992).

34. Whalen to Joanne Kyger, 2 or 3 November 1969 (he gives the Japanese date 44 X 27).

35. Whalen to Ginsberg, 13 November 1969.

36. Whalen to Joanne Kyger, 2 or 3 November 1969.

37. Whalen to Ginsberg, 13 November 1969.

CHAPTER 4: KALYANAMITRA

1. Located at 2273 California Street in San Francisco, spiritual issue of the American Academy of Asian Studies, the East-West House was a communal residence where East—especially Japan—and West could meet. Many writers lived there for shorter or longer periods, including Jack Kerouac, Philip Whalen, Joanne Kyger, Lew Welch, Albert Saijo, and Lenore Kandel. See Bill Morgan, *The Beat Generation in San Francisco: A Literary Tour* (San Francisco: City Lights Books, 2003).

2. Whalen to Ginsberg, 5 October 1959.

3. Author interview with Gary Snyder, 5 January 2006.

4. The tie was respectfully solemn and dark. Close inspection revealed it was decorated with a pattern of little red skulls.

5. Gary Snyder, "Highest and Driest: For Philip Zenshin's Poetic Drama/Dharma," in *Continuous Flame: A Tribute to Philip Whalen,* ed. Michael Rothenberg and Suzi Winson (New York: Fish Drum Inc, 2004), p. 31.

6. Ibid.

7. *The Gary Snyder Reader,* p. xxii.

8. The Chinese sense of "friends coming from afar" includes the idea of sharing learning.

9. Ezra Pound, *The ABC of Reading* (New York: New Directions, 1960), p. 36.

10. *Continuous Flame,* p. 32.

11. Private conversation with author, January 2006, Davis, California.

12. The Reed College alumni magazine has received letters begging it not to publish any more articles about "the Beats at Reed" or about one of their mentors, Professor Lloyd Reynolds!

13. "Far from the wicked city/Far from the virtuous town," from "Metaphysical Insomnia Jazz, Mumonkan XXIX," in *The Collected Poems of Philip Whalen,* ed. Michael Rothenberg (Middletown, CT: Wesleyan University Press, 2007).

14. Whalen, Hiking Notebook, July 1965, from unpublished papers of Philip Whalen, Bancroft Library, University of California, Berkeley. Leitswics = light switch, a mock vision quest name from Snyder's Reed days.

15. Ibid.

16. Author interview with Gary Snyder, 5 January 2006.

17. Author interview with Dr. Richard Levine, 5 January 2006.

18. Author interview with Gary Snyder, January 2006.

19. Snyder to Whalen, 3 November 1953, Reed College.

20. Whalen to Snyder, 24 March 1952.

21. *The Collected Poems of Philip Whalen.*

22. Jack Kerouac, *The Dharma Bums* (Harmondsworth: Penguin, 1976), p. 18.

23. Whalen to Ginsberg, 16 May 1966.

24. Whalen journal, 26 April 1969, Bancroft Library, UC Berkeley.

25. Matthew Davis and Michael Farrell Scott, *Opening the Mountain: Circumambulating Mount Tamalpais* (Emeryville, CA: Shoemaker and Hoard, 2006); Tom Killion and Gary Snyder, *Tamalpais Walking: Poetry, History, and Prints* (Berkeley, CA: Heyday, 2009). Most useful for this account has been a chapter from a book by David Robertson, an English professor colleague of Snyder's from UC Davis and a Tam hiker himself. In *Real Matter,* Robertson records excerpts from an interview he conducted with Philip and Gary in 1992.

26. "In the Pressure Tank," Naropa University lectures, class 3, part 1, 28 July 1980.

27. Whalen to Snyder, April 1959.

28. David Robertson, *Real Matter* (Salt Lake City: University of Utah Press, 1997).

29. Edward Conze, *Buddhist Wisdom Books* (London: George Allen and Unwin, 1958), p. 21.

30. Robertson, *Real Matter,* p. 127.

31. Whalen to Snyder, 28 November 1953. The drawing included in the letter shows a Buddha sitting beautifully in a temple and a very wide-butted fellow bent over among plants in a garden.

32. Robertson, *Real Matter,* p. 127.

33. Whalen to Diane di Prima, 1965.

34. See chapter 10.

35. Beyond telling the class (21 July 1976), Whalen wrote about it in *The Diamond Noodle* (Berkeley, CA: Poltroon Press, 1980), pp. 22–24.

36. Snyder to Whalen, 1955.

37. Lew Welch and Joanne Kyger were names that came up.

38. Interview with Gary Snyder, 5 January 2007.

39. It is one of the great paradoxes of Buddhist philosophy that the absence of a self does not excuse one from karmic retribution.

40. Jon Halper, ed., *Gary Snyder: Dimensions of a Life* (San Francisco: Sierra Club Books, 1991), p. 207.

41. Whalen was quite capable of writing a summary view of his relations with Snyder. In a 1968 letter to Stanworth Beckler, Philip recalls: "I first met Gary Snyder at Reed. He has been writing better & better ever since, & he has taught me an enormous amount about mountains and anthropology & Buddhism & girls & savoir vivre. . . . He & Allen & Jack & Rexroth have been my chief GURUS. But then so have the spirits of Aeschylus, Su T'ung Po, Lady Muraskai, Cezanne, Sesshu, Schönberg, Rachmaninoff . . . the series of debts is unlimited."

42. Whalen to Snyder, 7 June 1956.

43. Snyder to Whalen, 11 June 1956, Reed College.

44. Author interview with Gary Snyder, 5 January 2007.

45. Snyder to Whalen, 25 May 1956.

46. Snyder to Whalen, 30 September 1956.

47. Whalen to Snyder, 18 June 1957.

48. Whalen to Snyder, 1 November 1962.

49. Whalen to Snyder, 21 June 1960.

50. Whalen to Snyder, 4 July 1956.

51. Whalen to Snyder, 23 June 1961.

52. Whalen to Snyder, 22 May 1957.

53. Snyder to Whalen, 14 June 1957.

54. Whalen to Snyder, 15 December 1960.

55. Whalen to Snyder, 1 October 1958.

56. Snyder to Whalen, 9 Ocober 1958; *The Gary Snyder Reader,* p. 155.

57. Whalen to Snyder, 8 March 1963.

58. Snyder to Whalen, 2 May 1963.

59. Yet another JK who played an important role in Whalen's life was the poet and Whalen's publisher, Jim Koller.

60. See chapter 14.

61. Whalen to Snyder, 7 January 1984.

62. Whalen to Snyder, 16 September 1984.

63. Snyder to Whalen, 16 September 1987.

64. *The Gary Snyder Reader*, p. xxii.

65. *The Collected Poems of Philip Whalen*, p. 538.

66. "To the Muse," in *The Collected Poems of Philip Whalen*, p. 316.

67. Snyder to Whalen, 2 January 1955, Reed College.

68. Whalen to Snyder, 25 January 1955.

69. Whalen to Snyder, 24 April 1955.

70. Whalen to Snyder, 24 April 1955.

71. Snyder to Whalen, 16 June 1955, Reed College.

72. Whalen to Snyder, 2 May 1955. "Old original rice bag" is a fond Zen-style epithet for the Buddha.

73. Whalen, LSD Notebook, UC Berkeley.

74. Whalen to Snyder, 18 May 1955, for this and following references to Williams.

75. *The Collected Poems of Philip Whalen*, p. 304ff.

76. Snyder to Whalen, 9 June 1955, Reed College, for this and subsequent references to the Williams reading.

77. Whalen to Snyder, 13 June 1955.

78. Green Gulch Farm Zen Center, 10–12 April 1987. Transcripts of this conference were published in *Jimmy & Lucy's House of "K"* 9 (January 1989).

79. These included—beyond Sndyer and Whalen—Gail Sher, Norman Fischer, Steve Benson, Anne Waldman, Andrew Schelling, and Will Staple, with papers submitted to the conference by several more distinguished poets and artists.

80. Whalen to Ginsberg, May 1969.

CHAPTER 5: YOUR HEART IS FINE

1. Joanne introduced Gary Snyder to Weinpahl, who by this time had started to be interested in Zen. Later in 1959, Weinpahl went to Kyoto, where Snyder introduced him to Ruth Fuller Sasaki, who in turn arranged for him to study with Zuigan Goto Roshi. Weinpahl's *Zen Diary* from that time was published in 1970.

2. Members of the Spicer circle met at least weekly in small groups, under a variety of names and in varying constellations, to read work aloud and have it critiqued. Even Gary Snyder read to such a gathering. See Ellingham and Killian, *Poet Be Like God,* for a thorough, engaging account.

3. Author interview with Joanne Kyger, 23 September 2005.

4. Snyder to Whalen, 16 March 1959, Reed College.

5. Friends later in life wondered if Philip hadn't perhaps suffered a mild lifelong case of Tourette's syndrome, accounting for such outbursts.

6. Kyger to Whalen, 24 January 1959, Reed College.

7. Author interview with Kyger, 23 September 2005.

8. Hyphen House stood about five blocks from the East-West House and took its name from the hyphen between "East" and "West." It was founded at the beginning of October 1959, with Albert Saijo, Lew Welch, Les Thompson, Jay Blaise, Tom Field, and Philip Whalen as charter residents.

9. Kerouac, *Big Sur,* pp. 58–59.

10. "You all" clearly includes Joanne, since this was sent to Gary on the eve of his departure to Japan, a time when he was practically living with Joanne.

11. *Collected Poems of Philip Whalen,* pp. 76–77.

12. Whalen to Snyder, 9 March 1959.

13. Snyder to Whalen, 16 March 1959, Reed College.

14. Whalen to Snyder, 19 April 1959.

15. Author interview with Kyger, 23 September 2005.

16. *Collected Poems of Philip Whalen,* p. 134.

17. Whalen to Snyder, 8 June 1959; Whalen, Hiking Notebook, 4 July 1959.

18. Whalen, Hiking Notebook, 26 June 1959. Whalen was thirty-five at the time.

19. This stricture originated with Ruth Fuller Sasaki, Gary's employer and patron in Japan.

20. Author interview with Kyger, 23 September 2005.

21. Ibid.

22. Kyger to Whalen, 21 January 1960, Reed College.

23. Whalen to Kyger, March 1960, Mandeville Special Collections, UC San Diego.

24. Kyger to Whalen, 9 March 1960, Reed College.

25. Ibid.

26. UC San Diego, Register of Joanne Kyger Correspondence MSS 0008.

27. Whalen journal, 7 May 1964.

28. Ibid., 28 June 1964. Philip was forty-one at the time.

29. *Collected Poems of Philip Whalen,* p. 379.

30. Opstedal, "Dreaming as One: Poetry, Poets, and Community in Bolinas CA 1967–80," in *Big Bridge,* an online magazine, www. bigbridge.org; also Jim Koller, private correspondence with the author.

31. *Collected Poems of Philip Whalen,* p. 659. Joanne and Jack Boyce separated in 1970. At the time of Whalen's poem, Joanne Kyger was with ecologist Peter Warshall.

32. Kyger to Whalen, 21 February 1961, Reed College.

33. Cited in Brenda Knight, *Women of the Beat Generation* (Berkeley, CA: Conari Press, 1986).

34. Whalen to Kyger, November 1962, Mandeville Special Collections, UC San Diego.

35. Whalen to Kyger, 6 March 1963.

36. Whalen to Kyger, 30 August 1963.

37. Whalen to Kyger, 12 March 1963. Philip also called this "Graveyard Stew."

38. Kyger to Whalen, 4 December 1960. She also fairly reported what most sitters have noticed through the years: although the blows are *shoji*-shaking loud, they

do not generally cause pain. The sharp retort and the feelings around being singled out for discipline generally suffice to waken or still the meditator.

39. Personal conversation with the author, 3 November 1982.

40. Whalen to Kyger, 1969.

41. Author interview with Kyger, 12 August 2005.

42. David Schneider, "Side Effect: A Journal of Zen Life with Philip Whalen," unpublished manuscript.

43. *Collected Poems of Philip Whalen*, p. 140.

44. Joanne Kyger, *Just Space: Poems, 1979–1989* (Santa Rosa: Black Sparrow Press, 1991).

45. Author interview with Rick London, January 2009.

46. Kyger to Whalen, 3 February 1960, Reed College.

47. Expressed in Gary's own shipboard writings and known to them personally.

48. *Continuous Flame*, p. 33.

49. "Haiku: For Gary Snyder," in *Collected Poems of Philip Whalen*, p. 156.

50. Joanne Kyger, "Monday before the Recall," from *Ten Lovely New Poems*, available at http://mcclure-manzarek.com/friends/kyger.

51. "Basho Says Plants Stones Utensils," from ibid.

52. The second turning of the wheel of dharma, the first turning having been the Buddha's first sermon.

53. Joanne Kyger, *The Japan and India Journals, 1960–1964* (Bolinas: Tombouctou Books, 1981), p. 61.

54. *Collected Poems of Philip Whalen*, p. 692.

55. Joanne Kyger, "'JOANNE Is a Novel from the Inside Out,'" in *Joanne* (Bolinas, CA: Angel Hair, 1970).

56. *Collected Poems of Philip Whalen*, p. 373.

57. Ibid., p. 163.

58. Ibid., p. 417.

59. "Bodhicaryavatara," available in numerous translations, with or without learned commentary.

60. "Maha" = "great, large, broad"; "yana" = way, path, vehicle.

61. Joanne Kyger, *Again: Poems 1989–2000* (Albuquerque, NM: La Alameda, 2001).

CHAPTER 6: HAIL THEE WHO PLAY

1. Jay DeFeo, her husband Wally Hedrick, and Joan Brown.

2. Author interview with Michael McClure, 18 March 2005.

3. *Collected Poems of Philip Whalen*, p. 142.

4. Author interview with McClure, 18 March 2005.

5. *Continuous Flame*.

6. Hiking Notebook, 5 November 1959.

7. Snyder read "Berry Feast," long stretches of which are spoken by animals. The event was the Six Gallery reading.

8. Keith Abbott, private correspondence with the author, 3 July 2011.

9. The issue also included works by Snyder, Kerouac, Ginsberg, and Ferlinghetti.

10. See Ellingham and Killian, *Poet Be Like God,* p. 86.

11. Whalen to Ginsberg, 6 February 1957.

12. "ADDRESS TO THE BOOBUS, with her Hieratic Fomulas in reply" and "BOOBUS HIEROPHANTE Her Incantations," in *Collected Poems of Philip Whalen,* pp. 143–45.

13. Whalen to Snyder, 26 August 1963.

14. "The Magic Theatre, for John Lion," in *September Blackberries* (New York: New Directions, 1974), pp. 117–18.

15. Michael McClure, *The Mammals* (San Francisco: Cranium Press, 1972), p. 44.

16. Both excerpts from Michael McClure, *Jaguar Skies* (New York: New Directions, 1973).

17. *Collected Poems of Philip Whalen,* p. 546.

18. Whalen journal, 1967, p. 99.

19. See chapter 10.

20. "The Ode to Music: For Morton Subotnick," *Collected Poems of Philip Whalen,* p. 365.

21. "Warnings, Responses etc," in *Collected Poems of Philip Whalen,* p. 157.

22. Michael McClure, "Hollywood Hills," in *Jaguar Skies.*

23. Author interview with McClure, 18 March 2005.

24. Michael McClure, *Touching the Edge* (Boston: Shambhala, 1999).

CHAPTER 7: EARLY

1. Whalen journal, 12 November 1963.

2. Author interview with Velna Whalen, 21 June 2006.

3. Whalen, *The Diamond Noodle,* p. 62.

4. Naropa University lectures, talk on Alexander Pope, 18 July 1984.

5. One of Philip's Zen forbears, the great Dogen-zenji, wrote a fascicle he titled "Uji," which translates as "Being-Time" or, alternatively, as "The Time-Being." Brilliant and profound, it is also regarded as verging on opaque.

6. Allen, ed., *Off the Wall,* p. 37.

7. *Collected Poems of Philip Whalen,* p. 701.

8. This and subsequent portraits of his parents are from Whalen, *The Diamond Noodle.* This one is on p. 65.

9. Ibid.

10. Allen, ed., *Off the Wall.* p. 70.

11. "In the Pressure Tank," Naropa University lectures, class 3, part 1.

12. Whalen, *The Diamond Noodle,* p. 60.

13. Allen Ginsberg class in Naropa University lectures, 2.

14. Author interview with Velna Whalen, 21 June 2006.

15. Aram Saroyan interview, in Allen, ed., *Off the Wall*, p. 39.

16. Ibid.

17. Ibid.

18. Whalen to Stanworth Beckler, private correspondence, courtesy of S. Beckler.

19. *Diamond Noodle,* p. 31.

20. Philip Whalen in Allen Ginsberg's Spontaneous Poetics class, Naropa University lectures, July 1976, part 2.

21. Ibid.

22. Allen, ed., *Off the Wall*, p. 69.

23. Whalen in Allen Ginsberg's Spontaneous Poetics class, Naropa University lectures, July 1976, part 2.

24. Allen, ed., *Off the Wall*, p. 69.

25. Ibid.

26. Whalen in Allen Ginsberg's Spontaneous Poetics class, Naropa University lectures, July 1976, part 2.

27. Whalen journal, 1971, Bancroft Library, UC Berkeley.

28. Document in the possession of Velna Whalen.

29. Whalen in Allen Ginsberg's Spontaneous Poetics class, Naropa University lectures, July 1976, part 2.

30. *Diamond Noodle,* p. 101.

31. Naropa University lectures, July 1976, part 1.

32. *Collected Poems of Philip Whalen,* p. 157.

33. Bartlett interview, in Allen, ed., *Off the Wall*, p. 69.

34. Ibid.

35. "In the Pressure Tank," Naropa University lectures, part 1, 23 July 1980.

36. "In the Pressure Tank," Naropa University lectures, talk 13, part 1, 20 August 1980.

37. "In the Pressure Tank," Naropa University lectures, part 1, 23 July 1980.

38. Author interview with Richard Baker, 6 October 2005.

39. Whalen cites Lin Yutang, *The Gay Genius: The Life & Times of Su Tungpo.*

CHAPTER 8: FORCED ASSOCIATION

1. "In the Pressure Tank," Naropa University lectures, class 1.

2. Whalen to Stanworth Beckler, November 1945.

3. Ibid.

4. Ibid.

5. "In the Pressure Tank," Naropa University lectures, class 13, part 2.

6. These descriptions were written by hand in a booklet supplied by the U.S. Army for the purpose. The header running across both pages of the pamphlet's

spread read "My Buddies" and was adorned left and right with drawings of groups of servicemen walking arm-in-arm, polishing shoes, reading the paper, or otherwise enjoying down time together. The first page suggested direction to the bewildered: Name and Nickname—Where I Met Him—What I Liked & Disliked About Him—What We Did—Home Address—Picture. Philip was still going by the name "Pat" but preferred to be called "PG."

7. Beckler, "My Buddies."

8. Anne Waldman interview, in Allen, ed., *Off the Wall.*

9. Naropa University lectures, 1976, part 1.

10. Ibid.

11. Allen, ed., *Off the Wall,* p. 18.

12. Whalen journal, 16 March 1958.

13. Anne Waldman interview, in Allen, ed., *Off the Wall,* p. 16.

14. "Goldberry Is Waiting," in *Collected Works of Philip Whalen,* p. 828.

15. Ibid.

CHAPTER 9: REED'S FINE COLLEGE

"Reed's Fine College": "I sure am glad to be here, at Reed's fine college." Reverend Gary Davis, before a concert in 1970.

1. Anne Waldman interview, in Allen, ed., *Off the Wall.*

2. Ibid.

3. Private correspondence with Stanworth Beckler, June 1945.

4. "Life and Death and a Letter to My Mother Beyond Them Both," in *Collected Poems of Philip Whalen,* p. 301.

5. Yves le Pellec interview, in Allen, ed., *Off the Wall,* p. 58.

6. Lee Bartlett interview in ibid., p. 71.

7. Private correspondence with Stanworth Beckler, 15 January 1947.

8. Lee Bartlett interview, in Allen, ed., *Off the Wall.*

9. Private correspondence with Stanworth Beckler, 15 January 1947; Anne Waldman interview, in *Off the Wall,* p. 13; "In the Pressure Tank," Naropa University lectures, class 13, part 1, 1980.

10. Author interview with Georgianna Greenwood, 12 November 2013.

11. Ibid.

12. Steve Jobs, 2005 Stanford Commencement Address, available at www .youtube.com/watch?v=UF8uR6Z6KLc.

13. John Sheehy, *Comrades of the Quest: An Oral History of Reed College* (Corvallis: Oregon State University Press, 2012).

14. Ibid.

15. Gary's problems stemmed from association with other Northwest labor movements—the IWW specifically—but this was sufficiently anti-American. See Suiter, *Poets on the Peaks,* ch. 4.

16. Whalen to Snyder, 18 July 1954.

17. Lloyd knew Philip and Gary were sharing an apartment.

18. Lloyd Reynolds to Philip Whalen, 10 October 1964, 14 October 1963, and 19 July 1960, Special Collections, Eric V. Hauser Memorial Library, Reed College.

19. The three-dot ellipses are Philip's own.

20. Whalen to Mrs Lehman, Election Day 1965, Special Collections, Eric V. Hauser Memorial Library, Reed College.

21. Returning from the Vancouver Poetry Conference, 1963.

22. "Tribute to Lloyd Reynolds," *Oregonian,* 15 October 1978.

23. "In the Pressure Tank," Naropa University lectures, class 13, part 1.

24. Lew Welch, *I Leo,* ed. Donald Allen (Bolinas, CA: Grey Fox, 1977), p. 5.

25. For descriptions of these communal houses, see chapter 4.

26. He recounted in letters that all the events were "true." Lew Welch, *I Remain: The Letters of Lew Welch and the Correspondence of His Friends* (Bolinas, CA: Grey Fox, 1980), p. 143.

27. Welch, *I Leo,* pp. 53–54.

28. "In the Pressure Tank," Naropa University lectures, 1981. Lew's literary executor, Donald Allen, who published a great deal—nearly all—of Lew's poetry and prose, never got around to preparing that manuscript for publication.

29. "Adelaide Crapsey" makes some sense; she invented a five-line poetic form, the cinquain; the rest of the name seems purely fanciful.

30. Lew Welch, *How I Work as a Poet* (Bolinas, CA: Grey Fox, 1973), pp. 75–76.

31. Anne Waldman interview, in Allen, ed., *Off the Wall,* pp. 34–35.

32. "In the Pressure Tank," Naropa University lectures, class 10, part 2.

33. William Carlos Williams, *The Autobiography of William Carlos Williams* (New York: New Directions, 1967), p. 377.

34. Snyder to Whalen, 7 June 1971, Columbia University Libraries.

35. Whalen to Ginsberg, 12 June 1971.

36. "In the Pressure Tank," Naropa University lectures.

37. Welch, *I Remain,* vol. 1, p. 166.

38. Letter to Gary Snyder, in Welch, *I Remain,* vol. 1, p. 124.

39. Ibid., p. 111.

40. Ibid., p. 144.

41. Welch, *How I Work as a Poet,* p. 42.

42. Welch suffered at least two nervous breakdowns—one in Chicago in the midfifties and another in 1962, out west.

43. "In the Pressure Tank," Naropa University lectures, 1981.

44. Because at this writing Gary Snyder is alive, continuing to demonstrate effectively in word and deed the role of a poet, and because this book has already devoted a chapter to him, it will now focus on the other two.

45. Welch, *How I Work as a Poet,* p. 42.

"Solvitur Ambulando": "It is solved by walking."

1. *Evergreen Review* 2, the San Francisco Scene issue, 1957.

2. Whalen to Ginsberg, 3 September 1958.

3. Whalen to Ginsberg, Snyder, and Kerouac, 1958, Ginsberg letters, Stanford University.

4. Whalen to Ginsberg, 11 August 1959.

5. Bill Morgan, *The Beat Generation in San Francisco* (San Francisco: City Lights, 2003).

6. First McClure's *Hymns to St. Geryon,* then a book by Philip Lamantia, who'd organized the event, and finally Philip's.

7. Whalen to Ginsberg, 19 January 1960.

8. Whalen to Snyder, 19 January 1960.

9. Allen, ed., *Off the Wall.*

10. Hiking Notebook, 4 August 1957, p. 5.

11. Whalen journals, 27 March 1964.

12. Hiking Notebook, 1960.

13. Hiking Notebook, 1961.

14. Again capably organized by Elsa Dorfman.

15. Whalen to Snyder, 15 December 1960.

16. Hiking Notebook, 7 June 1960.

17. Whalen notebook, 24 October 1961.

18. Whalen, *You Didn't Even Try* (San Francisco: Coyote Books, 1967).

19.

> Sentient beings are numberless, I vow to save them.
> Desires are inexhaustible, I vow to put an end to them.
> The Dharmas are boundless, I vow to master them.
> The Buddha Way is unsurpassable, I vow to attain it.

20. All these come from Philip's journal, January to June 1963.

21. A mixture of amphetamine and barbiturate; a mood elevator and stimulant.

22. Whalen journal, 1 April 1963.

23. A review appeared in at least the *Times Literary Supplement,* 4 January 1968.

24. Whalen journal, 16 August 1962.

25. Whalen to Snyder, 23 June 1961.

26. Whalen to Diane di Prima, 12 December 1963.

27. Allen, ed., *Off the Wall,* p. 3.

28. *Collected Poems of Philip Whalen,* p. 360.

29. Whalen journal, 7 February 1966.

30. Whalen journal, 23 February 1963.

31. *San Francisco Chronicle,* 25 October 1963.

32. "Poetry at the Old Longshoreman's Hall," *The Don Carpenter Page,* www. doncarpenterpage.com/poetry.htm.

33. See chapter 9.

34. "Vancouver 1963 Poetry Conference & Miscellaneous Recordings," *Slought,* https://slought.org/resources/vancouver_1963.

35. Hiking Notebook, 22 August 1963.

36. "Vancouver 1963 Poetry Conference & Miscellaneous Recordings," *Slought,* https://slought.org/resources/vancouver_1963.

37. Hiking Notebook, 25 August 1963.

38. Naropa University lectures, 1977, parts 1 and 2.

39. Juliet McLaren published "Brief Season: The *Northwest Review* Crisis," an excellent account of the events at University of Oregon, in *Line,* nos. 7/8 (1986). The introductory essay to Simon Fraser's archive of materials from the *Northwest Review,* as well as *Coyote,* also provides a clear summary of the events. It is unattributed. My descriptions draw heavily on these two sources.

40. Artaud's play was translated for the first time into English by Guy Wernham and introduced by an essay from Michael McClure. The play was no stranger to scandal: a harsh work full of anger at the Catholic Church and at American "imperialism," it also contains lengthy, utterly unembarrassed meditations on flatulence and defecation. It was banned from the air on the eve of its French premiere in 1948.

41. "A Short History of the Second Millennium B.C.," in *Collected Poems of Philip Whalen,* p. 250.

42. Private correspondence, 8 June 1964.

43. Koller remarked that he was not at the *NWR* long enough to be on a printed masthead but only long enough to be fired.

44. *Coyote's Journal* continued healthily beyond that, and continues to exist, as of this writing, as an online magazine.

45. "The Best of It," in *Collected Poems of Philip Whalen,* pp. 392–93.

46. "Minor Moralia," in *On Bear's Head* (New York: Harcourt, Brace & World, 1969), p. 190.

CHAPTER 11: JAPAN, BOLINAS, JAPAN, BOLINAS

1. The show was a series titled *USA: Poetry.* National Educational Television, extinct since 1974, was a forerunner of much current public broadcasting.

2. Dick Moore.

3. "Tara," in *Collected Poems of Philip Whalen,* p. 483.

4. These and other descriptions of the voyage are taken from *Intransit,* the Philip Whalen issue (1967), p. 48.

5. See chapter 4.

6. Whalen to Jean Koller, 18 July 1966, Koller Papers, Dodd Research Center, University of Connecticut.

7. His address was % Kitamura, 73 Higashikubota-cho, Kita-shirakawa, Sakyo-ku, Kyoto.

8. Whalen journal, 9 June 1966. *Kami* are the gods and goddesses of the Shinto faith; larger-than-human energies, they are often associated with particular places and shrines in nature. An *Okami-sama* would be a great, important kami.

9. Whalen journal, June 1966.

10. Kyoto had not been Japan's official capital for one hundred years, and unofficially for much longer. Philip, typically, lived in the tenth-century city of Lady Murasaki and her *Tale of Genji* as much as he lived in a twentieth century of Pentel pens and beautiful neon.

11. Whalen to Ginsberg, 20 October 1966.

12. Whalen to Jim Koller, 2 March 1971.

13. Whalen to Donald Carpenter, 8 June 1969.

14. Whalen journal, 16 June 1969.

15. Whalen journal, 9 June 1966.

16. Kenneth Rexroth, *With Eye and Ear* (New York: Herder & Herder, 1969), pp. 210–11.

17. Whalen to Jim Koller, 24 April 1967.

18. Whalen journal, 27 November 1967.

19. Whalen to Ginsberg, 3 January 1968.

20. The phrase "on Bear's head" comes from the poem "The Sun Rises & Sets in That Child," in *Collected Poems of Philip Whalen*, p. 442.

21. *Continuous Flame*, p. 72. Philip had copies of the poems but not the handwriting he'd done for Poets Press.

22. Whalen to Jim Koller, 12 August 1969.

23. Whalen journal, 15 May 1969.

24. Whalen to Ginsberg, 24 January 1968.

25. Whalen journal, 21 July 1968.

26. David Chadwick interview with Whalen, *Cuke,* www.cuke.com /Cucumber%20Project/interviews/whalen.html.

27. Ibid.

28. Whalen to Don Carpenter, 28 October 1968.

29. Whalen to Don Carpenter, 15 April 1969.

30. Whalen journal, 16 May 1969.

31. Whalen journal, 22 March 1968.

32. *Imaginary Speeches for a Brazen Head.*

33. *Scenes of Life at the Capital* (Bolinas: Grey Fox Press, 1971).

34. *The Invention of the Letter* and *The Rise of William Johnson.*

35. Whalen journal, 24 May 1969.

36. *Continuous Flame,* p. 32.

37. Whalen journal, 22 October 1967.

38. Whalen journal, 20 May 1969.

39. Whalen journal, 11 September 1967.

40. Chadwick interview with Whalen.

41. Irmgard Schoegel had a distinguished Zen career as an author, translator, and roshi, ending up as senior teacher at several centers in England connected to the Buddhist Society. In some pictures of her as a nun, she looks startlingly like Philip as a monk.

42. Later known as Soko Morinaga Roshi, he was also liked and admired by Gary Snyder, Joanne Kyger, and Richard Baker.

43. Whalen journal, 30 April 1969.

44. Chadwick interview with Whalen.

45. Whalen journal, 10 January 1971.

46. Whalen to Jim Koller, 1 June 1970.

CHAPTER 12: NEW YEARS

1. Whalen to Ginsberg, 5 May 1971.

2. Whalen to Ginsberg, 29 June 1972.

3. *Continuous Flame,* p. 124.

4. Joe Brainard, *Bolinas Journal* (Bolinas, CA: Big Sky Books, 1971).

5. Whalen to Snyder, 18 June 1971; Whalen to Koller, 20 May 1971.

6. Coyote Books had been forced into retirement by Bay Area publishing machinations.

7. Don Allen was on Zen Center's board of directors; they spoke about once a week.

8. See chapter 1.

9. Cited in Michael Downing, *Shoes Outside the Door* (Washington, DC: Counterpoint, 2001), p. 185.

10. Allen, ed., *Off the Wall,* p. 48.

11. Whalen journal, 1 August 1972.

12. Whalen to Snyder, 3 March 1972.

13. Whalen journal, 6 September 1972.

14. *Roshi* transliterates Japanese and Chinese characters that mean "old master," "old teacher." Don Allen was the person who told Baker that Suzuki should be addressed with the title *roshi.*

15. Author interview with Richard Baker, 6 October 2005.

16. Downing, *Shoes Outside the Door,* p. 185.

17. Philip Whalen, *Canoeing Up Cabarga Creek* (Berkeley, CA: Parallax Press, 1996), p. xiii.

18. Interview with Richard Baker, 6 October 2005.

19. Whalen journal, 5 January 1971.

20. Richard Baker, introduction to Whalen, *Canoeing Up Carbarga Creek.*

21. Hiking Notebook, 28 June 1972.

22. Literally "touching mind," sometimes translated as "gathering mind" or "conveying mind."

23. Whalen journal, 13 August 1972.

24. Whalen journal, 15–27 September 1972.

25. *Ango* in Japanese. This period is meant to reproduce the rainy-season retreats from the Buddha's time.

26. Whalen journal, 20 September and 30 November 1972.

27. *Rohatsu* means literally "December 8"; the *sesshin* concludes on that date. It commemorates Buddha's enlightenment, which is imagined to have happened on that date some twenty-five centuries earlier.

28. Author interview with Zen Center students, 12 January 2009. Story told by Richard Levine, with corroboration from others.

CHAPTER 13: AN ORDER TO LOVE

"An Order to Love": "The community, the sangha, 'society'—an order to love; we must love more persons places and things with deeper and more various feelings than we know at present; a command to imagine and express this depth and variety of joys delights and understandings." "Minor Moralia (3)," in *Collected Poems of Philip Whalen,* p. 267.

1. Whalen to Snyder, 5 September 1972.

2. Whalen to Ginsberg, 19 February 1973.

3. This reproduces the original typography and punctuation; in seven pages of call-and-response promising extraordinary things, these are the only exclamation points.

4. Whalen to Ginsberg, 23 August 1972.

5. Whalen journal, 9 July 1972.

6. Whalen to Ginsberg, 19 February 1973.

7. Whalen to Jim Koller, 18 July 1974.

8. *Collected Poems of Philip Whalen,* pp. 700–701.

9. Quotations from Zen Center students are from an author interview conducted 12 January 2009.

10. The long ones run about six feet and have three rattling metal rings affixed to the top. Philip called them "Shingon jingle-sticks." He bought a short one for Allen when he was in Japan.

11. Chögyam Trungpa, *The Teacup and the Skullcup* (Halifax: Vajradhatu Publications, 2007), p. 131.

12. David Meltzer, *San Francisco Beat: Talking with Poets* (San Francisco: City Lights Books, 2001), p. 332.

13. Not all of the following stories occurred strictly during Philip's *ango.*

14. Richard Levine, private communication, 25 January 2014.

15. He may have seen steps like these in Japan. To those trying to clean their bowls, he appeared only as a huge presence in black robes, bouncing and clowning.

16. Naropa University lectures, 1977, part 3.

17. Whalen to Snyder, May 1981. "{The building is called Beginner's Mind Temple. The zendo is called Dai Bosatsu Zendo: Suzuki Roshi's idea.}"

18. Author interview with Richard Baker, 7 October 2005.

19. Whalen to Snyder, 6 September 1981.

20. Whalen to Snyder, 6 September 1981.

21. Author interview with Miriam Sagan, 2 January 2011.

22. Naropa University lectures, 1977, talk 1.

23. Whalen to Snyder, 25 March 1982. *Hojo* indicates the head priest at a temple; here Philip is referring to Baker.

CHAPTER 14: ROPE OF SAND

1. David Schneider, *Street Zen: The Life and Work of Issan Dorsey* (New York: Marlow, 2000).

2. Whalen to Snyder, 7 January 1984.

3. In the mid-1970s David Padwa commissioned the stupa, which was built by Dodrup Chen Rinpoche, to honor the U.S. visit of the head of the Nyingma School, H. H. Dudjom Rinpoche. Still other lamas—including the Vidyadhara Trungpa Rinpoche—personally blessed it.

4. Author interview with Miriam Sagan and Miriam Bobkoff, 2 January 2011.

5. Ibid. Stockton and Grant are streets in San Francisco's Chinatown, home to restaurants beloved by Philip.

6. Whalen to the author, January 1985.

7. Whalen journal, 26 September 1987.

8. Author interview with Jack Loeffler, 3 January 2011.

9. Whalen to Snyder, 9 May 1986.

10. Whalen to the author, January 1985.

11. Thomas Merton, *The Asian Journal* (New York: New Directions, 1975), p. 333.

12. Miriam Sagan recounted this wonderful story in a number of places, including *Continuous Flame*, p. 101.

13. Author interview with Miriam Sagan and Miriam Bobkoff, 2 January 2011.

14. Richard Baker, introduction to Whalen, *Canoeing Up Cabarga Creek*.

15. Author interview with Richard Baker, 6–7 October 2005.

16. David Meltzer, *San Francisco Beat: Talking to Poets* (San Francisco: City Lights, 2001), p. 332.

17. Whalen journal, 17 August 1987.

18. Whalen journal, 2 October–1 November 1987.

19. Philip notes after the July ceremonies, "So I am to wind up in the same boat as Reb," and explains that the papers will be unfinished. Whalen journal, 28 July 1987.

20. Whalen journal, 1 November 1987.

21. Interview with Britton Pyland, 22 September 2005.

22. Baker, introduction to Whalen, *Canoeing Up Cabarga Creek*.

23. Author interview with Jack Loeffler, 3 January 2011.

24. Author interview with Richard Baker, 6–7 October 2005.

1. Whalen to Snyder, 24 September 1987.

2. Whalen journal, 8 June 1988.

3. Whalen journal, 17 December 1988. *Godō* (literally "rear hall teacher") means the person in charge of the training of the monks in a monastery; this person is second only to the abbot.

4. Hartford Street Zen Center Newsletter, Winter 1994–95.

5. The little girl, Rose, goes through a great many trials trying to find out who she is. She seems satisfied by sitting in a chair on top of a mountain.

6. Hartford Street Zen Center Newsletter, Winter 1994–95.

7. Ibid.

8. Cited in Steve Silberman, *Thanks for Asking,* entry for 21 May 1993, available at www.stevesilberman.com/downloads/thanksforasking.doc.

9. Silberman, *Thanks for Asking.* Parts of this text appeared on *The Well* and in other online forms, and in *A Month with Philip Whalen* by poet Randy Roark, http://randyroark.com/category/journal/notebooks/a-month-with-philip-whalen-1993/.

10. Silberman, *Thanks for Asking,* entry for 12 June 1993.

11. Ibid., entry for 1 September 1993.

12. Hartford Street Zen Center Newsletter, Spring 1996.

13. Meltzer, *San Francisco Beat,* p. 333.

14. Hartford Street Zen Center group interview, 10 January 2009.

15. Roark, *A Month with Philip Whalen,* entry for 27 August 1993.

16. Ibid., entry for 9 September 1993.

17. Hartford Street Zen Center Newsletter, Fall 1996.

18. Hartford Street Zen Center Newsletter, 1995.

19. Whalen, *Some of These Days* (San Jose, NM: Desert Rose Press, 1999).

20. Author interview with Michael Rothenberg, 16 March 2008. The resultant book was *Overtime: Selected Poems* (Harmondsworth: Penguin Books, 1999).

21. The list of people who helped Philip here is too long and varied to reproduce accurately. No offense is intended by omission, and apologies are offered for any that occur.

22. Author interview with Michael Rothenberg, 8 March 2014.

23. Laura Burges, in the Hartford Street Zen Center group interview, 12 January 2009.

24. Author interview with Rick London, 10 January 2009.

25. Organized by Nancy Davis, the event took place on 30 June 2002.

26. Jennifer Birkett, in *Continuous Flame,* p. 110.

27. This is a nine-page folded, unbound, undated pamphlet, printed single-space and decorated with a line drawing of a bald, bespectacled Philip. He is shown in underpants, leaning on a shovel in a location called the "Nasturtium Bardo." Rosenthal imagines Philip's thought bubble saying, "At least no censorship here."

28. Author interview with Richard Baker, 6–7 October 2005.

29. For Gary Snyder's remarks, see chapter 4; for Michael McClure's, see chapter 6.

30. A videotape of Whalen's funeral is available from Cloud House Poetry Archives in San Francisco.

ACKNOWLEDGMENTS

1. In the course of doctoral research, Dr. Unger transcribed most, if not all, of Philip Whalen's journals. During the years of this work, Dr. Unger formed notions about Philip, and particularly about a love affair in the 1950s and 60s. With great respect, I've examined Dr. Unger's work. While I'm aware of his views, I have others.

PRIMARY SOURCES

Philip Whalen's journals, manuscripts, and letters to him are largely in three collections:

The Bancroft Library, University of California, Berkeley

Philip Whalen Papers, Oral History Project Collection, Special Collections, Eric V. Hauser Memorial Library, Reed College, Portland, Oregon

Columbia University, Rare Book & Manuscript Library, New York

Philip's letters to Allen Ginsberg are at Green Library, Stanford University, California.

Philip's letters to Gary Snyder are primarily at Special Collections, Shields Library, University of California, Davis.

Philip's letters to Jack Kerouac are housed at the Berg Collection, New York Public Library.

Philip's letters to Michael McClure are at Special Collections & Rare Books Division, Bennett Library, Simon Fraser University, Burnaby, British Columbia, Canada.

A large and valuable collection of recordings of classes and readings Philip Whalen gave at Naropa University is to be found online and at Naropa Poetics Audio Archive.

INDEX

Abbott, Keith, 130
About Now (Kyger), 121
"About the Beat Generation" (Kerouac), 46
"ADDRESS TO THE BOOBUS, with her
  Hieratic Formulas in reply" (poem;
  Whalen), 135
Adelaide Crapsey-Oswald Spengler Mutual
  Admiration Society, 75, 180–81, 303n29
"Aether" (poem; Ginsberg), 19
Again (Kyger), 118–19
AIDS epidemic, 268–70, 275–76
Alamogordo (NM), 161
Alderson, William, 157
Algren, Nelson, 198
Allen, Donald, 183, 229; as Berkeley Poetry
  Conference co-organizer (1965), 115;
  Bolinas residence of, 225; as Grove Press
  editor, 130–31, 188–89; Kyger published
  by, 108; as *New American Poetry* editor,
  130; as SFZC board member, 307n7;
  side business of, 199; as Welch's literary
  executor, 303n28; Whalen and, 130–31,
  137, 188–89, 190, 224, 225
Allen, Steve, 257, 258, 261, 269, 270–71, 280,
  284
American Academy in Rome, 216
American Academy of Asian Studies (San
  Francisco, CA), 52, 98, 294n1
American Indian Prose & Poetry, 192
Anderson, Ben Richard ("Dick"), 98,
  164–66, 167
Anderson, Reb, 261, 263
"Animism" (poem; M. McClure), 130

Antaiji (Kyoto, Japan), 221
anticommunism, 201–2
Apollinaire, Guillaume, 192
Armstrong, Karen, 282
Artaud, Antonin, 201, 305n45
Arts and Crafts movement, 172–73
Ashbery, John, 29
Auerhahn Press, 136, 189–90
Austen, Jane, 112
Avison, Margaret, 200
ayahuasca, 19

Baker, Richard, 222, 307n42; appearance
  of, 223, 229; as Berkeley Poetry
  Conference manager (1965), 115;
  Dongshan lineage of, 233, 261; Dorsey
  and, 268, 271; extramarital affair of, 254;
  as "Fast Talking Buddha," 231; as Grove
  Press employee, 130; HSZC founded by,
  268; "Invisible College" and, 244; Japan
  stays of, 62, 211; land purchases of, 217;
  as married Buddhist priest, 238;
  McClure and, 144; meditation practice
  of, 220; ordination ceremony liturgy
  rearranged by, 237; as political activist,
  69; resignation of, as SFZC abbot,
  254–55; as SFZC abbot, 131, 223, 225–26,
  228, 234–35, 243–44; SFZC satellite
  temple established by, 250–53; at
  Tassajara, 234–35; Whalen as
  ceremonial attendant to (*jisha*), 241–44;
  on Whalen as teacher, 6–7; Whalen's
  HSZC successor appointed by, 281;

Baker, Richard *(continued)*
Zen Center scandals and, 1. *See also* Baker-Whalen relationship
Baker, Sally, 217
Baker, Virginia, 62, 217, 222, 223, 244
Baker-Whalen relationship: dharma transmission, 260–64, 268; friendship, 131, 229–30, 262–63, 264; history of, 228–32; in Japan, 25, 131, 229–31; ordination, 238–39; SFZC residence and, 25, 140; significance of, 188; teacher-student, 17, 54, 131, 133, 186, 228, 231–32, 233, 235, 238, 246, 247 *fig. 17*, 263, 264–65; Whalen funeral service, 54, 132, 134, 284–85
Ball, Gordon, 27 *fig. 3*
Ballantine, Duncan, 174, 175
Banquet Years, The (Shattuck), 192
Baranowska, Sharon, 268
Barnard, Mary, 177
Basho, 93
"Basho Says Plants Stones Utensils" (poem; Kyger), 121
Baudelaire, Charles, 87, 192
Bay of Pigs invasion (1961), 201
Beard, The (play; M. McClure), 138, 142
Beat poets: Berkeley residences of, 291n1 (Ch. 1); Buddhist associations of, 4, 20, 41; cohabitation of, 14–15; friendships among, 2–6, 9–10, 41; Kerouac article about, 46; as literary school, 3–4; McClure (Joanna) and, 135; media coverage of, 81, 97; published works of, 188; readings/conferences, 115; sexuality of, 105; Six Gallery reading (1955), 3, 9–14, 41. *See also* Ginsberg, Allen; Kerouac, Jack; McClure, Michael; Six Gallery reading (1955); Whalen, Philip—as Beat poet; *specific poet*
Beckford, William, 87
Beckler, Stanworth ("Dan"), 163–64, 166, 296n41
"Bed of Old John Zoeller, The" (poem; Stevens), 157–58
Benson, Steve, 297n79
Berkeley (CA), 18, 36, 61; Beat poets' residence in, 2–3, 4, 9, 14–15; Beat poets' residences in, 291n1 (Ch. 1); Buddhist

study groups in, 52; Snyder's residence in, 62–63, 291n1 (Ch. 1); Whalen's residence in, 164, 291n1 (Ch. 1); writing groups in, 46
Berkeley, George, 157
Berkeley Bussei, 52
Berkeley Poetry Conference (1965), 68, 115–16
Berkson, Bill, 215, 224
Berlin Literarisches Colloquium, 216
Berman, Wallace, 136
Berrigan, Daniel, 216
Berrigan, Ted, 224, 235
Berry, Don, 58
"Berry Feast, The" (poem; Snyder), 87, 300n7 (Ch. 6)
Bhagavad Gita, 156, 166
Bible, 203
Big Bridge (online magazine), 279
Big Sur (Kerouac), 32–33, 35, 36, 38, 98–99
Biloxi (MS), 160
Birkett, Jennifer, 271, 273, 275, 283
Bishop, Elizabeth, 216
Black Mountain school, 18, 115
Blaise, Jay, 298n8
Blake, William, 36, 133, 140, 172, 178, 248–49
Blythe, R. H., 3, 60–61
Bobkoff, Miriam, 256, 257
Bodega Bay (CA), 109
bodhisattvas, 124–25, 250, 265, 291n7
body, 8
Bolinas (CA), 109, 116, 190, 213, 217, 222, 223–25
"BOOBUS HIEROPHANTE Her Incantations" (poem; Whalen), 135
Borregaard, Ebbe, 224
Boston (MA), 132
"Bow, The" (poem; M. McClure), 141
Boyce, Jack, 108, 109, 298n31
Brackett, Lambert, 229
Bragdon, Paul, 177
Brainard, Joe, 223, 224
Brain Candy (Whalen), 212, 214
Brautigan (dog), 136
Brautigan, Richard, 196, 224
Bread & Wine Poetry Mission (San Francisco, CA), 99

Brentano's Bookstore (San Francisco, CA), 96, 104
Brooklyn College, 29, 132
Brown, Bill, 110, 211, 213–14
Brown, Joan, 299n1
Brown, Zoe, 211, 213
Brownstein, Michael, 215
Buddha (Armstrong), 282
Buddha mind, 91–94
"Buddha Red Ears" (drawing; Kerouac), 33 *fig. 4*, 293n (Ch. 3)
Buddhism, 157; Beat poets' associations with, 20, 41; biographies in, 7–8; bodhisattvas in, 291n7; body/mind/speech division in, 8; death in, 282–83; emptiness in, 41, 74–75, 120–25; Four Vows of, 66, 304n19; funeral ceremonies, 276–78; impermanence in, 120, 125; priest ordinations in, 56, 276, 277 *fig. 20*; Second Turning in, 122, 124, 291n7, 299n52; sexuality and, 21; teacher-student dynamic in, 254, 263; time as viewed in, 147; Whalen's definition of, 67–68; Whalen's early interest in, 156–57; Whalen's readings in, 279–80. *See also* meditation; Zen Buddhism
Buddhist Bible, A (Goddard), 45
Buddhist Church of America, 52
Buddhist Society, 307n41
Bukowski, Charles, 201
Bullock, David, 280
Bunnell, Sterling, 140
Burges, Laura, 249, 281, 282
Burke, Clifford, 268, 279
Burroughs, William, 25 *fig. 1*, 26 *fig. 2*, 136
Burstein, Sandor, 272
Bush, Phyllis Aminta. *See* Whalen, Phyllis Aminta (Bush; mother)
Bush, Velna, 152
Bynner, Witter, 61

Caen, Herb, 198
Calendar (degree thesis; Whalen), 173
calligraphy, 170–72
Capote, Truman, 43
Carpenter, Don, 193, 198–99, 211–12, 213
Carpenter, Martha, 193

Cassady, Neal, 32, 35, 37, 41–42, 105, 198
Castro, Fidel, 201
Catholic Church, 305n45
censorship, 138, 142, 201–4, 305n45
Centralia (WA), 149
Chadwick, David, 244, 278
Charters, Ann, 44
Chaucer, Geoffrey, 137, 191
Chen, Dodrup, 309n3
Chicago (IL), 174, 235
Chicago Review, 40, 183, 293n18
Child, Frances, 157
"Chinese Written Character as a Medium for Poetry, The" (Fenellosa), 94
Christianity, 201–2, 203–4, 259
Christian Science, 93, 148, 169
City College of New York, 131
City of Paris department store (San Francisco, CA), 104
Civil War, 160
Clark, Tom, 224
Cleveland, SS, 206–7
Cobb, Ty, 33
Cochrane, Mickey, 34
Cocteau, Jean, 111
Coleman, Ornette, 140
Collected Poems of Philip Whalen, The (Whalen), 285
Colorado Springs (CO), 161
Columbia University (New York, NY), 9
Confucius, 55, 71
Connecticut College, 132
Connell, Evan, 198
Connor, Bruce, 136, 189
Conrad, Joseph, 192
conservatism, political, 139, 201–4
Continuous Flame (Whalen Festschrift), 128–29, 285
Coolidge, Clark, 199
COP Inc (Committee on Poetry), 16
Corinth Books, 189
Corman, Cid, 72
Corso, Gregory, 18, 28, 33–34, 50, 72, 110, 292n19
Coyote Books, 202–3, 204, 211, 212–13, 214, 307n6
Coyote's Journal, 202, 204, 305n39, 305n44
Crane, Hart, 183

Field, Tom, 198, 298n8
Fischer, Norman, 54, 92, 132, 243, 281, 283–84, 297n79
Flemming, Arthur, 202
Flower Ornament Sutra, 133
"For C." (poem; Whalen), 99
Fordham University (Bronx, NY), 132
formalism, poetic, 139
"For the Death of 100 Whales" (poem; M. McClure), 130
Fraser, Simon, 305n39
Freeway Reading (San Francisco, CA; 1964), 185 *fig. 14*, 199
Freud, Sigmund, 105–6
"Fuck Ode" (poem; M. McClure), 131
Fund for Poetry, 263
funeral ceremonies, 276–78

Gallup, Donald, 193
Gandavyuha Sutra, 144
Gary Snyder: Dimensions of a Life (ed. Halper), 75–76
Gary Snyder Reader, The (Snyder), 55, 56, 85
Gauguin, Paul, 157
Gehrig, Lou, 33–34
GI Bill, 167, 168–69, 174
Giles, Lionel, 61
Ginsberg, Allen, 146, 177; Berkeley residence of, 2–3, 4, 14–15, 41, 291n1 (Ch. 1); character of, 45; death of, 30, 293n21; drug use of, 19; early poems of, 52; hiking trips, 68; India visit of, 66, 113–14; Kerouac's literary portrayals of, 33–34; Kyger's view of, 113–14; land purchases of, 217; at literary awards banquet (San Francisco; 1963), 198; name-dropping of, 23; as Naropa University instructor, 2–3, 5, 24, 26–29, 26 *fig. 2*, 27 *fig. 3*; New York State farm of, 17; nonprofit foundation of, 16; as political activist, 22; promotional efforts of, 18–19, 23, 51, 132; readings/ conferences, 198, 199–200; relationship with Kerouac, 9, 41; sexual openness of, 21, 105; at Six Gallery reading (1955), 3, 10, 12–13, 292n3; Snyder and, 18, 68; in Snyder-Whalen correspondence, 72; spiritual visions of, 45; Welch and, 179;

Whalen's ordination and, 237–38; as Zen Buddhist, 19, 20–21; **works:** "Aether," 19; *Howl,* 10, 12–13, 28; "Laughing Gas," 19; *Reality Sandwiches,* 19–20
Ginsberg-Whalen relationship, 2; Buddhism in, 20–21, 24–25, 25 *fig. 1,* 237–38, 292–93nn19–20; correspondence, 5–6, 15, 16–20, 22–23, 29–30, 49–50, 62, 95, 98, 182, 188–90, 208, 213, 216, 237–38, 240, 292–93nn19–20; first meeting, 9–10; Ginsberg's death and, 30–31; hiking trips, 64–68; literary influence of, 41; politics and, 22; sexuality and, 21–22; Six Gallery reading (1955) and, 9, 23, 51; support, 15–17, 18–19, 23, 50, 51; teaching and, 23–29, 164; Vancouver Poetry Conference (1963), 200
Gloucester (MA), 131
Goddard, Dwight, 45
Gold, Herb, 198
Gold, Marianne, 173
Golden Gate Park (San Francisco, CA), 35–36, 196
Goofbook: For Jack Kerouac (Whalen), 40, 44–45
Gorf (play; M. McClure), 138
Gove, Robert, 69
Grabbing of the Fairy, The (play; M. McClure), 138
"Grace before Meat" (poem; Whalen), 141
Graves, Morris, 87
Graves, Robert, 45, 192
"graveyard stew," 235, 298n37
Great Wisdom Sutra, 66
Green Gulch Farm, 25, 54–55, 65, 132–34, 284–85
Grove Press, 77, 188–89, 229
Guggenheim Foundation, 216
Gysin, Byron, 136

Hadley, Drummond, 59
"Haiku, for Gary Snyder" (poem; Whalen), 121
"Haiku for Mike" (poem; Whalen), 128
haiku tradition, 121

Japan—Whalen's stays in: Baker and, 229–31; boat trip to (1966), 119–20, 206–7; correspondence during, 82–83, 114, 208, 211; decision to return, 216–17; employment, 53, 114, 207, 213, 221–22; first visit (1966–1967), 68, 82, 109, 176, 206–11, 213; free-time tourism, 138, 207–10, 218–19; Kerouac death during, 49–50; language difficulties, 95, 210–11, 218, 221; psychedelic adventures, 90; second visit (1969–1971), 82–83, 109, 182, 207, 215, 217–22; Snyder and, 53, 63–64, 64 *fig. 6*; Welch's disappearance and, 182; writings during, 86, 121, 208, 218, 225; Zen Buddhism and, 219–21, 297n1

Japanese poetry, 121
Japanese temple architecture, 78
Jarry, Alfred, 192
Jeffers, Robinson, 90
Jerusalem (Blake), 36
jisha (ceremonial attendant to abbot), 241–44
"JOANNE Is a Novel from the Inside Out" (poem; Kyger), 123
Jobs, Steve, 171–72
Jodo Shinshu Buddhism, 52
Johnson, Lyndon B., Whalen's broadside manifestos addressed to, 69–70
Johnson, Wendy, 243
Johnston, Edward, 172–73, 178
Jones, Leroi, 23, 72, 189, 190
Jovanovich, William, 212
Joyce, James, 90
jukai (priest ordination ceremony), 276

Kabuki theater, 210
Kagyu tradition, 23
kami (Shinto deities), 306n8
Kanaster, Joe, 281
Kandel, Lenore, 294n1
Kenner, Hugh, 96
Kentfield, Calvin, 198
Kerouac, Gabrielle ("Memere"; mother), 34–35, 36, 39
Kerouac, Jack: alcoholism of, 35–36, 44, 48–49; ancestry of, 34; appearance of,

32; as athlete, 32; as Beat poet, 2, 5; Berkeley residence of, 2–3, 291n1 (Ch. 1); character of, 45; death of, 49–50, 81; drawings of, 33 *fig. 4*, 293n (Ch. 3); early poems of, 52; as East-West House resident, 98–99, 294n1; in Ginsberg's correspondence, 18; Jackson suicide and, 41–42; literary skills of, 43; media coverage of, 97; poems of, 275; psychedelic adventures of, 36–37; relationship with Ginsberg, 9, 41; residences of, 14; Six Gallery reading as portrayed by, 292n3; Snyder and, 76, 81–82; in Snyder-Whalen correspondence, 72, 81–82; Welch and, 179; as Zen Buddhist, 4, 45, 48–49, 144; **works:** "About the Beat Generation," 46; *Big Sur,* 32–33, 35, 36, 38, 98–99; *Desolation Angels,* 33–34, 36, 38, 39, 48; *Lonesome Traveler,* 110; *On the Road,* 3. See also *Dharma Bums, The* (Kerouac)

Kerouac-Whalen relationship, 2, 5–6; blowups, 34, 39; Buddhism in, 20, 45, 47–49; correspondence, 5, 38, 39–41, 45–46; ethnicity and, 34, 293n5; first meeting, 41; as fraternal bond, 35–36, 49; influence on Whalen, 50; Jackson suicide and, 41–43; Kerouac's death and, 49–50; Kerouac's mother and, 34–35; as literary friendship, 38–45, 50; literary portrayals of, 32–34, 36, 45; in physical proximity, 36–38, 37 *fig. 5*, 39; sexuality and, 37–38; spirituality of, 45–49

Kesey, Ken, 198
KFPA (radio station), 185, 199
Kherdian, David, 196
King Jesus (Graves), 192
Kings Canyon, 59
Kittredge, Lyman, 157
Kiyooka, Roy, 49
koans, 80, 84, 192
Koller, Jim, 202, 204, 211, 214, 228, 240, 279, 296n59
Koya-san (Japan), 230
Krishnamurti, 170
Kyger, Joanne, 2, 100 *fig. 7*, 224, 279; on Allen, 225; appearance of, 96; divorce of,

sensibility of, 135; at Whalen memorial reading, 283; Whalen's first novel as viewed by, 137; Whalen's relationship with, 115, 127, 128–29, 251; Whalen's sexuality and, 101; **work:** "A Phil Whalen Specially Requested Evening Meal," 129

McClure, Michael, 2, 37, 212; animal consciousness of, 130; appearance of, 130; Artaud play introduced by, 305n45; birth of, 127; censorship attempts against, 138, 142; meditation practice of, 144; as playwright, 137–39, 142; psychedelic adventures of, 141–42; publishers of, 135–36, 201; reading performance style of, 137–38; readings/conferences, 23, 129–32, 137, 140, 198; religious sentiments of, 132–33; at Six Gallery reading (1955), 3, 12, 127, 292n3; in Snyder-Whalen correspondence, 72; on Whalen's character, 5; at Whalen's funeral, 54, 283; Whalen's sexuality and, 101; as Zen Buddhist, 144–45; **works:** "Animism," 130; *The Beard,* 138, 142; "The Bow," 141; *The Feast,* 139; "For the Death of 100 Whales," 130; "Fuck Ode," 131; *Gorf,* 138; *The Grabbing of the Fairy,* 138; "Hail Thee Who Play," 144; "Hollywood Hills," 143; "The Magic Theatre, for John Lion," 138; *Minnie Mouse and the Tap-Dancing Buddha,* 133, 138; *The Pink Helmet,* 138; *Touching the Edge,* 144–45

McClure-Whalen relationship, 133 *fig. 8,* 251; artistic bravery, 142–43; Berkeley Poetry Conference boycott and (1965), 115–16; Buddhism in, 20, 132–33, 144–45; cohabitations, 104; correspondence, 267; East Coast reading tour (1959), 23, 129–32, 137; first meeting, 127; as literary friendship, 134–40; literary influence of, 41; scientific interests, 140–41; sensual pleasures, 141–42; visits, 127–29; Whalen's funeral and, 132–34

McCorkle, Locke, 65, 76

McLaren, John, 196

McLaren, Juliet, 305n39

meditation: in Buddhism, 157; circumambulations and, 65–66; ethical conduct as arising from, 239–40; Kerouac and, 48–49; Kyger's practice of, 113, 298–99n38; McClure's practice of, 144; Snyder's practice of, 61, 68–69, 85–86, 184; Welch's practice of, 184; Whalen's definition of, 226–27; Whalen's practice of, 61, 68–69, 85–86, 92, 170, 184, 192, 220, 252–53; work meditation, 68–69

meditation mind, 85–86

meditation retreats (*sesshin*), 40, 232–33, 241

Meltzer, David, 136, 198, 224, 246, 274, 283

Memoirs of an Interglacial Age (Whalen), 43–44, 136–37, 189–90

Mendocino (CA), 268

Mercer, Jackie Gibson, 35

Merton, Thomas, 258–59, 273

mescaline, 90

Metaphysical Bookshop (San Francisco, CA), 60

Michigan, poetry festival in (1971), 223, 224

Miles, J., 201

Milk, Harvey, 105

mind, 8, 42–43, 123–24, 186; Buddha mind vs. poetry mind, 91–94; calligraphy mind, 94; hallucinogenic drugs and, 87–90; meditation mind, 85–86; "new," 95; poetry mind, 86–87, 91–94

Minnie Mouse and the Tap-Dancing Buddha (play; M. McClure), 133, 138

"Minor Moralia" (poem; Whalen), 308n (Ch. 13)

"Monday before the Recall" (poem; Kyger), 121

Monk, Thelonius, 140

Montgomery, John, 196

Moore, Stanley, 174

Morimoto Roshi, 221

Morinaga, Soko, 307n42

Morris, William, 172–73

Morrison, Jim, 144

Morte d'Arthur, Le, 192

Mountains and Rivers without End (poem; Snyder), 93

Mozart, Wolfgang Amadeus, 140

Whalen, Philip (*continued*)
59, 98, 104, 164–65, 193; kitchen wisdom of, 112–13; library of, 212; love interests of, 53; memorial reading, 283–84; military service of, 58, 160–66, 162 *fig. 11*, 227, 301–2n6; musical abilities of, 163–64; naming games of, 154; nightmares of, 274; political views of, 184–85, 205; popcorn habit of, 225; psychedelic adventures of, 36–37, 87–90, 122, 141–42, 224; reading interests of, 70, 151, 152, 155–57, 191–92; sexuality of, 101, 104–6, 271, 311n1; summer Forest Service lookout jobs of, 51, 61–62, 72, 165, 174; as teacher, 26–27, 186; temper fits of, 34, 39, 77, 194–95, 240, 272–73, 297n5; theater interests of, 51, 138–39, 210. *See also* Baker-Whalen relationship; Ginsberg-Whalen relationship; Kerouac-Whalen relationship; Kyger-Whalen relationship; McClure-Whalen relationship

Whalen, Philip—as Beat poet, 2, 5, 43–44, 183–84, 185–86; animal consciousness, 130; archive, 285; award nomination, 23, 83; Berkeley residence, 2–3, 291n1 (Ch. 1); correspondence, 4, 5 (*see also under specific relationship*); dramatic elements, 139; early poems, 52, 152; as East-West House resident, 99, 101, 294n1; editors, 44; fellowships/artist-in-resident stays, 16, 263; Festschrift for, 128–29, 285; financial difficulties, 68, 71, 101, 104, 128, 139, 184–85, 193–94, 195, 216, 224; friendships of, 2–6, 9–10, 58, 140, 146, 188; gay pornographic piece, 284, 310n27; as Hyphen House resident, 298n8; journal kept by, 30, 59, 108, 138, 150, 165, 191–92, 194, 196–97, 198, 207–8, 216–17, 221, 227, 229–30, 231, 242, 257, 262, 263, 268, 269, 274, 285, 311n1; Kerouac's drawings of, 33 *fig. 4*; Kerouac's literary portrayals of, 10, 13, 32–34, 38, 45; landscape descriptions, 150–51, 192; literary awards banquet incident (1963), 198; literary voice, 1, 12, 17–18; *Northwest Review* scandal, 142;

201–4, 305n44; novels, 43, 105, 137, 170, 176, 193–95, 203, 218; openness/sensitivity of, 143–44; poetic style, 178; publishers, 135–36, 188–90; radio recordings, 185, 199; reading performance style, 137, 249; readings/conferences, 15–16, 23, 42, 54, 68, 92–94, 103, 129–32, 137, 185 *fig. 14*, 189, 193, 198–201, 223, 224, 235; at Six Gallery reading (1955), 3, 10–12, 292n3; spiritual visions of, 45–46, 203; "takes" concept, 87, 121, 134–35; television interviews, 205–6, 305n1; Williams and, 90–91; women writers theory of, 112; **works:** "ADDRESS TO THE BOOBUS, with her Hieratic Formulas in reply," 135; "BOOBUS HIEROPHANTE Her Incantations," 135; *Brain Candy*, 212, 214; *Calendar*, 173; *The Collected Poems of Philip Whalen*, 285; "DEAR MR PRESIDENT," 69–70; *The Diamond Noodle*, 149, 157, 158–59, 176; "Different Ways of Being Nervous," 68; "A Distraction Fit," 102; "Dying Again," 108–9; *Every Day*, 196, 202, 211; "FAILING," 86; "For C." 99; *Goofbook: For Jack Kerouac*, 40, 44–45; "Grace before Meat," 141; "Haiku, for Gary Snyder," 121; "Haiku for Mike," 128; *Highgrade*, 94, 203, 211; "Home Again, Home Again . . . ," 109; "Hymnus Ad Patrem Sinensis," 93, 98; "If You're So Smart, Why Ain't You Rich," 11–12, 71; *The Invention of the Letter*, 112, 212; "Liberal Shepherds," 76; *Like I Say*, 164, 188–90; "Litany of the Candy Infant of Geneva," 106; "Mahayana," 48, 125; "The Martyrdom of Two Pagans," 11, 293n24; *Memoirs of an Interglacial Age*, 43–44, 136–37, 189–90; "Minor Moralia," 308n (Ch. 11); "Nobody Listening to YOU?" 69; "October 1st," 224–25; "The Ode to Music," 142; "O Goddess I call on you constantly," 203; *On Bear's Head*, 23, 117, 213–14, 215–16, 279, 306n20; "Plus ça change . . . ," 11, 87; "Poem for a Blonde Lady, " 117;

zazen. *See* meditation

Zen Buddhism: Beat poets' associations with, 4, 6; death and, 30–31; "dharma combat" in, 90, 246; hazing/testing rituals (*tangaryo*) in, 113, 234; koans in, 80, 84, 192; Kyger's readings in, 123; lineage transmission in, 238, 265; married priests in, 78–79, 238; the present moment in, 147; rules/regulations in, 242, 247; Snyder's readings in, 83; teacher-student dynamic in, 263; Western establishment of, 1, 85, 146, 225, 231; Whalen's readings in, 219, 279–80. *See also* Buddhism; meditation; Whalen, Philip—as Zen Buddhist

Zen in English Literature (Blythe), 60–61

Zen Mind, Beginner's Mind (Suzuki), 223

Zuigan Goto, 297n1